Ethics in
Public Management

Ethics in
Public Management

H. George Frederickson and Richard K. Ghere, editors

M.E.Sharpe
Armonk, New York
London, England

Library of Congress Cataloging-in-Publication Data

Ethics in public management / edited by H. George Frederickson and Richard K. Ghere.
    p. cm.
    Includes index.
    ISBN 0-7656-1460-X (cloth : alk. paper) ISBN 0-7656-1461-8 (pbk. : alk. paper)
    1. Public administration—Moral and ethical aspects. 2. Public administration—United
States. 3. Political ethics—United States. I. Frederickson, H. George. II. Ghere, Richard K.,
1945-

JF1525.E8E8567 2005
172'.2—dc22   2004023622

Printed in the United States of America

The paper used in this publication meets the minimum requirements of
American National Standard for Information Sciences
Permanence of Paper for Printed Library Materials,
ANSI Z 39.48-1984.

MV (c)   10   9   8   7   6   5   4
MV (p)   10   9   8   7   6   5   4   3

Contents

List of Tables and Figures

Tables

Figures

Part One

Ethics and Public Administration in the Twenty-First Century

1

Introduction

Richard K. Ghere

Published in 1993, *Ethics and Administration* included works adapted from papers presented at the Conference for the Study of Government Ethics in Park City, Utah, during the summer of 1991. The timing of the Park City conference coincided with an emergent interest in administrative ethics research that has since greatly expanded. Reliable evidence indicates that the number of published articles more than doubled between 1989 and 1991, and that number increased threefold before the beginning of the new century (Cooper 2001, p. 16). Many of the introductory questions that H. George Frederickson posed as editor of that volume focused on the status of ethics research as a systematic body of empirical knowledge. In chapter 2 of *Ethics in Public Management* (discussed in depth below), Donald C. Menzel revisits many of the same issues in reviewing research on ethics and integrity in governance within the U.S. experience. Yet these persisting research issues derive from an even more fundamental concern raised by Frederickson in 1993: "Does the ethics movement have staying power" or would attentiveness toward ethics and morality in government in the mid-1990s fade away?

With regard to staying power, the answer is resoundingly affirmative—indeed, issues of government corruption and attendant themes of morality in government do have substantial carrying capacity, sustained in large part by the drama of morality narratives that keep the media and citizenry engaged. Further, ethics concerns have long-term sustainability because they appear to be easily understood as elemental matters of right and wrong, in stark contrast to many vexing policy issues that are recognizably complex. Issues

3

that pertain to the moral conduct of government and public integrity *do* have staying power in the public eye as well as in the academy. Regarding the latter, many who are familiar with government ethics research would agree with Terry L. Cooper's recent observation, "[T]he numbers of journal articles, books, courses, conferences, and training exercises have proliferated beyond anyone's wildest expectations" (2004, p. 395). And as Cooper asserts, it is now time to take stock of this flourishing research interest by raising the tough, qualitative questions concerning the coherence and direction of research as well as the commitment to empirical inquiry relative to conceptual work. In short, it is fitting that *Ethics in Public Management* emerges as scholars examine the deportment of this flourishing, yet to some extent undisciplined, body of government ethics research.

In large part, however, it is *the event* that explains the dramaturgical staying power of government ethics that, in turn, stimulates reconsiderations of morality in a changing public arena. The world does not stand still while scholars fret about the stature of administrative ethics research against the standards of normal science, and it certainly has not done so since *Ethics and Public Administration* was published in 1993. Consider these events (some are discrete and others have unfolded more gradually) that have profoundly reshaped America's collective psyche, particularly with regard to expectations of morality and ethics in public life:

- The ongoing impact of the new public management (NPM) movement—triggered in part by the National Partnership for Reinventing Government—initiated by Vice President Al Gore—which reduced the size of the federal civilian workforce by 426,200 positions between January 1993 and September 2000.
- The ongoing impact of global economic activities—based on trade agreements that compromise national sovereignty.
- The 1997 impeachment (and later acquittal) of a U.S. president based on issues related to inappropriate sexual encounters with a female intern.
- The 1997–1998 incidents of misconduct within the Ramparts Division of the Los Angeles Police Department, which involved false arrests, perjured testimony, and the framing of innocent citizens.
- The violent demonstrations in 1999 that obstructed meetings of the World Trade Organization in Seattle and resulted in more than $2.5 million in damage.
- The terrorist attacks in 2001 that killed nearly 2,800 by crashing commercial airliners into the Twin Towers of New York's World Trade Center and into the Pentagon.
- The passage in 2001 of the U.S. Patriot Act, which substantially re-

stricted civil liberties in an effort to apprehend suspected terrorists.
- The ongoing administrative detention of prisoners of the U.S. war on Taliban forces in Afghanistan—prisoners held for indefinite time periods at the Guantanamo Bay Naval Base in Cuba without criminal due process rights.
- The accounting scandals in 2002 wherein a number of U.S. corporations admitted to misstating their accounts and overall financial positions. Big Five public accounting firms were found complicit in fraudulent accounting practices that certified misstated accounts.
- Seven U.S. astronauts died in 2003 in the Columbia Space Shuttle explosion; a subsequent accident investigation report faults NASA management culture.
- In 2003, the U.S. waged war against Ba'athist-ruled Iraq and sustained a coalition occupation pending creation of a new Iraqi constitution and government.
- In 2004, the abuse of Iraqi prisoners by U.S. military and civilian-contract personnel at the Abu Ghraib facility in Baghdad led to expedited military prosecutions and continued congressional and administrative investigations.

Clearly, issues such as these vie for attention in government ethics research. But to what extent can scholars treat such an expanding array of issues without compromising (but presumably enhancing) the standing of their research with regard to (1) the focus and coherence of the body of public-sector ethics and (2) the contribution of empirical research on government ethics for informing the study and practice of public administration? Although these questions address ethics research in general, they are nonetheless pertinent in placing the chapters in this volume in timely perspective.

Focus and Coherence

At this juncture, it is appropriate to assess research in administrative ethics in terms of relevance to core concerns that essentially define this body of scholarship. Although scholars may disagree on particulars, most would likely concur on a short list of research questions such as those that Cooper (2004) has identified as fundamental to the study of administrative ethics, which might include the nature of normative foundations, organization design as supportive of ethical conduct, and social justice concerns of what constitutes fair treatment. In addition, this set of core questions might now expand to consider "how administrative ethical norms fit into a global context" (Cooper 2004). Each chapter in this volume will address at least one of the above questions. Moreover, many of the chapters will deal specifically with ethics design issues, although some treat this concern at the organization/agency level while others focus on broader questions of public-sector accountability. For the sake of discussion in this introduction, these chapters fall under three design-related topics: organization designs that support ethical behavior; market forces that compromise administrative ethics; and unintended outcomes of anticorruption reforms. Three additional chapters in this book will treat the emerging question of how American administrative ethics fit into the global ethical context.

Part 2 will include five chapters that focus on organization design issues that influence moral conduct in public service. These discussions generally follow the widely held presumption that the *individual* assumes the critical role of moral agent in the organization setting—not surprising within U.S. culture, which has traditionally placed such a high premium on individualism. Yet at least by implication, these chapters call attention to a more complex web of human interaction. In chapter 3, Dennis P. Wittmer presents a general model of ethical decision making that conjoins several existing theoretical frameworks that address more specific components of ethical decision making. Wittmer adds breadth to the study of ethical decisions by linking scholarship on environmental influences with more common approaches that address individual development. Moreover, he supplements the strong empirical interest in moral cognitive development within public organization settings with other behavioral theories that focus on the individual. Some of the models that he incorporates are especially sensitive to the situation that directs the decision-making role, and as such they place the individual's moral cognition into a broader context of interaction. In regard to application, Wittmer's general model can affect the design of public organization as it informs public managers that the ethical character of public decisions is multifaceted—influenced by how situations and environmental factors are framed (or enacted) in the organization setting as well as by individual sensitivity.

Indeed, the breadth of Wittmer's model offers a fitting backdrop for chapter 4, in which Laura Lee Swisher, Ann-Marie Rizzo, and Marsha A. Marley present recent empirical findings about levels of cognitive development among public administrators as compared to other professional groups. After elaborating upon Lawrence Kohlberg's theory of cognitive moral development and how it has been operationalized in government ethics research, these authors present their own finding of an aggregate cognitive development score for public administrators surveyed, comparing this finding to those of similar studies of other professional groups. These comparisons suggest that practitioners in other professions (or graduate students pursuing entry in those career areas) are more likely to function at a higher, postconventional (or principled) level of moral development than are public managers. Implicit in this comparison is the cognitive tendency in public service to gravitate toward maintaining the norms of conventional reasoning. Thus, public managers tend to be more deferential to existing social order and its norms than to idealized principles of social justice and social cooperation. Although it raises questions about the effectiveness of teaching public administration ethics, Swisher, Rizzo, and Marley's chapter ultimately asks the critical design question: Is the politics-administration dichotomy in fact alive and well in the authoritative inertia of public bureaucracy?

The dichotomy tends to cast the political role within the organization as anathema to public morality within administrative structures. However, in chapter 5 Carole L. Jurkiewicz presents empirical research that supports the counterintuitive proposition that the prudent exercise of political power in the leadership role is instrumental both to the organization's effectiveness and to its ethical character. Contrary to Lord Acton's well-known dictum, power—rather than "corrupting absolutely"—*promotes* a principled work environment. Jurkiewicz's study builds upon research (such as that of Swisher, Rizzo, and Marley in chapter 4) that applies moral cognitive development theory to public management settings as it triangulates moral cognitive development, predisposition toward power, and leadership effectiveness. In so doing, her work empirically validates part of Wittmer's general decision model in chapter 3. In essence, Jurkiewicz's findings indicate that leaders who use power well guide their organizations toward a principled moral reasoning that rises above the pressures of majority opinion and obedience to authority. From a design perspective, her research offers robust insights into the nature of public management in general and into questions of managerial recruitment in particular.

A prevailing theme thus far relates to the capacity of those in public service to engage a principled moral reasoning that scrutinizes organization culture. Introducing the construct of administrative evil into the context of public service, chapter 6 extends this scrutiny to the deeply held values within modern culture that pull motives and actions toward the attainment of technical rationality in ways that perpetuate harm and injury to those affected. In their provocative book *Unmasking Administrative Evil*, Guy B. Adams and Danny L. Balfour update their thinking about the challenges of administrative evil in the public-service setting that promotes practical, utilitarian action. In effect, administrative evil indeed makes sense in horrendous scenarios (typically in other cultures) such as the Holocaust, wherein governmental officials pursue "rationally" efficient actions in ways that brutalize people. But Adams and Balfour's intent in chapter 6 is to sensitize readers to unmask evil of a lesser scale that public servants unknowingly perpetuate in their professional activities. Their work calls attention to a susceptibility to moral inversion, or an *agentic shift*, whereby professionals may unknowingly abdicate personal responsibility for their actions to meet expectations set within technical-rational bureaucracy. Although related to several of the significant events identified above, this agentic shift appears especially salient in the Abu Ghraib prison scandal related to the U.S. occupation of Iraq. In this recent example of administrative evil, enlisted military reservists have been accused of treating their Iraqi captors inhumanely in violation of the Geneva Convention. Adams and Balfour's chapter informs concern for organization design as it recommends a reconstruction of public ethics that incorporates values associated with deliberative democracy as a basis for administrative action. Specifically, deliberative democracy requires widely inclusive participation in decision making that is attentive to the social and economic outcomes of policy, especially as they affect the marginal and vulnerable in the community. Adams and Balfour's notions of deliberative democracy logically extend concern for principled moral reasoning toward a design strategy that can anticipate and avoid the unintended harms inflicted in pursuit of utility and effectiveness.

In chapter 7, Melvin Dubnick and Ciarán O'Kelly discuss behavior in response to how public officials cope with expectations imposed by accountability systems under which they work. Their analysis draws upon the behavior of two intelligence agency officials regarding events leading up to a British Parliament decision in the spring of 2003 to engage troops in Iraq based upon flawed evidence that Saddam Hussein possessed weapons of mass destruction. Dubnick and O'Kelly distinguish between "thin" and "thick" accountability, the latter based on expectations set by the normative ideas within the institutional and professional culture. In contrast to its thin counterpart based upon (thin) principled abstraction, thick accountability poses a critical dilemma for public officials. On one hand, deference to cultural expectations can lead to compromising and destructive outcomes, such as those Adams and Balfour described as administrative evil in chapter 6. Yet on the other hand, moral reasoning in democratic settings must proceed within the bounds of widely held societal and institutional expectations.

The next four chapters, included in Part 3, focus upon market perspectives on public organization that emerged in the 1990s. Often characterized as the new public management (NPM) movement, which was energized by Vice President Gore's National Partnership for Reinventing Government, these market-oriented reforms essentially call for a more limited, decentralized governmental role in public life. NPM advocates argue that public organizations ought to be concerned with end results rather than (bureaucratic) means and with facilitating entrepreneurship within both government and the private sector. Here the thinly veiled presumption is that businesses are better managed because the pressures of market competition are absent in government. From the standpoint of focus and coherence, these chapters hit directly on the core question of organization design to sustain ethical conduct, yet from a different angle than preceding work. Here the question turns to vulnerability with regard to how these market perspectives erode the capability of government organizations to operate in an ethical and accountable manner. This attention to vulnerability in turn raises a second core question concerning which *normative foundations* of governmental ethics are at particular risk in this strongly adversarial environment.

The authors of chapters 8 through 11 rely upon agency theory (focusing upon the contract between self-interested principals and agents) as a lens through which to examine how NPM reforms undermine institutional designs that promote ethical conduct in the public sector. In chapter 8, H. George Frederickson lays out the fundamental NPM arguments in recipe form as might be found in *Gourmet Magazine*. From there, he directs his analysis toward the contract—between government principals (buyers) and private sector agents (sellers)—that would replace hierarchical organization in the NPM vision of ideal governance. Frederickson then illustrates how each ingredient in the NPM recipe undercuts the ethical capacities of public institutions. *Cutting red tape* frees the principal from the obligations of accountability to assure fundamental constitutional protections (such as due process) and to compassion for and protection of citizens. *Privatization* assumes that governmental principals can act as smart buyers, with access to widely available information to select among numerous sellers. The realities of imperfect markets and information have in several cases led to corruption scandals in federal contracting. And *downsizing* shifts policy implementation to what Frederickson calls a "hidden bureaucracy" of countless contractual relationships that can skew public resources from the public interest toward mutual self-interest. With regard to the core question of normative foundations, Frederickson shows how each NPM ingredient limits government's capacity to steward the public interest.

In chapter 9, Lisa A. Dicke and Pitima Boonyarak pursue themes similar to Frederickson's, examining the impact of NPM reforms in the specific context of human services administration. In particular, they address the viability of the NPM argument that performance measurement technology can offer necessary accountability in the absence of thick bureaucratic controls. Yet in implicit reference to agency theory, these authors assert that performance measurements cannot provide the richly qualitative information that governmental buyers need in order to assess program impacts on the most vulnerable of clients—such as the aged and those with mental disabilities.

Despite the ideological insistence that performance measures *have to work*, public agencies for a variety of reasons did not, or could not, adopt these information technologies. Further, agencies that *do* have measurements in place may not actually use the information generated since it does not capture the qualitative nuances of ethical accountability critical to the delivery of human services.

Dicke and Boonyarak focus on the inability of government principals to utilize the information technologies touted in NPM rhetoric so as to assure ethical accountability in human service administration. Peter deLeon as well directs attention to principals—but as knowing culprits (or "cowboys") whose political actions led to five well-known corruption scandals in an era of government deregulation. In chapter 10, deLeon indicates that high-level political principals in federal bureaucracies are more likely to engage in corrupt activities than are administrative agents who, rising up through the ranks of civil service or other careerist routes, have benefited from ethics training. In assessing NPM practices as means to prevent corruption, deLeon notes that its advocacy for transparency in monitoring transactions between principals and agencies can to an extent limit the conditions that breed corruption scandals. Yet corruption often hinges on the ethical (mis)behavior of larger-than-life personalities (for example, that of Oliver North). DeLeon therefore reasons that the impersonal processes within NPM reforms cannot necessarily corral the cowboys in an era of diminished regulation.

Part 3 concludes with a discussion of the legal ambiguity that surrounds public-private partnerships, again focusing on the ethical implications of privatization as a key element in the NPM agenda. In chapter 11, Laura S. Jensen and Sheila Suess Kennedy elaborate on the judicial inability to articulate a systematic theory of *state action* that can determine when private parties in collaboration with government assume the legal responsibilities imposed on government. These authors recount how the courts have relied on differing criteria to determine whether private involvement with government involves assumption of a state role. The inconsistency among these rulings has led to what one scholar (quoted in chapter 11) terms a "conceptual disaster area" in its failure to differentiate a state role from private action that falls outside the parameters of legal accountability. The effects of this ambiguity become evident in the Abu Ghraib prison scandal since it is not known what, if any, legal responsibilities military intelligence contractors assume in their treatment of Iraqi prisoners. Jensen and Kennedy punctuate their conceptual discussion with a mini case concerning Mayor Stephen Goldsmith's initiatives to "marketize" municipal government in Indianapolis in the early 1990s. This case experience reveals many resulting accountability breaches that correspond to Frederickson's more generalized analysis of how the NPM ingredients compromise the public interest (chapter 8).

Although corruption control is rooted deeply in the reform tradition of public administration, might the cure sometimes prove more debilitating than the disease? Part 4 includes two chapters that both examine the unintended consequences of ethics control designs and also address workable alternative strategies. In chapter 12, Frank Anechiarico reviews the evolution of the "anticorruption project" in the United States, tracing it from the American Progressive Movement of the early twentieth century. He then associates the harmful aspects of various rule-bound anticorruption measures with Max Weber's assertions about the destructive tendencies that bureaucracies inflict upon humans. Anechiarico turns his focus to more innovative designs associated with deregulation, elaborating specifically on how recent New York City mayors relaxed bureaucratic rules so as to promote competition in municipal contracting while at the same time they created innovative measures to promote ethical compliance. In particular, the city's administration relied on an independent private-sector inspector general (IPSIG) to scrutinize the contracting activities of firms with historical links to organized crime. The author maintains that this new IPSIG approach served to expedite the recovery and clearance efforts at Ground Zero after the September 11, 2001, terrorist attacks.

In chapter 13, Kathryn G. Denhardt and Stuart C. Gilman concentrate on gift policy as an essential component of ethics regulation in government. These authors explain how gift regulations can be effective in avoiding corruption, sidestepping conflicts of interest, and instilling transparency in government operations. Nonetheless, Denhardt and Gilman assert that the imposition of a *zero-gift policy*—which forbids public officials to receive anything of value—casts a chill on legitimate governmental activities, on employee morale, and even on the enforcement of this strident measure. These difficulties prompt the authors to recommend a "bright line" de minimus design whereby public jurisdictions permit token gifts below a set value (for example, $25). If it were accompanied by a disclosure procedure or third party review, adoption of a de minimus gift policy could maintain material control without obstructing how public officials function in their spheres of interaction.

The last three chapters in this book shift attention from organizational design to emerging questions about the global relevance of public-sector ethics—specifically, whether administrative ethics norms in the United States fit into transnational and supranational contexts. To the extent that corruption control commands center stage in the global dialogue, there appears to be international consensus regarding the importance of ethics reform measures intended to remedy institutional corruption. In chapter 14, Gerald E. Caiden draws upon the recent experience of Transparency International—a Berlin-based nongovernmental organization that promotes anticorruption norms globally—to document a convergence of international opinion regarding types of behaviors that constitute corrupt practices. Caiden provides an analytical distinction between *individual* corruption—which can be rooted out by organization sanctions—and *institutional* corruption—which is pervasive within organization cultures. The latter constitutes a pattern of self-serving motivations that discredit the efforts of whistleblowers and others who strive to act ethically. These patterns of willful, unethical behavior in turn undermine trust in public institutions and counteract effective governance.

In chapter 15, Diane E. Yoder and Terry L. Cooper review various regional and international efforts to establish public management ethics standards. They indicate, however, that the motivations to fight corruption and promote integrity may vary among national and regional settings, perhaps subject to the complexities of increasing global interdependence. Thus, these authors understand regional and global declarations, agreements, and organizations as elements in a process of socially constructing a new international reality.

It has become evident that the thrust of global economic and political forces acts upon all nations—in ways both beneficial and tragically destructive—to fundamentally challenge the normative foundations of public service ethics. In chapter 16, Richard K. Ghere examines how the forces of globalization affect public service ethics both in professional practice and academic study in the aftermath of the September 11, 2001, terrorist attacks on the World Trade Center and the Pentagon. After asserting that administrative ethics need to adapt to a less stable "new normalcy," Ghere develops a research agenda that might lead scholars into some provocative areas of inquiry. For example, his recommendation to probe interactions among "globalization, public law, and regime values" could nudge researchers toward conflicts of obligation if requirements of international treaties eclipse traditional notions of national sovereignty and the regime values supporting it. At issue is whether the existing scope of administrative ethics is sufficient to address a complex and ambiguous set of global dynamics. Alternatively, there may be cause to incorporate a wider array of public morality and social/humanitarian justice concerns into a global perspective of public-service ethics.

Empirical Research and Theory Building

Referring back to chapter 2, Donald C. Menzel organizes his assessment of empirical research on government ethics and integrity around four sets of questions: (1) What has been the primary focus of empirical research on ethics in public administration and governance? What research questions are being asked? (2) How well does ethics research inform ethics theory? How well does ethics theory inform empirical research? (3) Are the research findings cumulative? Has progress been made toward building a body of knowledge? (4) Are there new avenues of research? Are there neglected areas of study?

Although they are directed toward articles published in ten public administration journals between 1995 and 2003, Menzel's questions can serve as pertinent benchmarks in a comparison of the research-theory linkages in this volume with a broader sample of ethics research. As they are applied to the chapters herein, two of the questions (specifically, 1 and 4) have been at least partially answered in the above discussion on focus and coherence. As has been discussed, several chapter authors focus on ethics design issues (which in essence combine Menzel's categories of ethical decision making, organization performance, and managerial experiences and strategies), although concerns of normative foundations and social justice surface in these discussions as well. So although the collective focus in this book is strong on design, the range of authors' concerns appears consistent with the core questions that are currently being examined in government-ethics scholarship. In addition, the three chapters that place public ethics and integrity into a global context appear to address a vital, new avenue of research, particularly amid critical international events that have unfolded recently.

Menzel's second and third (sets of) questions examine the extent to which empirical research and ethics theory inform each other and whether research findings are cumulative in building knowledge about government ethics and public integrity. On the first count, he finds only modest progress, primarily limited to studies of ethics decision making and moral development. In Part 2, chapters 4 (Swisher, Rizzo, and Marley) and 5 (Jurkiewicz) present empirical work that further tests Kohlberg's theory of moral cognitive development. Swisher, Rizzo, and Marley's reliance on cognitive theory contributes to accumulating evidence that, in aggregate, public managers are less likely to engage in principled reasoning than are those in other professions. In addition, Jurkiewicz's work has considerable potential to inform theory since it offers empirical evidence of managerial power as an important variable in ethics decision making. Such a finding adds substantially to an understanding of how principled reasoning translates into decisive action in public organizations.

Although it does not employ data analysis, Wittmer's integrative work (in chapter 3) also adds context to decision making as it incorporates moral development into a broader array of pertinent variables. Indeed, the tendency to dichotomize work as either *empirical data analysis* or *normative discourse* undervalues theory-building activities that both integrate existing knowledge (as Wittmer's chapter does) and posit causal explanations pertinent to ethical climates in the public arena. Years ago, Professor Arthur Goldberg (1963) called attention to "retroduction" as a scientific, imaginative leap to account for some observed phenomena. Such retroductive inference may be especially warranted if the causation asserted is societal by nature. For example, in chapter 6, Adams and Balfour posit a causal relationship between pervasive technical-rational thinking in Western society and their construct of administrative evil. Clearly, the independent variable remains constant, so they rely on case evidence to validate the plausibility of their argument. In similar fashions, the authors of chapters included in Part 3 construct chains of evidence that demonstrate how NPM initiatives erode the ethical capacities of public-sector entities. George Frederickson's recipe in chapter 8 outlines six causal assertions that link the various NPM ingredients to limited ethical capacity in government. In chapter 9, Dicke and Boonyarak explain why NPM's promises of accountable service delivery fall short in the administration of human services. And evidence that links NPM reforms to particular acts of misconduct (such as the scandals deLeon discusses in chapter 10) serves as building blocks for this theory-building activity. Further, Jensen and Kennedy offer a detailed explanation for the legal ambiguity that in many instances allows private collaborators in partnership with government to sidestep legal accountability. Collectively, these chapters contribute to theory in substantiating the impact of NPM reforms in weakening the capacity of public entities to act as stewards of the public interest.

Similar causal arguments are constructed in Part 4 to illustrate the relationship between overzealous anticorruption initiatives and adverse administrative outcomes. By probing these causal relationships, both chapters 12 and 13 point to particular administrative remedies (Anechiarico explains the functioning of the independent private-sector inspector general; Denhardt and Gilman recommend a de minimus gift policy) and in so doing, each discussion informs the practice of public administration.

As might be expected, the exploratory efforts that probe the contours of public service in global contexts engage in more preliminary forms of theory building. In chapter 14, Caiden's efforts articulate a coherent definition of corruption that has universal meaning. At first glance, it may appear that inquiries to determine whether or not U.S. ethical norms fit into transnational settings lend themselves well to empirical analysis—presumably, either "yes, they do" or "no, they do not." However, chapters 15 and 16 suggest that such inquiry may require researchers to reconsider the normative foundations of ethics and integrity within the context of national and regional experiences—

as well as to reassess our own public values amid global forces that challenge traditional national sovereignty assumptions.

There may be cause for disillusionment that, in the years since publication of *Ethics and Public Administration* in 1993, theory-grounded data analysis has not grown at a pace with the general literature in government ethics. It is to be hoped that the empirical payoff looms ahead in subsequent years as integrative research and causal theory building offer a richer array of testable questions and as more data-gathering alternatives to survey research are utilized. Yet perhaps the value consciousness inherent in the study of ethics and integrity cautions against the rush toward hard data manipulation found elsewhere in the social sciences. At any rate, one might err in discounting the value and extent of theory building in public-ethics research that has accrued over the past decade. The contributed chapters in this volume represent a variety of theory-building endeavors, and, in some cases, empirical theory that informs ethics research.

References

Cooper, Terry L. 2001. "The Emergence of Administrative Ethics as a Field of Study in the United States." In *Handbook of Administrative Ethics*, ed. Terry L. Cooper. New York: Marcel Dekker.
———. 2004. "Big Questions in Administrative Ethics: A Need for Focused, Collaborative Effort." *Public Administration Review* 64, no. 4: 394–407.
Goldberg, Arthur S. 1963. "Political Science as Science." In *Politics and Social Life*, ed. Nelson W. Polsby, Robert A. Dentler, and Paul A. Smith. Boston: Houghton Mifflin.

2

State of the Art of Empirical Research on Ethics and Integrity in Governance

Donald C. Menzel

Introduction

Before the 1990s, only a handful of scholars in the United States was engaged in empirical research that focused on public administration and government. Those efforts, such as Bowman's surveys (1977 and 1990) of public administration practitioners and Hejka-Ekins's (1988) study of ethics pedagogy in graduate public administration education, were laudable and valuable—yet very limited compared to the effort put into ethics theory (see Chandler 1983; Cooper 1982, 1984, 1986, 1987; Denhardt 1988, 1989; Dobel 1990; Frederickson and Hart 1985; Gawthrop 1984; Hart 1984; Nigro and Richardson 1990; Rawls 1971; Rohr 1976, 1978, 1989; Thompson 1985). Bowman's (1990, p. 345) comment aptly characterizes the pre-1990 state of empirical research on administrative and governmental ethics: "Empirical studies form a small part of this body of knowledge . . . many of them focus on business management, have a low and perhaps unreliable response rate, poll students, do not include attitudinal data, and/or are now outdated."

The times change, however. What has been a cottage industry of empirical ethics research has mushroomed into a robust and flourishing enterprise both within the United States and abroad. This chapter will describe and assess this promising new enterprise. More specifically, it will extend the research conducted by the author and subsequently published in *Public Integrity* (Menzel 1999). The following questions guide this review and assessment:

- What has been the primary focus of empirical research on ethics in public administration and governance? What research questions are being asked?
- How well does empirical research inform ethics theory? And, how well does ethics theory inform empirical research?
- Are the research findings cumulative? Has progress been made toward building a body of knowledge?
- Are there new avenues of research? Are there neglected areas of study?

Study Methodology

Articles published in ten public affairs and administration journals in the United States are the primary database for this study. Additionally, articles published in the volume edited by Frederickson (1993) are included since they are the products of a conference whose primary focus was to promote empirical research on ethics in government. Empirically based articles published in cognate fields such as business, psychology, education, and political science are omitted—although some references are made to the literature in these fields. In the study of business ethics, for example, there is a sizable literature, some of which is certainly relevant (e.g., studies of ethical decision making). In political science a modest literature deals with ethics, although most literature is normative or philosophical and often deals with issues such as war and human rights (Almond 1946; Mapel 1990; McKenna 1965; Tessitore 1990; Thompson 1978). There is also a sizable body of literature on political corruption that has an empirical base, and some of this literature is included in this review.

The review examines articles published between 1970 and 2003, with particular attention focused on the past five years—1999 through 2003.[1] The journals are *Public Administration Review; Public Administration Quarterly; American Review of Public Administration; Administration & Society; Public Productivity and Management Review; International Journal of Public Administration; Journal of Public Administration Research and Theory; Public Integrity Annual; Journal of Public Affairs Education;* and *State and Local Government Review.*

Five major research themes can be identified in the literature:

1. *Ethical decision making and moral development,* that is, what enters into the individual's reasoning process when confronted with an ethically challenging decision or situation? How does the stage

of one's moral development influence "right" and "wrong" decision making?

2. *Ethics laws and regulatory agencies*, that is, what and how do laws
   structure right and wrong behavior? How effective are regulatory
   bodies and commissions (local, state, and federal) in carrying out
   ethics laws and regulations?

3. *Organizational performance and ethics*, that is, how and to what
   extent do strong/weak ethics cultures or leaders influence organizational practices and outcomes? Do high performing public organizations adopt best-ethics management practices?

4. *Ethics management experiences and strategies*, that is, what constitutes "best-ethics management" practices? Are some ethics management strategies more/less effective than others?

5. *Community, culture, and the ethical environment*, that is, how does
   the culture of a community defined broadly as a collection of common values and interests influence the ethical environment of an
   organization, city, state, or nation? Why are some communities/
   cultures more likely than others to embrace strong/weak ethical
   environments?

Ethical Decision Making and Moral Development

Ethical decision making and moral development are subjects of long-stand-
ing interest to ethics theorists as well as to practicing public managers. It is at
the center of deontological and teleological approaches to ethics, regardless
of whether one is examining Kantian ethics or utilitarianism as espoused by
Jeremy Bentham or John Stuart Mill. Ethical decision making and moral
development also are central to Kohlberg's (1980) well-known writing and
research and to Dennis Thompson's (1985) exploration of the possibility of
administrative ethics.[2] It is therefore not surprising to find that a growing
number of investigators are drawing from these theories to devise empirical
research strategies. Among those are Stewart and Sprinthall (1993); Stewart,
Siemienska, and Sprinthall (1997), Stewart, Sprinthall, and Kem (2002);
Wittmer (1992, 2000); Jurkiewicz and Brown (2000); and White (1999b).

The Stewart-Sprinthall 1993 study analyzed data gathered from students
and local government managers in North Carolina in an effort to measure the
level of ethical reasoning exhibited by these groups. (The researchers employed Kohlberg's moral development theory and the Defining Issues Test
developed by Rest in 1986.) They also examined differences in ethical reasoning across demographic variables of gender, race, education, age, and
organizational responsibilities of line/staff and level of position. None of

these variables explained differences in ethical reasoning. As Stewart and Sprinthall note, "[P]ublic executives in this study are no more able to identify principled reasoning than mid-level or first-line managers" (1993, p. 217). However, what they did find is that there is a greater likelihood of higher-stage reasoning when a person is familiar with the content of the problem situation and there has been considerable discussion and analysis of the issues (p. 217). In Stewart and Sprinthall's judgment, open discussion and challenge can facilitate the growth process, even in an area as complex as ethical reasoning (p. 217).

Motivated by these findings, the authors secured a grant from the National Science Foundation to further explore the ethical attitudes and moral development of public officials in non-American settings, specifically in Poland and Russia. Their Polish research subjects were 485 local government officials in two provinces. Their primary research question was: "What system of moral reasoning is characteristic for newly appointed and elected officials in post-Communist Poland?" (Stewart, Siemienska, and Sprinthall 1997, p. 445). They expected to find a strong preference for principled reasoning when ethical decisions were made in the work setting. They discovered that their Polish respondents were remarkably similar to their U.S. subjects in their ethical reasoning. One striking difference, however, appeared when gender was taken into account. Polish women were much more likely to favor "a model of ethical reasoning characterized by concern for abstract principles of social cooperation than . . . their male counterparts" (Stewart, Siemienska, and Sprinthall 1999, p. 237). The authors discuss the implications of these findings for the future of governance in Poland.

White (1999b) also employed the Kohlberg framework to study the effect of gender upon moral development. His research compared 299 male and female members of the U.S. Coast Guard. The study found that the Coast Guard women scored higher on the Defining Issues Test (DIT). That is, women exhibited a higher level of ethical reasoning than did their male counterparts. White offered several explanations for this finding. First, "Coast Guard women may be a valid reflection of women in general and may confirm the argument that women score higher on the DIT. . . ." (p. 467). Second, Coast Guard women may be an "isolated segment of the population who join the Coast Guard for more altruistic reasons than do their male counterparts and this might indicate a higher level of moral development in the women" (p. 477).

Stewart, Siemienska, and Kern's 2002 study of ethical reasoning among Russian public administrators was conducted in 1998 and involved a survey administered to 113 public officials enrolled at the Russian Academy of Public Service. Using methodology and measurement instruments similar to those used in the United States and Poland, the researchers were able to compare and contrast ethical reasoning within and among Russian, Polish, and U.S. respondents. The study results found that gender was once again a significant variable in the ethical reasoning of Russians; female respondents exhibited a greater propensity to engage in principled reasoning than did their male counterparts. Differences among Russian, Polish, and U.S. respondents were not significant, although the Russian sample expressed the strongest preference for principled reasoning. However, Russian respondents scored low on "law and order" reasoning, which the researchers had some difficulty explaining. As they put it, "[F]rom the perspectives of theory, research, and practice, this study of Russian administrators challenged us on all fronts" (p. 294).

Wittmer (1992, 2000) also employs Kohlberg's theory to explore ethical decision making. His research focuses on questions such as: "Does ethical sensitivity result in more ethical decisions?" "What makes a person more ethically sensitive?" and "Are there significant differences in ethical decision making of those employed in public versus private sectors?"

In order to test hypotheses, he employed an experimental research design involving 156 university students drawn from programs in public administration, business management, and engineering at two universities. The students were presented with an ethical case and asked to decide what they should do. Wittmer found that greater ethical sensitivity fosters or promotes more ethical decision making and more personalized information enhances an individual's ethical sensitivity to the moral dimensions of a situation. To his surprise, he also found that business administration and engineering students scored higher than did public administration students on the general measure of principled reasoning. Public administration students scored higher than the others on Kohlberg's stage-three level—conventional ethical reasoning that emphasizes loyalty, trust, respect, and commitment to group. He suggests that this finding might be disturbing to those who hold the view that it is the responsibility of public administrators to protect individual citizen rights and uphold the fundamental values of American political culture. However, he concludes that "public managers are well served by recognizing that most adults tend to follow conventional moral reasoning" (2000, p. 191). Thus he implies that public managers may be more sensitive to, if not in touch with, ordinary Americans.

A final empirical study based on Kohlberg's theory of moral development is worth noting. This study was conducted by Jurkiewicz and Brown (2000). They examined the link between leadership defined as the effective exercise of power in an organization and ethics. They hypothesized that a positive relationship exists between one's level of ethical reasoning and effective leadership. Forty-two chief executive officers of nonprofit organizations in a large metropolitan community formed their database. Using a sophisticated screening process involving academic and practitioner judges who identified a sample of executives as highly effective, they surveyed two equal-sized samples of those judged highly effective and those judged noneffective. Their findings support their primary hypothesis—effective executives are more likely than are noneffective executives to evaluate moral decisions on the basis of calculated rights, values, or principles (p. 205).

The reader may be inclined to think that all empirical research on ethical decision making and moral development is driven by Kohlbergian theory and Rest's Defining Issues Test. This is not so. Other investigators have employed survey research (Strait 1996, 1997, 1999) and case studies (Frederickson and Newman 2001; Wheeland 2000) to gain insight into the ethical reasoning and moral development of public officeholders.

Strait (1996, 1997, 1999), for example, investigated ethical decision making and unethical behavior of university employees. Her research questions were: Are there gender differences in ethical/unethical behavior? Does age make a difference in ethical/unethical behavior? Are employees with more years of service more/less ethical than employees with fewer years of service? Basing her research on previous research (Ford and Woodrow 1994; Hahn, Colin, and Bart 1990), she hypothesized that (1) females would engage in more ethical behavior than would males, (2) older employees would engage in more ethical behavior than would younger employees, and (3) employees with longer service would be more ethical than would employees with shorter service. Strait tested these hypotheses and found that only the third hypothesis was valid. She concluded that "employees with seven or more years of service did appear to behave more ethically in the overall survey results" (1997, p. 47). She speculated that because vested employees have more time to be shaped and influenced by the policies and informal culture of their organizations, they are more likely to have a stronger ethical attachment to the organizations and are therefore less likely to engage in unethical behavior.

Frederickson and Newman (2001) explored the decision by a high-ranking manager in the U.S. Forest Service to resign her position. She "exited with voice" and, according to the investigators, is a moral exemplar. Their theoretical framework was based on Hart's (1992) notion of a moral episode. The episode had to do with Gloria Flora's judgment that, as the supervisor of a national forest in Nevada, she could no longer carry out her stewardship duties in the face of powerful economic and political pressures to exploit protected federal lands from mining, timber production, and livestock grazing. Gloria Flora's more than twenty years of service with the U.S. Forest

Service was terminated less than three years from vestment in the civil service retirement system. She paid a high price, emotionally and financially, for her moral courage. "Why?" asked Frederickson and Newman. Because she could not compromise her strong desire to do the right thing. "She was motivated to act as she did out of a sense of responsibility" (p. 360).

These studies and others that are not highlighted here (see Bowman, Berman, and West 2001; Pfiffner 2003; Swisher, Rizzo, and Marley 2001; Williams and Guy 2000; Folks 2000; Jurkiewicz 2002; Jurkiewicz and Nichols 2002; Jurkiewicz and Thompson 1999; Lovell 2003) break new intellectual ground. Collectively, they provide substantial motivation and guidance for probing even deeper and more systematically into the dynamics of ethical decision making and the moral development of men and women in public service.

Ethics Laws and Regulatory Agencies

Unethical and illegal acts spawned by the Watergate scandal in the 1970s and fueled by the Iran-Contra affair and the U.S. Department of Housing and Urban Development scandals of the 1980s, as well as less visible but still objectionable acts of public officials in state and local governments, have motivated lawmakers to pass numerous ethics laws. Nearly every state has an ethics statute or law, and thirty-eight states have established ethics offices or commissions. Many cities, including mega cities Los Angeles and Chicago, have established ethics commissions to investigate both real and alleged cases of wrongdoing. The United States government has also taken action, having established the Office of Government Ethics (OGE) with the passage of the Ethics in Government Act of 1978. Now, some twenty-five years later, nearly 15,000 full and part-time ethics officials can be found in the federal executive branch—excluding inspectors general (Gilman and Lewis 1996, p. 521).

These legislative and institution-building efforts have not gone unnoticed by researchers. Goodman, Holp, and Ludwig (1996), for example, studied state ethics laws to understand why some states adopt more/less stringent, comprehensive laws. They hypothesized that differences in political or institutional cultures could explain variation in state laws. Institutional cultures that foster highly professional legislative bodies, they contend, are more likely to adopt more stringent and comprehensive ethics laws than are less professionally oriented legislatures. "We posit that small, well paid legislatures, with sufficient staff, pass stronger legislation where ethical issues are concerned" (Goodman, Holp, and Ludwig 1996, p. 53).

Their study methodology included both building a "strength of state ethics legislation" index that incorporated sixteen broad categories of restrictions present or absent in a state's ethics laws and compiling political culture measures from 1990 census data. Additionally, they employed measures of legislative professionalization such as salary, size of staff, terms, and length of session in order to develop a regression model to explain variance in the strength of ethics legislation. Somewhat to their surprise, they found that "the degree of legislative institutionalization and the nature of the political culture are not strong effective explanatory variables in explaining the variance in ethics strength between the states" (1996, p. 54). The question of why there is variation in state ethics laws remains unanswered, although they speculate that "ethics legislation is a function of an ethics scandal process" (p. 55). They point to examples of significant ethics legislation passed in Ohio, California, South Carolina, Kentucky, and New York after intense media coverage of scandals.

Other investigators have focused on state ethics commissions. Williams (1996) studied the Florida Commission on Ethics to assess the agency's effectiveness in training public officials, conducting ethics audits, investigating complaints, and encouraging an ethical climate by management. Based on unstructured interviews with commissioners and a review of archival records of the agency, Williams concluded that the ethics commission was largely ineffective in all four areas. "Unfortunately," Williams asserts, "the commission apparently serves more effectively as a punitive agent than as an agent of constructive change" (p. 71).

Menzel (1996a) also studied the Florida Commission on Ethics but from a different vantage point—the view from the street. That is, he surveyed persons who had filed an ethics complaint (legally referred to as complainants) and public officials (legally referred to as respondents) who were the object of a complaint. These questions guided the research:

- What is the relationship between how an ethics complaint is handled and citizen trust/distrust in government?
- Do persons who file ethics complaints have a positive or negative experience? Are those experiences satisfactory and therefore helpful in building trust and confidence in government? Or are those experiences unsatisfactory and therefore contribute to the erosion of public trust and confidence in government?"
- What are the outcomes of the ethics complaint-making process?

Menzel's study methodology involved mail surveys of 303 complainants (144 responded) and 555 respondents (161 responded) between 1989 and 1992. Among other things, he found that complainants were much more likely to say they were dissatisfied with the outcomes of the complaints they filed than were respondents who were the objects of the complaints.

Furthermore, neither complainants nor respondents differentiated process outcomes from substantive outcomes. How one was treated and how things turned out—regardless of whether one was the person filing a complaint or the person who was the object of the complaint—seemed to go hand in hand. Finally, he concluded that "the ethics complaint-making process in Florida may be widening rather than closing the trust deficit" (p. 80).

Smith (2003a) also studied the practices of the Florida Ethics Commission as well as those of Connecticut and New York State. His comparative case study was based on anonymous interviews with sixty ethics officials and an examination of laws, rules, and regulations employed in these states. The central paradigm that emerged from his study was enforcement (Smith 2003a, p. 286). By this he means that "complaint making, investigations, and adjudicative proceedings all were geared toward, and products of, this enforcement function" (p. 287). His study primarily compares and contrasts the practices of the state agencies; it does not allow the reader to reach conclusions regarding "best practices," or which state ethics commission is more/ less effective than another, or why this might be the case.

Ethics agencies and practices at the local level of government have also been scrutinized (see Smith 1999). Van Noy (2000) reports on the Seattle experience, noting that the city has been a leader in developing and implementing legislation that reduces the influence of "money on elections and the conduct of government" (p. 303). She finds that public financing has proved to be the only successful tool for limiting the influence of money on elections and government conduct. The practices of another city, Houston, are detailed by Fain (2002). He reviews the zero-gift policy adopted by Houston and contends that it has deterred unethical behavior by city employees. This policy also enables two investigation and enforcement agencies—the Houston Office of Inspector General and the Harris County district attorney—to be effective. Fain notes that Houston has suffered no further embarrassment due to questionable acceptance of gifts since this policy was put into effect (p. 67).

Other investigators have focused on the legal or constitutional side of ethics issues (Brindle 2000; Brown 2000; Feigenbaum 2002; Gray 2002; Mackey 2003; Roberts 1999; Rohr 2002). Rohr offers a constitutional analysis of the ethical aftermath of privatization and contracting out. He explores the arguments developed by the justices of the U.S. Supreme Court and concludes that the "link between ethics and constitutional law is forged by the oath many public servants take to uphold the Constitution of the United States" (p. 1). Gray reviewed the legal history and justifications for affirmative action with attention on state and federal judiciary decision making. Brown reviewed the federal Hatch Act and Little Hatch Acts adopted by many states to regulate the political behavior of civil service employees. She found no pattern across the states' Little Hatch Acts to suggest why some state laws contain more/less strict provisions. Brown notes that since the federal act changed in 1993, however, to permit expanded political participation by federal civil service employees "there has been a definite trend toward loosening Little Hatch Acts" (2002, p. 118). One other legally oriented study is noteworthy. Roberts examined the role of the U.S. Supreme Court in "defining the nature of the law of public service ethics by using an individual responsibility model of official accountability" (1999, p. 20). His study covered issues such as the immunity doctrine and its evolution, codes of ethics and the appearance of impropriety, administrative investigations of official misconduct, mail fraud, and more.

These studies and others (see Dobel 1993; Herrmann 1997; Light 1993) add significant insight into ethics laws and the practices of regulatory agencies. Nonetheless, additional study of ethics statutes and regulatory agencies is needed. As in other areas of empirical research, this subject area remains a work in progress.

Organizational Performance and Ethics

Efficiency, economy, and effectiveness have been the hallmark values of modern public administration since Woodrow Wilson declared that "the field of administration is a field of business" (1887, p. 20). Public officeholders, so presumed Wilson and his intellectual successors, were expected to be men and women of high moral character. Thus there was little reason to be concerned about the need to add a fourth "e"—ethics—to this holy trilogy. But times change and ethics has become academic talk and shoptalk. Indeed, it is increasingly common to find public affairs graduate programs that offer ethics courses and public organizations that provide in-house ethics training (see Bowman and Menzel 1998).

At first one might think this trend is the result of an increasing incidence of wrongdoing. Upon closer examination, however, one may discover a more compelling explanation—the growing recognition by private- and public-sector managers that productive, high-performing units can add value to their organizations' performance by adhering to practices and behavior that promote ethics and integrity in their organizations. Both practicing public managers and public affairs scholars are devoting greater time and energy to understanding and building ethical workplaces (see Berman and West 1997; Bohte and Meier 2000; Bowman 1990; Bruce 1994, 1996; Burke and Black

1990; Jurkiewicz and Brown 2000; Menzel 1992, 1993, 1995a, 1995b, 1996b; Perry 1993; Zajac and Comfort 1997; Zajac and Al-Kazemi 2000). They are also gaining greater appreciation of the roles that professional associations and ethics codes play in fostering organizational integrity.

Among the earliest investigators of the ethics-performance linkage were Burke and Black (1990) and Bruce (1994). Burke and Black conducted an exploratory study of organizational ethics and productivity by surveying sixty-nine executives and managers, approximately one-third of whom were from the public and nonprofit sectors. Their findings did not demonstrate a firm empirical link between ethics and performance but did motivate them to recommend that agencies should create "a leadership group focused on identifying ethical concerns and productivity measures" (1990, p. 132). Bruce also used survey research to obtain data from municipal clerks about ethics in the workplace. Municipal clerks, according to her survey, are members of a highly ethical group who believe that city employees are basically ethical and highly productive. She concludes that managers and supervisors have a "substantial influence on employee ethics and, by extension, on organizational performance" (1994, p. 251).

Menzel (1992, 1993, 1995a, 1995b, 1996b) also has conducted research that probes the ethics-performance link. He surveyed several different populations—city and county managers in Florida and Texas and city and county employees in two Florida governments. One study (1993) question was "Do ethical climates of public organizations reinforce or detract from organizational values such as efficiency, effectiveness, excellence, quality, and teamwork?" He hypothesized that as the ethical climate of an organization becomes stronger, organizational performance values such as efficiency, effectiveness, teamwork, excellence, and quality will be strongly supported. The findings led him to accept the hypothesis that an organization's ethical climate has an important positive influence on an organization's performance.

Similar findings are reported by Berman and West (1997) in their survey of city managers and the adoption of ethics management strategies in their cities. They note that "commitment to workforce effectiveness and the adoption of pay-for-performance policies are associated strongly with ethics management practices. Efforts to decrease absenteeism and to adopt a customer-orientation also are significantly associated with ethics management" (p. 26).

Other research by Menzel (1996b) focused on the organizational consequences of ethics-induced stress in the public workplace. Ethics-induced stress was defined as a form of cognitive dissonance between an employee's sense of ethics and the ethical or not-so-ethical values found in the employee's workplace. He asked: Does ethics-induced stress result in decreased employee productivity? Does it result in lower levels of job satisfaction? Higher levels of conflict? Higher levels of employee turnover? Drawing on a surveys of several hundred city and county managers in Florida and Texas, he found strong statistical associations between managers' high levels of ethics-induced stress and impaired organizational performance. Specifically, as the level of ethics-induced stress increases, job satisfaction decreases, organizational conflict increases, and employee turnover is likely to be greater.

Organizational consequences associated with whistle-blowing also have been studied, although admittedly not nearly so often as why an employee blows the whistle or what the consequences are for the whistle-blower.[3] As Perry (1993) notes, considerable attention has been given to finding out how whistle-blowers are treated by their organizations, but little attention has been given to how blowing the whistle impacts organizational performance and control. His study set out to investigate this complex phenomenon. Drawing on archival data, interviews, and self-administered surveys in federal agencies, he found that whistle-blowing "has a very limited role to play in correcting specific abuses and promoting organizational change" (p. 94).

An innovative study of cheating within and by organizations also notes the undesirable organizational outcomes that may result. Boht and Meier (2000) studied organizational cheating in Texas public schools and concluded that important organizational goals are displaced, thus impairing their effective performance, which is to produce educated members of society. Moreover, this study pays particular attention to identifying the motivations for organizational cheating. They argue that cheating occurs because of inadequate performance measurement, resource scarcity, overwhelming workload demands, and a lack of accountability (pp. 177–78).[4] Boht and Meier's research points to ethics failure in organizations, a subject that has been studied by Zajac and Comfort (1997) and Zajac and Al-Kazemi (2000).

Zajac and Comfort (1997) examined organizational learning strategies as responses to ethics failures. Their study focused on three county health departments in three states and relied on field observations, interviews, and self-administered surveys. They asked, "How much and what kind of organizational learning takes place when an organization experiences ethics failure?" (1997, p. 553). They developed several models of organizational ethics learning and auditing and tested these using vignettes that indicate several types of ethics failure—marginal, malicious, or symptomatic. They concluded that the greatest organizational learning effort is in response to symptomatic failure, which they define as severe dysfunctions within the organization.

Zajac and Al-Kazemi (2000) investigated ethics failure and organizational learning in a study of public agencies in a non-American setting, Kuwait. Adopting the methodology employed to study county health departments, the researchers surveyed and interviewed 254 employees in six Kuwait agencies. Three questions guided their study: How do public agencies in Kuwait respond to ethics failures? How much effort is committed to organizational learning when failure occurs? When organizational learning is found, what are its specific features? (pp. 22–23). They found that only low to moderate levels of organizational effort have been directed toward learning from ethics failures, both in the American counties and in Kuwait agencies; effort toward preventative ethics learning (ethics audits) is high in all sampled agencies in both countries; none of the agencies in either country engage in formal ethics scanning, that is, they do not routinely seek information about potential ethics problems (p. 39). Zajac and Al-Kazemi contend that "the significance of this research is found primarily in the high cost of ethics failure, both for public agencies and the public" (p. 23). These costs include misappropriating of public resources (corruption), additional expenditure of agency and law enforcement resources to remedy failures, and the time and attention that the agency devotes to its response to the failure that might otherwise be spent in the pursuit of its mission (p. 23).

One response to public-sector ethics failure is codification, either in the form of law or in the adoption and enforcement of a code of ethics. Many states have opted for ethics laws. Advocates of codes typically presume that codes contribute to a healthy organization and thus to a higher performing organization.[5] Surveys (Bowman 1990; Bowman and Williams 1997) of practitioner members of the American Society for Public Administration (ASPA) show that practitioners strongly embrace codes and believe that they have a positive influence on organizational life. Bruce's research (1996) also adds to the believed real world impact of codes. Her study of members of the International Institute of Municipal Clerks found that clerks "rank a code of conduct as the most powerful way a city can prevent corruption" (p. 29).

In summary, there is a substantial and growing interest in probing the relationship between ethics and organizational performance. The literature reviewed here might suggest that this subject has been exhaustively examined. This is not so—many studies rely heavily on perceptions and attitudes and therefore only partly close the gap in our knowledge of the relationship between behavior and organizational performance. The work past and present is promising, but much more study is needed.

Ethics Management Experiences and Strategies

Can agency leaders and public officials manage ethics in the workplace in a manner similar to that by which budgets, policies, or people are managed? Does ethics management imply controlling the hearts and minds, not to mention behaviors, of employees? Perhaps. Yet even the acts of developing and adopting a code of ethics or a statement of principles can be viewed as managing ethics in the workplace (Bowman 1981).[6] Thus ethics management is not a new enterprise; what is new is how we think about it. If we think about it as a systematic and conscious effort to promote organizational integrity, as Article IV of the American Society for Public Administration's Code of Ethics declares, then there is such a thing as ethics management.[7] If we think about it only as "control," then it may be arguable to suggest that there can be anything approaching effective ethics management.

Bowman's research (1990) is helpful when one thinks about these matters. When he asked public managers in 1989 if their agencies had a consistent approach toward dealing with ethical concerns, he found that nearly two-thirds said their organizations did not have a consistent approach. When he asked the same question in 1996, he found that a smaller (58 percent) yet still large percentage of respondents replied in the same fashion—"my agency does not have a consistent approach toward dealing with ethical concerns." Do these responses suggest that there is little in the way of ethics management in the public sector? Possibly—but not necessarily. Indeed, the empirical research in this area has grown enormously over the past decade. The attention focused on ethics management experiences and strategy development ranges from local to national to international, and it is especially rich when the subject of corruption is added to the matter of promoting integrity and ethics in governance. Recent published research concerned with ethics management includes Berman, West, and Cava (1994), Berman and West (1997), Cava, West, and Berman (1995), Cooper and Yoder (2002), Gilman (2000), Grundstein-Amado (2001), Glor and Greene (2003), Holland and Fleming (2003), Huberts (2000), Kim (2000), Quah (1999), Smith (2003b), and West and Berman (2003).

Among the first researchers to explore empirically ethics management strategies were Berman, West, and Cava (1994). They surveyed more than 1,000 directors of human resource agencies in municipalities with populations over 25,000 to learn what ethics management strategies are employed, how they are implemented, and how effective they are. They posited that ethics management strategies could be placed on a continuum ranging from formal to informal (p. 189).

> *Formal* ethics management strategies involve mandatory employee training, use of ethics as a criterion in the reward structure, and the adoption of organizational rules that promote the ethical climate, such as requiring financial disclosure and approval of outside activities. *Informal* ethics management strategies involve reliance on role models and positive reinforcement and are behaviorally based.

After factor-analyzing the responses, they identified four categories of ethics management strategies—two of which they label as formal, one informal, and one a combination of formal and informal. The two formal strategies are code-based strategies and regulatory-based strategies. Adopting a code of ethics or establishing a standard of conduct would constitute a code-based strategy. Using ethics as a criterion in personnel hiring and promotion and requiring approval of outside activities would reflect a regulatory-based strategy. Leadership-based strategies, such as the demonstration of exemplary moral leadership by senior management, constitutes an informal ethics management strategy. Employee-based strategies that incorporate ethics training, protect whistle-blowers for valid disclosures, or solicit employees' opinions about ethics constitute a mixed strategy.

With regard to which ethics management strategies are employed in municipalities, the findings of Berman, West, and Cava confirm in part Bowman's research about the lack of a consistent approach—if *consistent* means *formal.* A minority of the cities that were surveyed reported the use of formal ethics management strategies, while a majority said their cities relied primarily on leadership-based strategies—an informal strategy. But does a reliance on an informal strategy result in ineffective ethics management? Not necessarily. Berman, West, and Cava's research concludes that moral leadership strategies are more effective than are regulatory- or code-based strategies in enabling cities to achieve ethics management objectives such as avoiding conflicts of interest, reducing the need for whistle-blowers, and fostering fairness in job assignments.

West and Berman (2003) extended their research in 2000 with another survey of city managers in all 338 U.S. cities with populations over 65,000. This study focused on the use and effectiveness of municipal audit committees, including an analysis of how audit committees promote accountability and help to resolve ethical issues that are related to financial management. Their research found, among other things, that there is a positive relationship between audit committee activities and the presence of ethics training in a municipality and that audit committees actively seek to detect ethical wrongdoing (p. 356).

Another investigator who has examined ethics management approaches and strategies is Smith (2003b). His most recent study focuses on ethics administrators in government agencies and corporate ethics officers in the private sector. Who and what are ethics administrators and officers? Why are they needed? Are they effective? What difference do they make? His research answers the who, what, and why questions but, as he acknowledges, does not answer the two latter and perhaps most significant questions. He asserts that his inquiry raises more questions than it answers. Still, Smith's study offers helpful insight into initiatives that contribute to organizational integrity.

The research highlighted above takes important steps toward improving our understanding and knowledge of what it means to manage ethics, how it can be done, and what outcomes agency managers can expect. As Berman, West, and Cava (1994) note, however, their efforts are exploratory, and much more needs to be done to understand the dynamics of mixing and matching strategies to fit particular organizational and governance circumstances. Their research is limited as well to survey research on American municipalities. What variation in strategies and consequences might be found in state or federal agencies or nonprofit organizations? The same question could be asked of public organizations in countries around the globe.

Are nations embracing ethics management strategies? Yes, to some extent—but not exactly. That is, there has been a substantial effort past and present to understand and control, if not manage, unethical behavior from a corruption perspective. This literature is so vast—see Cooper and Yoder (2002), Gilman (2000), Grundstein-Amado (2001), Glor and Greene (2003), Holland and Fleming (2003), Huberts (2000), Kim (2000), Quah (1999), Seligson (2001)—that it can only be touched upon in this review. Huberts's study of the anticorruption strategies and practices of the twenty-five-year-old Hong Kong Independent Commission Against Corruption offers a detailed assessment of the strategies employed in the fight against corruption. Kim offers a similar assessment of the strategies adopted by South Korea to strengthen the integrity of governance. Studies of Canada have also found their way into the empirical literature on ethics and corruption. Glor and Greene provide a detailed analysis of ethical reform in the governance of Canada as do Holland and Fleming, who compare Canadian ethics initiatives with those in Australia. Others who add their voices to understanding the two-sided coin of integrity and corruption in governance are Gilman (2000) and Cooper and Yoder (2002). Gilman, who served in the U.S. Office of Government Ethics, reviews what this office has done since its creation in 1978 to assist governments worldwide to develop and implement strategies and practices that foster integrity and ethics in governance. Cooper and Yoder examine the efforts of the United Nations and the Organization for Economic Cooperation and Development to combat corruption. They document what international organizations have done to establish international ethical standards that promote consistent public management ethics practices.

Community, Culture, and the Ethical Environment

Empirical research on community, culture, and the ethical environment is wide ranging in theory, methodology, and geography. Some investigators (Holbrook and Meier 1993), for example, ask whether there are systemic, institutional, cultural, or sociohistorical influences on incidences of wrong-doing or corrupt behavior. Others muse about why the incidence of wrong-doing is higher or lower in some local governments than in others (Menzel 1995a; Menzel and Benton 1991). Still others question how the ethical environment of one's city or community is interwoven with the ethical conduct of public officials (Eimicke, Cohen, and Salazar 2000; Ghere 1996, 1999; Thomas 2001). Finally, a stream of research examines the relationship between ethics and trust building in one's agency or community (Berman 1996; Carnevale and Wechsler 1992; Daly and Vasu 1998; De Vries 2002).

Political corruption was the focus of Holbrook and Meier's (1993) research. They developed and tested four models that could explain political corruption: historical-cultural, political, structural, and bureaucratic. Using data from the archives of the United States Department of Justice regarding the number of public officials in each American state who had been convicted of corruption over a ten-year period, Holbrook and Meier employed regression analysis to determine which model is the most powerful predictor of corrupt behavior. The weakest model (and in their words the "most devastating finding") is the structural model.[8] This model is essentially the traditional reform or transparency model (e.g., having state computer auditing capability of political campaigns, mandating campaign report filing, operating with initiative-referendum-recall requirements). In contrast, the most powerful model is the bureaucratic model, which includes measures of the total government employment, salaries of employees, budget size, and gambling arrests—with the latter being the most important variable in the model.

Using similar models, Menzel and Benton (1991) examined the incidence of ethics complaints in Florida counties over a sixteen-year period. Their research questions included:

1. Are there historical or cultural factors that motivate citizens to file ethics complaints against local government officials?
2. Are there political factors that motivate citizens to file ethics complaints against local government officials?
3. Are more complaints filed against local government officials in unreformed than in reformed local governments?
4. Do officials in larger governments have more complaints filed against them than officials in smaller governments?

They tested a series of hypotheses and found that Florida residents file more complaints against local government officials in those counties that experience high population growth, possess a more educated public, and have unreformed county governments (i.e., less professional management).

In a separate study, Menzel (1995a) investigated the ethical environment in Florida communities by surveying members of the Florida City and County Management Association, citizens who filed ethics complaints, and local government officials who had complaints filed against them. This research explored the ethical outlooks of these three groups to determine how congruent or incongruent their ethical outlooks were. Among the findings were that local government managers' perceptions of wrongdoing by officials at different levels of government (local, state, federal) were more similar to those of public officials who have been accused of unethical behavior than they were to those of citizen complainants. Moreover, managers cast a more wary eye on elected officials than on appointed officials. Furthermore, they perceive more wrongdoing by appointed officials than by public employees, and more wrongdoing by public employees than by colleagues in the public management profession.

How public managers, elected officials, and citizens view each other ethically and do or do not hold common outlooks may influence or condition private-public partnerships in their communities. Ghere's research (1996), for example, of the ethics of a public-private partnership effort to stimulate economic development in a midwestern county resulted in ethical mismatches that cast suspicion on the entire enterprise. The case involved a contractual relationship between a county government and a local chamber of commerce and, eventually, serious ethical lapses on the part of chamber officials and serious accountability lapses on the part of the county government. Ghere's study raised pertinent questions about whether or not public officials can "facilitate a flexible and collaborative relationship to enlist the market prowess of the private sector yet at the same time impose a tightly structured contract that wards off ethical abuse" (1996, p. 618). Additional study by Ghere (1999) involved an analysis of statements and materials at the 1996 and 1997 annual meetings of the National Council for Public-Private Partnerships. He concluded that ethical risks are associated with privatization. As he put it, "[T]hese conversations between public officials and business executives appear troubling in view of stewardship responsibilities to promote open and candid dialogue" (1999, p. 147).

Privatization, contracting out, and a commitment to competition are viewed by some scholars as the tools of entrepreneurial behavior and decision making in the public sector. Are there significant ethical risks associated with employing these tools? Eimicke, Cohen, and Salazar (2000) sought an answer to this question through case studies of Orange County, California; Indianapolis, Indiana; San Diego, California; and Bogotá, Colombia. They contended that these cases were fairly typical of privatization and contracting out in cities, and "although many decisions are carried out without controversy and with beneficial results, ethical questions abound" (p. 240). In other words, public-sector entrepreneurialism involves a high level of ethical risk taking (see also Cohen and Eimicke 1999).

Thomas (2001) approaches privatization from a different angle—the extent to which privatization contributes to a loss of public trust and confidence in governmental leaders and political representatives. Her research focuses on two questions: Will privatization result in a "new spate of loss of public trust nationally and internationally? How can trust and integrity be integrated into privatized functions?" (p. 242). She draws on two case studies in Great Britain to formulate answers. One case is the privatization of British Rail and the other is the proposed privatization of British Nuclear Fuels Limited. These cases, especially the British Rail case, have "led to a backlash in the UK, with calls for a halt to future privatizations, such as the National Air Traffic Services and London Underground" (p. 250). In sum, she feels that privatization is undermining public trust in and the integrity of government.

Berman (1996) is another researcher who has probed the linkage between ethics and trust. His study sought to find out how much trust there is among local government officials and community leaders, what municipal strategies are employed to increase trust levels, and how socioeconomic conditions may influence perceptions of trust in local government. He surveyed city managers and chief administrative officers in all 502 U.S. cities with populations of more than 50,000 to obtain their perceptions of trust levels. The findings indicated that "community leaders have only moderate levels of trust in local government" but that cities with a council-manager form of government experience a significantly higher level of trust than do cities with the mayor-council form of government (p. 33).

Berman identified three principal trust-building strategies—communication, consultation and collaboration, and minimization of wrongdoing. Communication strategies emphasize providing information about the cities' programs and performance. Consultation/collaboration strategies involve engaging community leaders via partnerships, meetings, panels, and so forth. Strategies to minimize wrongdoing emphasize adopting ethics codes, providing ethics training, and so forth. Strategies vary from community to community, and no single strategy appears to be more effective than the others. However, some evidence suggests that "using a range of strategies by local officials increases trust, even though the impact of individual strategies is modest" (1996, p. 34). Socioeconomic conditions, Berman concluded, have an influence on trust levels. Positive conditions in a community, such as high economic growth and cooperation among local groups, inspire trust in government. "Negative community conditions, such as economic stagnation, low income levels, racial strife and high levels of crime reduce economic and political resources . . . for dealing with community problems" contribute to a distrust of government (p. 34).

Carnevale and Wechsler (1992) and Daly and Vasu (1998) also have focused on trust building within public organizations. Carnevale and Wechsler, for example, build a model of organizational trust that combines characteristics of the individual (e.g., gender, salary, and efficacy) and the organization (e.g., in-group status, fairness of rewards and punishment, ethical environment). Their database involved a survey of more than 1,000 employees of an American state agency responsible for issuing drivers' licenses and performing related tasks. Among other things, their findings confirmed the hypothesis that "individuals who perceive the organization as ethical in its treatment of themselves and others will report higher levels of organizational trust" (Carnevale and Wechsler 1992, p. 480).

Taken together, studies of community, ethics, and trust building provide a firm foundation for further research. There can be little argument about the need to more fully understand what community leaders can and should do to foster ethical and trustworthy government. By the same measure, government leaders need to know what they can and should do to build trustworthy relationships with community leaders. The slope here is slippery, but it is surmountable.

Equally challenging is the matter of the honesty of politicians and administrators. It is widely presumed that both politicians and administrators often find it difficult to be honest in carrying out their duties. Systematic empirical research documenting this presumption is, however, rare. One of those rare studies is De Vries's (2002) investigation of the honesty of local government politicians and administrators in seventeen countries. His study is also an example of the effort to link traditional ethics theory with empirical study. Four philosophical views—teleological and deontological ethics theories, virtue ethics, and dialogic ethics—are used to frame the study. Nearly 10,000 respondents were asked "questions about their valuation of honesty in general and more specific questions about their opinions on the disclosure of facts and the presentation of one-sided facts" (2002, p. 313). Subsets of 15 politicians and administrators in each of 408 communities in 13 countries enabled De Vries and his colleagues to analyze community as well as individual proclivities toward honesty. At the individual level, his statistical model could explain only 5 percent of the variance. However, at the community level, his statistical model performed much better, explaining 26 percent of the variance in the politicians' responses and 13 percent among administrators. These findings, he concluded, suggest that "opinions on ethical behavior are foremost socially-culturally determined" (p. 330). Furthermore, "public officials will tell the truth when they can afford it, and when they are dishonest, this can be explained by the circumstances that do not allow them to tell the truth" (p. 332). How well does ethical theory explain these outcomes? Not very well at all, concluded De Vries. Rather, as suggested above, social-cultural influences appeared to make the more significant difference in actual behaviors. Perplexing? So it would seem.

Another empirical study that explored the interface between ethics as an individual trait and one's organizational environment is by Montjoy and Slaton (2002). Their study examined the infamous Palm Beach, Florida, butterfly ballot controversy in the U.S. presidential election debacle in 2000. Was the butterfly ballot design an ethics failure of the Palm Beach County Supervisor of Elections? Many observers thought so. Montjoy and Slaton disagreed. Their case study and ethical analysis concluded that the failure was a product of complexity and the unwillingness of many actors in a highly interdependent election process to assume responsibility for their behavior. As they put it, "[D]etermining who is responsible and for what in the decentralized and often fragmented electoral system of the United States requires an appreciation of interdependence" (p. 196).

Do ethical/unethical communities and cultures beget ethical/unethical governments and governance? Or is it the converse? It is, of course, just as difficult to develop a meaningful measure of an ethical community as it is to develop a meaningful measure of an ethical government. Still, there seems to be an inexorable logic that one is not likely to find ethical government in a community that does not embrace a strong set of ethical values. It also seems logical to suggest that no matter how difficult the challenge might be, managers and public officials who do not seem to embrace strong ethical values can make a contribution to raising the ethical consciousness of members of the community by promoting and exemplifying strong ethical principles and integrity. Empirical research on community and the ethical milieu does not provide us with clear signals or guidelines. Rather, we are left to our sense of intuition and the rules of reason and logic to sort through this matter.

Summary and Conclusion

Empirical research on ethics and integrity in public administration and governance is healthy and growing, both quantitatively and qualitatively. The past decade has seen an enormous outpouring of empirical research. Moreover, there is every indication that the next decade will be even more promising in blending theory and observation, building a cumulative body of knowledge, opening new avenues of research, and attending to overlooked areas of study.

As the reader may recall, this review and assessment has been guided by the following questions:

- What has been the primary focus of empirical research on ethics in public administration and governance? What research questions are being asked?
- How well does empirical research inform ethics theory? How well does ethics theory inform empirical research?
- Are the research findings cumulative? Has progress been made toward building a body of knowledge?
- Are there new avenues of research? Are there neglected areas of study?

This chapter will conclude with a brief summary response to each question.

The research subject matter and the questions that are addressed range across ethical decision making and moral development, laws and regulatory agencies, organizational performance, ethics management experiences and strategies, and the community-culture-ethical environment. The primary questions addressed include:

Ethical Decision Making and Moral Development

- To what extent and why do public officials engage in ethical reasoning?
- What variables, personal and contextual, influence ethical decision making?
- At what stage (Kohlberg model) of moral development do public administrators function?
- How does the stage of one's moral development influence right and wrong decision making?

Ethics Laws and Regulatory Agencies

- Have ethics laws and regulatory bodies made a difference in the ethical behaviors and practices of appointed and elected public officials?
- How effective are regulatory bodies and commissions (local, state, and federal) in carrying out ethics laws and regulations?

Organizational Performance and Ethics

- How does the ethical environment of a public organization contribute to organizational performance?
- How and to what extent do strong/weak ethics cultures or leaders influence organizational practices and outcomes?
- Do high-performing public organizations adopt best-ethics management practices? Why or why not?

Ethics Management Experiences and Strategies

- What experiences do we have with ethics management?
- What ethics management strategies are employed by public organizations to strengthen the ethical environment of the workplace?
- What constitutes best-ethics management practices?

Community, Culture, and the Ethical Environment

- How does the culture of a community, defined broadly as common values and interests, influence the ethical environment of an organization, city, state, or nation?
- Why are some communities/cultures more likely than others to embrace a strong/weak ethical environment?

These are challenging questions, and it would be misleading to suggest that the research reviewed here has produced definitive answers to them. Nevertheless, considerable progress has been made toward definitive answers.

How well does empirical research inform ethics theory? Conversely, how well does ethics theory inform empirical research? Is there an intellectual bridge between theory and reality? Some empirical research is informed by ethics theory (especially in the study of ethical decision making and moral development), but much is not. Similarly, it is difficult to argue that empirical research has had a substantial influence on ethics theory. More theory-observation bridge building remains for future investigators.

Is there progress in building a body of knowledge in public administration and governance ethics? Here the answer is "yes," but this task also remains unfinished. The pace of empirical research has quickened considerably over the past decade, but the size of the task is daunting. Much more has been accomplished in cognate fields, especially business administration. Public administration and governance scholars have much catching up to do. Empirical research in this domain has certainly moved beyond a cottage industry, but it is not yet a mature enterprise. There are many encouraging signs, though, of maturity. First, new ethics journals such as *Public Integrity* and the e-journal *Global Virtue Ethics Review* are stimulating ethics scholarship and promoting improved communication of ideas and findings among investigators. Ethics research findings to date have been scattered about public administration journals in the United States, but with the launching of these journals, especially *Public Integrity*, new publication outlets have been put into place. Indeed, the articles selected for this review were drawn heavily from *Public Integrity*. Second, the creation of the Ethics Section of the American Society for Public Administration is an important organizational link for ethics scholars and practitioners. Third, the quest for a tighter fit between ethics theory and empirical findings remains important. More empirical research across a spectrum of subjects, as this review and assessment has documented, is needed to build a cumulative body of knowledge.

This review and assessment is a work in progress. While ethics articles published in leading U.S. public administration journals since 1970 were incorporated into this review, there is a growing body of empirical research published in European journals that was not included. Moreover, ethics research that examines similarities and differences between private- and public- sector organizations was only touched upon here (see Berman, West, and Cava 1994; Wittmer and Coursey 1996). A body of research on pedagogical issues also has not been reviewed here (see Bowman and Menzel 1998; Menzel 1997, 1998a). Finally, new study horizons are associated with the ethical applications of information technology, the Internet, and the World Wide Web (Menzel 1998b, 1998c). Another avenue of new research might examine the influence of organizational structure on the "formation and development of public officials' ethical disposition toward administrative action" (Kim 2001, pp. 80–81). It should be noted that research in the field of policy ethics is rapidly expanding, and this literature is not incorporated in this review (see Brainard 2000; Di Norcia 2003; Gonzalez 2001; Wisensale 1999; Zundel 2002).

Beyond these developments, the research strategies for ethics scholars should include greater methodological rigor with perhaps less reliance on survey research methods. Such rigor, of course, could include contextually rich case studies as well as trend or longitudinal analyses that were largely absent from the studies examined here. Ethics as a study subject remains sensitive to participants as well as to organizations and scholarly observers. Methodologies that produce candid and valid data are critical to the development of theory and building a cumulative body of knowledge.

Public administration and governance researchers can gain much by more closely examining empirical research in other fields. The literature reviewed here, while not altogether uninformed by other bodies of literature, is probably not as well informed as it could be. Greater cross-fertilization of ideas and study approaches across fields such as business, psychology, education, and engineering is needed.

Notes

1. The journals selected here do not constitute the universe of public affairs/administration journals. Journals published in other countries, for example, are not included.

However, in the author's judgment and as reflected by published rankings of U.S. journals, this collection represents the leading public affairs/administration journals.

2. An excellent overview of Lawrence Kohlberg's theory of moral development and its implications for ethical decision making by public administrators can be found in White (1999a).

3. Brewer and Selden (1998) provide a concise summary of recent research on the motivation of whistle-blowers.

4. Similar conclusions are drawn by Ott, Boonyarak, and Dicke (2001) in a study of performance measurement as a vehicle for achieving ethical accountability in the delivery of human services.

5. The Code of Ethics of the American Society for Public Administration, Article IV, Promote Ethical Organizations states: [To] strengthen organizational capabilities to apply ethics, efficiency and effectiveness in serving the public, ASPA members are committed to

1. Enhance organizational capacity for open communication, creativity, and dedication.
2. Subordinate institutional loyalties to the public good.
3. Establish procedures that promote ethical behavior and hold individuals and organizations accountable for their conduct.
4. Provide organization members with an administrative means for dissent, assurance of due process and safeguards against reprisal.
5. Promote merit principles that protect against arbitrary and capricious actions.
6. Promote organizational accountability through appropriate controls and procedures.
7. Encourage organizations to adopt, distribute, and periodically review a code of ethics as a living document.

6. See Grundstein-Amado (2001) for an in-depth discussion of how public service organizations can formulate and implement codes of ethics as an ethics management strategy.

7. They contend this is a devastating finding because the structural model is the most amenable to control and manipulation—intervention by policy makers.

8. Holbrook and Meier (1993) explain that greater enforcement in such areas as gambling, drugs, and prostitution will likely increase the need for police protection, and thus generate more bribe attempts.

References

Almond, Gabriel A. 1946. "Politics, Science, and Ethics." *American Political Science Review* 40 (April): 283–93.
Berman, Evan M. 1996. "Restoring the Bridges of Trust: Attitudes of Community Leaders toward Local Government." *Public Integrity Annual*: 31–49.
Berman, Evan M., and West, Jonathan P. 1997. "Managing Ethics to Improve Performance and Build Trust." *Public Integrity Annual*: 23–31.
Berman, Evan; West, Jonathan; and Cava, Anita. 1994. "Ethics Management in Municipal Governments and Large Firms: Exploring Similarities and Differences." *Administration & Society* 26 (August): 185–203.

Bohte, John, and Meier, Kenneth J. 2000. "Goal Displacement: Assessing the Motivation for Organizational Cheating." *Public Administration Review* 60 (March/April): 173–82.
Bowman, James S. 1977. "Ethics in the Federal Service: A Post-Watergate View." *Midwest Review of Public Administration* 11 (March): 3–20.
———. 1981. "Ethical Issues for the Public Manager." In *A Handbook of Organization Management*, ed. William B. Eddy, pp. 92–115. New York: Marcel Dekker.
———. 1990. "Ethics in Government: A National Survey of Public Administrators." *Public Administration Review* 50 (May/June): 345–53.
Bowman, James S., and Williams, Russell L. 1997. "Ethics in Government: From a Winter of Despair to a Spring of Hope." *Public Administration Review* 57 (November/December): 517–26.
Bowman, James S.; Berman, Evan M.; and West, Jonathan P. 2001. "The Profession of Public Administration: An Ethics Edge in Introductory Textbooks?" *Public Administration Review* 61 (March/April): 194–205.
Bowman, James S., and Menzel, Donald C., eds. 1998. *Teaching Ethics and Values in Public Administration Programs*. Albany: State University of New York Press.
Brainard, Lori A. 2000. "Presidential Leadership, Interest Groups, and Domestic Policymaking Summitry." *Public Integrity* 2 (Spring): 91–104.
Brewer, Gene A., and Selden, Sally Coleman. 1998. "Whistle Blowers in the Federal Civil Service: New Evidence of the Public Service Ethic." *Journal of Public Administration Research and Theory* 8 (July): 413–39.
Brindle, Jeffrey M. 2000. "Mission and Method: Regulating Campaign Financing in New Jersey." *Public Integrity* 2 (Fall): 289–302.
Brown, Alysia J. 2000. "Public Employee Political Participation." *Public Integrity* 2 (Spring): 105–20.
Bruce, Willa. 1994. "Ethical People Are Productive People." *Public Productivity & Management Review* 18 (Spring).
———. 1996. "Codes of Ethics and Codes of Conduct: Perceived Contribution to the Practice of Ethics in Local Government." *Public Integrity Annual*: 23–39.
Burke, Frances, and Black, Amy. 1990. "Improving Organizational Productivity: Add Ethics." *Public Productivity & Management Review* 14 (Winter).
Carnevale, David G., and Wechsler, Barton. 1992. "Trust in the Public Sector: Individual and Organizational Determinants." *Administration & Society* 23: 471–94.
Cava, Anita C.; West, Jonathan; and Berman, Evan. 1995. "Ethical Decision-Making in Business and Government: An Analysis of Formal and Informal Strategies." *Journal of State Governments* 2 (March): 28.
Chandler, Ralph C. 1983. "The Problem of Moral Reasoning in American Public Administration: The Case for a Code of Ethics." *Public Administration Review* 43: 32–39.
Cohen, Steven, and Eimicke, William. 1999. "Is Public Entrepreneurship Ethical?" *Public Integrity* 1 (Winter): 54–74.
Cooper, Terry L. 1982. *The Responsible Administrator: An Approach to Ethics for the Administrative Role*. Port Washington, NY: Kennikat Press.
———. 1984. "Citizenship and Professionalism in Public Administration." *Public Administration Review* 44: 143–49.
———. 1986. *The Responsible Administrator: An Approach to Ethics for the Administrative Role*, 2d ed., Millwood, NY: Associated Faculty Press.
———. 1987. "Hierarchy, Virtue, and the Practice of Public Administration: A Per-

spective for Normative Ethics." *Public Administration Review* 47 (July/August): 320–28.

Cooper, Terry L., and Yoder, Diane E. 2002. "Public Management Ethics Standards in a Transnational World." *Public Integrity* 4 (Fall): 333–52.

Daly, Dennis M., and Vasu, Michael L. 1998. "Fostering Organizational Trust in North Carolina: The Pivotal Role of Administrators and Political Leaders." *Administration & Society* 30 (March): 62–84.

Denhardt, Kathryn G., 1988. *The Ethics of Public Administration: Resolving Moral Dilemmas in Public Organizations.* New York: Greenwood.

———. 1989. "The Management of Ideals: A Political Perspective on Ethics." *Public Administration Review* 49 (March/April): 187–92.

De Vries, Michiel S. 2002. "Can You Afford Honesty? A Comparative Analysis of Ethos and Ethics in Local Government." *Administration & Society* 34 (July): 309–34.

Di Norcia, Vincent. 2003. "Mr. Bush's National Energy Plan: A Case Study in Ethical Policy Assessment." *Public Integrity* 5 (Spring): 113–26.

Dobel, J. Patrick, 1990. "Integrity in the Public Service." *Public Administration Review* 50 (May/June): 354–66.

———. 1993. "The Realpolitik of Ethics Codes." In *Ethics and Public Administration*, ed. H. George Frederickson, pp. 158–76. Armonk, NY: M.E. Sharpe.

Eimicke, William B.; Cohen, Steven; and Salazar, Mauricio Perez. 2000. "Ethical Public Entrepreneurship." *Public Integrity* 2 (Summer): 229–45.

Fain, Herbert. 2002. "The Case for a Zero Gift Policy: Commentaries," *Public Integrity* 4 (Winter): 61–80.

———. 1999. "The City of Houston's Office of Inspector General." *Public Integrity* 1 (Fall): 417–26.

Feigenbaum, Edward D. 2002. "Beating around the Roudebush: Abandoning Precedent in the Bush Presidential Recount." *Public Integrity* 4 (Summer): 239–50.

Folks, Susan R. 2000. "A Potential Whistle-blower." *Public Integrity* 2 (Winter): 61–74.

Ford, Robert, and Richardson, Woodrow, 1994. "Ethical Decision Making: A Review of the Empirical Literature." *Journal of Business Ethics* 13 (March): 205–21.

Frederickson, H. George, and Hart, David K. 1985. "The Public Service and the Patriotism of Benevolence." *Public Administration Review* 45: 547–53.

Frederickson, H. George, and Newman, Meredith A. 2001. "The Patriotism of Exit and Voice: The Case of Gloria Flora." *Public Integrity* 3 (Fall): 347–62.

Frederickson, H. George, ed., 1993. *Ethics and Public Administration.* Armonk, NY: M.E. Sharpe.

Gawthrop, Louis C. 1984. *Public Sector Management Systems and Ethics.* Bloomington: Indiana University Press.

Ghere, Richard K. 1996. "Aligning the Ethics of Public-Private Partnership: The Issue of Local Economic Development." *Journal of Public Administration Research and Theory* 6 (October): 599–621.

———. 1999. "Public Integrity, Privatization, and Partnership: Where Do Ethics Fit?" *Public Integrity* 1 (Spring): 135–48.

Gilman, Stewart C. 2000. "An Idea Whose Time Has Come." *Public Integrity* 2 (Spring): 135–55.

Gilman, Stuart C., and Lewis, Carol W. 1996. "Public Service Ethics: A Global Dialogue." *Public Administration Review* 56 (November/December): 517–24.

Glor, Eleanor D., and Greene, Ian. 2003. "The Government of Canada's Approach to Ethics: The Evolution of Ethical Government." *Public Integrity* 5 (Winter 2002–3): 39–65.

Gonzalez, George A. 2001. "Democratic Ethics and Ecological Modernization: The Formulation of California's Automobile Emission Standards." *Public Integrity* 3 (Fall): 325–44.

Goodman, Marshall R.; Holp, Timothy J.; and Ludwig, Karen M. 1996. "Understanding State Legislative Ethics Reform: The Importance of Political and Institutional Culture." *Public Integrity Annual*: 51–57.

Gray, W. Robert. 2002. "The Four Faces of Affirmative Action: Analysis and Answers." *Public Integrity* 4 (Winter): 43–59.

Grundstein-Amado, Rivka. 2001. "A Strategy for Formulation and Implementation of Codes of Ethics in Public Service Organizations." *International Journal of Public Administration* 24: 461–78.

Hahn, William; Colin, George; and Bart, Barbara. 1990. "Ethical Business Behavior: The Perspectives of Minority and Majority Students." *Proceedings, Society for the Advancement of Management.*

Hart, David K. 1984. "The Virtuous Citizen, the Honorable Bureaucrat, and 'Public' Administration." *Public Administration Review* 44: 111–20.

———. 1992. "The Moral Exemplar in an Organizational Society." In *Exemplary Public Administrators*, ed. Terry L. Cooper and N. Dale Wright, pp. 9–29. San Francisco: Jossey-Bass.

Hejka-Elkins, April. 1988. "Teaching Ethics in Public Administration." *Public Administration Review* 48 (September/October): 885–91.

Herrmann, Frederick M. 1997. "Bricks without Straw: The Plight of Government Ethics Agencies in the United States." *Public Integrity Annual*: 13–22.

Holbrook, Thomas M., and Meier, Kenneth J. 1993. "Politics, Bureaucracy, and Political Corruption: A Comparative State Analysis." In *Ethics and Public Administration*, ed. H. George Frederickson, pp. 28–51. Armonk, NY: M.E. Sharpe.

Holland, Ian, and Fleming, Jenny. 2003. "Reforming Ministerial Ethics: Institutional Continuity and Change." *Public Integrity* 5 (Winter 2002–3): 67–82.

Huberts, Leo W.J.C. 2000. "Anticorruption Strategies: The Hong Kong Model in International Context." *Public Integrity* 2 (Summer): 211–28.

Jurkiewicz, Carole L. 2002. "The Influence of Pedagogical Style on Students' Level of Ethical Reasoning." *Journal of Public Affairs Education* 8 (October): 263–74.

Jurkiewicz, Carole L., and Brown, Roger G. 2000. "Power Does Not Corrupt Absolutely: An Empirical Study." *Public Integrity* 2 (Summer): 195–210.

Jurkiewicz, Carole L., and Nichols, Kenneth L. 2002. "Ethics Education in the MPA Curriculum: What Difference Does It Make?" *Journal of Public Affairs Education* 8 (April): 103–14.

Jurkiewicz, Carole L., and Thompson, Carolyn R. 1999. "An Empirical Inquiry into the Ethical Standards of Health Care Administrators." *Public Integrity* 1 (Winter): 41–53.

Kim, Ho-Seob. 2001. "Organizational Structure and Ethics Attitudes of Public Officials." *Public Integrity* 3 (Winter): 69–86.

Kim, Pan S. 2000. "Improving Ethical Conduct in Public Service." *Public Integrity* 2 (Spring): 157–71.

Kohlberg, Lawrence. 1980. *The Meaning and Measurement of Moral Development.* Worcester, MA: Clark University Press.

Light, Paul C. 1993. "Federal Ethics Controls: The Role of the Inspector General." In

Ethics and Public Administration, ed. H. George Frederickson, pp. 100–20. Armonk, NY: M.E. Sharpe.

Lovell, Alan. 2003. "The Enduring Phenomenon of Moral Muteness: Suppressed Whistleblowing." *Public Integrity* 5 (Summer): 187–204.

Mackey, Earl S. 2003. "Dismantling the Kentucky Legislative Ethics Law." *Public Integrity* 5 (Spring): 149–58.

Mapel, David R. 1990. "Prudence and the Plurality of Value in International Ethics." *Journal of Politics* 52 (May): 433–56.

McKenna, Joseph C. 1965. "Reason and Revelation in Hooker's Ethics." *American Political Science Review* 59 (September): 647–58.

Menzel, Donald C. 1992. "Ethics Attitudes and Behaviors in Local Governments: An Empirical Analysis." *State and Local Government Review* 24 (Fall): 94–102.

———. 1993. "The Ethics Factor in Local Government: An Empirical Analysis." In *Ethics and Public Administration*, ed. H. George Frederickson, pp. 191–204. Armonk, NY: M.E. Sharpe.

———. 1995a. "The Ethical Environment of Local Government Managers." *American Review of Public Administration* 25 (September): 247–62.

———. 1995b. "Through the Ethical Looking Glass Darkly." *Administration & Society* 27: 379–99.

———. 1996a. "Ethics Complaint Making and Trustworthy Government." *Public Integrity Annual*: 73–82.

———. 1996b. "Ethics Stress in Public Organizations." *Public Productivity & Management Review* 20: 70–83.

———. 1997. "Teaching Ethics and Values in Public Administration: Are We Making a Difference?" *Public Administration Review* 57 (May/June): 224–30.

———. 1998a. "To Act Ethically: The What, Why, and How of Ethics Pedagogy." *Journal of Public Affairs Education* 4 (January): 11–18.

———. 1998b. "WWW.ETHICS.GOV: Issues and Challenges Facing Public Managers." *Public Administration Review* 58 (September/October): 445–52.

———. 1998c. "Cyber-Management and Public Administration." *Journal of Public Administration and Management*. Available at www.hbg.psu.edu/Faculty/jxr11/98_3_1.html.

———. 1999. "A Review and Assessment of Empirical Research on Public Administration Ethics: Implications for Scholars and Managers." *Public Integrity* 1 (Summer): 239–64.

Menzel, Donald C., and Benton, Edwin. 1991. "Ethics Complaints and Local Government: The Case of Florida." *Journal of Public Administration Research and Theory* 1 (October): 419–35.

Montjoy, Robert S., and Slaton, Christa Daryl. 2002. "Interdependence and Ethics in Election Systems: The Case of the Butterfly Ballot." *Public Integrity* 4 (Summer): 195–210.

Nigro, Lloyd G., and Richardson, William D. 1990. "Between Citizen and Administrator: Administrative Ethics and PAR." *Public Administration Review* 50 (November/December): 623–36.

Ott, J. Steven; Boonyarak, Pitima; and Dicke, Lisa A. 2001. "Public Sector Reform, and Moral and Ethical Accountability." *Public Integrity* 3 (Summer): 277–89.

Perry, James L. 1993. "Whistleblowing, Organizational Performance, and Organizational Control." In *Ethics and Public Administration*, ed. H. George Frederickson, pp. 73–99. Armonk, NY: M.E. Sharpe.

Pfiffner, James P. 2003. "Elliot L. Richardson: Exemplar of Integrity and Public Service." *Public Integrity* 5 (Summer): 251–70.
Quah, Jon S.T. 1999. "Corruption in Asian Countries: Can It Be Minimized?" *Public Administration Review* 59 (November/December): 483–94.
Rawls, John A. 1971. *A Theory of Justice*. Cambridge, MA: Belknap Press of Harvard University Press.
Rest, James. 1986. *Moral Development: Advances in Research and Theory*. New York: Praeger.
Roberts, Robert. 1999. "The Supreme Court and the Law of Public Service Ethics." *Public Integrity* 1 (Winter): 20–40.
Rohr, John, 1976. "The Study of Ethics in the PA Curriculum." *Public Administration Review* 36 (July/August): 398–406.
———. 1978. *Ethics for Bureaucrats: An Essay on Law and Values*. New York: Marcel Dekker.
———. 1989. *Ethics for Bureaucrats: An Essay on Law and Values*, 2d ed. New York: Marcel Dekker.
———. 2002. "The Ethical Aftermath of Privatization and Contracting Out: A Constitutional Analysis." *Public Integrity* 4 (Winter): 1–12.
Seligson, Mitchell A. 2001. "Corruption and Democratization: What Is to Be Done?" *Public Integrity* 3 (Summer): 221–41.
Smith, Robert W. 1999. "Local Government Ethics Boards." *Public Integrity* 1 (Fall): 397–416.
———. 2003a. "Enforcement or Ethical Capacity: Considering the Role of State Ethics Commissions at the Millennium." *Public Administration Review* 63 (May/June): 283–95.
———. 2003b. "Corporate Ethics Officers and Government Ethics Administrators." *Administration & Society* 34 (January): 632–62.
Stewart, Debra W., and Sprinthall, Norman A. 1993. "The Impact of Demographic, Professional, and Organizational Variables and Domain on the Moral Reasoning of Public Administration." In *Ethics and Public Administration*, ed. H. George Frederickson, pp. 205–19. Armonk, NY: M.E. Sharpe.
Stewart, Debra W.; Sprinthall, Norman A.; and Kem, Jackie D. 2002. "Moral Reasoning in the Context of Reform: A Study of Russian Officials." *Public Administration Review* 62 (May/June): 282–97.
Stewart, Debra W.; Siemienska, Renata; and Sprinthall, Norman. 1997. "Ethical Reasoning in a Time of Revolution: A Study of Local Officials in Poland." *Public Administration Review* 57 (September/October): 445–53.
———. 1999. "Women and Men in the Project of Reform: A Study of Gender Differences among Local Officials in Two Provinces in Poland." *American Review of Public Administration* 29 (September): 225–39.
Strait, Patricia Bellin. 1996. "Unethical Actions of Public Servants: A Voyeur's View." *Public Integrity Annual*: 41–50.
———. 1997. "An Empirical Investigation of 'Suspect' Employees in the Public Sector: A Voyeur's View, Part Two." *Public Integrity Annual*: 43–48.
———. 1999. "The Voyeur Trilogy, Part Three: Anecdotal Evidence of the Ethical Behavior of Public Employees." *Public Integrity* 1 (Spring): 167–74.
Swisher, Laura Lee; Rizzo, Ann-Marie; and Marley, Marsha Ann. 2001. "Moral Reasoning among Public Administrators: Does One Size Fit All?" *Public Integrity* 3 (Winter): 53–68.

Tessitore, Aristide. 1990. "Making the City Safe for Philosophy: Nicomachean Ethics, Book 10." *American Political Science Review* 84 (December): 1251–62.

Thomas, Rosamund Margaret. 2001. "Public Trust, Integrity, and Privatization." *Public Integrity* 3 (Summer): 242–61.

Thompson, Dennis F. 1985. "The Possibility of Administrative Ethics." *Public Administration Review* 45: 555–61.

Thompson, Kenneth. 1978. "New Reflections on Ethics and Foreign Policy: The Problem of Human Rights." *Journal of Politics* 40 (November): 984–1010.

Van Noy, Carolyn M. 2000. "The City of Seattle and Campaign Finance Reform." *Public Integrity* 2 (Fall): 303–16.

West, Jonathan P., and Berman, Evan M. 2003. "Audit Committees and Accountability in Local Government: A National Survey." *International Journal of Public Administration* 26: 329–62.

Wheeland, Craig M. 2000. "Partisan Politics, Ethics, and the Home Rule Charter." *Public Integrity* 2 (Fall): 347–62.

White, Richard D. Jr. 1999a. "Public Ethics, Moral Development, and the Enduring Legacy of Lawrence Kohlberg." *Public Integrity* 1 (Spring): 121–34.

———. 1999b. "Are Women More Ethical? Recent Findings on the Effects of Gender upon Moral Development." *Journal of Public Administration Research and Theory* 9 (July): 459–71.

Williams, Russell L. 1996. "Controlling Ethical Practices Through Laws and Rules: Evaluating the Florida Commission on Ethics." *Public Integrity Annual*: 65–72.

Williams, Russell L., and Guy, Mary E. 2000. "The Archer's Conundrum: Why Don't More Arrows Add More Virtue?" *Public Integrity* 2 (Fall): 317–28.

Wilson, Woodrow. 1887. "The Study of Administration." Reprinted in *Political Science Quarterly* 56 (December 1941): 481–506.

Wisensale, Steven K. 1999. "Grappling with the Generational Equity Debate." *Public Integrity* 1 (Winter): 1–19.

Wittmer, Dennis. 1992. "Ethical Sensitivity and Managerial Decisionmaking: An Experiment." *Journal of Public Administration Research and Theory* 2 (October): 443–62.

———. 2000. "Individual Moral Development: An Empirical Exploration of Public- and Private-Sector Differences." *Public Integrity* 2 (Summer): 181–94.

Wittmer, Dennis, and Coursey, David. 1996. "Ethical Work Climates: Comparing Top Managers in Public and Private Organizations." *Journal of Public Administration Research and Theory* 6 (October): 559–72.

Zajac, Gary, and Al-Kazemi, Ali A. 2000. "Administrative Ethics and Organizational Learning in Kuwait and the United States: An Empirical Approach." *International Journal of Public Administration* 23: 21–52.

Zajac, Gary, and Comfort, Louise K. 1997. "The Spirit of Watchfulness: Public Ethics as Organizational Learning." *Journal of Public Administration Research and Theory* 23: 21–52.

Zundel, Alan F. 2002. "The Futility of Empirical Policy Analysis without Normative Policy Analysis." *Public Integrity* 4 (Spring): 101–14.

Part 2

Organization Designs That Support Ethical Behavior

3

Developing a Behavioral Model for Ethical Decision Making in Organizations: Conceptual and Empirical Research

Dennis P. Wittmer

An applicant is being interviewed for a position in an organization. The human resources manager asks, "Do you lie, steal, or cheat?" The applicant replies, "No, but I am willing to learn." Or so the joke goes. While character is formed at an early age, human behavior is pliable, and it certainly behooves those charged with managing society's institutions and organizations to understand what the important factors and influences are when it comes to ethical choices and behavior in their organizations.

One critical outcome of ethical decision making and conduct is a sense of trust among individuals, which is an important factor in organizational productivity and success. At the macro level of society, as well as in the international community, trust is important not only for growing economies but also for peace and stability in communities. Robert Putnam (2000) has developed these ideas through his extensive study of social capital, and Francis Fukuyama (1995) titled an entire book *Trust*, in which he examined trust in different cultures and economies. Fukuyama says, " . . . a nation's well-being, as well as its ability to compete, is conditioned by a single, pervasive cultural characteristic: the level of trust" (p. 7). To the extent that trust results at least in part from ethical decisions and ethical conduct, the importance of understanding ethical decision making is underscored.

More than ever, it seems, the success of organizations and the well-being of society are affected by the ethical choices made by all in the organization.

Simon (1948) argued that a science of administration is fundamentally about decision making. At least part of that science should involve ethical decision making. The past decade has seen a clear movement to submit the study of administrative or organizational ethics to empirical study and testing. The results of such research have clear implications for how organizations are structured and managed. The implications may involve protective and reactive strategies to avoid unethical behavior, but from a positive and proactive perspective findings can provide managers with insights for engendering ethical decision making and action.

The purpose of this chapter is to present a general model of ethical decision making, including a summary of empirical research that relates to various relationships expressed in the model.

Descriptive Frameworks and Models of Ethical Decision Making

> When a man sets out to solve a problem, he embarks on a course of mental activity more circuitous, more complex, more subtle, and perhaps more idiosyncratic than he perceives. . . . Dodging in and out of the unconscious, moving back and forth from concrete to abstract, trying chance here and there, soaring, jumping, backtracking, crawling, sometimes freezing on point like a bird dog, he exploits mental processes that are only slowly yielding to observation and systematic description. (Braybrooke and Lindblom 1970, p. 81)

A prefatory remark is pertinent at the outset of this discussion. Braybrooke and Lindblom capture the messy and complex nature of decision making. Any effort to conceptualize this process will necessarily produce a model that simplifies by providing structure to phenomena. Such conceptualizations should illuminate and help us understand. But the very act of modeling will reduce reality to the structure proposed, thereby usually leaving out important features of reality. Some might simply abandon such modeling efforts because they are doomed to failure. The view taken here, while recognizing the limitations of such conceptualization, is that efforts to model can improve our understanding. Thus the spirit of the following discussion is curiosity and hope, tempered with humility.

In the past fifteen to twenty years, theoretical models have been proposed for understanding ethical/unethical decision-making behavior, especially in managerial and organizational contexts. The models have generally become increasingly complex and more sophisticated, containing common elements and often building on previous models. There have been efforts to synthesize proposed managerial models (e.g., Ferrell and Fraedrich 1991; Jones 1991).

What follows is a brief summary of several of the more important conceptual models, which provide the basis for the model proposed in the next chapter.

James Rest (Four-Component Model)

An important contribution to the development of an ethical decision-making model is the work of James Rest (1984, 1986), who proposed a four-component model for understanding moral behavior or psychology. Rest's approach to the complexity of moral behavior was to ask the following question: "When a person is behaving morally, what must we suppose has happened psychologically to produce that behavior" (p. 3)? His answer was a framework of individuals working through four psychological processes to produce ethical/unethical behavior. These components include: ethical interpretation or perception of situations in terms of alternative courses of actions and the effects on the welfare of those involved or affected; ethical judgment or formulation of what would be the morally right course of action (i.e., reasoning to some conclusion about the ethically right action); selection or actual choosing of the moral values and actions; and finally, implementing or executing the moral course of action, which involves behavioral follow-through or doing what is determined to be morally right.

Rest (1984) offered the four-component model in response to a three-part division for studying ethical behavior: moral thought, moral emotion, and moral behavior. According to this threefold scheme, behavior is studied by behaviorist psychologists, moral thinking is studied by cognitive-developmentalists, and moral emotion or affect is studied typically by psychoanalysts. Rest argued that this kind of division hinders our understanding of moral psychology and behavior because morality is more a set of processes, each of which includes cognitive and affective components. He contended that proper functioning of all components is necessary in moral behavior, and that research and moral education will be enhanced by adopting a process model.

Trevino Model (Person-Situation Interactionist Model)

Linda Trevino (1986) proposed a "person-situation interactionist model" to explain ethical decision-making behavior in organizations. Citing the lack of a comprehensive theory to guide empirical research in organizational ethics, Trevino proposed a model that posits cognitive moral development of an individual as the critical variable in explaining ethical/unethical decision-making behavior. However, improving on previous models that emphasize either individual or organizational variables, Trevino proposed an interactionist model that posits individual variables (e.g., locus of control, ego strength, field dependence) and situational variables (e.g., reinforcement contingencies, organizational culture) as moderating an individual's level of moral development in explaining ethical decision making.

Trevino's theory is important for several reasons. First, it clearly recognizes the complexity of ethical decision making and the numerous factors affecting decision making in managerial contexts. Second, while recognizing complexity, her model is illuminating by simplifying and grouping the expected influences on ethical decision making (i.e., individual and organizational factors). Third, while the theory offers a behavior model, it clearly recognizes the importance of cognitive processes in explaining ethical behavior.

Clarkson Group

A group of researchers from Clarkson University represents another effort to develop a theoretical framework for understanding ethical behavior in organizations. Their model portrays ethical behavior as a function of individual characteristics and environmental influences, but as mediated through an individual's decision-making process.

Both the Trevino and Clarkson models are similar in viewing ethical behavior as a product of individual and environmental influences. However, the Clarkson group (Bommer et al. 1987) expanded the Trevino model, both internally and externally. Their model expanded the Trevino model externally by including environmental influences outside the organization. Trevino's model appropriately focused on critical organizational factors in the environment (immediate job context, organizational culture, and characteristics of the work itself). The Clarkson model expanded external influences to include various environments (work environment, government/legal environment, social environment, professional environment, and personal environment).

Internally, the theory is expanded to include an individual decision process as mediating both environmental factors and individual attributes (e.g., level of moral development). The decision process of an individual is theorized to be a kind of central processing unit that functions both as a selective perceptual filter and as a mechanism individuals employ to build an internal conceptual model that represents the situation and appropriate solutions for ethical problems.

Besides generally expanding the variables and factors included in a behavioral model of ethical decision making, the Clarkson model is important because it makes explicit the importance of perception to the decision process and outcomes. Information about either the nature of the situation or the character of the environment is seen as selectively filtered by a manager or decision maker. Cognizant of the literature that challenges rational decision-making models, the authors emphasized the subjective nature of the filtering process and individual difference in perceptual orientation (e.g., cognitive style). Thus the model included individual differences in perception, expected to have effects on decision outcomes.

Ferrell, Gresham, and Fraedrich (A Synthesis Model)

Ferrell and Gresham (1985) proposed a "contingency framework" for understanding ethical decision making in marketing situations. Besides individual factors and the existing organizational environment, this model included the influence of "significant others" (differential association and role-set configuration) and "opportunity" on individual decision making.

Expanding on that model and incorporating other models, Ferrell, Gresham, and Fraedrich (1989) proposed a "synthesis model" that specifically incorporated "awareness" and "perception" as the first step of the ethical decision-making process. In fact, perception is theorized as related to the stage of cognitive moral development (i.e., whether one perceives a situation as an ethical dilemma will depend on one's level of moral development). Awareness and perception of an ethical dilemma leads to the development and evaluation of various options or alternatives, which produces an intention or determination to pursue some course of action (the final stage of the model). As these several stages are perceived, each is influenced by individual factors, opportunity, and organizational culture.

More recently Ferrell, Fraedrich, and Ferrell (2002) have offered a model in which ethical/unethical behavior is a product of ethical evaluation and intentions, a process that is affected by intensity of the ethical issue, individual factors (e.g., moral development), and the organizational culture (e.g., opportunity and the behavior of significant others in the organization).

An Issue-Contingent Model of Ethical Decision Making (Jones)

Thomas Jones (1991) added another important construct into behavior models of ethical decision making, that of "moral intensity" or characteristics of the moral issue itself. He argued that ethical decision-making outcomes will be contingent on the character of the issue itself, as well as factors or characteristics of the individual or the environment. The components of moral intensity include magnitude of consequences, social consensus, probability of effect, temporal immediacy, proximity, and concentration of effect.

A Proposed General Ethical Decision-Making Model

Incorporating the models discussed above, the general model (Figure 3.1) offered here serves to integrate different aspects of previous work. For ex-

Figure 3.1   **General Behavioral Model for Ethical Decision Making**

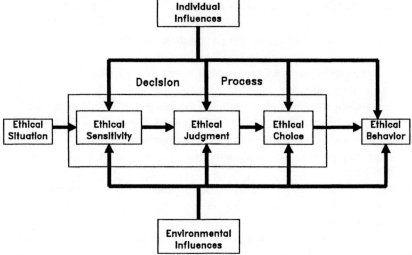

ample, as seen in Figure 3.1, the processes of Rest's (1984, 1986) four-component model are placed at the center of the model, such that ethical decisions are a product (in part) of sensitivity and perception of the ethical issues
and the reasoning used to arrive at some conclusion about what to do in the
situation. Following more managerially oriented models (Jones 1991; Trevino
1986; Bommer et al. 1987; and Ferrell, Gresham, and Fraedrich 1989), this
model provides for the influence of various individual and environmental
factors that may influence the decision processes in managerial and organizational settings. The general descriptive model can be summarized:

Ethical decision making = f(ethical decision processes, individual attributes,
environmental factors)

This general model posits a cognitive process for resolving moral or ethical decisions. The theory presents a process that begins with awareness, perception, or sensitivity to the moral issue. A decision maker proceeds through
judgment as to what is reasoned to be the ethically justified course of action
to a decision or choice of action, ending with the actual behavior of the decision maker. While cognitive processes occupy center stage, the model incorporates both noncognitive individual variables (e.g., ego strength) and
environmental variables internal and external to an organization (e.g., ethical climate or reward/punishment structures).

Empirical Studies of Ethical Decision Making

As can be seen in the behavioral models discussed above, in one form or another, individual characteristics and environmental forces are thought to influence ethical behavior. Several studies have tested theorized relationships. In the next section, I will discuss studies that are related to the decision process and to individual attributes and environmental influences on elements of this process. The following summary is not intended to be exhaustive; rather, it is indicative of empirical studies that are emerging in the area of ethical decision making. More extensive summaries of this body of research provide valuable overviews (e.g., Ford and Richardson 1994; Fritzsche 1997; Loe, Ferrell, and Mansfield 2000).

Ethical Situation—Issue Intensity

Following Jones (1991) research has focused on dimensions of the issue itself and the relationship to ethical awareness or sensitivity. One such study found that the magnitude of consequences, issue framing, and social consensus about the problematic ethical character of the situation were related to moral awareness (Butterfield, Trevino, and Weaver 2000).

Moral/Ethical Sensitivity

The fundamental idea with ethical or moral sensitivity or perception is that ethical decision making implies ethical detection. Ethical perception and sensitivity can accordingly be defined as the recognition of ethical dimensions (e.g., ethical norms) in decision situations.

Efforts in several professional fields have developed measures of ethical sensitivity. Muriel Bebeau, a colleague of James Rest, pursued one of the earliest empirical programs attempting to measure ethical sensitivity. Applying her approach to the profession of dentistry, she developed the Dental Ethical Sensitivity Test (DEST) as a tool to assess the ability of dental students to recognize ethical issues in situations commonly confronted by dentists (Bebeau 1986; Bebeau, Reifel, and Speidel 1981; Bebeau, Oberle, and Rest 1984; Bebeau, Rest, and Yamoor 1985). Stemming from Bebeau's work, Volker (1984) devised an assessment of moral sensitivity in the counseling profession. Another application has been to the profession of medicine. An instrument was developed to measure ethical sensitivity among medical students. Clinical vignettes were used "to assess one aspect of ethical sensitivity: the ability to recognize ethical issues" (Herbert et al. 1990).

In organization and management contexts Wittmer (2000) devised and empirically tested an instrument to measure ethical sensitivity, relating sensitivity to decision outcomes. This same instrument was also used in an experimental context to test the effect of "personalized information" as an exogenous variable on ethical sensitivity (Wittmer 1992). The general approach was to use an in-basket exercise that involved subjects acting on various tasks. Subjects were not cued as to an "ethical situation's" presence, but they were asked to assess their perceptions of situations and decisions made. Some of these items were "ethical dimensions." The instrument was styled after Rest's DIT. Results showed a range of ethical sensitivity scores that were related to decision outcomes.

An important qualification should perhaps be made at this juncture. Moral behavior (indeed, most behavior) is extremely complex, and while the four decision processes provide a logical or conceptual framework, the general model should not be understood as a rigid, linear process. The different components can overlap in time and may influence one another. For example, as discussed in Rest (1986), there are studies to support the idea that the reasoning process or selection process can influence sensitivity. Subjects may use defensive strategies to deny feelings of obligation. Schwartz (1977) found that as the costs of moral actions became clearer to subjects, they began to deny personal responsibility or they reappraised situations to make alternatives more acceptable. Rest argued that as subjects engaged in components 2 and 3, they altered their interpretations of situations, in effect they desensitized themselves to the ethical aspects of the situation. Thus sensitivity can be influenced by reasoning.

In another classic study of the influence of situational factors in ethical or prosocial behavior (Darley and Batson 1973), seminary students (those with the highest expressed standards of morality) were given the task of preparing a lecture on the parable of the Good Samaritan or on job opportunities for graduates. However, half of the students were told they had ample time to prepare, while the others were told that they must hurry. On the way to deliver the lecture, all subjects were confronted with a person in distress. Significantly more of the subjects who were under perceived time constraints failed to help the person in distress. Rest interpreted this as an example of how engaging intently in the action component influenced the subjects' sensitivity to a new ethical situation.

Ethical Judgment

Cognitive moral development (CMD) is the most widely tested measure of ethical judgment. An individual's level of cognitive moral development (or moral reasoning/judgment) has been the single, most important individual characteristic studied in the theoretical and empirical research related to moral psychology and moral judgment. Based on the pioneering work of Piaget (1932), Kohlberg (1969, 1984) proposed a six-stage theory of moral reasoning, or differences in the kinds of reasons individuals employ in resolving moral dilemmas. Kohlberg's assessment instrument involved an interview process, while Rest (1986) developed the Defining Issues Test (DIT), a paper-and-pencil test to measure CMD. Stewart and Sprinthall (1991, 1993, 1994) have developed the Stewart-Sprinthall Management Survey (SSMS), which adopts a moral development stage sequence similar to Kohlberg and Rest, but the SMSS uses dilemmas or situations adapted to public service or public management.

Research that has focused on CMD, using subjects in the public sector, has continued. Regarding public/private sector differences, Wittmer (1992) found that engineering and business students had higher scores on principled reasoning for CMD, while public administration students tended to have higher scores in the conventional stages of moral development. Peek (1999) studied 266 employees in the General Services Administration (GSA) of the federal government. She concluded that CMD was related to level of education but not to either gender or age. Swisher (2000) assessed a sample of 344 members of the American Society for Public Administration, and concluded that the level of CMD was equivalent to that of the general population, although she did find a statistically significant difference between males and females, with females scoring higher on postconventional reasoning. Mobley (2002) studied managers from Virginia's Commerce and Trade agency, and Osgood (2003) studied the CMD of municipal government officials. Gibson (2001) assessed the CMD level of Designated Agency Ethics Officials (DAEOs), and discovered that the subjects exhibited a conventional "law and order" orientation. Other studies from the public sector will be cited in the following sections.

Level of individual CMD has been found to be related to individual ethical decision making and ethical behavior in organizational and managerial contexts. Trevino and Youngblood (1990) tested students in an experimental, in-basket design. Cognitive moral development was found to be a significant predictor of ethical decisions. In another study of ethical decision making (Stratton, Flynn, and Johnson 1981), students were asked to recommend whether or not to pad an expense account. All students who recommended padding the expense account used reasons categorized in the first three stages of moral development, while students who recommended against padding used reasoning in stages four through six.

Besides managerial decision-making situations, moral development has been found to be significantly related to other ethical and prosocial behaviors, for example, cheating (Malinowski and Smith 1985); helping behavior (Kohlberg and Candee 1984); and whistle-blowing (Brabeck 1984). In a comprehensive and critical review of empirical studies that relate moral judgment and moral behavior, Blasi (1980) reported that fifty-seven of seventy-five studies showed a statistically significant relation between moral judgment and behavior, although the strengths of the relationships were generally moderate (correlations of approximately .30). In a review of studies relating the DIT to behavioral measures, there was a pervasive and modest relationship in approximately thirty studies reviewed (Thoma 1985). Thus empirical studies tend to support the proposition that cognitive moral development is related to moral judgments and decision outcomes.

Individual Influences

Besides an individual's level of CMD the general model assumes that there are individual influences that can affect different elements or stages in the decision process.

Locus of Control

An individual characteristic studied in managerial decision making is locus of control, which is conceived as the relative perception of how much control an individual feels over events in one's life. As Rotter (1966) originally conceived, individuals are located on an internal/external scale. Internal types are more inclined to view outcomes such as reinforcements as contingent on one's own efforts and behavior, while external types are more inclined to view outcomes as a result of luck, chance, fate, or powerful others. Locus of control may affect different elements of the decision-making process. For example, externals may be inclined to make judgments based on the rules of the organization rather than on self-generated principles. On the other hand, internals may be more apt to make choices and act on their own judgments, since they take more personal responsibility for their judgments.

Relating this characteristic to ethical decision making in a managerial context, Trevino and Youngblood (1990) reported locus of control as having the strongest direct effect on ethical/unethical decision outcomes, higher scores as internals related to more ethical decision making. Hegarty and Sims (1978 and 1979) included locus of control as a variable in several laboratory decision-making experiments. Decision tasks such as kickback payments were examined, and in two of the three experiments locus of control was found to be related to unethical decision outcomes. On the other hand, Wittmer (1992) found no statistically significant relationship to decision outcome when he studied student responses to a managerial decision with ethical dimensions.

In addition to managerial decision-making behavior, locus of control has been related to other moral behaviors such as whistle-blowing (Dozier and Miceli 1985) as well as to resistance to social pressure, willingness to harm another person if directed to by an authority, helping behavior, and cheating (Lefcourt 1982).

Age

As reported in Ford and Richardson (1994), a number of studies have examined the relationship of age and ethical behavior. They found eight studies; only three had found a significant relationship, and of those the results were mixed. Gentle (1997) found a positive relationship between CMD and age as well as between CMD and education. There is limited empirical evidence that age is related to ethical behavior and decision making.

Experience or Employment Tenure

The evidence is mixed here as well, but Fritzsche (1997, p. 62) concluded, "Age and/or tenure also appear to have some bearing on the ethics of decision making." Choi (2003), using subjects in public service, found a positive association of CMD with tenure in position, participative and collaborative environments, and ethical climates. In one study (Harris 1990) tolerance for unethical behavior decreased as the years of service increased. In another study (Kelley, Ferrell, and Skinner 1990) subjects age fifty and over and with ten or more years of experience perceived themselves as more ethical. Ford and Richardson (1994) found some studies where years of employment were related to decision-making behavior, but generally they found the support mixed, concluding that "further study is warranted on both age and employment related factors" (p. 211).

Gender

Another characteristic that has received increasing attention is the role gender plays in ethical decision making. Gilligan (1982) has argued that women tend to define themselves in terms of relationships in which they are involved, making decisions that will maintain those relationships. If this is true, decisions may be based more on caring and fostering cooperative relationships than on the application of rules and principles of justice, the focus and structural principle guiding Kohlberg's typology of moral development. Consequently, gender may influence the level of cognitive moral development, the ethical judgments made, the choice, and the ultimate behavior.

White (1999) studied 299 subjects from the U.S. Coast Guard and found that women scored higher than men. Barnett and Karson (1989) found that gender did have an effect on decisions that were made in response to hypothetical scenarios. For example, women were more likely to keep (rather than dismiss) an employee for the summer, although the employee was not motivated or competent but was the child of close friends who had asked that the child be hired for the summer.

But the empirical results are mixed here as well. Ford and Richardson (1994) found that the sex of the subjects is reported more than other variables. They reported fourteen studies, seven of which indicated that females are likely to act more ethically. The other seven studies showed that the sex of the subjects had no impact on ethical behavior. Fritzsche (1997) reported two other studies that support the hypothesis that females act more ethically (Akaah 1989; Arlow 1991), while other studies show mixed results (e.g., Fritzsche 1988). Other studies support the idea that women are more ethical in decision making (e.g., Franke, Crown, and Spake 1997).

Machiavellianism

One other interesting variable that has been related to ethical decision making is Machiavellianism, a measure of preference for manipulative behavior. Hegarty and Sims (1978 and 1979) found that Machiavellianism explained significant variance in ethical behavior. Singhapakdi and Vitell (1990) found that managers who were more Machiavellian tended to perceive ethical problems less seriously and were less likely to take corrective action, thus relating Machiavellianism both to ethical sensitivity and to ethical behavior.

Other Individual Variables

Other individual characteristics have been related to ethical behavior and decision making in organizational managerial contexts, but the above summary provides a brief introduction and overview to the kinds of variables and relationships studied. What can we conclude from the empirical research on individual variables as related to ethical decision making? While the evidence is sometimes conflicting, as a broad generalization we might say that more ethical decision-making behavior tends to be associated with those who have higher levels of moral development, who have greater awareness or sensitivity to the ethical dimensions of situations, who have greater sense of personal control, who are older and more experienced, who are female, and who are less manipulative.

Environmental Variables

Besides individual or personal attributes, the general model that has been presented here proposes the influence of environmental variables on the stages in the ethical decision-making process. While environment can be thought of as including a wide range of influences (social, legal, organizational, professional, and personal), most of the empirical research on ethical behavior in management has focused on the organizational or immediate job environment. One example of current research (White 2002) relates the influence of environmental variables on cognitive moral development. The study involved the use of Coast Guard subjects in two environments, one in the intense, hierarchical environment of a warship and the other in a less-intense land assignment. Differences in CMD were assessed and attributed to differences in the environments.

Reward (and Punishment) Structures

One of the most obvious factors that influences ethical decision making concerns organizational sanctions, or rewards and punishments. In one of their decision-making experiments, Hegarty and Sims (1978) found that extrinsic reward explained the greatest variance in unethical behavior, the number of kickback payments recommended. In another laboratory study of decision making and direct reinforcement (Trevino, Sutton, and Woodman 1985), subjects whose ethical behavior was punished or whose unethical behavior was rewarded were more likely to make unethical decisions. Ethical decisions were more likely to occur when unethical behavior was punished. In yet another decision-making experiment, Trevino and Youngblood (1990) studied the effect of indirect learning, which is based in social learning theory, and they found that vicarious reward had an indirect influence on ethical decision making. Tenbrunsel (1998) studied subjects in a negotiation task. When subjects had an incentive, they were more like to deceive the other party in the negotiation. Other studies have found a relationship between sanctions and ethical decision making (Fritzsche and Becker 1984; Hunt, Chonko, and Wilcox 1984; Laczniak and Inderrieden 1987).

Significant or Referent Others

Another important and intuitively obvious environmental variable would be the behavior and attitudes of others in the organization or one's peer group. This has been studied as the influence of significant others or referent others in organizations. In a survey of practicing marketing managers, Zey-Ferrell, Weaver, and Ferrell (1979) found that perceptions of peer behavior was a significant predictor of their own self-reported ethical behavior. Peer behavior was found to be more strongly related to ethical/unethical behavior than to the subjects' own beliefs or what they thought management believed. In a later study, Zey-Ferrell and Ferrell (1982) expanded referent others to include individuals outside the organization, such as clients. Another survey of the perceptions and self-reported ethical behavior of two groups of practicing advertisers (ad agency account executives and corporate clients) found that the perceived behavior of referent groups was strongly related to ethical behavior of subjects, and for both groups intraorganizational relationships were more important than interorganizational relationships.

Organizational Policies and Codes of Conduct

Another organizational factor expected to influence ethical/unethical decision making concerns the policies and codes of the organization. The articulation of clearly stated organizational policies is considered to be important in providing guidance to decision makers. Hegarty and Sims (1979) found that the presence of an organizational ethics policy reduced unethical decision behavior. On the other hand, at the organizational level of analysis, Mathews (1987) analyzed 485 top corporations in terms of the relationship of corporate codes of conduct and illegal corporate activity. He found that the existence of codes was not related to the number of legal violations. Ford and Richardson (1994) reported nine studies that examined the relationship of codes or policies to ethical decision making and ethical perception. They concluded that codes or policies are "consistently and significantly related to ethical behavior" (p. 216). The greatest effect, however, seems to occur when policies are accompanied by good communication and clear sanctions.

One study (McCabe, Trevino, and Butterfield 1996) examined the relationship of ethical conduct both to corporate ethics codes and to previous experience with honor codes in college. One of the intriguing findings was that unethical behavior was lowest among those who worked in organizations with strong codes of conduct and who came from colleges with honor codes.

Top Management Commitment

The results of Mathews's study from the previous section would not come as a surprise to many who believe that a serious commitment of top management, as well as appropriate sanctions, must accompany any organizational code of conduct for it to have a positive effect on ethical decision making and behavior. In a decision-making study that used students as subjects, the influence of stated organizational concern was examined as a major independent variable on ethical decision making. The study found that only when a code existed and top management concern was combined with sanctions (dismissal for unethical conduct) was there a significant effect on ethical decision making (Laczniak and Inderrieden 1987). Hegarty and Sims (1979) found that when subjects were given a letter from the corporate president that supported ethical behavior, ethical decision-making behavior increased while unethical decision making decreased. Ford and Richardson (1994) reported that a number of studies follow the results of Brenner and Molander (1977) and Baumhart (1961). In these studies *Harvard Business Review* readers were asked what they believed had most influenced their own ethical behavior. The highest-ranked factor was the behavior of superiors.

Ethical Work Climates

Other factors that have been studied in more recent years are organizational culture/climate and ethical work climates. Victor and Cullen (1987, 1988) developed a framework that was empirically tested. Following the idea that organizational culture involves shared beliefs, customs, and values, they conceived of ethical climate as the "shared perceptions of what is ethically correct behavior and how ethical issues should be handled" (1987, p. 52). Their empirical studies produced five dimensions of ethical climates: caring, law and code, rules, instrumental, and independence. Relating ethical climates to decision making, Akaah and Riordan (1989) determined that healthier ethical environments improved the likelihood that marketing professionals would make ethical decisions. In terms of public administration research, Wittmer and Coursey (1996) examined the effect of sector on ethical climates, concluding that "public managers generally perceive the ethical climates of their organizations less favorably than do their private sector counterparts."

Other Environmental Variables

Besides the factors reported here, other environmental variables have been examined in terms of their impact on ethical decision making and ethical behavior: opportunity (Zey-Ferrell, Weaver, and Ferrell 1979; Zey-Ferrell and Ferrell 1982); scarcity-munificence in the environment (Staw and Szwajkowski 1975); ethics training programs (Delaney and Sockell 1992); structural factors such as formalization, centralization, and controls (Ferrell and Skinner 1988); and organizational size (Browning and Zabriskie 1983; Murphy, Smith, and Daley 1992; Weber 1990).

What can we conclude from this body of empirical research on environmental influences? Generally there is support that ethical decision making is affected by the behavior of peers and associates, by the actions of supervisors and top management, by the existence of policies and codes of conduct, by the rewards and punishments, and by the general atmosphere or climate of the organization.

Conclusion

It is important for managers, in creating ethical behavior in organizations, to have an understanding of the factors that contribute to ethical/unethical decisions and conduct. Empirically grounded theory can provide a more solid basis for decisions made with respect to formal codes of conduct, the role of senior management in promoting ethical conduct, what kinds of rewards and sanctions should be in place, and even the kinds of individuals who will best fit into the culture of the organization. This chapter has been a brief introduction to the current state of science and knowledge with respect to ethical decision-making behavior. Conceptual models have emerged, and relationships have been tested in the past twenty years that provide some guidance to managers and administrators. Indeed, there has been a growing body of studies from public administration students and researchers in recent years. This is encouraging for the future in terms of general managerial knowledge as well as information concerning what might be unique about public-sector organizations.

This leads to a final point: the possible use and advantage of such knowledge in educational programs. There is at least a hope not only that we might be able to understand ethical decision making and behavior, but also that we might actually be able to improve ethical decision making and conduct. According to Rest (1984, p. 36), "[D]eficiencies in any component can result in failure to behave ethically." By breaking ethical decision making into its component parts and studying theorized relationships, educational programs can perhaps be better designed to address separately sensitivity, reasoning, or strategies for carrying out ethical choices.

Note

This chapter draws from, expands, and updates material from Dennis Wittmer, "Ethical Decision-Making," in *Handbook of Administrative Ethics*, ed. Terry L. Cooper, pp. 481–507 (New York: Marcel Dekker, 1994).

References

Akaah, I.P. 1989. "Differences in Research Ethics Judgments between Male and Female Marketing Professionals." *Journal of Business Ethics* 8, no. 5: 375–81.

Akaah, I. P., and Riordan, E. A. 1989. "Judgments of Marketing Professionals about Ethical Issues in Marketing Research." *Journal of Marketing Research* 26, 112–20.

Arlow, P. 1991. "Personal Characteristics in College Students' Evaluations of Business Ethics and Corporate Social Responsibility." *Journal of Business Ethics* 10, no. 1: 63–69.

Barnett, J.H., and Karson, M.J. 1989. "Managers, Values, and Executive Decisions: An Exploration of the Role of Gender, Career Stage, Organizational Level, Function, and the Importance of Ethics, Relationships and Results in Managerial Decision-Making." *Journal of Business Ethics* 8: 747–71.

Baumhart, R. 1961. "Problems in Review: How Ethical Are Businessmen?" *Harvard Business Review* 39 (July/August): 6–9.

Bebeau, M.J. 1986. *Dental Ethical Sensitivity Test*. Minneapolis: University of Minnesota, Center for the Study of Ethical Development.

Bebeau, M.J.; Oberle, M.; and Rest, J.R. 1984. "Developing Alternate Cases for the Dental Sensitivity Test (DEST)." *Journal of Dental Research* 63, no. 196, program abstracts no. 228.

Bebeau, M.J.; Reifel, N.M.; and Speidel, T. M. 1981. "Measuring the Type and Frequency of Professional Dilemmas in Dentistry." *Journal of Dental Research* 60, program abstracts, no. 891.

Bebeau, M.J.; Rest, J.R.; and Yamoor, C.M. 1985. "Measuring Dental Students' Ethical Sensitivity." *Journal of Dental Education* 49: 225–35.

Blasi, A. 1980. "Bridging Moral Cognition and Moral Action: A Critical Review of the Literature." *Psychological Bulletin* 88: 1–45.

Bommer, M.; Gratto, C.; Gravander, J.; and Tuttle, M. 1987. "A Behavioral Model of Ethical and Unethical Decision Making." *Journal of Business Ethics* 6: 265–80.

Brabeck, M. 1984. "Ethical Characteristics of Whistle Blowers." *Journal of Research in Personality* 18: 41–53.

Braybrooke, D., and Lindblom, C. 1970. *A Strategy of Decision*. New York: Free Press.

Brenner, S.N., and Molander, E.A. 1977. "Is the Ethics of Business Changing?" *Harvard Business Review* 55 (January/February): 57–71.

Browning, J., and Zabriskie, N.B. 1983. "How Ethical Are Industrial Buyers?" *Industrial Marketing Management* 12: 219–24.

Butterfield, K.; Trevino, L.K.; and Weaver, G.R. 2000. "Moral Awareness: Influences of Issue-Related and Social Context Factors." *Human Relations* 53, no. 7: 981–1018.

Choi, D.L. 2003. "Moral Reasoning in Public Service: Individual, Organizational, and Societal Determinants." Dissertation Abstracts, International Section A: Humanities and Social Sciences, vol. 64, 2–A.

Colby, A., and Kohlberg, L. 1987. *The Measurement of Moral Judgment*, vol. 1: *Theoretical Foundations and Research Validation*. New York: Cambridge University Press.

Darley, J., and Batson, C. 1973. "From Jerusalem to Jericho: A Study of Situational and Dispositional Variables in Helping Behavior." *Journal of Personality and Social Psychology* 27: 100–8.

Delaney, J.T., and Sockell, D. 1992. "Do Company Ethics Training Programs Make a Difference? An Empirical Analysis." *Journal of Business Ethics* 11: 719–27.

Dozier, J., and Miceli, M.P. 1985. "Potential Predictors of Whistleblowing: A Prosocial Perspective." *Academy of Management Review* 10: 823–36.

Ferrell, O.C., and Fraedrich, J. 1991. *Business Ethics: Ethical Decision Making and Cases.* Boston: Houghton Mifflin.

Ferrell, O.C., and Gresham, L.G. 1985. "A Contingency Framework for Understanding Ethical Decision Making in Marketing." *Journal of Marketing* 49 (Summer): 87–96.

Ferrell, O.C., and Skinner, S.J. 1988. "Ethical Behavior and Bureaucratic Structure in Marketing Research Organizations." *Journal of Marketing Research* 25 (February): 103–9.

Ferrell, O.C.; Fraedrich, J.; and Ferrell, L. 2002. *Business Ethics: Ethical Decision Making and Cases.* New York: Houghton Mifflin.

Ferrell, O.C.; Gresham, L.G.; and Fraedrich, J. 1989. "A Synthesis of Ethical Decision Models for Marketing." *Journal of Macromarketing* 9: 5–16.

Ford, R.C., and Richardson, W.D. 1994. "Ethical Decision-Making: A Review of the Empirical Literature." *Journal of Business Ethics* 13, no. 3: 206–24.

Franke, G.R.; Crown, D.F.; and Spake, D.F. 1997. "Gender Differences in Ethical Perceptions of Business Practices: A Social Role Theory Perspective." *Journal of Applied Psychology* 82, no. 6: 920–35.

Fritzsche, D.J. 1988. "An Examination of Marketing Ethics: Role and Decision Maker, Consequence of Decision, Management Position and Sex of the Respondent." *Journal of Macromarketing* 8, no. 3: 29–39.

———. 1997. *Business Ethics: A Global and Managerial Perspective.* New York: McGraw-Hill.

Fritzsche, D.J., and Becker, H. 1984. "Linking Management Behavior to Ethical Philosophy—An Empirical Investigation." *Academy of Management Journal* 27: 166–75.

Fukuyama, F. 1995. *Trust: The Social Virtues and the Creation of Prosperity.* New York: Free Press.

Gentle, L.M. 1997. "Ethical Decision-Making by Federal Managers." Dissertation Abstracts International Section A: Humanities and Social Sciences, vol. 58, 2–A.

Gibson, P.A. 2001. "Ethics of the Ethics Official: The Impact of Demographic and Professional Characteristics on the Moral Reasoning of Federal Designated Agency Ethics Officials." Dissertation Abstracts International Section A: Humanities and Social Sciences, vol. 61, 10–A.

Gilligan, C. 1982. *In a Different Voice: Psychological Theory and Women's Development.* Cambridge, MA: Harvard University Press.

Harris, James R. 1990. "Ethical Values of Individuals at Different Levels of the Organizational Hierarchy of a Single Firm." *Journal of Business Ethics* 9: 741–49.

Hegarty, W.H., and Sims, H.P. 1978. "Some Determinants of Unethical Behavior: An Experiment." *Journal of Applied Psychology* 63: 451–57.

———. 1979. "Organizational Philosophy, Policies, and Objectives Related to Unethical Behavior: A Laboratory Experiment." *Journal of Applied Psychology* 64: 331–38.

Herbert, P.; Meslin, E.M.; Dunn, E.V.; Byrne, N.; and Reid, S.R. 1990. "Evaluating Ethical Sensitivity in Medical Students: Using Vignettes as an Instrument." *Journal of Medical Ethics* 16: 141–45.

Hunt, S.D.; Chonko, L.B.; and Wilcox, J.B. 1984. "Ethical Problems of Marketing Researchers." *Journal of Marketing Research* 21: 304–24.

Jones, T.M. 1991. "Ethical Decision Making by Individuals in Organizations: An Issue-Contingent Model." *Academy of Management Review* 16: 366–95.

Kelley, E.K.; Ferrell, O.C.; and Skinner, S.J. 1990. "Ethical Behavior among Marketing Researchers: An Assessment of Selected Demographic Characteristics." *Journal of Business Ethics* 9, no. 8: 681–88.

Kohlberg, L. 1969. "Stage and Sequence: The Cognitive-Developmental Approach to Socialization." In *Handbook of Socialization Theory and Research*, ed. D.A. Goslin, pp. 347–80. Chicago: Rand McNally.

———. 1984. *Essays on Moral Development*, vol. 2: *The Psychology of Moral Development*. New York: Harper and Row.

Kohlberg, L., and Candee, D. 1984. "The Relationship of Moral Judgment to Moral Action." In *Morality, Moral Behavior and Moral Development*, ed. W.M. Kurtines and J.L. Gewirtz, pp. 52–73. New York: Wiley.

Laczniak, G.R., and Inderrieden, E.J. 1987. "The Influence of Stated Organizational Concern upon Ethical Decision Making." *Journal of Business Ethics* 6: 297–307.

Lefcourt, H.M. 1982. *Locus of Control: Current Trends in Theory and Research*, 2d ed. Hillsdale, NJ: Erlbaum.

Loe, T.W.; Ferrell, W.L.; and Mansfield, P. 2000. "A Review of Empirical Studies Assessing Ethical Decision Making in Business." *Journal of Business Ethics* 25: 195–204.

Malinowski, C., and Smith, C.P. 1985. "Moral Reasoning and Moral Conduct: An Investigation Prompted by Kohlberg's Theory." *Journal of Personality and Social Psychology* 49: 1016–27.

Mathews, M.C. 1987. "Codes of Ethics: Organizational Behavior and Misbehavior." In *Research in Corporate Social Policy*, vol. 9: *Empirical Studies of Business Ethics and Values*, ed. W.C. Frederick and L.E. Preston, pp. 107–30. Greenwich, CT: JAI Press.

McCabe, D.; Trevino, L.K.; and Butterfield, K. 1996. "The Influence of Collegiate and Corporate Codes of Conduct on Ethics-related Behavior in the Workplace." *Business Ethics Quarterly* 6: 441–60.

Mobley, S.E. 2002. "The Study of Lawrence Kohlberg's Stages of Moral Development Theory and Ethics: Considerations in Public Administration." Dissertation Abstracts International, Section A: Humanities and Social Sciences, vol. 63, 5–A.

Murphy, P.R.; Smith J.E.; and Daley, J.M. 1992. "Executive Attitudes, Organizational Size, and Ethical Issues: Perspectives on a Service Industry." *Journal of Business Ethics* 11: 11–19.

Osgood, R.V. 2003. "A Study of the Cognitive Moral Development Theory and Ethics in Municipal Government." Dissertation Abstracts International Section A: Humanities and Social Sciences, vol. 63, 7–A.

Peek, K.L. 1999. "The Good, the Bad, and the 'Misunderstood': A Study of the Cognitive Moral Development Theory and the Ethics in the Public Sector." Dissertation Abstracts International Section A: Humanities and Social Sciences, vol. 60, 5–A: 1787.

Piaget, J. 1932. *The Moral Judgment of the Child*. New York: Free Press.

Putnam, R.D. 2000. *Bowling Alone: The Collapse and Revival of American Community*. New York: Simon and Schuster.

Rest, J.R. 1984. "The Major Components of Morality." In *Morality, Moral Behavior, and Moral Development*, ed. W. Kurtines and J. Gewirtz, pp. 24–40. New York: Wiley.

———. 1986. *Moral Development: Advances in Research and Theory.* Westport, CT: Praeger.

Rotter, J.B. 1966. "Generalized Expectancies for Internal versus External Control of

Reinforcement." *Psychological Monographs: General and Applied* 80, no. 1: 1–28.
Schwartz, S.H. 1977. "Normative Influences on Altruism." In *Advances in Experimental Social Psychology*, vol. 10, ed. L. Berkowitz, pp. 221–79. New York: Academic Press.
Simon, Herbert A. 1948. *Administrative Behavior*. New York: Macmillan.
Singhapakdi, A., and Vitell, S.J. 1990. "Marketing Ethics: Factors Influencing Perceptions of Ethics Problems and Alternatives." *Journal of Macromarketing* (Spring): 4–18.
Staw, B.M., and Szwajkowski, E. 1975. "The Scarcity-Munificence Component of Organizational Environments and the Commission of Illegal Acts." *Administrative Science Quarterly* 20: 354–54.
Stewart, D.W., and Sprinthall, N.A. 1991. "Strengthening Ethical Judgment in Public Administration." In *Ethical Frontiers in Public Management*, ed. J.S. Bowman, pp. 243–60. San Francisco: Jossey-Bass.
———. 1993. "The Impact of Demographic, Professional, and Organizational Variables and Domain on the Moral Reasoning of Public Administrators." In *Ethics and Public Administration*, ed. H.G. Frederickson, pp. 205–19. Armonk, NY: M.E. Sharpe.
———. 1994. "Moral Development in Public Administration." In *Handbook of Administrative Ethics*, ed. T.L. Cooper, pp. 325–48. New York: Marcel Dekker.
Stratton, W.E.; Flynn, W.R.; and Johnson, G.A. 1981. "Moral Development and Decision-Making: A Study of Student Ethics." *Journal of Enterprise Management* 3: 35–41.
Swisher, L.L. 2000. "Measuring Moral Development in Public Administration." Dissertation Abstracts International Section A: Humanities and Social Sciences, vol. 60, 8–A.
Tenbrunsel, A.E. 1998. "Misrepresentation and Expectations of Misrepresentation in an Ethical Dilemma: The Role of Incentives and Temptation." *Academy of Management Journal* 41, no. 3: 330–39.
Thoma, S.J. 1985. "On Improving the Relationship between Moral Reasoning and External Criteria: The Utilizer/Nonutilizer Dimension." Ph.D. dissertation, University of Minnesota.
Trevino, L.K. 1986. "Ethical Decision Making in Organizations: A Person-Situation Interactionist Model." *Academy of Management Review* 11: 601–17.
Trevino, L.K.; Sutton, C.D.; and Woodman, R.W. 1985. "Effects of Reinforcement Contingencies and Cognitive Moral Development on Ethical Decision-Making Behavior: An Experiment." Paper presented at the annual meeting of the Academy of Management, San Diego.
Trevino, L.K., and Youngblood, S. 1990. "Bad Apples in Bad Barrels: A Causal Analysis of Ethical Decision Making Behavior." *Journal of Applied Psychology* 75, no. 4: 378–85.
Victor, B., and Cullen, J.B. 1987. "A Theory and Measure of Ethical Climate in Organizations." In *Research in Corporate Social Performance and Policy: Empirical Studies of Business Ethics and Values*, ed. W.C. Frederick, pp. 51–71. Greenwich, CT: JAI Press.
———. 1988. The Organizational Bases of Ethical Work Climates." *Administrative Science Quarterly* 33 (March): 101–25.
Volker, J.M. 1984. "Counseling Experience, Moral Judgment, Awareness, and Moral Sensitivity in Counseling Practice." Ph.D. dissertation, University of Minnesota.

Weber, J. 1990. "Managers' Moral Reasoning: Assessing Their Responses to Three Moral Dilemmas." *Human Relations* 43: 687–702.

White, R.D. 1999. "Are Women More Ethical? Recent Findings on the Effects of Gender upon Moral Development." *Journal of Public Administration Research and Theory* 9, no. 3: 459–72.

———. 2002. "Do Employees Act Like They Think? Exploring the Dichotomy between Moral Judgment and Ethical Behavior." *Public Administration Quarterly* 25, no. 4: 391–411.

Wittmer, D.P. 1992. "Ethical Sensitivity and Managerial Decision Making: An Experiment." *Journal of Public Administration Theory and Research* 2: 443–62.

———. 2000. "Ethical Sensitivity in Management Decisions: Developing and Testing a Perceptual Measure among Management and Professional Student Groups." *Teaching Business Ethics* 4: 181–205.

Wittmer, D.P., and Coursey, D. 1996. "Ethical Work Climates: Comparing Top Managers in Public and Private Organizations." *Journal of Public Administration Research and Theory* 6, no. 4: 559–72.

Zey-Ferrell, M., and Ferrell, O.C. 1982. "Role-Set Configuration and Opportunity as Predictors of Unethical Behavior in Organizations." *Human Relations* 35: 587–604.

Zey-Ferrell, M.; Weaver, K.M.; and Ferrell, O.C. 1979. "Predicting Unethical Behavior among Marketing Practitioners." *Human Relations* 32: 557–69.

4

Update on Moral Reasoning Research and Theory in Public Administration: A Neo-Kohlbergian Perspective

Laura Lee Swisher, Ann-Marie Rizzo, and
Marsha A. Marley

Introduction

Relatively few ethical theories have been the subject of research to validate or refine their central tenets. Lawrence Kohlberg's theory of cognitive moral development and the neo-Kohlbergian approach[1] of James Rest and associates (Rest et al. 1999a) provide examples of an ethical framework that has evolved in response to ongoing research. This chapter outlines the major features of Kohlberg's original theory of moral development, describes criticisms and limitations of Kohlberg's six-stage framework, delineates changes made to the Kohlbergian approach in formulating the neo-Kohlbergian perspective, describes a study of moral reasoning among public administrators with the Defining Issues Test (DIT) of James Rest (1979, 1986, 1993; Rest and Narvaez 1998a), and highlights differences between the Kohlbergian and neo-Kohlbergian interpretations of its results for public administration ethics. The chapter concludes with a discussion of the manner in which ethical theory and descriptive research in public administration can be enriched through the ongoing cycle of descriptive research and subsequent reflection.

Behavioral research and writing concerning moral reasoning begins with Lawrence Kohlberg's body of work, which contends that ethical conduct for

Table 4.1

Comparison of Kohlberg and Neo-Kohlbergian Approaches to Moral Reasoning

	Kohlberg	Neo-Kohlberg
Approach	Cognitive, developmental, and social constructionist	Cognitive, developmental, and social constructionist
Framework	Six stages	Three schemas (stages)
Stages/schemas	1. Obedience 2. Instrumental egoism 3. Interpersonal concordance 4. Law and duty 5. Consensus building 6. Social cooperation	1. Personal interest (stages 2–3) 2. Maintaining norms (stage 4) 3. Postconventional (stages 5–6)
Consolidation/transition types	Not applicable	6 types—Consolidated or in transition in each schema
Development	Hard stage model Hard staircase model—subject is in only one stage	Soft stage model Shifting distribution between schemas—not a staircase
Highest moral reasoning	Principled reasoning	Postconventional reasoning
Evaluation	Interview—subject must articulate (production task)	Multiple choice test (Defining Issues Test)—subject must select (recognition task)

Source: Adapted with permission from the ideas of Rest et al. (1999a)

all human beings, irrespective of profession, depends on moral cognition and the ability to identify and reason through ethical dilemmas. From this perspective, ethical behavior is not merely about "doing the right thing." What one decides to do depends upon how one conceptualizes the dilemma within a specific moral worldview.

Kohlberg (1969, 1976, 1981a, 1981b) characterized the individual's moral worldview as progressing through six distinct stages, each of which uses a different type of moral reasoning to resolve ethical problems. As Kohlberg described it, moral development progresses from making decisions based on obedience, self-interest, laws and rules, and ultimately is based on social arrangements. (Table 4.1 summarizes important aspects of Kohlberg's theory as they compare to the later neo-Kohlbergian one.) In this regard, he argued that the higher stages of reasoning were more sophisticated and comprehensive and were superior to simpler, more conventional thinking.

Kohlberg's work stimulated considerable controversy, research, and re-

---

Table 4.2

Criticisms and Limitations of Kohlberg's Theory

1. By focusing on moral judgment (or deciding), Kohlberg presented a very limited view of moral behavior.
2. By focusing on abstract global stages of moral development, Kohlberg ignored the role of intermediate concepts (such as conflict of interest or confidentiality) that are commonly used in ethical decision making.
3. Kohlberg found very few examples of stage 5 or 6 moral reasoning.
4. Kohlberg focused on justice or macro morality (the formal structures of society) at the expense of caring or micro morality—face-to-face interactions (Rest et al. 1999a, p. 15).
5. Kohlberg's emphasis of abstract top-down foundational principles favors certain ethical approaches (like Kant and Rawls) at the expense of other acceptable ethical positions.
6. The hard-staircase development approach (one can be in one and only one stage) is no longer accepted in psychology.
7. The Moral Judgment Interview overemphasizes verbal skills by requiring the subject to produce verbal responses.
8. Kohlberg's research focused on male subjects, and the moral developmental process that he described is limited to the experience of men (see Gilligan 1982).

Source: Adapted with permission from the ideas of Rest and Narvaez (1994) and Rest et al. (1999a).

---

action. While his theory was the subject of initial praise and later intense criticism (Table 4.2), there can be no doubt that Kohlberg introduced an important line of research. At a later date, James Rest developed a written multiple choice alternative to Kohlberg's Moral Judgment Interview, the Defining Issues Test (DIT) (1993), which became the focus of numerous research publications.

Kohlberg had expressed doubts about the ability of a written instrument, such as the DIT, to result in a determination of the moral reasoning of the subject (Rest et al. 1999a and 1999b). However, findings with the DIT generated new insights into moral reasoning and development that pushed beyond the limits of Kohlberg's work. In contrast to Kohlberg's work, the DIT produced a large database of findings that were amenable to exploration and analysis with new scales and theories.

Differences between Kohlberg and Neo-Kohlbergian Perspectives

James Rest and his associates produced the neo-Kohlbergian or Minnesota perspective (Walker 2002) based on Kohlberg's original with the DIT. Results of over 400 published studies (Rest et al. 1999a, p. 62) allowed Rest and insights and research colleagues to evaluate criticisms leveled at Kohlberg. DIT research provided a scholarly lens through which the neo-Kohlbergians viewed criticisms of Kohlberg. This evaluation process resulted in revision of Kohlberg's theoretical framework and publication of their neo-Kohlbergian perspective (Rest et al. 1999a, 1999b).

Although there are many differences between the neo-Kohlbergian perspective and Kohlberg's theory (see Table 4.1), this part of the chapter will focus on just a few of these major differences: stages versus schema, the nature of the developmental process, the theoretical moral framework for interpretation of moral reasoning, the issue of gender in moral development, and evaluation of moral reasoning. Discussion will focus on the critique of Kohlberg and changes that these criticisms stimulated in the neo-Kohlbergian approach.

Stages versus Schemas

In place of six stages, the neo-Kohlbergians proposed three *schemas:* personal interest, maintaining norms, and the postconventional. Each schema bases ethical decisions on different criteria (Table 4.3) and serves as a different lens or worldview to provide guidance for action in responding to an ethical problem. The creators of the DIT further describe schema:

> Schema are general cognitive structures in that they provide a skeletal conception that is exemplified (or instantiated) by particular cases or experiences. That is, a schema has "slots" that can be filled in by particular instances. (Rest et al. 1999a, p. 136)

In the personal-interest moral judgment schema, decisions are based on self-interest and personal welfare without regard for society. The maintaining-norms moral judgment schema (formerly Kohlberg's stage 4 or conventional reasoning) bases ethical decisions on obeying the law, norms, rules, convention, and authority. Recognizing that laws and social conventions may be biased, the postconventional schema bases ethical decisions on the moral purposes, principles, and ideals that undergird social law and order (Rest et al. 1999a, pp. 36–43). At the heart of these differences about the criteria for each stage or schema of ethical decision making are differences in conceptualizing how social arrangements and cooperation ought to be organized.

Because DIT research has demonstrated steadily decreasing moral reasoning from the personal interest schema, the main concern in evaluating adult populations is the shift from maintaining-norms reasoning to

74 LAURA LEE SWISHER, ANN-MARIE RIZZO, AND MARSHA A. MARLEY

Table 4.3

Maintaining Norms versus Postconventional

Maintaining norms	Postconventional
Need for norms	Moral criteria most important. Laws and rules may be flawed, so moral considerations are critical.
"Society-wide scope"— recognizes need for social order.	Appeals to ideals (justice, rights, etc.)
Uniform application— laws and rules apply to everyone.	Ideals must be able to be shared.
Partial reciprocity (reversibility)— each person must perform roles and duties even though these laws and rules may benefit some more than others.	Full reciprocity (reversibility)— laws and rules should not be biased.

Source: Adapted with permission from the ideas of Rest and Narvaez (1994) and Rest et al. (1999a).

Table 4.4

Comparison of Three Schemas' Ethical Decision-Making Criteria

Personal interest	Maintaining norms	Postconventional
(Kohlberg's stages 2–3) Personal stake Decisions are based on consequences for me or for my loved ones.	(Kohlberg's stage 4) Existing social order Decisions are based on societal norms, laws, authority, and standards. (Includes religious and cultural norms.)	(Kohlberg's stages 5–6) Ideal social cooperation Decisions are based on "sharable ideals for organizing cooperation in society, and are open to debate and tests of logical consistency, experience of the community, and coherence with accepted practice" (Rest et al. 1999a, p. 41).

Source: Adapted with permission from the ideas of Rest et al. (1999a and 1999b).

postconventional reasoning. Acts of civil disobedience provide a practical illustration of how the maintaining-norms and postconventional schemas might differ in guiding ethical actions. While the maintaining-norms schema might emphasize that every person in society has an obligation to obey the law, the postconventional schema might emphasize the underlying principle of justice in protesting a biased law that places some citizens at a disadvantage.

Table 4.4 compares the moral decision making used by the three schema.

Nature of Developmental Process—Not a Staircase

Psychologists took issue with Kohlberg's hard-stage "staircase" description of the developmental process. Like stairs, a person could be in one and only one stage. Recognizing that development does not proceed in this fashion, the neo-Kohlbergian approach frames moral reasoning in terms of shifting patterns of schema. While Kohlberg attempted to identify whether a subject was a stage 5 or a stage 6 moral reasoner, the neo-Kohlbergian approach is concerned more with the extent to which a person uses maintaining-norms or postconventional reasoning.

Similarly, Kohlberg's theory was also criticized because he identified very few subjects as having reached stage 6. If this were an accurate developmental framework, critics reasoned, some subjects should progress to the highest stage of development. In contrast to Kohlberg's lack of highest levels of moral judgment, DIT studies demonstrated a strong developmental pattern with many subjects engaging in postconventional reasoning.

Theoretical Moral Framework

Neo-Kohlbergians have departed from Kohlberg's theoretical moral legacy in four areas: by developing a more comprehensive view of moral behavior, by distinguishing between macro- and micromorality, by not equating particular types of moral philosophy with more developed moral thinking, and by delineating different levels of abstraction in moral thinking. In the following section, we will discuss each of these contributions.

Kohlberg's theory of moral development was frequently criticized for its focus on moral cognition and its failure to recognize the complexity of moral actions. In response to these criticisms, Rest and associates adopted a multi-dimensional model of moral behavior, the four-component model of moral behavior. The four-component model delineates four overlapping psychological processes of moral behavior: moral sensitivity, interpreting the situation; moral judgment, making a decision about right or wrong action; moral motivation, giving priority to moral values; and moral courage, persevering and implementation (Rest 1994). From this perspective, the DIT provides information about only one process of moral behavior, moral judgment or moral reasoning.

The neo-Kohlbergians also enhanced the theoretical basis by distinguishing between macromorality and micromorality. Whereas macromorality involves the ethics of social and organizational structures, micromorality refers to the ethics of personal face-to-face ethics. This distinction addressed Kohlberg's lack of attention to personal ethics in favor of justice in social structures. The neo-Kohlbergian perspective values both macro and micromorality, and it admits that the DIT provides more information about macromorality.

Kohlberg has been criticized by philosophers for equating the highest stages of moral reasoning ("principled reasoning") with particular ethical theorists like Rawls and Habermas. Indeed, Kohlberg self-consciously attempted to blend his ideas of stage thinking with the philosophy of John Rawls (Rest et al. 1999b, p. 302), thus giving rise to the famous care-versus-justice debates. In contrast to this endorsement of specific abstract philosophical positions, the neo-Kohlbergian perspective suggests that thinking from a variety of ethical theories can be postconventional moral reasoning. The neo-Kohlbergian perspective embraces "common morality" and views most contemporary moral theories as compatible with postconventional thinking. According to Rest and associates, the only moral philosophies not compatible with the highest schema are emotivism, philosophies, like that of Nietzsche, which oppose social cooperation, and philosophies that base ethical actions on direct knowledge of the divine will (Rest et al. 1999b, p. 303).

A final neo-Kohlbergian contribution was the distinguishing of levels of abstraction in moral theories. In their formulation, developmental schema and moral theories (for example, deontology and utilitarianism) are relatively abstract and offer limited guidance to specific moral behavior. Rules and laws are very specific in their guidance. In between these extremes are "intermediate concepts" (Bebeau and Thoma 1999). Intermediate concepts include principles such as informed consent, conflict of interest, privacy, paternalism, and autonomy. Intermediate concepts provide a middle level of abstraction versus specificity in making decisions, and they are often a focus for professional ethics.

Gender in Moral Development

One important criticism of Kohlberg alleges that his theory is gender biased and that females receive lower moral development scores. Although Gilligan (1982) is widely regarded as having discredited Kohlberg's theories on the basis of gender bias, empirical studies with the DIT have consistently found few significant differences in moral judgment based on gender (Rest et al. 1999a). Ironically, women typically have scored slightly higher in postconventional reasoning on the DIT when gender differences do exist. A metanalysis of 56 studies involving over 6,000 subjects found that gender accounted for only .002 of the variance in DIT moral judgment scores (Rest et al. 1999a, p. 116; Thoma 1986; Rest 1986). It is not uncommon to find significant gender differences in traditionally male-dominated professional fields, such as medicine (Baldwin, Daugherty, and Self 1991; Self, Wolinsky, and Baldwin 1994; Self, Wolinsky and Baldwin 1989) and veterinary medicine (Self, Olivarez, and Baldwin 1994).

Evaluation of Moral Reasoning

Kohlberg used the Moral Judgment Inventory to classify each subject into one of the six stages of moral reasoning, so a person might be described as a stage 4 moral reasoner. In contrast, the DIT provides information about the relative proportions of thinking from each of the major schemas, with particular attention to the proportion of postconventional versus maintaining-norms thinking.

The DIT is a multiple choice instrument that consists of three (short-form) or six (long-form) story dilemmas, followed by a series of questions and items to rate and rank. After each story, the subject identifies what action should be taken, rates the importance of twelve issues raised by the dilemma from "no importance" to "great importance," and finally, ranks the four most important issues. Each issue represents a fragment of one of the three moral reasoning schemas: personal interest, maintaining norms, or postconventional (Rest et al. 1999a).

Scoring of the DIT yields the P or P percent, which essentially indicates the percentage of postconventional issues that the subject ranks as most important and represents the importance placed on postconventional thinking. Ongoing research with the DIT has shown it to be a valid and reliable test of moral judgment, with test-retest reliability of .7 to .8 (Rest et al. 1999a, p. 93). Based on more than twenty years of DIT testing, Cronbach's alpha for the P percent score on the DIT is in the range of .76 to .83 (Rest et al. 1999a, p. 92). Test-retest reliability and Cronbach's alpha are slightly lower for the shorter three-story version of the DIT (Rest 1993) than for the longer six-story version.

DIT research also generated new indices, other than the P percent score, to evaluate moral reasoning. Although some indexes failed to improve on the P percent, the $N2$ index is in the process of replacing the P percent score. In contrast to the P score, which primarily considers the *rankings* of postconventional items, the $N2$ score also considers the difference in *rating* the schema. In a sense, $N2$ evaluates the ability to select and distinguish postconventional items from items from lower schema. Based on research with the DIT, the $N2$ index is now considered a more sensitive index than the P percent (Rest et al. 1999a).

In addition to new indexes, the Minnesota group has also created a new DIT (DIT-2) to address concerns about the dated scenarios in the DIT. Recently, the Center for the Study of Ethical Development created a second version, DIT-2. This version is shorter, with only five story dilemmas, and it has updated scenarios. In preliminary testing, DIT-2 has performed similarly to DIT-1 and has .79 correlation with DIT-1 results (Rest and Narvaez 1998b, p. 27; Rest et al. 1999a).

As is indicated by this summary, the neo-Kohlbergian perspective of James Rest and associates has effectively used research with the DIT to address many of the criticisms of Kohlberg's original theory. This description of the evolution of the neo-Kohlbergian perspective provides a foundation for interpretation of a study of moral reasoning that will be described in the following section.

Cognitive Developmental Research and Public Administration

Public administration research in cognitive developmental has been primarily from the Kohlbergian perspective, with scant attention to the neo-Kohlbergian perspective. In fact, little research in public administration had used the cognitive developmental perspective until the pioneering work of Debra Stewart and Norman Sprinthall (Stewart and Sprinthall 1991, 1993, 1994). They developed an instrument, the Stewart-Sprinthall Management Survey (SSMS), to assess the moral development of public administrators using public administration dilemmas. Stewart, Sprinthall, and Siemienska later (1997) expanded their use of the SSMS to include work with government officials from Poland utilizing dilemmas specific to the Polish context. While Stewart and Sprinthall (1991) found no differences based on gender in studies of public administrators in the United States, studies in Poland (Stewart, Sprinthall, and Siemienska 1997) and Russia (Stewart, Sprinthall, and Kem 2002) revealed higher postconventional (principled) reasoning and lower maintaining-norms (law and duty) thinking among females than among their male counterparts. Surprisingly, Russian officials differed from their Polish and American counterparts by choosing stage 4 reasoning significantly less often.

White's study of Coast Guard and enlisted personnel found no differences in DIT postconventional scores (mean $P\% = 33.5$) based on rank, age, education, or race. However, females scored significantly higher than males, scoring a mean P percent of 37.22 versus 32.76 (White 1999, 465).

As has been discussed, the issue of gender differences in moral judgment has historically been a major source of contention. Although the bulk of research suggests that level of formal education has a much stronger influence on ethical schema than does gender, women in male-dominated fields may score higher than men do. Within public administration, White's (1999) research with Coast Guard personnel and Stewart, Sprinthall, and Siemienska's (1997) research in Poland and Stewart, Sprinthall, and Kem's research in Russia (2002) supported the existence of gender differences.

Purpose and Hypotheses

This study had three main purposes: to establish a baseline measurement of postconventional reasoning with the DIT in a random sample of public administrators; to examine differences in ethical schema preference among public administrators based on age, gender, race, formal education, organizational context, or organizational function; and to compare the moral judgment of public administrators to that of other professional groups. The researchers posed the following questions:

- What types of moral reasoning do public administrators use?
- Are there significant differences in preference for moral reasoning schema based on age, gender, race, formal education, organizational context, or organizational function?

Since formal education has such a significant impact on moral judgment (Rest et al. 1999b; McNeel 1994), the researchers hypothesized that those with masters or doctoral level education would have a significantly higher preference for postconventional reasoning (P % score) than for maintaining norms (law and order). Based on the educational background of the sample, it was anticipated that the postconventional score would be comparable to other similarly educated professional groups (Rest 1994a, p. 14).

Age, gender, race, formal education, region, organizational context, and organizational function or title (independent variables) were operationalized as the subject's response to a demographic questionnaire. Type of moral reasoning schema (dependent variable) was operationalized as the P or P percent score indicating the percentage of preference for postconventional reasoning and the maintaining-norms percentage score.

Given the respondents' educational backgrounds, and based on previous DIT research, it was anticipated that the mean P percent score would be 45 or more and the mean maintaining-norms percentage score would be less than 35.

Methods

This cross-sectional study examined moral reasoning among public administrators using the DIT created by James Rest (1979, 1993). The terms "moral judgment," "moral thinking," "ethical reasoning," and "moral reasoning" are used interchangeably here to refer to the cognitive process of determining a right or wrong action (Rest 1994). As Rest and his associates describe it, "the special function of the construct of moral judgment is to provide conceptual guidance for action choice situations in which moral claims conflict" (1999a, p. 10).

The membership of the American Society for Public Administration (ASPA) was chosen as the study population because it is the oldest and most widely known association for public administrators. In addition, ASPA has a diverse membership with members from all fifty states; from the municipal, state, and federal organizational contexts; and with a variety of occupational functions. A computer-generated random sample of 1,000 of the 11,185 ASPA members was obtained after obtaining permission from the organization. This sampling frame included academic and student members. The survey was mailed to 1,000 ASPA members. A follow-up reminder postcard was mailed to the entire sample four weeks after the initial mailing.

Sample respondents were predominantly white (93.8 percent) and male (67 percent). Mean age was 48.45 years ($n = 262$, $sd = 10.31$). Respondents had a high degree of formal education with more than 85 percent holding a graduate degree. Most (30.7%, $n = 264$) worked in municipal government as top or middle managers (35.2 percent). About 14 percent of respondents were college or university teachers or administrators and 1.1 percent were students. This sample appeared demographically congruent with the profile of ASPA (demographic information obtained from the American Society for Public Administration in late 1998). That is, the sample was composed predominantly of middle-aged white males who were middle or top managers, most of whom held a graduate degree.

Instrumentation involved a brief demographic questionnaire and the short form of the DIT. Completed DIT results were sent to the Center for the Study of Ethical Development (University of Minnesota, Minneapolis) for scoring. Standard reliability checks eliminated subjects who did not understand the directions, provided random answers, or selected numerous meaningless responses.

These data and information from the demographics survey were entered into the Statistical Program for the Social Sciences, version 7.0 (SPSS 1995) and descriptive statistics were calculated. Raw maintaining-norms scores were converted to a percentage of total items to enable comparison to the P percent and $N2$ scores. Analysis of variance was used to analyze differences between groups on postconventional moral reasoning and maintaining-norms reasoning. Since not everyone agrees that DIT data meet the criteria for parametric statistical analysis, the Mann Whitney statistical test assisted in analyzing differences in moral reasoning based on gender and education. One-sample t-test was employed to compare the group postconventional mean of 41.45 to the score of other groups obtained in previous DIT research.

Results

Response rate to the DIT survey was 34.4 percent. Standard DIT consistency checks eliminated another 70 subjects, leaving a usable sample of 274 subjects. This somewhat low response rate may reflect the complexity and length of the survey, and that it was administered in the summer. In addition, a number of surveys were returned because of a wrong address. Table 4.5 summarizes the results and indicates that, in general, the ASPA members show a slight preference for postconventional moral reasoning (41.45 percent versus 37.13 percent maintaining-norms reasoning). This preference for postconventional reasoning contrasted with Stewart and Sprinthall's findings among public administrators in the United States of a preference for maintaining-norms reasoning—42 percent to 44 percent versus 38 percent postconventional (Stewart and Sprinthall 1994).

Mann-Whitney analysis of difference revealed that females used significantly more postconventional reasoning and significantly less maintaining norms reasoning than males (Table 4.6) in analyzing ethical dilemmas on the DIT. There were no significant differences in P percent scores based on other variables related to organizational context or job function.

Based on the educational background of the sample the researchers had predicted that the sample's P percent score would not differ from P percent scores of other comparably educated groups. Table 4.7 summarizes the results of one-sample t-tests comparing the sample's mean postconventional score (41.45) to that of other groups.

The sample's postconventional score was significantly lower than the score of moral philosophy students, physicians, and staff nurses, but it was higher than the score of Coast Guard personnel in White's study. The mean postconventional score was also significantly higher than that of accountants and managers in Stewart and Sprinthall's studies whose P percent was 39 ($t = 2.392$, $df = 273$, $p = .013$). One-sample t-test also demonstrated that public administrators used significantly more maintaining-norms reasoning than did college students ($t = 9.26$, $df = 273$, $p = .000$) reported in previous DIT research (Rest 1993, p. 20).

Since formal education is the strongest predictor of moral reasoning scores, one would expect this highly educated group of public administrators to have had higher P percent values than adults in general, who pre-

Table 4.5

Summary of Preference for Postconventional Moral Reasoning

Group		P% Scores				N2 Scores		
	n	Range	Mean	sd	n	Range	Mean	sd
Males	177	0.0–83.3	39.73	15.92	171	7.52–71.86	45.71	12.34
Females	87	3.4–83.3	45.23	18.02	86	8.42–73.07	48.40	13.39
Undergraduate degree or less	38	6.7–66.7	36.93	15.13	38	7.52–68.24	42.05	14.54
Master's or doctoral degree	225	0.0–83.3	42.14	17.08	218	9.19–73.07	47.25	12.34
Entire sample	274	0.0–83.3	41.45	16.95	267	7.52–73.07	46.43	12.86

Table 4.6

Summary of Mann-Whitney Test for Influence of Gender on Moral Reasoning

Source	N	Mean rank	Sum of ranks	Z
Postconventional P%				
Male	177	125.05	22133.50	–2.266*
Female	87	147.66	12846.50	
Total	264			
Postconventional N2				
Male	171	125.57	21130.50	–1.651[a]
Female	86	139.80	12022.50	
Total	257			
Maintaining norms				
Male	177	140.67	24898.00	–2.483**
Female	87	115.89	10082.00	
Total	264			

$**p = .013; *p = .023; {}^{a}p = .099$

Table 4.7

Summary of One-sample T-Tests Comparing Public Administrators' Postconventional Reasoning (P %) to That of Other Groups

Group (data source)	P% score	df	Std. error mean	t
Moral philosophy/political science graduate students (Rest 1994a, p. 14)	65.20	273	1.02	–23.3**
Law students (Rest 1994a, p. 14)	52.20	273	1.02	–10.5**
Practicing physicians (Rest 1994a, p. 14)	49.20	273	1.02	–7.6**
Staff nurses (Rest 1994a, p. 14)	46.30	273	1.02	–4.737**
College students (Rest 1994a, p. 14)	42.30	273	1.02	–.8
Public administrators in this study	41.50	—	—	—
Adults in general (Rest 1994a, p. 14)	40.00	273	1.02	1.4
Accountants (Ponemon 1992b)	38.06	273	1.02	3.3*
Coast Guard personnel (White 1999)	33.50	273	1.02	7.8**

$**p = .000; *p = .001$

sumably have less education. However, the group was not significantly different in its use of postconventional reasoning than were adults in general or college students.

It is interesting to note that the *P* percent and *N2* indexes produced slightly different evaluations of this sample. Although the *P* percent score was significantly different for males and females, the *N2* score was not significantly

Table 4.8

Summary of Mann-Whitney Test for Influence of Education (two categories) on Postconventional Moral Reasoning (P% versus $N2$)

Source	N	Mean rank	Sum of ranks	Z
Postconventional $N2$ score				
Undergraduate degree or less	38	105.96	4026.50	–2.033*
Master's or doctor's degree	218	132.43	28869.50	
Total	256			
Postconventional P% score				
Undergraduate degree or less	38	111.11	4222.00	–1.834[a]
Master's or doctor's degree	225	135.53	30494.00	
Total	263			

$*p = .042$; [a]$p = .067$

different (Table 4.6). Similarly, the $N2$ score was significantly different for education (undergraduate degree or less versus master's degree or higher), but not different for P percent (Table 4.8).

Discussion

Preference for Postconventional Thinking

The purpose of this study was to examine public administrators' moral reasoning by using a valid and reliable measure of moral reasoning, the DIT. As the researchers had anticipated, results demonstrated that public administrators employ more postconventional moral reasoning than maintaining-norms reasoning. This preference for postconventional thinking differs from Stewart and Sprinthall's conclusions in previous studies (1991, 1993, 1994). Using the SSMS with county, municipal, and state managers in the United States, Stewart and Sprinthall (1991, 1993, 1994) found a preference for maintaining norms (42 percent), with P percent values of 38 and 39. Using the neo-Kohlbergian framework, the schema mix for this public administration sample looks like Figure 4.1.

Gender Differences and Public Administrators' Moral Thinking

As illustrated by Figure 4.2 and reflected in the significant differences in P percent scores, the schema mix for men and women was different. Women in this public administration sample seemed to slightly prefer postconventional thinking to maintaining-norms thinking. Male administrators, on the other

Figure 4.1 **Moral Schema Mix for Sample of American Society for Public Administration (ASPA) Members**

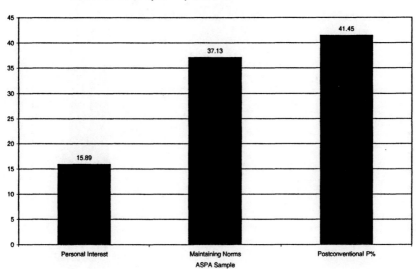

hand, seemed to have about equal preference for the two types of thinking or to slightly prefer maintaining-norms moral reasoning.

Gender differences in moral reasoning in this study contrast with Stewart and Sprinthall's (1991, 1993, 1994) work in the United States, and coincide with findings among Polish (Stewart, Sprinthall, and Siemienska 1997) and Russian (Stewart, Sprinthall, and Kem 2002) public administrators and with White's (1999) study of Coast Guard personnel. From the neo-Kohlbergian perspective, these results are not entirely surprising. Although DIT research has found very few gender differences, it is not uncommon for women to score higher than men do on postconventional reasoning in male-dominated professions.

In a comparison of moral reasoning scores obtained by the DIT-2 and the SSMS among members of the Ethics Section of the ASPA, Rizzo and Swisher (2004) found that females scored slightly higher on postconventional reasoning on both the DIT and SSMS, but this difference was not statistically significant. Results also demonstrated that SSMS maintaining-norms scores were significantly higher than the corresponding DIT maintaining-norms scores. SSMS postconventional scores were lower than DIT scores, but this difference was not significant. Additionally, individuals who identified themselves as liberals had significantly higher DIT postconventional scores than did conservatives. These findings suggest that the two instruments may tap into slightly different aspects of moral reasoning.

Figure 4.2 **Comparison of Moral Schema Mix for Males and Females in American Society for Public Administration (ASPA) Sample**

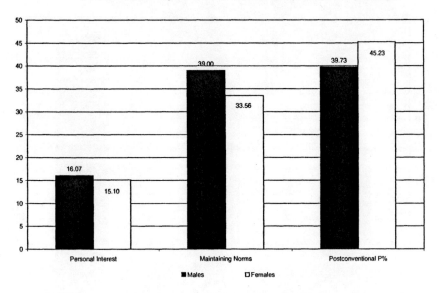

An interesting finding in this study of ASPA members was the differing results for P percent and $N2$ scores in comparing men and women. While the P percent and $N2$ scores were both higher for females than for males, only the P percent scores were significantly different (see Tables 4.5 and 4.6). Given that the P percent scores include ranked data only while $N2$ scores incorporate both ranking and rating, it is possible that men and women rate the ethical issues similarly but rank them differently.

Importance of Education

From the neo-Kohlbergian perspective, perhaps the most surprising result in this study is the relatively small impact of education on moral thinking. In spite of the sample's overall preference for postconventional thinking, the P percent score was lower than predicted based on amount of formal education; the sample did not differ significantly from adults in general in the use of postconventional moral reasoning. A review of over 100 citations about the effect of demographic variables on P percent scores concluded that "the level of formal education is the strongest predictor of DIT scores" (Rest et al. 1999a, p. 70; Rest and Thoma 1985). College education has had a particularly significant impact on moral reasoning. Based on a review of thirty longitudinal studies, Rest and associates concluded that each level of formal education increases the DIT P percent score by about ten points (Rest et al. 1999a, p. 73). From the perspective of this previous research, it is surprising that the group did not score higher on postconventional thinking. Considering that 85 percent of those in this sample held graduate degrees, is there something about the profession or the job or about their particular education or training that nullifies the impact of education on the moral reasoning of public administrators?

Given the relatively low postconventional scores and lack of differences in P percent scores between educational groups in this study, it is interesting that only $N2$ scores were different for those with graduate degrees than for those with undergraduate education or less. However, the P percent results are consistent with White's study of Coast Guard and enlisted personnel, which found no differences in DIT postconventional scores (mean $P\% = 33.5$) based on education.

Limitations

These findings should be interpreted with an understanding of the study's limitations. The four-component model of moral behavior provides one basis for understanding the limitations of this research. The purpose was to examine moral reasoning among public administrators. Moral reasoning is merely one component of moral behavior, a complex multidimensional process composed of at least four component processes: moral sensitivity, interpreting the situation; moral judgment, deciding what is right or wrong; moral motivation, prioritizing moral values over others; and moral character or courage, persisting against adversity (Rest 1994). This research examined only the second component: moral judgment. It does not provide information about contextual, personal, or organizational factors that may influence ethical sensitivity (component one), motivation (component three), or moral courage (component four). Given the complexity of moral behavior, it does not tell us whether administrators, individually or collectively, behave morally.

In addition this study provides more insight into macromorality than micromorality. That is, the results tell us more about public administrators' worldview and implicit framework for conceptualizing societal structure. Data from this study provide a window into the default schemas with which public administrators conceptualize society. They tell us considerably less about the interpersonal ethics and virtues necessary for the successful negotiation of microethical situations.

Another limitation relates to instrumentation and sample. The short form of the DIT has somewhat decreased reliability compared to the longer form, and this may have affected results. In addition, instrument complexity and the mail survey format may have affected the quantity and quality of responses on the DIT; it should also be noted that only about one-third of the sample was comprised of females, approximately the proportion of females in the ASPA.

New Questions and Issues in Research in Public Administration Ethics

This chapter has illustrated how one ethics theory, the neo-Kohlbergian approach, has used research to refine, validate, critique, and improve its underlying model. The authors have highlighted the differences between the original and revised models in discussing the results of a study of moral reasoning among members of the ASPA. The success of the Minnesota group demonstrates that ethics can utilize research to generate questions, improve theoretical models, and create perspectives.

This study raises questions for more research, and it points to deficits in our knowledge of the moral behavior of public administrators. The following list represents some examples of questions raised by the study:

- What typical or common moral dilemmas do administrative professionals in government routinely encounter, and how do they work through the decision process?
- Does type of moral reasoning make a difference in moral behavior?
- Since the DIT uses hypothetical dilemmas, do administrators rely more on maintaining-norms moral reasoning than do other professional groups in actual work situations?
- How do organizational and institutional factors constrain moral reasoning?
- What are the critical moral sensitivity issues for public administrators, the motivational factors and moral character governing their behavior?
- What is the preprofessional ethics training for public administrators?
- Do ethics training programs have an impact on moral judgment?
- What are the intermediate ethical concepts that guide the ethical decision making of public administrators?
- In what ways does hierarchical level or position constrain or shape moral reasoning in public managers?
- Do contextual factors influence moral behavior differently for men and women?
- Why do women in public administration—ostensibly with the same training and education as men occupying the same work context if not comparable positions—reason differently about moral situations?
- What is the significance for moral behavior of differences between find-

ings of the DIT and the SSMS with regard to gender, political orientation, and measurement of maintaining norms reasoning?

As illustrated by these questions, the impact of education, leadership, and organizational culture on moral thinking and action are some especially important areas for further research in public administration ethics.

Previous studies with the DIT suggest that leaders and organizational culture may have both positive and negative impacts on moral reasoning. In a study of nonprofit chief executives, Jurkiewicz and Brown (1999) found that effective executives scored higher on both postconventional moral reasoning and power than did those who were not effective. A similar study of nonprofit executives by Jurkiewicz and Massey (1998) found that effective executives scored much higher on postconventional thought ($P\%$ score of 65.14) than those who were not effective ($P\%$ score of 33.57). This suggests that leadership has a moral dimension.

Ponemon's (1992a) study of the accounting profession concluded that selection, socialization, and promotion patterns within the organizational culture resulted in senior managers with lower mean P percent scores (38.05):

> In summary, cross-sectional and longitudinal studies yield consistent findings. That is, DIT P scores increase from 40 to 42 for staff and seniors and then sharply decrease from 42 to 36 for seniors and managers. As advanced earlier, the root causes of this are two-fold. First, socialization pressures cause auditors with lower ethical reasoning capacities to leave the firm rather than develop to higher levels. This was reflected by auditors with lower DIT P scores leaving the firm one year after promotion to senior. Second, and perhaps more disconcerting, selection-socialization results in only certain types of auditors being promoted within the firm. Evidence of this process was revealed in audit manager promotions where only those seniors with relatively low DIT P scores were advanced. (Ponemon 1992a, p. 252)

Taken together, these studies indicate that organizational leadership and culture may impact organizational ethics and moral decision making. The fact that this study found no differences in moral reasoning between staff and managers in moral reasoning could stimulate further research into the reasons for and effects of this lack of difference.

Gender differences in moral reasoning found in this study suggest either that men and women in public administration perceive their roles differently or that they bring different worldviews to the same roles. Alternatively, different organizational factors may shape men's and women's professional role concept in government. Following Ponemon (1992b), women with relatively higher P percent scores might find that promotion eludes their grasp not only because of traditional organizational and career obstacles but also because they fail to fit the ethical profile of those in top echelons. Indeed, if public administration professions correspond to accounting, senior officials' prospects to serve as ethical role models or mentors in government would be compromised.

The current study also raises issues for further research in the area of education. Lower than anticipated postconventional scores may be the result of the content, type of educational intervention, or effectiveness of the ethics curricula of public administration programs. Previous research indicates that both time and format are important considerations in teaching moral reasoning (Self, Olivarez, and Baldwin 1994, p. 167; Rest and Thoma 1985). The small group dilemma discussion format is more effective in increasing moral judgment scores than the traditional academic lecture format (Rest et al. 1999a, p. 74; Self, Olivarez, and Baldwin 1994). Self and associates found that forty-four contact hours produced significant change in medical students' moral reasoning but fifteen contact hours did not (Self, Wolinsky, and Baldwin 1989; Self, Olivarez, and Baldwin 1994, p. 167). Menzel's study of MPA graduates reveals how little we know about the types and effects of different pedagogical approaches to teaching public administration ethics (Menzel 1997). Do courses that emphasize compliance rather than moral decision making increase moral judgment?

An ongoing concern in cognitive developmental research is the link between judgment and action. A number of authors have commented on the link between high postconventional scores and positive ethical actions. Similarly, low P percent scores have been associated with underreporting of audit tasks (Ponemon 1992b) and decreased likelihood of predicting whistle-blowing in experimental situations (Arnold and Ponemon 1991). This suggests that low P percent scores among public administrators, if tied to behavior, could have deleterious consequences. Further research could establish whether differences in moral reasoning have these effects on behavior.

The neo-Kohlbergian framework might also stimulate questions about whether schema scores are the most relevant measures of professional ethics. Bebeau and Thoma (1999) developed a measure of intermediate concepts for dentistry. This tool evaluates the ability of professionals to utilize ethical concepts in commonly encountered professional ethical situations. An instrument to evaluate the use of intermediate ethical principles could provide valuable information about the moral reasoning of public administration students.

Conclusion

The historical debate about the nature of administrative discretion provides another context for interpreting these findings. In spite of the theoretical rejection of the politics-administration dichotomy (White 1939), these results may support the argument that public administrators view their role as that of applying law and policy through use of the maintaining-norms moral reasoning schema. As Stewart and Sprinthall suggest, "Finally, [the pull toward law and duty] could reflect the grip that the Wilsonian dichotomy has on the culture of public administration: a dichotomy which casts ideal public administrators as unwavering implementors of the politically forged law" (Stewart and Sprinthall 1994, p. 342).

Results may also reflect the longstanding dual mind-set on the subject of ethics in public administration. On the one hand, there is increasing recognition that public administrators make complex ethical decisions, as discussed in this passage:

> [P]ublic officials are confronted with a host of issues, problems, and dilemmas of an ethical nature, all of which require sharp skills of critical thinking. Put another way, it seems as if a new requirement for public administration is the ability to solve a moral problem. Hence, there may have been some truth in Plato's famous dictum found in his *Republic* that holds: "Unless kings become philosophers or philosophers become kings, there is no hope for humanity." We might say that at a bare minimum, what *is* necessary is that public administrators become proficient at moral reasoning. (Madsen and Shafritz 1992, p. 212)

On the other hand, there is a longstanding resistance to ethical reflection in public life. In part, this may be attributed to the scientific rational-technical worldview and the positivist history of public administration (Adams 1992). In addition, this resistance may be the result of an aversion to issues of value that can be politically divisive (Amy 1992).

The Kohlbergian and neo-Kohlbergian moral theory stand in sharp contrast to the positivist understanding of the public administrator. Research from the neo-Kohlbergian perspective affirms that how one views the moral world and society makes a difference. Indeed, Rest and associates have suggested that type of moral reasoning has an important effect on public-policy decisions (Rest et al., p. 312). At the same time, the neo-Kohlbergian perspective reminds us that ongoing research can change how we view the moral world:

> Successful research is never final or completed. One solid finding leads to further questions, conjecture, and theorizing, which in turn lead to further research. Sometimes—happily—the new directions lead to fruitful new

theories and findings. As active areas of research gain prominence, they invite the scrutiny of critics. Appropriately, critics have a way of coming up with challenges and proposals that call for readjustments and redirection in the plans conceived by the original researchers. DIT research also has been redirected this way. (Rest et al. 1999a, p. 99)

As these comments suggest, ethical theories benefit from the cycle of research in which propositions are tested and results subjected to the critique of peers.

Although DIT research has provided a foundation for improvement and validation of the cognitive developmental perspective, many questions remain about the moral sensitivity, judgment, motivation, and courage of public administrators. Policy implementation and regulation inevitably have social and ethical dimensions, and public administrators often serve in a consultative role to political leaders, providing information and advice regarding policy analysis and implementation. Further research from the neo-Kohlbergian perspective could provide even greater insight into the moral dimensions of these roles.

Notes

The authors would like to thank the members of the American Society for Public Administration who contributed their time and efforts to complete the questionnaire used in this research.
1. Several scholars have attempted to adapt and update Kohlberg's theories and could lay claim to the title "neo-Kohlbergian." In this chapter the term "neo-Kohlbergian" refers to the perspective of James Rest and associates as articulated in *Postconventional Moral Thinking: A Neo-Kohlbergian Approach* (1999a).

References

Adams, Guy B. 1992. "Enthralled with Modernity: The Historical Context of Knowledge and Theory Development in Public Administration." *Public Administration Review* 52, no. 4: 363–73.

Amy, Douglas J. 1984. "Why Policy Analysis and Ethics Are Incompatible." *Journal of Policy Analysis and Management* 3 (Summer), pp. 573–591.

Arnold, Donald F. Sr., and Ponemon, Lawrence A. 1991. "Internal Auditors' Perceptions of Whistle-blowing and the Influence of Moral Reasoning: An Experiment." *Auditing* 10, no. 2: 1.

Baldwin, DeWitt C. Jr. Daugherty, Steven, and Self, Donnie J. 1991. "Changes in Moral Reasoning during Medical School." *Academic Medicine* 66: 1–3.

Bebeau, Muriel J., and Thoma, Stephen J. 1999. "Intermediate Concepts and the Connection to Moral Education." *Educational Psychology Review* 11, no. 4: 343–60.

Gilligan, Carol. 1982. *In a Different Voice: Psychological Theory and Women's Development*. Cambridge, MA: Harvard University Press.

Jurkiewicz, Carole L., and Brown, Roger G. 1999. "Power, Ethics, and Executive

Effectiveness." Paper presented at the 60th national conference of the American Society for Public Administration. Orlando, FL, April 10-14.

Jurkiewicz, Carole L., and Massey, Tom K. 1998. "The Influence of Ethical Reasoning on Leader Effectiveness: An Empirical Study of Non-profit Executives." *Non-Profit Management and Leadership* 2, no. 2: 173–86.

Kohlberg, Lawrence. 1969. "Stage and Sequence: The Cognitive-Developmental Approach to Socialization." In *Handbook of Socialization Theory and Research*, ed. D. Goslin, pp. 347–480. Chicago: Rand McNally.

———. 1976. "Moral Stages and Moralization: The Cognitive-Developmental Approach." In *Moral Development and Behavior*, ed. Thomas Lickona, pp. 31–53. New York: Holt, Rinehart and Winston.

———. 1981a. "From *Is* to *Ought*: How to Commit the Naturalistic Fallacy and Get Away with It." In *The Philosophy of Moral Development: Moral Stages and the Idea of Justice*, pp. 101–89. San Francisco: Harper and Row.

———. 1981b. *The Philosophy of Moral Development: Moral Stages and the Idea of Justice*. San Francisco: Harper and Row.

Madsen, Peter, and Shafritz, Jay M., eds. 1992. *Essentials of Government Ethics*. New York: Penguin Books.

McNeel, Steven P. 1994. "College Teaching and Student Moral Development." In *Moral Development in the Professions: Psychology and Applied Ethics*, ed. James R. Rest and Darcia Narvaez, pp. 27–50. Hillsdale, NJ: Erlbaum.

Menzel, Donald C. 1997. "Teaching Ethics and Values in Public Administration: Are We Making a Difference?" *Public Administration Review* 57, no. 3: 224–30.

Ponemon, Lawrence A. 1991. "Internal Auditors' Perceptions of Whistle-blowing and the Influence of Moral Reasoning: An Experiment." *Auditing* 10, no. 2: 1.

———. 1992a. "Ethical Reasoning and Selection-Socialization in Accounting. *Accounting, Organizations, and Society* 17, nos. 3–4: 239–58.

———. 1992b. "Auditor Underreporting of Time and Moral Reasoning: An Experimental Lab Study." *Contemporary Accounting Research* 9, no. 1: 171.

Rest, James R. 1979. *Development in Judging Moral Issues*. Minneapolis: University of Minnesota Press.

———. 1986. *Moral Development: Advances in Research and Theory*. New York: Praeger.

———. 1993. *Guide to the Defining Issues Test*, version 1.3. Minneapolis: Center for the Study of Ethical Development.

———. 1994. "Background: Theory and Research." In *Moral Development in the Professions: Psychology and Applied Ethics*, ed. James R. Rest and Darcia Narvaez, pp. 1–26. Hillsdale, NJ: Erlbaum.

Rest, James R., and Narváez, Darcia, eds. 1994. *Moral Development in the Professions: Psychology and Applied Ethics*. Hillsdale, NJ: Erlbaum.

———. 1997. *Ideas for Research with the DIT*, version 1.3. Minneapolis: Center for the Study of Ethical Development.

———. 1998a. *Supplement to the Guide for DIT-1*. Minneapolis: Center for the Study of Ethical Development.

———. 1998b. *Guide for DIT-2-2*, version 2.3. Minneapolis: Center for the Study of Ethical Development.

Rest, James; Narváez, Darcia; Bebeau, Muriel J.; and Thoma, Stephen J. 1999a. *Postconventional Moral Thinking: A Neo-Kohlbergian Approach*. Mahwah, NJ: Erlbaum.

————. 1999b. "The Neo-Kohlbergian Approach: The DIT and Schema Theory."
    Educational Psychology Review 11, no. 4: 291–324.
Rest, James R., and Thoma, Stephen J. 1985. "The Relation of Moral Judgment
    Development to Formal Education." *Developmental Psychology* 21, no. 4:
    709–14.
Rizzo, Ann-Marie, and Swisher, Laura Lee. 2004. "Comparing the Stewart–Sprinthall
    Management Survey and the Defining Issues Test-2 as Measures of Moral Rea-
    soning in Public Administration." *Journal of Public Administration: Research and
    Theory* 14: 335–48.
Self, Donnie J., and Baldwin, DeWitt C., Jr. 1994. "Moral Reasoning in Medicine."
    In *Moral Development in the Professions: Psychology and Applied Ethics*, ed.
    James R. Rest and Darcia Narvaez, pp. 163–72. Hillsdale, NJ: Erlbaum.
Self, Donnie J.; Olivarez, Margie; and Baldwin, DeWitt C. Jr. 1994. "Moral Reason-
    ing in Veterinary Medicine." In Rest and Narvaez, 1994.
Self, Donnie J.; Wolinsky, F.D.; and Baldwin, DeWitt C., Jr. 1989. "The Effect of
    Teaching Medical Ethics on Medical Students' Moral Reasoning." *Academic Medi-
    cine* 64: 755–59.
SPSS, version 7.0. 1995. Statistical Program for the Social Sciences, Chicago.
Stewart, Debra W., and Sprinthall, Norman A. 1991. "Strengthening Ethical Judg-
    ment in Public Administration." In *Ethical Frontiers in Public Management*, ed.
    James S. Bowman, pp. 243–60. San Francisco: Jossey-Bass.
————. 1993. "The Impact of Demographic, Professional, and Organizational Vari-
    ables and Domain on the Moral Reasoning of Public Administrators." In *Ethics
    and Public Administration*, ed. H. George Frederickson, pp. 205–19. Armonk, NY:
    M.E. Sharpe.
————. 1994. "Moral Development in Public Administration." In *Handbook of
    Administrative Ethics*, ed. Terry L. Cooper, pp. 325–48. New York: Marcel
    Dekker.
Stewart, Debra W.; Sprinthall, Norman A.; and Kem, Jackie D. 2002. "Moral Reason-
    ing in the Context of Reform: A Study of Russian Officials." *Public Administra-
    tion Review* 62, no. 3: 282–97.
Stewart, Debra W.; Sprinthall, Norman A.; and Siemienska, Renata. 1997. "Ethical
    Reasoning in a Time of Revolution: A Study of Local Officials in Poland." *Public
    Administration Review* 57, no. 5: 445–53.
Thoma, Stephen J. 1986. "Estimating Gender Differences in the Comprehension and
    Preference of Moral Issues." *Developmental Review* 6, no. 2: 165–80.
Walker, Lawrence J. 2002. "The Model and the Measure: An Appraisal of the Minne-
    sota Approach to Moral Development." *Journal of Moral Education* 31, no. 3:
    353–67.
White, Leonard. 1939. *The Study of Public Administration*. New York: Macmillan.
White, Richard D. 1999. "Are Women More Ethical? Recent Findings on the Effects
    of Gender upon Moral Development. *Journal of Public Administration Research
    and Theory* 9, no. 3: 459–71.

_____ **5**

Power and Ethics: The Communal Language of Effective Leadership

Carole L. Jurkiewicz

What do power and ethics have in common? More, and less, than one may believe. The most recognized association between the two is Lord Acton's definitive admonition that "power corrupts and absolute power corrupts absolutely." That statement underlies a belief that is near ubiquitous in the United States, and tends to serve as a framework for our experience. When we read of the seemingly unending instances of organizational corruption, from Enron to Tyco to Martha Stewart, each scenario seems to lend credence to the notion that power and ethics are incompatible at best, and most probably at opposite ends of a continuum. This belief is bolstered as well by martyr-tinged vignettes of purportedly ethical people who fail to achieve high levels of power and widespread influence, the self-proclaimed do-gooders thwarted in their attempts to get hired/promoted/elected.

In societies characterized by egalitarian ideologies such as our own, power and those who possess it are viewed as potentially—if not inherently—unethical and immoral. As the definition of power embodies a purposeful influence of one person over another, possibly entailing overcoming some resistance or opposition, we tend to view its exercise as an infringement of basic human rights—that in some nebulous sense no one should have power over anyone else (Pfeffer 1998; Solomon and Hanson 1983). It comes as no real surprise, then, that those who hold power in organizations are viewed as basically corrupt (e.g., Giacalone and Jurkiewicz 2003) and becoming increasingly more so with the passage of time. Power and ethics have been so closely intertwined that it is nearly impossible to consider one without considering the other within the context of organizations. They are two of the most important influences upon our behavior, particularly behavior within organizations (Pfeffer 1998; Torbert 1991; Clegg 1989; Boulding 1990; Lukes 1986), so it is natural that one would ask whether effective and noneffective leaders differ in regard to their power motive and level of ethical reasoning.

Yet the question of causality implied in Acton's phrase had not been empirically tested prior to a study (Jurkiewicz and Brown 2000) that focused on nonprofit executives. The results demonstrated strong statistical significance between high power motive and executive effectiveness, as well as high levels of ethical reasoning and executive effectiveness. Scores on instruments measuring each of these constructs were extraordinarily successful in predicting executive effectiveness for that sample. In summarizing the findings, the following questions for future research were posed: Was the executive sample unique in some way that was not measured? Would a different method of effectiveness classification lead to different predictive accuracy of the instruments? Would effective executives in public and private sectors score at the same high levels as the nonprofit executive sample? It was postulated that answering these questions could establish a basis for selection and promotion criteria, address the efficacy of ethics training, and contribute to an understanding of the influence of ethical reasoning on organizational performance.

Two subsequent empirical studies (Jurkiewicz 2002a; Jurkiewicz and Nichols 2002) reported significant positive behavioral effects of ethics training on public administration students, and other findings have supported the correlation between executive effectiveness and levels of ethical reasoning beyond the nonprofit realm (Duffield and McCuen 2000; Rest et al. 1999). To further address the questions regarding definitions of effectiveness and sector specificity, the study was recently replicated with a sample of public-sector executives and with a slightly modified definition of effectiveness. That study and those findings are reported here. While many questions remain to be answered and new ones have arisen, the findings mirror those reported in 2000: Effective executives, in the public sector as well as in the nonprofit sector, tend to have high levels of power motivation and exhibit high levels of ethical reasoning. Furthermore, scores on these construct measures have strong predictive power regarding executive effectiveness. It is hoped that these data will further the ability to understand the communal language of power and ethics.

Power and Effective Leadership

The theoretical links between power and effective leadership are deeply rooted. Sterling's (1958) pioneering work long ago stipulated a key organizational foundation: An organization's chief concern is the optimum allocation of its resources to ensure its own survival, which requires that, at least to some extent, it subordinate the needs and values of the individual to its own interests—that being the supreme need for power. Pfeffer's Law of Political Entropy states that once politics is introduced into a situation, it is very difficult if not impossible to restore rationality, which means that over time more and more organizations will come to be characterized by the political model. To configure organizations as political entities aligns them with governments, where power is critical to executive effectiveness, while at the same time it is diffused among warring parties (Clegg 1979). To understand such politicized organizational environments necessitates both knowledge of organizational politics and political will and expertise (Pfeffer 1998).

Today's "leadership crisis" is ascribed by scholars and practitioners alike to the lack of an understanding and use of power and political skill (e.g., Prilleltensky 2000; Pfeffer 1998; Gardner 1990). Prilleltensky (2000) and Kotter (1998) emphasize that it is almost impossible for managers to achieve their goals through persuasion or formal authority alone, that what they need is power; this is essentially an amplification of Mintzberg's (1983) classic view. The increasing politicization of organizations in the United States requires that an effective leader be a skilled political operator (Prilleltensky 2000; Pfeffer 1998) in order to manage issues of resource scarcity; conflict; heterogeneous collections of values, beliefs, and attitudes; eroding institutional and authoritative confidence; and a growing movement toward corporate accountability and social responsibility. Zaleznik and Kets de Vries (1985) maintain that the ability to control and influence others is the basis for directing organizations and attaining social goals, that leadership in its essential form is the exercise of power, that successful executive careers depend upon securing power, and that power transforms individual interests into coordinated activities that accomplish specific, valuable ends. Boonstra and Bennebroek Gravenhorst (1998) and Bradshaw (1998) postulate that leader effectiveness is rooted in the awareness that power and vested interests permeate all aspects of their organizations and the interactions of people within them. Fernandez and Hogan (2002) and McClelland and Burnham (1976) offer empirical evidence that effective leaders have strong power motives and relatively weak needs for achievement and affiliation. Conversely, they contend that the most ineffective leaders have strong affiliative motives and low needs for power and achievement. In support of these theoretical notions is Heimovics, Herman, and Jurkiewicz's (1993) empirical finding that effective executives are much more likely to think and act in accordance with a political frame than are a group of noneffective executives. It can be postulated, then, that leaders need power in order to achieve desirable outcomes in organizations, and, hence, to be perceived as effective.

Ethics and Effective Leadership

In contrast to the relatively ample body of literature correlating power and effective leadership, the ethics-effectiveness link is considerably less substantive.

Ample evidence supports the notion that leaders are the primary influencers of ethical conduct in organizations (e.g., Fernandez and Hogan 2002; Mendonca 2001; Baumhart 1961; Schmidt and Posner 1983; Hitt 1990; Jansen and Von Glinow 1985). Bennis and Nanus (1985) claim that leaders are responsible for the ethical standards that govern the behavior of individuals in the organization, that leaders set the moral tone, and that they are personally responsible for the set of ethics or norms that govern behavior. In fact, Jurkiewicz (2002), Jurkiewicz and Nichols (2002), Jurkiewicz and Thompson (2000), Cooper (1990), and Denhardt (1988) go so far as to say that unethical organizations pose an actual threat to the ethical individual who becomes employed there.

Ethical behavior in organizations is generally attributable to the ethical standards of top executives and to the culture that they substantively direct (Duffield and McCuen 2000; Weaver, Trevino, and Cochran 1999; Block 1993). Even if leaders' espoused positions are of organizational amorality, their behavior defines their organizations' ethical frameworks via social influence processes (Jurkiewicz 2002; Mendonca 2001; Conger and Kanungo 1998), implying an inextricable connection between ethics and leadership. Mendonca (2001, p. 268) asserts that an "organization's success, in fact its very survival, over the long term is dependent on ethical leadership."

Baumhart, early on (1961), and later Brenner and Molander (1977), established that individuals in positions of power in organizations set the standards of ethical conduct for their firms. Bok (1978) maintains that unethical behavior, in the form of lying or any other overt or implicit manifestation, is counterintuitive to effective leadership. Lewis (1991) adds support for the argument that effective leaders must have an ethical orientation if their organizations are to prosper. Her contention is that, even given myriad opportunities for moral compromise, ethical survival ensures professional success. Duffield and McCuen (2000) and Andrews (1989) expansively document how ethical decision making and ethical behavior are essential to effective leadership. Jackall (1988) offers additional theoretical support to the notion that effective leadership and career success are synonymous with a strong moral code that guides behavior. While the structure of organizations allows for a diverse range of evaluative rules and standards among the people employed there, success is defined by adherence to the organization's overriding ethic. Trevino and colleagues (1999) maintain that leader effectiveness is inextricably tied to a concern for the nature of that ethic. It is thus postulated that effective leadership is linked to ethical action and that responsible moral judgment is viewed as inextricably tied to leader effectiveness.

The Power-Ethics Link

The link between power and ethics was likely forged long before history makes note of it, though Plato is often credited with advancing the idea that power is a necessary feature of "the good" (Kreiger and Stern 1968). Aristotle, following the Greek tradition that power can be used to achieve good ends, pointed to reciprocity between the power wielder and the power subject's capacity to respond, thereby establishing the separation between means and ends that is still very much a focus of the debate about the exercise of power and ethical conduct today. Plato and Aristotle, in fact, adopted the Greek word *ethos* to describe their studies of Greek values and ideals (Solomon 1992).

Modern day attempts to address the connection between power and ethics present considerable variability, suggesting that while no clear paradigm of inquiry has yet emerged, there is progress toward that end. Chambliss (1996) argues that ethical decision making has more to do with power relationships than with any other aspect of problem solving. Cavanaugh, Moberg, and Velasquez (1981) developed a decision tree theoretical model to determine whether engaging in a particular act of power is ethically just or unjust, emphasizing that the complexity of political behavior makes it quite difficult to use simple judgmental rules in evaluating it (Velasquez, Moberg, and Cavanaugh 1983). They state that the ethicality of such behaviors depends upon the intentions of the power wielders and the congruence between their goals and the goals of the organization. DiTomaso and Hooijberg (1996) and Brumback (1991) demonstrate that power affects how individuals perceive the ethical aspects of situations. Dokecki (1996), Bowden (1997), and Brown (1997) contend that ethical thought is inextricably bound to the power relationships associated with any particular situation.

Jurkiewicz and Thompson (2000), Siguaw and colleagues (1998), and Brief and colleagues (1996) found that instances of unethical behavior were more frequent when such behavior was rewarded, under circumstances of increased competition, and under directives by a supervisor. Additionally, Hegarty and Sim (1978) identified the following personality variables as significant covariates of unethical behavior: locus of control, economic and political value orientation, and Machiavellianism. This strict definition of unethical behavior as acceptance of kickback payments, however, limits the generalization of their results. Studies on workplace spirituality have demonstrated strong statistical significance between those who hold a defined set of ethical values (thus scoring high on measures of workplace spirituality) and their recognition of unethical behaviors (Giacalone and Jurkiewicz 2003). Prilleltensky, Walsh-Bowers, and Rossiter (1999) offer evidence that the development of ethical values is consequent to the exercise of power. A theory integrating the exercise of power with an unwritten code of ethics (Jurkiewicz 2002b) has been advanced as a framework for understanding the dynamics between the two constructs.

Some view power as a catalyst to increase ethicality. Cartwright and Zander (1968) theorize that the burdens and responsibilities associated with power are likely to lead to compassionate, rather than exploitive, behavior on the part of the power wielder. Berle (1967) theorizes that power ennobles the individual by expanding and deepening one's understanding of oneself; he also notes that possessing organizational power frequently obliges the individual to ignore and rise above conventional morality. Rogow and Lasswell (1963) purport that the possession of power leads neither to corruption nor to ennoblement. They contend that the connection between power and corruption is dependent upon the various combinations of individual ego needs and the types of social organizations to which the individual belongs. This finding is supported by Zahra's (1984) research, which indicates that managers do not perceive power-related behavior as either inherently unethical or immoral and further indicates that becoming skillful at power-related behavior is seen as key to the advancement of one's career.

In summary, the link between power and ethics, at least theoretically, is strong and compelling. Attempts to understand this relationship would benefit from an expanded empirical examination of the variables.

Operationalizing Power

Measures of power can be separated into those that seek to uncover a predisposition toward power, or power motive, and those that record behavior and inductively measure presence/absence or degree of power. Three basic propositions influence the choice of power measure used in this study: (1) Attributions of power can be misdirected. (2) The usefulness and generalizability of any power measure is essential to the strength of the inferences one may hope to draw from the research. (3) Generally speaking, those who are the most powerful tend to deny it and downplay their impact, while the less powerful tend to boast and overestimate their influence (Pfeffer 1981). Therefore, it has been decided to discount ex post facto measures and focus instead on ab initio measures, or the motives or intentions of the power wielder that guide, consciously or unconsciously, powerful behavior. Psychological theory provides strong support for making assessments of individual power based upon determinants rather than consequences, knowing that in order to exercise power one must first have the need or desire for it within oneself (Pfeffer 1992). People's behavior is thought to be guided and directed by underlying motives as they are given opportunity to express themselves in specific environments. (For a full discussion of the reasoning behind this approach, see Jurkiewicz and Brown 2000.) Thus the Machiavellian Scale, Mach V (Christie and Geis 1970), is the measure of power motive selected for this study of executives for three reasons: its strength as an ab initio measure; its high levels of reliability and validity; and the normative scales developed from its previous use.

Operationalizing Ethics

Empirical measures of ethical constructs with established reliability and validity indexes are few. Because this study approached the research questions from the perspective of an executive reasoning about ethical issues, the widely accepted Developmental Theory and Moral Maturity Index ([DTMMI]; see Kohlberg 1969, 1976, 1981; Kohlberg et al. 1976, 1978) as operationalized by Rest (1979a) in the Defining Issues Test (DIT) was selected. The six stages of ethical reasoning as conceptualized by Kohlberg present a progression of moral decision making from the simplest level, wherein one defines "right" by those actions that do not result in punishment (stage 1), to the most complex, wherein "right" represents the universal moral principles determined through rational, informed personal reflection (stage 6), as outlined in Table 5.1. Cognitive identification and reconciliation of competing moral perspectives characterize the highest levels, while the lowest are rooted in egocentrism (for a complete typology of the stages see Kohlberg 1981). The DIT does not measure these stages directly, but scores on the DIT correlate with Kohlberg's scores on the DTMMI measure of moral maturity and are much easier to compute (Rest et al. 1999). (For a full discussion of the reasoning behind this approach, see Jurkiewicz and Brown 2000.)

The DIT is a self-administered instrument with a standardized scoring procedure. Scoring indicates an individual's level of ethical reasoning, and produces an intervally scaled P-score. The P-score indicates the relative importance, described as a percent score, a subject gives to principled moral considerations when making decisions about moral dilemmas. In effect, the DIT attempts to tap the basic conceptual framework an individual uses to analyze a social-moral problem and to judge what the proper course of action is. Offered as an assessment of conceptual adequacy of moral thinking (Rest 1979b; Rest et al. 1999) that can be used to typify subjects, it is applied

Table 5.1

Kohlberg's Six Stages of Moral Judgment, Measured by the Defining Issues Test

Stage 6
  The preeminence of universal ethical principles
    Self-determined principles of justice
    Respect for persons as ends, not means
    Principles supersede laws, social agreements

Stage 5b
  Uphold basic rights, values, social contracts
    Rules are relative and compromise the social contract
    Obligated only to obey laws, contracts freely chosen
    Good based on rational calculation of overall utility

Stage 4
  Social system and conscience maintenance
    Right is fulfillment of duties to society
    Laws upheld except when in conflict with social duties
    Concerned with "what if everyone else did it?"

Stage 3
  Mutual expectations, relationships, conformity
    Concern with others' feelings, keeping trusts, living up to expectations
    Obeyance of Golden Rule
    Loyalty, respect, and gratitude

Stage 2
  Individual instrumental purpose and exchange
    Right is acting to meet one's own interests and needs
    Awareness that others' interests may not match one's own
    Sense of fairness, following through on the "deal"

Stage 1
  Punishment and obedience
    Right is to avoid breaking rules
    Obedience to authority, authority always knows what is best
    Avoiding punishment for doing wrong

Note: For full text, see Kohlberg (1981).

here to determine whether the level of ethical reasoning varies between the effective and noneffective executives.

In accordance with the literature and the previous study on nonprofit executives, the following was anticipated:

  1. The average score of effective executives on the Mach V will be significantly higher than the average score of noneffective executives.

2. The average level of ethical reasoning of effective executives on the DIT will be significantly higher than the average score of the noneffective executives.
3. The average *P*-score of effective executives on the DIT will be significantly higher than the average *P*-score of the noneffective group.
4. Higher scores on the Mach V and the DIT will be predictive, in part, of public-sector executive effectiveness.

Method

Participants included 202 upper-level administrators, randomly selected from a large state agency in the southeastern United States, who had been employed in their current positions for a minimum of six months. An effective versus noneffective criterion was established for this sample through confidential surveys of all subordinates who directly reported to them, and of those to whom the administrators reported; survey respondents were identified by a coding system known only to the researcher. Information on reporting relationships was obtained through the support of the human resources personnel at that agency, who also approved the study as part of a larger administrative analysis. Surveys were distributed in hard copy form by human resource personnel during regularly scheduled meetings, completed individually by the respondents, and mailed directly to the researcher in a postage-paid, preaddressed envelope. The survey was distributed again two weeks after the initial delivery, and all were encouraged to respond if they had not already done so. Questions on the survey included both subordinate and superordinate open-ended assessments of the potential subjects as well as Likert-type scales of the degree to which the potential subject exhibited specific leadership behaviors culled from the literature. Additionally, performance evaluations of the potential subjects were examined, as were records of hiring, firing, and transfers of their subordinates. Completed, usable surveys from a minimum of three-fourths of their subordinates and all their superordinates were required for inclusion in the sample. In analyzing the data, those administrators who received average ratings (as determined by two judges with no knowledge of the study's intent and working independently) were eliminated from the study, leaving a working sample of seventy-one administrators: thirty-one effective and forty noneffective. Neither survey respondents nor administrators were made aware of the purpose of the study or the results. All seventy-one subjects were mailed a packet containing a letter requesting their participation, the Mach V, the DIT, and a postage-paid return envelope. With the use of the coding system to track returns, subjects who had not returned their instruments within two weeks were contacted by phone and were asked whether they had received the packets; if so, they were asked for their participation in the study. Packets were again sent to those who could not recall receiving them. Nonrespondents from this group were phoned again in two weeks, and the same protocol was used. Of the seventy-one subjects, sixty-five executives completed and returned usable instruments: thirty effective and thirty-five noneffective.

Results

> Hypothesis 1. The average score of effective executives on the Mach V will be significantly higher than the average score of noneffective executives.
>
> Hypothesis 2. The average level of ethical reasoning of effective executives on the DIT will be significantly higher than the average score of the noneffective executives.

Hypotheses 1 and 2 were both confirmed. The effective group scored significantly higher on both instruments than did the noneffective group. The t-value for the differences in mean scores on the DIT's measure of level of ethical reasoning was 2.997, with $p < .01$. The t-value for the differences in mean scores on the Mach V was 2.89, again with a level of significance less than .01. The results of these one-tailed tests of the first and second hypotheses based on scores on the DIT and the Mach V are reported in Table 5.2. Scores on the DIT were computed two ways for this analysis. As reported in Table 5.2, average stage and level of the two groups were computed and compared. Table 5.2 also reports the more commonly used P-score, which indicates the relative importance, described as a percent score, a subject gives to principled moral considerations when deciding about moral dilemmas. Both scoring methods follow the recommended scoring protocol as detailed by Rest (1979a; 1986).

To assess whether the preference for principled moral reasoning among effective executives is significantly higher than is the preference for principled moral reasoning among noneffective executives, a t-test was used to compare the P-scores of the two groups (see Table 5.2). The difference in means between the two groups was conclusively in the direction anticipated, with effective public-sector executives scoring an average of 64.10 and noneffective executives scoring an average of 31.44. Effective executives exhibited significantly higher preferences for principled ethical reasoning, at a confidence level of over 99 percent, than did their less effective counterparts.

Table 5.2

Test of Difference in Defining Issues Test (DIT), Mach V, and *P*-Scores for Effective and Noneffective Executives

	Effective executives	Noneffective executives	*t*-value	Significance
DIT	3.905	3.419	2.997	$p < .01$
	(.494)	(.479)		
Mach V	104.03	96.12	2.89	$p < .01$
	(8.97)	(6.59)		
P-Score	64.10	31.44	19.473	$p < .001$
	(4.83)	(5.28)		

Notes:
DIT values range from 1 to 6 (see Kohlberg, 1981).
P-scores on the DIT can range from 0 to 95, with a score of 35 being average (Rest et al. 1997).
Scores on the Mach V can range from 40 to 160, with a score of 100 being average (Christie and Geis 1970).
Standard deviations are shown in parentheses.
The assumption of equal variances between the two groups was supported ($p = .852$).

> Hypothesis 3. The average *P*-score of effective executives on the DIT will be significantly higher than the average *P*-score of the noneffective group.

A test of correlation of the scores on the two instruments reveals a significant positive relationship between the two measures, as was postulated in our third hypothesis. Pearson's *r* in this instance is .419, with $p > .01$.

> Hypothesis 4. Higher scores on the Mach V and the DIT will be predictive, in part, of public-sector executive effectiveness.

In order to test the fourth hypothesis, a discriminant analysis was used to determine the strength of any relationship between the predictor and dependent variable, effectiveness. Additionally, this technique permits the user to predict group membership and assign respondents to one or the other group based upon their Mach V or *P*-score values. Table 5.3 reports the results of the analysis wherein the Mach V and the *P*-scores are the predictor variables and effective/noneffective leadership is the dependent variable.

In addressing the hypothesis on whether scores on these two instruments could be in part predictive of executive effectiveness, discriminant analysis using stage and level scores successfully predicted group membership for

Table 5.3

Discriminant Analysis of Effective and Noneffective Executives by Scores on the Mach V and Defining Issues Test Instruments

		Classification results	
		group membership	
Actual group	No. of predicted cases	effective	noneffective
Effective	30	21	9
		70.0%	30.0%
Noneffective	35	8	27
		22.86%	77.14%

Note: Percent of grouped cases correctly classified: 73.85%.

70.0 percent of the effectives and for 77.14 percent of the noneffectives. Overall, the percentage of grouped cases correctly classified was 73.85 percent. The individual scores of those subjects whose group membership was not predicted, 30.0 percent of the effectives and 22.86 percent of the noneffectives, reveal some consistency in scores across both variables. Eight of the nine effectives scored lower than their group average on both instruments, and six of the eight noneffectives scored higher than their group average on both instruments.

As Table 5.4 shows, level of ethical reasoning was predictive of executive effectiveness. In fact, P-score alone successfully predicted group membership for 93.33 percent of the effective executives and 91.43 percent of the less effective ones. This outcome demonstrates strong support for Hypothesis 2 since, all things being equal, one would have expected to correctly classify only one-half of the executives to the correct group by chance alone.

Discussion

These findings very closely replicate those that employ the same instruments with a sample of nonprofit executives (Jurkiewicz and Brown 2000). Questions posed at the conclusion of that study suggested the importance of examining public-sector executives using the same constructs as well as a triangulated criterion of effectiveness. That the statistically significant relationships hold for both populations contributes strength to the developing theory on the interrelationship between power and ethics, and leader and organizational effectiveness. Whether the results will hold true for executives in the proprietary sector is the next natural area of inquiry in expanding this effort. If so, the dynamics of power and ethics may be universally associated with executive effectiveness, rather than mediated

Table 5.4

Predicting Effective and Noneffective Executives by Level of Ethical Reasoning

| | | Classification results | |
| | | Group membership | |
Actual group	No. of predicted cases	effective	noneffective
Effective	30	28	2
		93.33%	6.67%
Comparison	35	3	32
		8.57%	91.43%

Notes: This test utilized a two-group discriminant analysis.
Percentage of grouped cases correctly classified: 92.3%.

by sector-specific or environmental influences. It would be an important finding, indeed.

What does this study tell us? Effective public-sector executives tend to have stronger power motives than noneffective public-sector executives have. Furthermore, when they are confronted by ethical dilemmas, effective executives engage in significantly more complex cognitive reasoning than do noneffective executives. Although they are driven to gain positions of influence over others, effective executives are more likely to view the ethical issues they encounter from the broadest possible perspective, taking into account multiple stakeholders, principles, circumstances, issues of rights and justice, and the consequences of their decision for all affected by it.

The results provide further empirical evidence linking power, ethics, and executive effectiveness. Although it is not conclusive, evidence indicates that effective executives are more ethical than are executives who are not deemed effective. The results point to a difference between the two groups in the cognitive complexity of their ethical frameworks. Kohlberg (1981) characterizes the move up through the higher levels of moral reasoning as taking numerous and complicated factors into account to determine what is right and good. Noneffective executives reason at the conventional level, wherein doing the right thing is construed as doing one's duty in society, upholding the social order, and maintaining the social welfare. Effective executives, on the other hand, reason on average at a significantly higher level than either the noneffective group or the general populace (only 28 percent reportedly reach this stage of moral development). They tend to reason at the postconventional or principled level, wherein moral decisions are generated from a complex set of rights, values, or principles.

This research suggests that effective executives evaluate moral decisions more upon the basis of calculated rights, values, or principles than upon public opinion. Further, they are more likely to make decisions regarding moral dilemmas that may be unpopular with the majority, yet decisions they have reasoned as right, and are therefore willing to accept the ensuing conflict that may result from the decision. Less-effective executives, on the other hand, reason about the same moral dilemmas within a framework where doing the right thing is construed as doing one's duty in society, upholding the social order, and displaying obedience to authority. Less-effective executives would tend to concern themselves to a greater extent with how their decisions regarding the moral dilemmas their organizations face would be viewed by others, both within and outside the organization.

These findings are consistent with research in the area of effective leadership. The proclivity to face conflict rather than avoid it when one's decisions are challenged by others is characteristic of many of the findings on effective leadership. Additionally, the dependence upon oneself to engage and communicate an organizational vision rooted in firmly held principles is a hallmark of effective leadership, and is one that is supported by this research. It is a vision that transcends the mere written code of an organization (Jurkiewicz 2002b; Kanungo and Mendonca 1996), and incorporates the dynamic power relationships of the people within the organization (Bowden 1997). Rather than a preoccupation with trying to please others, effective leaders earn respect by making tough decisions based upon principled criteria, taking responsibility for those decisions and proceeding on that path with conviction (Prilleltensky 2000). That perspective on effective leadership is echoed in these findings.

The validity of these findings is grounded on the premise that the triangulated criterion for effectiveness used here (commentaries from knowledgeable others, performance ratings, documented rates of hiring/firing/transfers) is a valid measure of executive effectiveness. Even though the study of effectiveness is an increasingly problematical concept in the management literature, it has been reported elsewhere (Jurkiewicz and Brown 2000; Heimovics, Herman, and Jurkiewicz 1993, 1995) that the findings of this body of research are not methodological artifacts of the use of the reputational approach. The indispensability of executive leadership to organizational success in the public sector has been well established. Progress has been made in identifying those skills distinct to effective public-sector executives and lacking in a comparison group. Replication of this study in a continued variety of organizational settings would enable these hypotheses to be generalized to a broader population, with the pivotal nexus being an accepted effectiveness criterion. The empirical link demonstrated in this study between ethical reasoning and effective leadership is an important first step in examining these issues more closely.

The unequivocal nature of these results replicates the earlier study (Jurkiewicz and Brown 2000), especially with regard to the predictive strength of principled ethical reasoning on leader effectiveness. Directions for future research include expansion of the study to other populations, including private-sector executives and also federal- and local-level public executives. What about professional groups? Do these findings hold equally true for different age cohorts, genders, and ethnic groups? Given that the empirical research and theoretical contentions from which the hypotheses for this study were drawn are rooted in a broad-based literature, one could reasonably anticipate similar results, suppositions supported by other research in leader effectiveness (Robie et al. 2001). While not discounting the differing contexts in which the two sectors operate or the impact that has on organizational structure and evaluation, leadership skills such as influencing to effect outcomes, using oneself as a symbol of the organization, and rallying individual efforts toward a collective end are arguably the same. Would the study yield the same findings if replicated in other countries and cultures? There is evidence that organizational ethics varies widely across the globe, so perhaps dissimilarities would emerge in this area. Would a different method of effectiveness classification lead to different predictive accuracy of the DIT? The empirical evidence now established between power, ethics, and effective leadership is an important first step to a closer examination of these issues. These results are bolstered by findings on the effectiveness of other professionals as it correlates to scores on the DIT (Rest et al. 1999). The need for further research on ethical decision making and executive effectiveness in the public sector is clear. Such research could establish a basis for selection and promotion criteria, ethics training, development of organizational culture and policies, and enhancement of individual and organizational performance. The importance of ethics education and its relevance to executive performance is strengthened by these findings.

The common belief that power or its pursuit is divisive and harmful keeps effectiveness beyond the reach of many otherwise skillful organizational members. To deny that power is necessary in organizations, to disassociate oneself from the exercise of power in order to appear irreproachable, to be naive about the use of power in organizations is to render oneself ineffective at best, and to block one's personal and organizational progress at worst. A much larger question is: Does power corrupt? Such a fascinating inquiry as this may very well build upon the research reported here. How, when, and why it does or does not corrupt are important questions yet to be answered.

The conclusion drawn here is that power and ethics are integral to discussions of effective leadership. The notion that power corrupts and absolute power corrupts absolutely has again been empirically challenged. Power motive, given its concomitant correlation with ethical reasoning in this study, is not necessarily more corruptive than any other need. By recognizing that power is essential to an organization's functioning and by teaching organizational members how to capitalize and operate from an ethical power base—and thereby bringing the exercise of power out into the open—more efficient, effective, and possibly more ethical workplaces can be created. Power separated from superstition and treated as a skill on par with other abilities considered necessary for success in business can transform organizations into empowering institutions that are more responsive to environmental changes, that are characterized by more cohesive and loyal employees, and that foster enhanced communication.

What do power and ethics have in common? They are two of the most important influences upon our behavior, particularly behavior within organizations. Questions concerning these concepts continue to reside at the forefront in much of today's literature on organizations, and they are a concern of practicing administrators as well.

References

Andrews, Kenneth.1989. *Ethics in Practice*. Boston: Harvard Business School Press.

Baumhart, Raymond. 1961. "How Ethical Are Businessmen?" *Harvard Business Review* (July/August): 6–176ff.

Bennis, Warren G., and Nanus, Burt. 1985. *Leaders: The Strategies for Taking Charge*. New York: Harper and Row.

Berle, Adolf. 1967. *Power*. New York: Harcourt, Brace & World.

Block, Peter. 1993. *Stewardship: Choosing Service over Self-Interest*. Berrett-Koehler Publishers.

Bok, Sissela. 1978. *Lying: Moral Choice in Public and Private Life*. New York: Random House.

Boonstra, Jaap, and Bennebroek Gravenhorst, Kilian. 1998. "Power Dynamics and Organizational Change: A Comparison of Perspectives." *European Journal of Work and Organizational Psychology* 7: 97–120.

Boulding, Kenneth. 1990. *Three Faces of Power*. London: SAGE.

Bowden, Peta. 1997. *Caring: Gender-Sensitive Ethics*. London: Routledge and Kegan Paul.

Bradshaw, Patricia. 1998. "Power as Dynamic Tension and Its Implications for Radical Organizational Change." *European Journal of Work and Organizational Psychology* 7: 121–43.

Brenner, Steven, and Molander, Earl. 1977. "Is the Ethics of Business Changing?" *Harvard Business Review* (January/February): 57–71.

Brief, Arthur; Dukerich, Janet; Brown, Paul; and Brett, Joan. 1996. "What's Wrong with the Treadway Commission Report?" *Journal of Business Ethics* 15, no. 2: 183–92.

Brown, Laura. 1997. "Ethics in Psychology: Who Benefits by It?" In *Critical Psychology: An Introduction*, ed. D. Fox and I. Prilleltensky, pp. 51–67. London: SAGE.

Brumback, Gary.1991. "Institutionalizing Ethics in Government." *Public Personnel Management* 20: 353–64.

Cartwright, Dorwin, and Zander, Alvin. 1968. *Group Dynamics*. New York: Harper.

Cavanaugh, Gerald; Moberg, Dennis; and Velasquez, Manuel. 1981. "The Ethics of Organizational Politics." *Academy of Management Review* 6: 363–74.

Chambliss, Daniel. 1996. *Beyond Caring*. Chicago: University of Chicago Press.

Christie, Richard, and Geis, Florence. 1970. *Studies in Machiavellianism*. New York: Academic Press.

Clegg, Stewart. 1979. *The Theory of Power and Organization*. Brisbane, UK: Routledge and Kegan Paul.

———. 1989. *Frameworks of Power*. London: SAGE.

Conger, Jay, and Kanungo, Rabindra. 1998. *Charismatic Leadership in Organizations*. Thousand Oaks, CA: SAGE.

Denhardt, Kathryn G. 1988. *The Ethics of Public Service*. New York: Greenwood Press.

DiTomaso, Nancy, and Hooijberg, Robert. 1996. "Diversity and the Demands of Leadership." *Leadership Quarterly* 7: 163–87.

Dokecki, Paul. 1996. *The Tragi-comic Professional: Basic Considerations for Ethical Reflective-Generative Practice*. Pittsburgh: Duquesne University Press.

Duffield, James F., and McCuen, Richard H. 2000. "Ethical Maturity and Successful Leadership." *Journal of Professional Issues in Engineering Education and Practice* 126, no. 2 (April): 79–82.

Fernandez, Jorge E., and Hogan, Robert T. 2002. "Values-Based Leadership." *Journal for Quality and Participation* 25, no. 4 (Winter): 25–27.

Gardner, John. 1990. *On Leadership*. New York: Free Press.

Giacalone, Robert, and Jurkiewicz, Carole L. 2003. "Toward a Science of Workplace Spirituality." In *The Handbook of Workplace Spirituality and Organizational Performance*, ed. R. Giacalone and C. Jurkiewicz. Armonk, NY: M.E. Sharpe.

Hegarty, William, and Sim, Henry Jr. 1978. "Some Determinants of Unethical Decision Behavior: An Experiment." *Journal of Applied Psychology* 63, no. 4: 451–57.

Heimovics, Richard; Herman, Robert; and Jurkiewicz, Carole. 1993. "Executive Leadership and Resource Dependence in Nonprofit Organizations: A Frame Analysis." *Public Administration Review* 53, no. 5: 419–27.

———. 1995. "The Political Dimension of Effective Nonprofit Executive Leadership." *Nonprofit Management & Leadership* 5, no. 3: 233–48.

Hitt William D. 1990. *Ethics and Leadership*. Columbus OH: Battelle Press.

Jackall, Robert. 1988. *Moral Mazes*. New York: Oxford University Press.

Jansen, Erik, and Von Glinow, Mary Ann 1985. "Ethical Ambivalence and Organizational Reward Systems. *Academy of Management Review* 10, no. 4: 814–22.

Jurkiewicz, Carole L. 2002. "The Influence of Pedagogical Style on Students' Level of Ethical Reasoning." *Journal of Public Affairs Education* 8, no. 4: 263–74.

———. 2002b. "The Phantom Code of Ethics and Public Sector Reform." *Journal of Public Affairs and Issues* 6, no. 3: 1–19.

Jurkiewicz, Carole L., and Brown, Roger. 2000. "Power Corrupts Absolutely . . . Not." *Public Integrity* 2, no. 3: 195–210.

Jurkiewicz, Carole L., and Nichols, Kenneth L. 2002. "Ethics Education in the MPA Curriculum: What Difference Does It Make?" *Journal of Public Affairs Education* 8, no. 2: 103–14.

Jurkiewicz, Carole L., and Thompson, Carolyn R. 2000. "Conflicts of Interest: Organizational vs. Individual Ethics in Healthcare Administration." *Journal of Health and Human Services Administration* 23, no. 1: 100–23.

Kanungo, Rabindra, and Mendonca, Manuel. 1996. *Ethical Dimensions of Leadership*. London: SAGE.

Kohlberg, Lawrence. 1969. " Stage and Sequence: The Cognitive-Developmental Approach to Socialization." In *Handbook of Socialization Theory and Research*, ed. David A. Goslin, pp. 347–80. Chicago: Rand McNally.

———. 1976." Moral Stages and Moralization: The Cognitive-Developmental Approach." In *Moral Development and Behavior*, ed. Thomas Lickona, pp. 31–58. New York: Holt, Rinehart, and Winston.

———. 1981. *Philosophy of Moral Development*. New York: Harper and Row.

Kohlberg, Lawrence; Colby, Anne; Gibbs, John; and Speicher-Dubin, Betsy. 1976. *Moral Stage Scoring Manual*. Cambridge, MA: Center for Moral Education, Harvard University.

———. 1978. *Standard Form Scoring Manual*. Cambridge, MA: Center for Moral Education, Harvard University.

Kotter, John P. 1998. *The Leadership Factor*. New York: Free Press.

Krieger, Leonard, and Stern, Fritz. 1968. *The Responsibilities of Power*. London: Macmillan.

Lewis, Carole. 1991. *The Ethics Challenge in Public Service*. San Francisco: Jossey-Bass.

Lukes, Steven. 1986. *Power*. Oxford, UK: Blackwell.

McClelland, David, and Burnham, David. 1976. "Power Is the Great Motivator." *Harvard Business Review* (March/April): 100–10.

Mendonca, Manuel. 2001. Preparing for Ethical Leadership in Organizations." *Canadian Journal of Administrative Sciences* 18, no. 4: 266–76.

Mintzberg, Henry. 1983. *Power in and Around Organizations*. Englewood Cliffs, NJ: Prentice Hall.

Pfeffer, Jeffrey. 1981. *Power in Organizations*. Marshfield, MA: Pitman.

———. 1992. *Managing with Power*. Boston: Harvard Business School Press.

———. 1998. *The Human Equation*. Boston: Harvard Business School Press.

Prilleltensky, Isaac. 2000. "Value-Based Leadership in Organizations: Balancing Values, Interests, and Power among Citizens." *Ethics and Behavior* 10, no. 2: 139–59.

Prilleltensky, Isaac; Walsh-Bowers, Richard; and Rossiter, Amy. 1999. "Clinicians' Lived Experience of Ethics: Values and Challenges in Helping Children." *Journal of Educational and Psychological Consultation* 10, no. 4: 315–42.

Rest, James. 1979a. *Revised Manual for the Defining Issues Test*. Minneapolis: University of Minnesota Press.

———. 1979b. *Development in Judging Moral Issues*. Minneapolis: University of Minnesota Press.

———. 1986. *DIT Manual*. Minneapolis: University of Minnesota Press.

Rest, James R., and Narvaez, Darcia. 1997. *Ideas for Research with the DIT*, version 1.3. Minneapolis: Center for the Study of Ethical Development.

Rest, James; Narváez, Darcia; Thoma, Stephen; and Bebeau, Muriel. 1999. "DIT2: Devising and Testing a Revised Instrument of Moral Judgment." *Journal of Educational Psychology* 91: 644–59.

Robie, Chet; Johnson, Karin M.; Nilsen, Dianne; and Hazucha, Joy Fisher. 2001. "The Right Stuff: Understanding Cultural Differences in Leadership Performance." *Journal of Management Development* 20, no. 7: 639–49.

Rogow, Arnold, and Lasswell, Harold. 1963. *Power, Corruption and Rectitude.* Englewood Cliffs, NJ: Prentice Hall.

Schmidt, Warren H., and Posner, Barry Z. 1983. *Managerial Values in Perspective.* New York: American Management Association.

Siguaw, Judy; Rockness, Joanne; Hunt, Tammy; and Howe, Vincent Jr. 1998. *Ethical Values and Leadership: A Study of AACSB Business School Deans.* Proceedings, Academy of Management conference, San Diego, August 7 to 9.

Solomon, Robert. 1992. *Morality and the Good Life.* New York: McGraw-Hill.

Solomon, Robert, and Hanson, Kristine. 1983. *Above the Bottom Line: An Introduction to Business Ethics.* New York: Harcourt Brace Jovanovich.

Sterling, Richard. 1958. *Ethics in a World of Power.* Princeton, NJ: Princeton University Press.

Torbert, William. 1991. *The Power of Balance.* Newbury Park, CA: SAGE.

Trevino, Linda; Weaver, Gary; Gibson, David; and Toffler, Barbara. 1999. "Managing Ethics and Legal Compliance: What Works and What Hurts." *California Management Review* 41, no. 2: 131–51.

Velasquez, Manuel; Moberg, Dennis; and Cavanaugh, Gerald. 1983. "Organizational Statesmanship and Dirty Politics: Ethical Guidelines for the Organizational Politician." *Organizational Dynamics* 11: 65–80.

Weaver, Gary R., Trevino, Linda K., and Cochran, Philip L. (1999). "Integrated and Decoupled Corporate Social Performance: Management Commitments, External Pressures, and Corporate Ethics Practices." *Academy of Management Journal* 42 no. 5: 539–52.

Zahra, Shaker. 1984. "Managerial Views of Organizational Politics." *NRECA Management Quarterly* 25 no. 1: 31–37.

Zaleznik, Abraham, and Kets de Vries, Manfred. 1985. *Power and the Corporate Mind.* Chicago: Bonus Books.

6

Public-Service Ethics and Administrative Evil: Prospects and Problems

Guy B. Adams and Danny L. Balfour

A Century of Progress.
—*Title of the 1933 Chicago World's Fair*

Science Explores, Technology Executes, Mankind Conforms.
—*Motto of the 1933 Chicago World's Fair*

In the acclaimed novel *The Remains of the Day,* by Kazuo Ishiguro (1988), the central character, Mr. Stevens, reflects on his life of faithful service as butler to Lord Darlington, a British aristocrat and diplomat. Mr. Stevens takes great pride in his high standards of professionalism and the supporting role he played in Lord Darlington's attempts to keep the peace in Europe and support accommodative policies toward a defeated Germany during the years between the two world wars. Lord Darlington arranged numerous informal meetings of key politicians and diplomats at his palatial home in the English countryside where great affairs of state were negotiated over fine food, wine, and cigars. But Mr. Stevens must also struggle with the fact that his employer lost faith in democracy, succumbing to the temptations of fascism in difficult times, and failed to appreciate the true nature of Hitler and his regime, even to the point of supporting anti-Semitism and lauding the economic and social "achievements" of Nazism in the mid-1930s. Lord Darlington's efforts were ultimately discredited and he died in disgrace soon after World War II.

Mr. Stevens, a consummate professional, sees no connection between his actions and the moral and strategic failures of his employer. In a remarkable example of perverse moral reasoning, Stevens comes to the conclusion that his professional behavior shields him from any moral responsibility for his employer's actions (Ishiguro 1998, p. 201):

> How can one possibly be held to blame in any sense because, say, the passage of time has shown that Lord Darlington's efforts were misguided, even foolish? Throughout the years I served him, it was he and he alone who weighed up evidence and judged it best to proceed in the way he did, while I simply confined myself, quite properly, to affairs within my own professional realm. And as far as I am concerned, I carried out my duties to the best of my abilities, indeed to a standard which many may consider "first rate." It is hardly my fault if his lordship's life and work have turned out today to look, at best, a sad waste—and it is quite illogical that I should feel any regret or shame on my own account.

Mr. Stevens's justification of his role and abdication of responsibility in Lord Darlington's affairs is a clear example of what we have termed *administrative evil*. The common characteristic of administrative evil is that ordinary people within their normal professional and administrative roles can engage in acts of evil without being aware that they are doing anything wrong. While a butler may perhaps seem an odd exemplar of administrative evil, Stevens pursues every new technique and practice in his chosen profession with the greatest diligence. Yet, it is his myopic focus on his administrative role and professional standards that serve to mask his own contributions to the evil that stemmed from Darlington's moral failures. "Just following orders," his dismissal of two housekeepers whose only offense was that they were Jewish does not stir his conscience, among many other such examples in the novel. Mr. Stevens carries on by stubbornly denying that he did anything wrong and by asserting instead that he actually did everything "right," that is, professionally correctly.

Administrative evil is regrettably a recurring aspect of public policy and administration in the modern era. The same reasoning and behavior employed by Mr. Stevens mask the supporting (and at times, primary) role played by far too many professionals and administrators in acts that dehumanize, injure, and even kill their fellow human beings. Our reluctant and tragic conclusion is that administrative evil is unlikely to disappear from a world order that depends so heavily on organizations and professions that systematically enable its reproduction.

In recent times, we have seen an escalation of violence and uncertainty worldwide, punctuated for Americans by the terrible events of September 11, 2001 (for analyses of this escalation, see Juergensmeyer 2000; Lifton 1999; Volkan 1997). While those events were not an example of administrative evil, they certainly have led to a dramatic increase in references to evil in public discourse. Richard Bernstein provides us an important assessment (2002, p. x):

> Few would hesitate to name what happened on that day as evil—indeed, the very epitome of evil in our time. Yet, despite the complex emotions and responses that the events have evoked, there is a great deal of uncertainty about what is meant by calling them evil. There is an all too familiar popular rhetoric of "evil" that becomes fashionable at such critical moments, which actually obscures and blocks serious thinking about the meaning of evil. "Evil" is used to silence thinking and to demonize what we refuse to understand.

Although it might initially seem odd for us not to welcome greater use of a term that we have argued is in fact underused in the social science literature, we agree completely with Bernstein that the proliferation of "evil talk" in public discourse undermines our understanding of dynamics about which we very much need all the insight we can gain. At the same time, there has been increased attention to the topic of evil in the scholarly literature, epitomized by Bernstein (2002) and Neiman (2002), and this development we welcome wholeheartedly because much of this new scholarship offers support for our argument in key areas (Adams and Balfour 2004).

What Is Administrative Evil?

We begin with the premise that evil is an essential concept for understanding the human condition. As one examines the sweep of human history, clearly there have been many great and good deeds and achievements as well as real progress in the quality of at least many humans' lives. But we also see century after century of mind-numbing, human-initiated violence, betrayal, and tragedy. We name as evil the actions of human beings that unjustly or needlessly inflict pain, or suffering, or death on other human beings. However, evil is one phenomenon in human affairs that defies easy definition and understanding (see Garrard 2002; Katz 1988; McGinn 1997; Sanford 1981; Steiner 2002). As Reinhold Niebuhr (1986, p. 246) wisely noted, "We see through a glass darkly when we seek to understand the cause and nature of evil. . . . But we see more profoundly when we know it is through a dark glass that we see, than if we pretend to have clear light on this profound problem."

Evil is defined in the *Oxford English Dictionary* as the antithesis of good in all its principal senses. Staub (1992, p. 25) offers a more expansive characterization: "Evil is not a scientific concept with an agreed meaning, but the idea of evil is part of a broadly shared human cultural heritage. The essence of evil is the destruction of human beings. . . . By evil I mean *actions* that have such consequences." And Fred Katz (1993, p. 5) provides a useful, behavioral definition of evil as "behavior that deprives innocent people of their humanity, from small scale assaults on a person's dignity to outright murder . . . [this definition] focuses on how people behave toward one another—where the behavior of one person or an aggregate of persons is destructive to others."

These definitions, while helpful, can be further refined. Rather than a continuum of evil as suggested in Katz's definition, we propose a continuum of evil and wrongdoing with horrible, mass eruptions of evil such as the Holocaust and other genocides at one extreme and the "small" white lie, which is somewhat hurtful, at the other (Staub 1992, p. xi). Somewhere along this continuum, wrongdoing turns into evil, and, depending on both context and particulars, this changeover may occur at differing locations on the continuum. At the white-lie end of the continuum, use of the term *wrongdoing* seems more apt than does use of the term *evil*. However, Sissela Bok (1978) has argued persuasively that even so-called white lies can have serious personal and social consequences, especially as they accrue over time. For the most part, we are concerned with the end of the continuum where the recognition of evil may be easier and more obvious. Nonetheless, the small-scale, wrongdoing end of the continuum remains of importance, because the road to great evil often begins with seemingly small, first steps of wrongdoing. Staub (1992, p. xi) notes correctly that "[e]xtreme destructiveness . . . is usually the last of many steps along a continuum of destruction."

Technical Rationality and Administrative Evil

The modern age, especially the twentieth century, has had as its hallmark what we call *technical rationality*. Technical rationality is a way of thinking and living (a culture) that emphasizes the scientific-analytic mind-set and faith in technological progress. For our purposes here, the culture of technical rationality has enabled a new and bewildering form of evil that we call *administrative evil*. What is different about administrative evil is that its appearance is *masked*. Administrative evil may be masked in many ways, but the common characteristic is that people can engage in acts of evil without being aware that they are in fact doing anything at all wrong. Indeed, ordinary people may simply be acting appropriately in their organizational roles—

in essence, just doing what those around them would agree they should be doing—and at the same time, participating in what a critical and reasonable observer, usually well after the fact, would call evil. Even worse, under conditions of what we call *moral inversion*, in which something evil has been redefined convincingly as good, ordinary people can all too easily engage in acts of administrative evil while believing that what they are doing is not only correct but, in fact, good.

The basic difference between evil as it has appeared throughout human history, and administrative evil, which is a fundamentally modern phenomenon, is that the latter is less easily recognized as evil. People have always been able to delude themselves into thinking that their evil acts are not really so bad, and we have certainly had moral inversions in times past. But there are three very important differences in administrative evil. One is our modern inclination to *un-name* evil, an old concept that does not lend itself well to the scientific-analytic mindset (Bernstein 2002; Neiman 2002). The second difference is found in the structure of the modern, complex organization, which diffuses individual responsibility and requires the compartmentalized accomplishment of role expectations in order to perform work on a daily basis (Staub 1992, p. 84). The third difference is the way in which the culture of technical rationality has analytically narrowed the processes by which public policy is formulated and implemented, so that moral inversions are now more likely.

Evil and Administrative Evil in the Modern Age

Evil is only a barely accepted entry in the lexicon of the social sciences. Social scientists much prefer to *describe* behavior, avoiding ethically loaded or judgmental rubrics—to say nothing of what is often considered religious phraseology. Yet evil reverberates down through the centuries of human history, showing little sign of weakening in the opening years of the twenty-first century and the apex of modernity (Lang 1991). In the modern age, we are greatly enamored with the notion of progress, of the belief that civilization develops in a positive direction, with the present age at the pinnacle of human achievement. These beliefs constrain us from acknowledging the implications of the fact that the twentieth century was the bloodiest, both in absolute and relative terms, in human history, and that we continue to develop the capacity for even greater mass destruction (Rummel 1994).

Nearly 200 million human beings were slaughtered or otherwise killed as a direct or indirect consequence of the epidemic of wars and state-sponsored violence in the twentieth century (Rummel 1994; Eliot 1972; Bauman 1989; Glover 1999). Administrative mass murder and genocide have become a demonstrated capacity within the human social repertoire (Rubenstein 1975, 1983), and simply because such events have occurred, new instances of genocide and dehumanization become more likely (Arendt 1963). As Bernstein states (2002, p. iv):

> Looking back over the horrendous twentieth century, few of us would hesitate
> to speak of evil. Many people believe that the evils witnessed in the twentieth
> century exceed anything that has ever been recorded in past history. Most of us
> do not hesitate to speak about these extreme events—genocides, massacres,
> torture, terrorist attacks, the infliction of gratuitous suffering—as evil.

If we are to have any realistic hope for ameliorating this trajectory in the twenty-first century, administrative evil needs to be better understood, especially by those likely to participate in any future acts of mass destruction— professionals and citizens who are active in public affairs.

Despite its enormous scale and tragic result, it took more than twenty-five years for the Holocaust to emerge as the major topic of study and public discussion that it is today. But knowing more about the Holocaust does not necessarily mean that we really understand it, nor does it mean that future genocides will be prevented (Power 2002). Within our own culture and closer to our own time, the dynamics of administrative evil become progressively more subtle and opaque. Administrative evil is not easily identified as such, because its appearance is masked.

That administrative evil is masked suggests that evil also occurs along another continuum: from acts that are committed in relative ignorance to those that are known and deliberate acts of evil, or what we would characterize as masked and unmasked. Individuals and groups can engage in evil acts and not recognize the consequences of their behavior, or they can engage in evil acts when they are convinced that their actions are justified or serve the greater good, as Staub (1992, p. 25) notes:

> We cannot judge evil by conscious intentions, because psychological dis-
> tortions tend to hide even from the perpetrators themselves their true inten-
> tions. They are unaware, for example, of their own unconscious hostility or
> that they are scapegoating others. Frequently, their intention is to create a
> "better world," but in the course of doing so they . . . destroy the lives of
> human beings. Perpetrators of evil often intend to make people suffer but
> see their actions as necessary or serving a higher good. In addition, people
> tend to hide their negative intentions from others and justify negative ac-
> tions by higher ideals or the victims' evil nature.

Administrative evil falls within the range of the continuum in which people engage in or contribute to acts of evil without recognizing that they are doing anything wrong.

Lang (1991) argues that, in the case of genocide, it is difficult to maintain that evil occurs without the knowledge of the actor. Genocide is a deliberate act; mass murderers know that they are doing evil. Fred E. Katz (1993) recounts several instances in which deliberate acts of evil have occurred in bureaucratic settings (such as those based on the testimonies of the commandants of Auschwitz and Sobibor). However, the direct act of mass murder, even when it is facilitated by public institutions, is not what we call administrative evil—or at least mass murder represents the most extreme and unmasked manifestation of administrative evil. Both before and surrounding such overt acts of evil are many more, and much less obvious, evil administrative activities that lead to and support the worst forms of human behavior. Moreover, without these instances of masked evil, the more overt and unmasked acts are less likely to occur (Staub 1992, pp. 20–21).

If administrative evil means that people inflict pain and suffering and death on others, but do so *not* knowingly or deliberately, can they be held responsible for their actions? We believe the answer is yes, but when ordinary people inflict pain and suffering and even death on others in the course of performing their "normal" organizational or policy role, they usually justify their actions by saying that they were just following orders and doing their job. This reflects the difficulty of identifying administrative evil, and the possibility of missing it altogether, or perhaps worse, calling mistakes or misjudgments evil. We maintain that identifying administrative evil is most difficult within one's own culture and historical time period.

Administrative evil poses a fundamental challenge to the ethical foundations of public life. Our reluctance to recognize the importance of administrative evil as part of the identity and practice of public policy and administration reinforces its continuing influence and increases the possibility of future acts of dehumanization and destruction, even in the name of the public interest. The Holocaust and other eruptions of administrative evil strongly suggest that the assumptions and standards for ethical behavior in modern, technical-rational systems are ultimately incapable of preventing or mitigating evil in either its subtle or more obvious forms. The problems for public-service ethics begin with the evolution of professionalism in a culture of technical rationality.

Professionalism, Technical Rationality, and Public-Service Ethics

Within the first two decades of the twentieth century, professionalization had come to mean the reliance on science and the scientific-analytic mindset, and the growing specialization and expertise of the professions. It also meant the sloughing off of reform and advocacy as a trademark of professionalism. We want to suggest here that the tenets of advocacy and reform, when they were part and parcel of the ethos of professionalism (as they were in the latter half of the nineteenth century), represented a large part of the substance of both the *public-service ideal* and the *ethical standards* of the professions (Adams 2000). Their loss left a technically expert, but morally impoverished professionalism—professionalism more susceptible to moral inversion and administrative evil (Browne, Kubasek, and Giampetro-Myer 1995).

One result has been confusion within the professions over behavior that benefits a profession and ethical behavior. As both MacIntyre (1984) and Poole (1991) have argued, modernity has produced a way of thinking—an epistemology—that renders moral reasoning necessary but superfluous. Note how ethics is simply subsumed in professionalism in this statement by Kearney and Sinha (1988, p. 575):

> In a sense, the profession provides the professional administrator with a Rosetta Stone for deciphering and responding to various elements of the public interest. Professional accountability as embodied in norms and standards also serves as an inner check on an administrator's behavior. . . . When joined with a code of ethics or conduct and the oath of office, professionalism establishes a value system that serves as a frame of reference for decision making . . . and creates a special form of social control conducive to bureaucratic responsiveness.

Professionals do not see the technical rational model of professionalism as eschewing ethics. Quite the contrary: They see the role model of *professional* as satisfying the need for a system of ethical standards. To be professional is to be ethical.

Ethics and Public-Service Ethic

Ethics is the branch of philosophy concerned with systematic thought about character, morals, and right action. In the modern age, until recently, two versions of ethics have dominated Anglo-American philosophical thinking, namely *teleological* (or consequentialist) ethics and *deontological* ethics (Frankena 1973). Both share an interest in determining the rules that should govern—and therefore be used to judge—individual behavior as good or bad, right or wrong. Teleological ethics, based on utilitarianism and tracing its lineage to Bentham (1989) and others, offers the overarching principle of the greatest good for the greatest number. Oriented toward the results or consequences of actions, teleological ethics tends to elevate the ends over the means used to achieve those ends. Deontological ethics, founded in the thought of Kant (1959) and his support of duty and order, reverses this emphasis, holding that the lower-order rules that govern means are essential for the higher-order rules that concern the ends to be achieved. For our purposes, it is important that both traditions have focused on the individual as the relevant unit of analysis.

Both public-service and professional ethics in the technical-rational tradition draw upon both teleological and deontological ethics and focus on the individual's decision-making process in the modern, bureaucratic organization and as a member of a profession. In the public sphere, deontological ethics are meant to safeguard the integrity of the organization by helping individuals conform to professional norms, avoid mistakes and misdeeds that violate the public trust (corruption, nepotism, etc.), and assure that public officials in a constitutional republic are accountable to the people through their elected representatives. At the same time, public servants are encouraged to pursue the greater good by using discretion in the application of rules and regulations and creativity in the face of changing conditions (teleological ethics). The good public servant should avoid both the extremes of rule-bound behavior and undermining the rule of law with individual judgments and interests.

It is fairly self-evident that public (and private) organizations depend on at least this level of ethical judgment in order to function efficiently and effectively and to maintain public confidence in government (and business). At the same time, it is important to recognize that these ethical standards of an organization or profession are only safeguards, not fail safes, against unethical behavior. Nor do they necessarily help individuals to resolve tough moral dilemmas that are often characterized by ambiguity and paradox. Indeed, these problems provide the grist for the discourse on professional ethics in the technical-rational tradition. The Friedrich-Finer (1940;1941) debate on public-service ethics is still a useful way to describe the ethical terrain in public life. Finer argued for a version of ethics that emphasizes external standards and controls, laws, rules, regulations, and codes. By contrast, Friedrich maintained that ethics is of necessity a matter of the individual's internal standards of conduct—a moral compass that guides the public servant through the morass of ethical dilemmas.

The Finer position of external controls is most compatible with a view of the public servant as a neutral functionary who carries out, in Max Weber's phrase, *sine ira ac studio* (without bias or scorn), policy decisions made in the political sphere or by those in higher echelons of the organizational hierarchy. Dennis Thompson (1985; see also Ladd 1970) has gone so far as to argue that both an ethic of neutrality (decisions from politics) and an ethic of structure (decisions from higher up) preclude public-service ethics altogether because they deny the legitimacy of administrative and professional discretion. More recently, arguments in the literature are primarily over just which ethical grounds might justify such discretion. Prominent among the arguments for administrative and professional discretion are: (1) justice-based claims, usually following Rawls (Hart 1984); (2) citizenship (Cooper 1991); (3) American regime values (Rohr 1978); (4) stewardship (Kass 1990); (5) conservation (Terry 2002); and (6) countervailing responsibility (Harmon 1995).

The Challenge of Administrative Evil

Despite the extensive literature on public-service ethics, there is little recognition of the most fundamental ethical challenge to the professional within a technical-rational culture; that is, one can be a good or responsible professional and at the same time commit or contribute to acts of administrative evil. As Harmon (1995) has argued, technical-rational ethics has difficulty dealing with what Milgram (1974) termed the "agentic shift," where the professional or administrator acts responsibly toward the hierarchy of authority, public policy, and the requirements of the job or profession but abdicates any personal, much less social, responsibility for the content or effects of decisions or actions. There is little in the way of coherent justification for the notion of a stable and predictable distinction between the individual's personal conscience guided by higher values that might resist the agentic shift, and the socialized professional or administrator who internalizes agency values and obedience to legitimate authority. In the technical-rational conception of public-service ethics, the personal conscience is always subordinate to the structures of authority. The former is subjective and personal, while the latter is characterized as objective and public.

This paradox is starkly illustrated in the Third Reich and the Holocaust. Many of the administrators directly responsible for the Holocaust were, from the technical-rational perspective, effective and responsible administrators who used administrative discretion to both influence and carry out the will of their superiors. Professionals and administrators such as Adolph Eichmann and Albert Speer obeyed orders, followed proper protocol and procedures, and were often innovative and creative in carrying out their assigned tasks efficiently and effectively (Keeley 1983; Hilberg 1989; Harmon 1995; Lozowick 2000). Ironically, the SS was very concerned about corruption in its ranks and about strict conformance to the professional norms of its order (Sofsky 1997).

As Rubenstein (1975) points out, no laws against genocide or dehumanization were broken by those who perpetrated the Holocaust. Everything was legally sanctioned and administratively approved by a legitimated authority, while at the same time, a number of key programs and innovations were initiated from within the bureaucracy (Browning 1989; Sofsky 1997). Even within the morally inverted universe created by the Nazis, professionals and administrators carried out their duties within a framework of ethics and responsibility that was consistent with the norms of technical rationality (Lifton 1986). Hilberg (1989) has shown that the professions were "everywhere" in the Holocaust. Lawyers, physicians, engineers, planners, military professionals, accountants, and others all contributed to the destruction of the Jews and other "undesirables." Scientific methods were used in ways that dehumanized and murdered innocent human beings, showing clearly how the technical-rational model of professionalism empties out moral reasoning. The moral vacuity of professional ethics is clearly revealed by the fact that the vast majority of those who participated in the Holocaust were never punished. In fact, many were placed in responsible positions in postwar West German government or industry as well as in NASA and other public and private organizations in the United States. The need for "good" managers to rebuild the German economy and to develop our own rocket program outweighed any consideration of the reprehensible activities in which they were complicit.

The historical record is such that we must conclude that the power of the individual's conscience is very weak relative to that of legitimated authority in modern organizations and social structures more generally, and that current ethical standards do too little to limit the potential for evil in modern organizations. Even if the individual finds the moral strength to resist administrative evil, the technical-rational perspective provides little in the way of guidance regarding how to act effectively against evil. As public-service ethics is now construed, one cannot be a civil servant and be in public disagreement with legally constituted political authorities (Trow 1997). A public servant can voice disagreement with a public policy privately, but if this does not result in a change of policy the only acceptable courses of action that remain are exit or loyalty (Hirschman 1970; Harmon 1995). One can either resign and seek to change policy from the outside (leaving only silent loyalists in the organization) or remain and carry out the current policy. This was the choice faced by German civil servants in the early 1930s, as observed by Brecht (1944). If legitimate authority leads in the direction of administrative evil, it will certainly not provide legitimate outlets for resistance. In a situation of moral inversion, when duly constituted authority leads in the direction of evil, public-service ethics is of too little help. Within the technical-rational tradition, there seems to be little or no room for allowing or encouraging public servants to publicly disagree with policies that threaten the well-being of members of the polity, particularly policies that may produce or exploit surplus populations. Rather than expect the individual public servant to exit voluntarily when in serious disagreement with such public policies, public disagreement might press those in authority either to dismiss the offending administrator or to engage in a public debate over the policy. In either case, policy makers would have to take responsibility for their policies, rather than place that responsibility on the shoulders of functionaries.

One can only imagine whether things might have been different in Germany had the civil service spoken out against Nazi policies in the early days of the regime. True, individual civil servants would have done so at considerable personal risk, but, at the same time, the newly constituted government could not have sustained itself without their collective support. That the vast majority of the German civil service willingly carried out their duties once the legal basis for the new regime was established (Brecht 1944), and that U.S. government scientists continued the Tuskegee experiments long after a cure for syphilis had been developed are but two of many examples that reveal how the ethical framework within a culture of technical rationality leaves little room for moral choice or for resistance to administrative evil that is sanctioned by legitimate authority.

If the Holocaust teaches us anything, it is that individual administrators and professionals, far from resisting administrative evil, are most likely to be either helpless victims or willing accomplices. The ethical framework within a technical-rational system posits the primacy of an abstract, utility-maximizing individual, while it binds professionals to organizations in ways that make them into reliable conduits for the dictates of legitimate authority, which is no less legitimate when it happens to be in pursuit of an evil policy. An ethical system that allows an individual to be a good administrator or professional and at the same time commit acts of evil is necessarily devoid of moral content, or, perhaps better, is morally perverse. Given the reality of administrative evil, no public servant should be able to rest easy with the notion that ethical behavior is defined by doing things the right way. Norms of legality, efficiency, and effectiveness—however "professional" they may be—do not necessarily promote or protect the well-being of humans, especially that of society's most vulnerable and superfluous members, whose numbers are growing in the early years of the twenty-first century.

Globalization, the Corrosion of Character, and Surplus Populations

Since the fall of the Berlin Wall in 1989, a new, global world order has emerged (see Friedman 1999; Farazmand 1999; Bauman 1999; Sassen 1998; Huntington 1996; Fukuyama 1992). The relatively stable and predictable system of the Cold War, at least for most industrialized nations, has given way to a new global system that is more complex and unpredictable (Balfour and Grubbs 2000), a process that was accelerated by the events of September 11, 2001. Where once two great nation-states defined many of the parameters of the world's political and economic systems, we now find a constantly shifting balance of powers in the relationships between nation-states, between these states and super-markets (such as the North American Free Trade Agreement and the European Union), and between states, super-markets, and super-empowered individuals (Friedman 1999). Old boundaries no longer restrict movement as the world moves toward greater integration of markets, nation-states, and technology. These developments have created both prosperity and phenomenal opportunities to create wealth, but they also have opened the doors to new conflicts and to deepening poverty among those who lack access to these new opportunities.

One consequence of this new world order is that individuals are becoming less tied to the traditional moorings of organization, community, and nation that once nurtured and protected them, although these moorings had already loosened considerably during the past century. For some, this represents a great opportunity to explore new horizons and possibilities. Many others, however, have found themselves adrift in a world that offers no safe haven in which to land and settle into a stable life. At the extreme end of this spectrum are millions of refugees and displaced persons—surplus populations. The dimensions of this problem are such that no nation or community remains untouched by it (Fritz 1999, p. 5):

> An estimated 50 million people were either driven from their countries or uprooted within them by the mid-1990s, roughly one out of every hundred people on earth. Counting those who emigrated for what were viewed as dire economic reasons, the figure more than doubles. The impact of this great migration has been enormous. It has compelled U.S.-led armies to intervene in faraway wars. It has led to a reactionary wave of restrictive immigration laws around the world. And it has planted the seeds of countless future conflicts.

Each new refugee crisis challenges already overstressed nation-states and nongovernmental organizations to find ways to absorb and care for these people with limited resources within an increasingly unsupportive political and social environment.

On another level, millions more individuals feel threatened by the new world order, fearful that they too will be uprooted and left hanging without a safety net. The underlying anxiety of the Cold War era was the fear that the conflict between the two superpowers would escalate into a nuclear holocaust. While that concern has diminished since the upheavals of the early 1990s, new anxieties have emerged. People feel threatened by terrorism and by the rapid changes and painful dislocations caused by unseen and poorly understood global forces. They fear that their jobs, communities, or workplaces can be changed or even taken away at any moment by anonymous and turbulent economic, political, and technological forces. A new technology can transform an industry in a matter of months, making an individual's skills obsolete, or one's organization can disappear overnight in a new wave of mergers. The mass of refugees throughout the world serves as a constant reminder of how anyone can be overtaken and made superfluous by the dynamics of the new global system.

In his book, *The Corrosion of Character: The Personal Consequences of Work in the New Capitalism,* Richard Sennett (1998) discusses how organizations are changing in the new global system and some of the effects of these changes on the individual worker. He encapsulates many of these developments in his conversations with Rico, a successful businessman in the electronics industry, whose wife is also a working professional. While in many ways they exemplify success in the contemporary economy, they also suffer from deep anxieties about the future and the quality of their lives— anxieties that have become all too real for many thousands of people like them in the wake of the "tech bust."

Rico struggles to maintain a sense of identity and ethical integrity in an atmosphere of continual change and low levels of commitment to anything other than short-term gains (Sennett 1998, pp. 20–21):

> He feared that the actions he needs to take and the way he has to live in order to survive in the modern economy have set his emotional, inner life adrift . . . his deepest worry is that he cannot offer the substance of his work life as an example to his children of how they should conduct themselves ethically. The qualities of good work are not the qualities of good character.

One result of the increasing focus on the short term is low levels of trust and commitment. The pace of change in contemporary organizations means that for most workers there is "no long term." Rico values the independence he has found in the new economy but he also feels adrift, with no strong bonds of commitment or trust (Sennett 1998, p. 25), "'No long term' means keep moving, don't commit yourself, and don't sacrifice." For managers and policy makers, this means that individual employees are all expendable. Any notion that organizations should care for their employees or make long-term commitments to them is seen as an anachronism, an impossible luxury. Translated to the individual level, the short-term orientation of the new global economy tends to undermine character, especially those qualities that bind people to each other and furnish the individual with a stable sense of self.

Under these conditions, the changing requirements for success in organizations make moral inversions and administrative evil more likely. Although once bureaucracy and stable lines of authority and routine were valued, today the emphasis is on flexibility and autonomous action. Corporations and governments want employees who can think on their feet and adroitly adjust to rapid change, but they also want to retain the right (in the name of adaptability) to terminate these employees at any time for the good of the organization. It would be a mistake to conclude, therefore, that more flexibility means more freedom for employees ("Freedom's just another word for nothin' left to lose," to paraphrase the Foster/Kristofferson song). Instead, the move away from bureaucratic structure to more flexible forms of organization has replaced one structure of power and control with other, less visible forms of control and compliance (Barker 1993). The threat of expendability and fear of social breakdown make people all the more prone to protect their self-interest rather than consider the implications of their actions for the well-being of others. The context these developments provide for ethics in public life is a difficult one.

The Prospects for Reconstructing Public Ethics

As the twenty-first century unfolds, two trends seem clear: First, interdependence is greater than it has ever been—people's fates are deeply intertwined—and this is less recognized than ever. Second, social and ethnic groups around the world are more and more fractionated and fractious—socially centripetal forces are as powerful as they have ever been, with more surplus populations appearing—and being created—at the fringes of society. We live at a time in the United States when politics has become more sharply partisan, when public discussion in many forums has degenerated well below hard-edged debate, when hyperpluralism underlines our differences perhaps beyond repair, and when the relentless pressure to entertain in the media has made even the somewhat thoughtful sound bite seem deliberative by comparison with the serial-monologue-by-interruption so common on public-affairs television.

Without the cohesion provided by a much greater sense of community, it is hard to see how American society can be kept from literally flying apart except through coercive power, which carries the potential to degenerate into public policies of elimination, the most perversely tempting technical-rational solution to social and political disorder (Rubenstein 1975, 1983). As a response to serious social fragmentation and economic dislocation, an authoritarian America now seems to be in the realm of the possible, one in which the barriers to "final solutions" can all too easily fail. Many political, economic, and social responses to these conditions have been suggested from a variety of perspectives. However, we would suggest that any viable response must be plausible within the American political system of liberal democracy.

Liberal Democracy

Liberalism and democracy came together in the American founding period. A clear account of the marriage between the two appears in C.B. Macpherson's *The Life and Times of Liberal Democracy* (1977). The core values of classical liberalism are individualism; the notion of rights (particularly to property); the sanctity of contracts; and the rule of law. Classical liberalism sets the philosophical foundation for American society, which allows for and encourages differential achievement by individuals. Democracy's chief value—equality—is often outweighed within this framework. Americans of the founding period lived, as we twenty-first century Americans do, in an order fraught with tension between the liberal and the democratic traditions.

Democratic principles were a driving force in the American Revolution (Countryman 1985). While political beliefs were widely divergent, there was widespread popular support for the democratic aims of the revolution; there had to be in order for the armies to be manned and for the struggle to be successfully pressed against the British.

What lingers decisively, however, is not a polity based on the revolutionary rhetoric, but on the state that was built following the war during a time that has been appropriately called "counterrevolutionary." The constitutional framework that was laid down during the founding period was formed more from the principles of liberalism than from those of democracy. The core value of the more democratic, revolutionary period—equality—was given a severe reduction in rank by the founding fathers. The value of liberty—and its repository in the individual—was elevated and buttressed by law, by contract, and by right. The American liberal democracy is thus predominantly procedural—civil liberties, voting, fair procedures in decision making, and technical-rational policy making (Adams et al. 1990). Within this context of American liberal democracy appear at least two divergent scenarios in which public ethics will either flourish or wither.

Putting Cruelty First

"Putting cruelty first," our initial scenario, is more apparent in American public life at the national level, gives precedence to liberty within the pantheon of American political values, and offers a public ethics that at best provides a scant defense against administrative evil. This version of liberal-ism is perhaps best articulated by Judith Shklar in *Ordinary Vices* (1984), in which she advances a "liberalism of fear" predicated on the rather dismal track record of human beings, particularly in the twentieth century. Among the pantheon of human vices, including treachery, disloyalty, tyranny, dis-honesty, and cruelty, Shklar argues for "putting cruelty first" (1984, pp. 7–44). If our first consideration in public life is the cruelty that human beings all too often inflict on one another, our normal response is a healthy fear of cruelty, leading us to a liberalism of fear; one whose foremost mission is to avoid the worst excesses of state power run amok (Shklar 1984, p. 5):

> Tolerance consistently applied is more difficult and morally more demand-ing than repression. Moreover, the liberalism of fear, which makes cruelty the first vice, quite rightly recognizes that fear reduces us to mere reactive units of sensation. . . . The alternative . . . is . . . between cruel military and moral repression and violence, and a self-restraining tolerance that fences in the powerful to protect the freedom and safety of every citizen, old or young, male or female, black or white.

A polity based on the liberalism of fear is focused on avoiding our worst proclivities. At the same time, it paradoxically makes strenuous ethical de-mands on citizens (Shklar 1984, p. 249): "[L]iberalism imposes extraordi-nary ethical difficulties on us: to live with contradictions, unresolvable conflicts, and balancing between public and private imperatives which are neither opposed to nor at one with each other." In a liberalism of fear, into which we are prompted by our "ordinary vices" and by the forces of global-ization, we are dependent on the development of character in our citizens—too many weak characters and we lapse into the excesses of evil. Too much of an organized, systematic program by government or by religious or social institutions to reform character on a large, social scale, and we risk falling into evil through arrogance, as Shklar notes (1984, p. 39): "Nothing but cru-elty comes from those who seek perfection and forget the little good that lies directly within their powers." It is just as easy to overreach, as to underreach for character development within a liberalism of fear, leading to those cruel consequences that surely warrant our fear.

In this first scenario, one is left with a minimalist public ethics. Transpar-ency becomes the chief principle, under the assumption that when people can see the worst excesses they will respond to correct them. A system of laws and regulations that makes public deliberations and decisions *visible* to the public becomes the pillar of public ethics. Along with a system of trans-parency, public ethics under a liberalism of fear would include a program of laws and regulations that would set minimum floors below which we would not want to allow people's behavior to sink (in full knowledge and expectation that at least from time to time it would).

This is not a version of public ethics that inspires much optimism about future instances of administrative evil. The assumptions about human nature under a liberalism of fear tend toward the misanthropic, anticipating the worst from human beings, having been given so little encouragement from the events of the twentieth century. Indeed, the difficulties of getting a liberalism of fear right, along with the corrosion of character exacerbated by globalization, suggest that administrative evil may well increase, perhaps even dramatically.

Deliberative Democracy

The second scenario for public ethics focuses on the democratic aspect of our political heritage—in particular, deliberative democracy—and has been more visible at the local level of our polity (Box 1998; Chaskin et al. 2001). In its most basic sense, deliberation is careful thought and discussion about issues and decisions. Deliberative processes comprise discussion and consideration by a group of persons of the reasons for and against a measure, or, put another way, consulting with others in a process of reaching a decision (Fishkin 1991). According to Dryzek (2000), deliberation is a process of social inquiry in which participants seek to gain understanding of themselves and others, to learn, and to persuade. Thus one of the cornerstones of deliberative processes is the nature of the communication involved: participants strive to rise above win-lose exchange; over time, they may aspire to dialogue and even to become a learning community (Yankelovich 1999).

Participants in deliberative processes are expected to be open to change in their attitudes, ideas, and positions, although such change is not a required outcome of deliberation. It is a process that can, over time, foster growth in citizens, both in the capacity for practical judgment and in the art of living together in a context of disagreement—hence, a public ethics. As in a liberalism of fear, tolerance is elevated to a central virtue in public life. Deliberative democracy insists on a meaningful role for citizens in public decisions, although sorting out which citizens and what decisions are appropriate for deliberation represents ongoing problems. There is a considerable theoretical literature on both deliberative democracy (Gutmann and Thompson 1996; Dryzek 1990) and deliberative governance (Forester 1999; Hajer and Wagenaar 2003; Fischer 2000; deLeon 1997). Deliberative processes have been used at all levels of government (although mostly at the local level) and share in common involving citizens in public discussion and decision making (Dryzek and Torgerson 1993). Insistence on full deliberation sets a very high standard that has been met only rarely, and then only after multiple iterations (Scott, Adams, and Wechsler forthcoming).

A public ethics appropriate for deliberative democracy offers a possible alternative to the technical-rational approach to administrative ethics and to the complex of problems associated with administrative evil. Alastair MacIntyre (1984) provided the groundbreaking work within this literature (also known as neo-Aristotelian, character, or virtue ethics). This tradition does not locate ethics in the autonomous individual, but within the community. That is, ethics emerges from the relational context within which people act—within the public square.

The process of building a community, in this case, an inclusive, democratic community, develops public life and public ethics at the same time. As detailed by Deborah Stone, a political community has the following characteristics (1988, p. 25):

> It is a community.
> It has a public interest, if only an idea about which people will fight.
> Most of its policy problems are common problems.
> Influence is pervasive, and the boundary between influence and coercion is always contested.
> Cooperation is as important as competition.
> Loyalty is the norm.
> Groups and organizations are the building blocks.
> Information is interpretive, incomplete, and strategic.
> It is governed by the laws of passion as well as of matter.
> Power, derivative of all those elements, coordinates individual intentions and actions into collective purposes and results.

Publicness is a key aspect in this development as Ventriss (1993, p. 201) notes: "A public, therefore, is a community of citizens who attempt to understand the substantive interdependency of social and political issues on the community, and who maintain a critical perspective on the ethical implications of governmental policy making." In this view, it would be unethical for public servants *not* to speak publicly to policy issues. As citizen professionals and administrators in a democratic community, they would have a special responsibility to guard against policies and practices that might engender eruptions of administrative evil.

This critical and active citizenship is a key aspect of building a viable deliberative democracy. Camilla Stivers (1993, p. 441) has articulated the following characteristics of democratic citizenship:

the exercise of authoritative power, using sound judgment and relying on practical knowledge of the situation at hand;

the exercise of virtue, or concern for the public interest, defined substantively in particular contexts through reasoned discourse;

the development of personal capacities for governance through their exercise in practical activity; and

the constitution of community through deliberation about issues of public concern.

In summary, then, active citizenship means participation in governance and the exercise of decisive judgment in the public interest, an experience that develops the political and moral capacities of individuals and solidifies the communal ties among them.

Deliberative democracy clearly makes very high demands on individuals, and on individuals acting together in the public interest. It views exclusion and nonparticipation in public life as major problems in and of themselves. Public policies based on exclusion and exploitation are entirely inimical to a deliberative democracy because they "weaken the community by undermining the civic bonds that unify it, while eroding the political process by converting what should be a dialogue between fellow citizens into a repressive hierarchy" (Farber 1994, p. 929). This, of course, is precisely what occurred in Nazi Germany. Under the rhetoric of a unified community, the Nazis' racist and exclusionary policies created a polity held together not by civic bonds but by the terror of the concentration camps (Gellately 2001; Sofsky 1997).

A public ethics within a deliberative democracy would require that professionals and administrators be attentive to social and economic outcomes of public policy, as well as to their proper and faithful implementation. Public servants could not ethically implement a policy that was overtly detrimental to the well-being of any segment of the population. It would be unethical, for example, to cooperate with the cutting off of disability benefits to legal immigrants, many of whom are elderly and are likely to wind up malnourished, or homeless, or both. Such a policy amounts to defining this group as a surplus population, and an ethical public service cannot be complicit in that sort of public policy.

Cruelty, Deliberation, and Administrative Evil

Within our liberal democratic polity, at least these two versions of public ethics can be imagined. The first, based on a liberalism of fear, stems from an essentially misanthropic view of human nature: We have repeatedly seen the worst from human beings, and we should expect no better. In this scenario, we should understand that only a minimalist public ethics can be expected to be workable, but even more important, we must beware the arrogance of a public ethics based on grand designs about human perfectibility—such designs are the well-traveled avenues to those horrific eruptions of evil that we have seen throughout human history, but especially during the past century (Glover 1999; Berlin 1991).

The second version, based on deliberative democracy—while not blind to human vices, including cruelty—does assume that we humans can, with hard work and great vigilance, do better. In this scenario, we can strengthen our public life and our public ethics through the rigor and tribulations of deliberative processes. This is not an easy road; not only does it risk arrogance and a concomitant descent into evil, but it assumes more—perhaps far more—than we have yet achieved. Yet it does have the considerable attraction of imagining a future in which we can hope for fewer lapses into administrative evil.

The most likely future involves some mixture of both of these scenarios (and perhaps others as well). However, regardless of which assumptions about human nature one holds—and which version of public ethics one thus finds persuasive—no human communities, even deliberative and democratic ones, offer any guarantees against administrative evil. And they certainly offer no escape from evil itself, which remains a part of the human condition. Still, one might hope—perhaps without lapsing into fantasy— that administrative evil might not be so easily masked in deliberative democratic communities. And public servants might not so easily wear the mask of administrative evil when their roles entail a critically reflexive sense of the context of public affairs as well as a duty to educate and build an inclusive and active citizenry. Understanding administrative evil thus provides no easy or sentimental solutions, nor does it promise that the future will be better. It offers only an inevitably small and fragile bulwark against things going really wrong—those genuinely horrific eruptions of evil that our global culture of technical rationality has exacerbated very nearly beyond our willingness to comprehend.

> Do not despair. You need not worry so much about the
> future of civilization, for mankind has not yet risen so far,
> that he has so very far to fall.
> —*Sigmund Freud, Vienna, the 1920s*
> *(personal recollection of Raul Hilberg)*

References

Adams, Guy B. 2000. "Administrative Ethics and the Chimera of Professionalism: The Historical Context of Public Service Ethics." In *Handbook of Administrative Ethics*, 2d ed., ed. Terry L. Cooper, pp. 291–308 . New York: Marcel Dekker.

Adams, Guy B., and Balfour, Danny L. 2004. *Unmasking Administrative Evil*, rev. ed. Armonk, NY: M.E. Sharpe.

Adams, Guy B.; Bowerman; Priscilla V.; Dolbeare, Kenneth M.; and Stivers, Camilla. 1990. "Joining Purpose to Practice: A Democratic Identity for the Public Service." In *Images and Identities in Public Administration*, ed. Henry D. Kass and Bayard L. Catron, pp. 219–40. Newbury Park, CA: SAGE.

Arendt, Hannah. 1963. *Eichmann in Jerusalem: A Report on the Banality of Evil.* New York: Viking Press.

Balfour, Danny L., and Grubbs, Joseph W. 2000. "Character, Corrosion and the Civil Servant: The Human Consequences of Globalization and the New Public Management." *Administrative Theory and Praxis* 22: 570–84.

Barker, James R. 1993. "Tightening the Iron Cage: Coercive Control in Self-Managing Teams." *Administrative Science Quarterly* 38: 408–37.

Bauman, Zygmont. 1989. *Modernity and the Holocaust.* Ithaca, NY: Cornell University Press.

———. 1999. *In Search of Politics.* Stanford, CA: Stanford University Press.

Bentham, Jeremy. 1989 [1789]. *Vice and Virtue in Everyday Life.* New York: Harcourt Brace Jovanovich.

Berlin, Isaiah. 1991. *The Crooked Timber of Humanity.* New York: Knopf.

Bernstein, Richard J. 2002. *Radical Evil: A Philosophical Investigation.* Cambridge, UK: Polity Press.

Bok, Sissela. 1978. *Lying: Moral Choice in Public and Private Life.* New York: Vintage.

Box, Richard C. 1998. *Citizen Governance: Leading American Cities in the 21st Century.* Thousand Oaks, CA: SAGE.

Brecht, Arnold. 1944. *Prelude to Silence.* New York: Oxford University Press.

Browne, M. Neil; Kubasek, Nancy K.; and Giampetro-Meyer, Andrea. 1995. "The Seductive Danger of Craft Ethics for Business Organizations." *Review of Business* 17 (Winter): 23–29.

Browning, Christopher. 1989. "The Decision concerning the Final Solution." In *Unanswered Questions: Nazi Germany and the Genocide of the Jews*, ed. F. Furet, pp. 96–118. New York: Schocken Books.

Chaskin, Robert J.; Brown, Prudence; Venkatesh, Sudhir; and Vidal, Avis. 2001. *Building Community Capacity.* New York: Aldine.

Cooper, Terry L. 1991. *An Ethic of Citizenship for Public Administration.* Englewood Cliffs, NJ: Prentice Hall.

Countryman, Edward. 1985. *The American Revolution.* New York: Hill and Wang.

deLeon, Peter. 1997. *Democracy and the Policy Sciences.* Albany: State University of New York Press.

Dryzek, John. 1990. *Discursive Democracy: Politics, Policy and Political Science.* Cambridge: Cambridge University Press.

———. 2000. *Deliberative Democracy and Beyond.* Oxford: Oxford University Press.

Dryzek, John, and Torgerson, Douglas. 1993. "Democracy and the Policy Sciences: A Progress Report." *Policy Sciences* 26: 127–49.

Eliot, Gil. 1972. *The Twentieth Century Book of the Dead*. New York: Scribner.

Farazmand, Ali. 1999. "Globalization and Public Administration." *Public Administration Review* 59: 509–22.

Farber, Daniel A. 1994. "The Outmoded Debate over Affirmative Action." *California Law Review* 82: 893–934.

Finer, Herbert. 1941. "Administrative Responsibility in Democratic Government." *Public Administration Review* 1: 335–50.

Fischer, Frank. 2000. *Citizens, Experts and the Environment: The Politics of Local Knowledge*. Durham, NC: Duke University Press.

Fishkin, James S. 1991. *Democracy and Deliberation*. New Haven, CT: Yale University Press.

Forester, John. 1999. *The Deliberative Practitioner: Encouraging Participatory Planning Processes*. Cambridge, MA: MIT Press.

Frankena, William. 1973. *Ethics*, 2d ed. Englewood Cliffs, NJ: Prentice Hall.

Friedman, Thomas. 1999. *The Lexus and the Olive Tree*. New York: Farrar, Strauss and Giroux.

Friedrich, Carl J. 1940. "Public Policy and the Nature of Administrative Responsibility." In *Public Policy*, ed. C.J. Friedrich and E.S. Mason, pp. 3–24. Cambridge, MA: Harvard University Press.

Fritz, M. 1999. *Lost on Earth: Nomads of the New World*. Boston: Little, Brown.

Fukuyama, Francis. 1992. *The End of History and the Last Man*. New York: Free Press.

Garrard, Eve. 2002. "Evil as an Explanatory Concept." *Monist* 85 (April): 320–37.

Gellately, Robert. 2001. *Backing Hitler: Consent and Coercion in Nazi Germany*. New York: Oxford University Press.

Glover, Jonathan. 1999. *Humanity: A Moral History of the Twentieth Century*. New Haven, CT: Yale University Press.

Gutmann, Amy, and Thompson, Dennis F. 1996. *Democracy and Disagreement*. Cambridge, MA: Harvard University Press.

Hajer, Maarten, and Wagenaar, Hendrik. 2003. *Deliberative Policy Analysis: Understanding Governance in the Network Society*. Cambridge: Cambridge University Press.

Harmon, Michael M. 1995. *Responsibility as Paradox: A Critique of Rational Discourse on Government*. Thousand Oaks, CA: SAGE.

Hart, David K. 1984. "The Virtuous Citizen, the Honorable Bureaucrat and 'Public' Administration." *Public Administration Review* 44: 111–20.

Hilberg, Raul. 1989. "The Bureaucracy of Annihilation." In *Unanswered Questions: Nazi Germany and the Genocide of the Jews*, ed. F. Furet, pp. 119–33. New York: Schocken Books.

Hirschman, Albert O. 1970. *Exit, Voice and Loyalty*. Cambridge, MA: Harvard University Press.

Huntington, Samuel. 1996. *The Clash of Civilizations and the Remaking of the World Order*. New York: Touchstone.

Ishiguro, Kazuo. 1988. *The Remains of the Day*. New York: Knopf.

Juergensmeyer, Mark. 2000. *Terror in the Mind of God: The Global Rise of Religious Violence*. Berkeley: University of California Press.

Kant, Immanuel. 1959. *Metaphysical Foundations of Morals*. Indianapolis, IN: Bobbs-Merrill.

Kass, Henry D. 1990. "Stewardship as a Fundamental Element in Images of Public Administration." In *Image and Identity in Public Administration*, ed. Henry D.

Kass and Bayard L. Catron, pp 113–31. Newbury Park, CA: SAGE.

Katz, Fred E. 1993. *Ordinary People and Extraordinary Evil: A Report on the Beguilings of Evil*. Albany: State University of New York Press.

Katz, Jack. 1988. *Seductions of Crime: Moral and Sensual Attractions in Doing Evil*. New York: Basic Books.

Kearney, Richard C., and Sinha, C. 1988. "Professionalism and Bureaucratic Responsiveness: Conflict or Compatibility." *Public Administration Review* 48: 571–79.

Keeley, M. 1983. "Values in Organizational Theory and Management Education." *Academy of Management Review* 8, no. 3: 376–86.

Ladd, John. 1970. "Morality and the Ideal of Rationality in Organizations." *Monist* 54: 488–516.

Lang, Berel. 1991. "The History of Evil and the Future of the Holocaust." In *Lessons and Legacies: The Meaning of the Holocaust in a Changing World*, ed. Peter Hayes, pp. 90–105. Evanston, IL: Northwestern University Press.

Lifton, Robert Jay. 1986. *The Nazi Doctors: Medical Killing and the Psychology of Genocide*. New York: Basic Books.

———. 1999. *Destroying the World to Save It: Aum Shinrikyo, Apocalyptic Violence and the New Global Terrorism*. New York: Henry Holt.

Lozowick, Yaacov. 2000. *Hitler's Bureaucrats: The Nazi Security Police and the Banality of Evil*. New York: Continuum.

MacIntyre, Alastair. 1984. *After Virtue*, 2d ed. Notre Dame, IN: Notre Dame University Press.

Macpherson, Crawford B. 1977. *The Life and Times of Liberal Democracy*. New York: Oxford University Press.

McGinn, Colin. 1997. *Ethics, Evil and Fiction*. Oxford, UK: Clarendon Press.

Milgram, Stanley. 1974. *Obedience to Authority*. New York: Harper and Row.

Neiman, Susan. 2002. *Evil in Modern Thought: An Alternative History of Philosophy*. Princeton, NJ: Princeton University Press.

Niebuhr, Reinhold. 1986. *The Essential Reinhold Niebuhr: Selected Essays and Addresses*, ed. Robert McAfee Brown. New Haven, CT: Yale University Press.

Poole, Ross. 1991. *Morality and Modernity*. London: Routledge, Chapman and Hall.

Power, Samantha. 2002. *"A Problem from Hell": America and the Age of Genocide*. New York: Basic Books.

Rohr, John A. 1978. *Ethics for Bureaucrats*. New York: Marcel Dekker.

Rubenstein, Richard L. 1975. *The Cunning of History*. New York: Harper and Row.

———. 1983. *The Age of Triage: Fear and Hope in an Overcrowded World*. Boston: Beacon Press.

Rummel, Rudolph J. 1994. *Death by Government*. New Brunswick, NJ: Transaction.

Sanford, J.A. 1981. *Evil: The Shadow Side of Reality*. New York: Crossroad.

Sassen, S. 1998. *Globalization and Its Discontents*. New York: Free Press.

Scott, James A.; Adams, Guy B.; and Wechsler, Barton. 2004. "Deliberative Governance: Lessons from Theory and Practice." In *Tampering with Tradition*, ed. Peter Bogason, Hugh Miller, and Sandra Kenson, pp 11–21. Lanham, MD: Lexington Books.

Sennett, Richard. 1998. *The Corrosion of Character: The Personal Consequences of Work in the New Capitalism*. New York: Norton.

Shklar, Judith N. 1984. *Ordinary Vices*. Cambridge, MA: Harvard University Press.

Sofsky, Werner. 1997. *The Order of Terror: The Concentration Camp*. Princeton, NJ: Princeton University Press.

Staub, Ervin. 1992. *The Roots of Evil: The Origins of Genocide and Other Group Violence*. New York: Cambridge University Press.

Steiner, Hillel. 2002. "Calibrating Evil." *Monist* 85 (April): 183–94.

Stivers, Camilla. 1993. "Citizenship Ethics in Public Administration." In *Handbook of Administrative Ethics*, ed. Terry L. Cooper, pp. 433–55. New York: Marcel Dekker.

Stone, Deborah A. 1988. *Policy Paradox and Political Reason*. New York: Harper-Collins.

Terry, Larry D. 2002. *Leadership of Public Bureaucracies: The Administrator as Conservator*, 2d ed. Armonk, NY: M.E. Sharpe.

Thompson, Dennis F. 1985. "The Possibility of Administrative Ethics." *Public Administration Review* 45: 555–61.

Trow, M. 1997. "The Chiefs of Public Universities Should Be Civil Servants, not Political Actors." *Chronicle of Higher Education* 44 (May 16): A48.

Ventriss, Curtis. 1993. "The 'Publicness' of Administrative Ethics." In *Handbook of Administrative Ethics*, ed. Terry L. Cooper, pp. 199–218. New York: Marcel Dekker.

Volkan, Vamik. 1997. *Blood Lines: From Ethnic Pride to Ethnic Terrorism*. Boulder, CO: Westview Press.

Yankelovich, Daniel. 1999. *The Magic of Dialogue: Transforming Conflict into Cooperation*. New York: Simon and Schuster.

7

Accountability Through Thick and Thin: Moral Agency in Public Service

Melvin Dubnick and Ciarán O'Kelly

As in other aspects of life, the most challenging ethical choices in public administration are not between right and wrong, but among contrasting perceptions of proper behavior. This general dilemma is particularly difficult in the complex world of public-sector decision making where various forms of accountability come into play. In this chapter we will examine the dynamic role of alternative conceptions of accountability in shaping the ethical choices of administrative officials. We will argue that the expectations of public administrators are rooted in thick or thin normative approaches to their work. Our analysis will focus on the behavior of two officials involved in one of the most scrutinized public events of recent decades: the events leading up to the decision of the British Parliament in the spring of 2003 to permit the Blair government's commitment to engage troops in a war against Iraq in an effort to overthrow the regime of Saddam Hussein.

Relying on evidence and testimony provided by the official inquiry into the suicide of Dr. David Kelly (the Hutton Inquiry), which followed a scandal over the uses of intelligence in justifying the 2003 war on Iraq, we will examine the implications of distinct views of accountability reflected in the behavior of two prominent members of the British intelligence community, John Scarlett and Brian Jones. Brian Jones was, at the time he provided evidence to the Hutton Inquiry, the former branch head in the Scientific and Technical Directorate of the Defense Intelligence Analysis (DIA) staff, which had worked on the British government dossier, "Iraq's Weapons of Mass Destruction," which was central to the events leading to Kelly's death. John McLeod Scarlett headed the Joint Intelligence Committee (JIC), the body that formally issued the report in question. Both had long and notable careers as civil service professionals in the British intelligence community, and each came to his job with a clear perspective on what was expected of him as an intelligence professional. Central to our analysis is the nature of those perspectives on accountability, which we consider to be "thick" and "thin" variations of that important concept.

We will begin with an account of the events leading up to the Hutton Inquiry, and then we will describe our theoretical framework: that expectations shape public administrator perceptions of accountability within organizations. These perceptions are, in turn, motivated by the administrators' normative approaches. If the administrator relies more on conceptions of principle, then they exercise a thin ethic. If their decisions are based on concrete relationships, then they are motivated by a thick moral framework. Finally, we will return to the Hutton Inquiry, describing how the two key players we examine approached the challenges they faced.

Background: The War on Iraq and the Hutton Inquiry

"Iraq's Weapons of Mass Destruction"

When the United Kingdom, the United States, and other countries invaded Iraq in 2003, they did so largely on the presumption that Saddam Hussein had stockpiled weapons of mass destruction (WMD) and, crucially, that he was prepared to use them. Hussein had, it was claimed, a chemical and biological weapons (CBW) program and was acquiring materials for the construction of nuclear weapons. Given that his WMD program was "active, detailed, and growing" (Blair 2002), the governments maintained that something had to be done.

In Britain, Prime Minister Tony Blair had a problem. The majority opinion among the British public was set against an invasion of Iraq. Likewise, a large proportion of the governing Labour Party's members of Parliament (MPs) wanted to prevent military action. Suspicion of the push toward war was rooted in concern for international law and the United Nations (UN), in concern for the independence of European policy-formation processes, and, not least, in distrust of the Bush administration's methods, motives, and tone. If MPs voted against military intervention, or placed barriers on its taking place (making it conditional on United Nations Security Council approval, for example), Blair's hands would have been tied.[1]

In an effort to bring public and parliamentary opinion behind his proposed policies, Blair decided to publish a dossier, outlining the intelligence assessment of the threat that Iraq posed. This dossier, titled "Iraq's Weapons of Mass Destruction," was published on September 24, 2002.[2]

The publication of intelligence assessments was largely unprecedented. Intelligence is normally passed from the Intelligence Services to the Joint Intelligence Committee (JIC), which is based in the Cabinet Office,[3] and includes intelligence professionals and civil servants drawn from several major intelligence-gathering agencies. As the "main instrument for advising on priorities for intelligence gathering," the JIC is tasked with making high-level intelligence judgments drawn from the assessments of the various units and services that report to them (Cabinet Office 2001). It is worth emphasizing that the JIC is not a political committee. It prepares and provides information from which politicians may make decisions.

The dossier set out to display the evidence that Iraq was maintaining a WMD program and was prepared to employ WMD, both against Iraqi civilians (as had happened in Halabja in 1988) and in pursuit of Saddam Hussein's strategy of regional domination. It was divided into three parts, outlining in turn Iraq's chemical, biological, nuclear, and ballistic missile programs, the history of UN inspections, and Iraq under Saddam Hussein. The dossier was prefaced both by a foreword, signed by Tony Blair, and by an executive summary. Blair's foreword set out the case that could be drawn from the information contained in the dossier, while, strangely, the executive summary "took the form of a judgment. It was not a summary of the main points in the text" (Scarlett 2003a, 101:10–13; 79:10–21).

One serious allegation was that Iraq was capable of activating WMD within 45 minutes after an order to deploy was given. This charge was repeated four times, including in the prime minister's foreword. The 45–minute claim was a key part of the evidence presented in the dossier.[4]

Parliament was recalled when the dossier was published, and Tony Blair repeated the allegations, including the 45–minute claim, in his statement (White, Watt, and Wintour 2002). Although much of the information in the dossier was not new, the new elements were sufficiently serious that they had an effect. When members of Parliament voted,[5] the government's motion was carried. The effect on public opinion was more difficult to measure, but several newspapers carried front page stories about the 45–minute claim the day after the dossier was published.

Andrew Gilligan, David Kelly, and the 45–Minute Claim

On May 29, 2003, BBC radio's early morning news program, *Today*, broadcast a report on the dossier in general, and about the 45–minute claim in particular.[6] Andrew Gilligan, BBC radio's defense correspondent reported that "one of the senior officials in charge of drawing up that Dossier" had alleged the following:

- The intelligence community was concerned about some of the claims in the dossier, notably the 45–minute claim, which came from a single, unreliable source.
- During the week before the dossier was published, pressure was brought to bear on the intelligence agencies to "sex it up."
- The government had inserted the 45–minute claim in the knowledge that it was probably wrong.
- Tony Blair's director of communications and strategy, Alastair Campbell, had been at the center of attempts to make the dossier more appealing. He had had caveats removed and had, in effect, spun the dossier to make Saddam Hussein appear to be more menacing than the intelligence services could reliably ascertain.

In the wake of this report, and a series of others originating from the same source,[7] the government, led by Alastair Campbell, launched an "unprecedented attack" (Dyke 2003, 151:1) on the BBC, claiming not only that these allegations were incorrect, but that the BBC's reporting of the war had been biased from the start. The government denied that there was dissent in the ranks of the intelligence services over the dossier's claims. The controversy went on for some weeks, with the government pressuring the BBC to name its source so that his or her veracity could be tested.

Simultaneously, the Foreign Affairs Select Committee (FAC) of the House of Commons began an investigation into the allegations that the cause for war had been spun. They interviewed, among others, Andrew Gilligan and Alastair Campbell. Another investigation was carried out by the Intelligence and Security Committee (ISC) which, unlike the FAC, holds hearings in camera and reports directly to the prime minister.

On June 30, as the public argument was going on, Dr. David Kelly, an official in the Ministry of Defence (MoD), wrote a letter to his line manager in which he expressed concern that he would be identified as Gilligan's source.

Kelly was based in, and responsible to, the MoD, but he was formally working there on secondment from the Defence Evaluation and Research Agency (DERA). A biologist by training, he had been at the forefront of assessing Soviet BCW capabilities after the end of the Cold War. Once weapons inspections began in Iraq, he was drafted there, too. He was "the Ministry of Defence's chief scientific officer and senior adviser to the proliferation and arms control secretariat, and to the Foreign Office's non-proliferation department. The senior adviser on biological weapons to the UN biological weapons inspections teams (UNSCOM) from 1994 to 1999, he was also, in the opinion of his peers, pre-eminent in his field, not only in this country, but in the world" (Fountain and Smith 2003).

While he claimed that he could not have been Gilligan's primary source, he realized that it might appear that he had been. He was a well-known expert on the subject, and he had had an informal meeting with Gilligan on May 22 in order to discuss a trip Gilligan had taken to Iraq. Issues of WMD had come up then, but Kelly insisted that he provided no more than background.[8]

In the following two weeks, Kelly attended a series of meetings with MoD personnel in which he was questioned further about his meetings with Gilligan and other journalists. His managers and senior officials concluded (mistakenly, as it turned out) that, although Kelly might have been a corroboratory source for Gilligan's story, he was not Gilligan's primary source,[9] or if he was, Gilligan had seriously misrepresented him.

The issue of what to do with Kelly complicated things for Number 10. The spat with the BBC over Gilligan's report had focused increasingly on who Gilligan's source might be. Number 10 pressured the BBC to reveal its source, in order to verify that he was in a position to make the comments he had made about the dossier. Once they were aware that Kelly might have been the source, they stepped up pressure on the BBC, believing that the differences between Gilligan's and Kelly's stories would undermine the BBC's case. As Alastair Campbell wrote in his diary, "it would fuck Gilligan if that [Kelly] was his source."[10]

In any case, if they kept Kelly's identity secret and it still came out, Number 10 would be accused of a cover-up. Because Kelly had come forward before the FAC had wrapped up its inquiry, this question would be asked: Why had Number 10 not made his existence known to the committee?[11] It was felt that both the FAC and the ISC would have to be notified of Kelly's coming forward. If this were to be done, however, his name would have to be made public, given that the FAC met in public.

In the end, a decision was made both to release a statement that an unnamed official had come forward and to name Kelly to the chair of the ISC on an informal basis.[12] This statement was released on July 8. Simultaneously, it was decided that if a journalist were to ask whether Kelly was the source, press spokespersons would confirm it. They would not volunteer his name. Strangely, MoD press officers handed to journalists a statement set in a question and answer format. This statement narrowed the possible sources down to a very few people. Once journalists were aware that the source would be confirmed if a name were suggested, they simply ran through a list of names until they came to Kelly's name, and it was confirmed.

Despite the FAC's publishing their report regarding intelligence and the Iraq war on July 7, 2003,[13] they summoned Kelly to make an appearance. He also appeared before the ISC. In his testimony to the FAC, he insisted that there were inconsistencies between what he recalled from his meeting with Gilligan and what Gilligan had reported his source as saying. Kelly again suggested that either he was not actually Gilligan's primary source or that Gilligan had embellished his words.

Kelly was "thrown" (Clark 2003, 125:1), however, when two MPs, David Chidgey and Richard Ottaway, quoted a transcript of a telephone conversation he had had with *Newsnight*'s Susan Watts. Apparently, this transcript had been leaked by Andrew Gilligan, who had an interest in having Kelly reveal himself as the primary source.[14] In her transcript, Watts's source, who subsequently was confirmed to be Kelly, had made most of the allegations that Gilligan's source had made. Kelly had committed perjury when he denied that the words quoted were his. He had stated that Number 10 had been behind pressure to "word-smith" the dossier.[15]

The controversy came to a head when, three days after he appeared before the FAC (and two days after he appeared, in camera, before the ISC), Kelly killed himself. Tony Blair, already under fire over WMD and Iraq, called an inquiry into the circumstances behind Kelly's death, to be chaired by Lord Brian Hutton, a senior judge. The results of the Hutton Report, while finding against the BBC for lax editorial monitoring of correspondents' reports, did not find that anyone had been directly to blame for Kelly's death.

The inquiry placed an enormous amount of information in the public realm. This information gives an insight into the processes through which the dossier had been constructed. It is this information that is of interest for our purposes.

The Dilemma: Between Precision and Accessibility

When a public document is constructed, there is a tension between precision and accessibility. An intelligence document that focused solely on accuracy would risk being so obscure as to render it indigestible both to the media and to the public. The dossier was billed as an intelligence assessment of Iraq's WMD programs. Given that 10 Downing Street also had an interest in making the strongest case possible for their chosen course of action, it was almost inevitable that pressure, direct or otherwise, would be brought to bear to favor accessibility over precision. Whereas the language of an intelligence assessment will inevitably be rather dry and will include many caveats, a media-friendly document will include language that can be utilized by journalists and their editors.

Although the dossier was commissioned because Blair's administration believed that its assessments would help them make a case for war, we should remember that intelligence professionals, on the other hand, are not tasked with deciding upon courses of action. Ideally, an intelligence assessment is aimed at making the best possible report of the facts, given the (insufficient) information available. Raw intelligence information is not a sound basis for decision making. Instead, intelligence analysts must bring their experience and knowledge to bear, judge the reliability of sources and the veracity of information, and contextualize it in a stock of "collateral intelligence," to use Brian Jones's phrase (2003, 92:8). This perspective is accompanied by a strong standard in the intelligence community that favors objectivity and neutrality. As one U.S. careerist said of the Central Intelligence Agency (CIA), "The CIA is neither a policy nor a law-enforcement agency":

> Analysts do not have policy preferences. Analytic products do not lean in specific policy directions. The Agency produces intelligence free from political bias. . . .
> Remaining relevant but neutral is a noble goal, but not an easy one. The lure of conforming to the view of reality held by interested players in the [political] Branches is strong, although our culture in the Intelligence Community alerts us to resist. (Armstrong 2002)[16]

In the case of the British WMD dossier, the "lure of conforming" was particularly strong. There was a great deal of controversy over the dossier within the intelligence community. The JIC appears to have approved an almost complete version, but they did so in the face of concerns expressed by other intelligence participants over the intemperate use of language in the dossier's drafting. We suggest that this division reflected an ethical dilemma within the group caused by different conceptions of the appropriate form of accountability to be applied under the conditions of uncertainty and political sensitivity that characterized the situation.

The government's ambiguity about the purpose of the dossier placed intelligence officials in a difficult ethical position. If they were to cooperate fully, they would compromise their own standards of professional conduct. If they were to refuse to cooperate, they would have to defy the will of elected officials and those superordinates with responsibility toward them. This tension was even more complicated because of the consensus in the WMD section of British intelligence that Saddam Hussein was a problem.

In the run-up to the publication of the dossier, a series of drafts was distributed among intelligence staff, seeking advice and further information. In his judgment, Lord Hutton wrote,

> I consider that the possibility cannot be completely ruled out that the desire
> of the Prime Minister to have a dossier which, whilst consistent with the
> available intelligence, was as strong as possible in relation to the threat
> posed by Saddam Hussein's WMD, may have subconsciously influenced
> Mr Scarlett and the other members of the JIC to make the wording of the
> Dossier somewhat stronger than it would have been if it had been con-
> tained in a normal JIC assessment. (Hutton 2003, p. 320)

One way in which pressure was brought to bear was simply through the
returning of dossier drafts to the JIC when Downing Street was not satisfied.
In the two weeks before the publication of the dossier, officials at Number 10
made a series of suggestions for the strengthening of the dossier's language.
Significantly, on September 17, Alastair Campbell sent John Scarlett a six-
teen-point memo, making "drafting points" on the dossier.[17] Scarlett incorporated some of these points into another draft and refused to incorporate
others. Then, on September 19, Jonathan Powell (Downing Street's chief of
staff) requested that a claim—that Saddam Hussein would use WMD if he
felt threatened—be changed. According to Powell, this claim "backs up
the . . . argument that there is no CBW threat and we will only create one if
we attack him. I think you should redraft the para[graph]."[18] Scarlett amended
it to say, "As part of Iraq's military planning, Saddam is willing to use chemical and biological weapons."

Although it is entirely credible that the suggestions made on drafting had
no motive beyond improving the presentation of the intelligence assessment,
it is also possible that people in the JIC and in the intelligence community
responded to repeated drafting demands by making "the wording of the Dossier somewhat stronger" than it would otherwise have been. There is a thin
line between bargaining and negotiating over the use of language and doing
so over the substance of the document.

On September 11, 2002, an e-mail was sent to the intelligence agencies
from a member of the JIC assessment staff. In the e-mail that staff member
wrote: "No. 10 through the Chairman wants the document to be as strong as
possible within the bounds of available intelligence. This is therefore a last
(!) call for any items of intelligence that agencies think can and should be
included" (Hutton 2003, p. 132).

Although calls for information did reflect a wish to remain within "the
bounds of available information," it is likely that members of the intelligence community, when faced with such requests, presented information
that was more uncertain. It is evident that the 45–minute claim was one of
these pieces of information, and it was the government's use of it as a
headline-grabbing piece in the public and parliamentary debates over com-

mitments to taking military action in Iraq that eventually became the focal point of the Kelly affair.

In the analysis below, we will consider the role that accountability played in the approach by two prominent actors in the dossier-drafting process: John Scarlett and Brian Jones. Testimony they (and others) provided at the Hutton Inquiry provides insights into how differing impressions of what was expected of them as intelligence professionals impacted on their responses to the dilemmas posed by the Iraqi WMD dossier. Before considering the roles of Scarlett and Jones, we turn to a general account of expectations and accountability.

Expectations and Accountability

Much of the behavior of public administrators is driven by the need to effectively cope with expectations, and these are shaped by the accountability systems under which they work. Expectations—or at least the perceptions one develops about what others expect of oneself—can thus be seen as rational responses to the institutional settings within which an individual operates (Dubnick and Romzek 1993). They are rooted in three levels of rational calculation.

1. Given the goal orientation of institutional actors, a primary root of expectations lies in thinking about the consequences of certain actions, in the context of the public administrator's aims. Given the erratic social context in which public administrators operate, the development of expectations is obviously a complex affair (Klingner, Nalbandian, and Romzek 2002).
2. Expectations also will be a function of purely self-interested responses to environmental factors. The public administrator will respond to institutional signs suggesting either paths of least resistance or behavior most likely to lead to promotion and other forms of reward (Niskanen 1971; Blais and Dion 1991; Bendor and Moe 1985).
3. Expectations are set by the normative ideals that are set within the institutional or professional culture.[19] Culture, in this context, refers to agreed behavior norms not rooted in explicit threat-and-reward frameworks (Dolan 2002). It reflects, in short, membership of a moral community. The normative element of the individual's professional identity will be set, in part, by current behavior in and the basic principles of the institutions to which they belong. These "standards of performance," or "domain values" (Gardner, Csikszentmihalyi, and Damon 2001), can shape expectations in a profound way.

While individuals are not the moral slaves of their organizations, individual choice cannot fully be understood without comprehending the setting in which it takes place. The power of institutional contexts to shape expectations is profound.

The manner in which expectations might be shaped can be considered to be a function of a range of formal and informal accountability mechanisms. These mechanisms often have an overlapping and simultaneous impact on an individual's sense of what type of response or reaction others expect of him or her under given conditions. Moreover, the mechanisms are as likely to generate conflicting expectations as they are to produce consistent and reinforcing expectations (Dubnick and Romzek 1993). Much seems to depend on how the individual processes these expectations, and this issue has been the subject of a range of psychological theories and models from cognitive dissonance and groupthink (Janis and Mann 1977; Festinger 1957) to heuristics and other forms of second-order decision making (Sunstein and Ullmann-Margalit 1999).

The accountability mechanisms can be categorized into four broad types, each highlighting a different aspect of social identity (Dubnick 2003). Most often, accountability is associated with the idea of answerability, based on the premise that individual identity is determined by one's position in a structured (usually hierarchical) relationship. Liability, a second form of accountability, sees individual identity rooted in more-formalized expectations developed through rules, contracts, legislation, and similar relationships based on legalistic standing. Still another form of accountability is associated with role-based expectations. Such roles foster blameworthiness as a basis for shaping and directing one's behavior. Finally, accountability expectations are derived from an individual's perceived status in a community where attributions come into play. Being characterized as powerful and influential, as a successful or a failed entrepreneur, or, importantly, as a person in pursuit of truth or as a person in pursuit of results, can have consequences for what one regards as relevant expectations.

The strategies an individual develops in order to cope with the multiple, diverse, and often conflicting sets of expectations that emerge from these accountability mechanisms are central to determining both specific reactions and one's general approach to tasks. Often, within the highly institutionalized contexts of many professions, some parameters for strategic choices are set through the formalization of expectations (Stinchcombe 2001) or expectations embedded in established relationships (Granovetter 1985). This is most evident in military organizations, for example, where accountability systems are well defined and severely limit the range of choices an individual might make. Soldiers or sailors of given ranks and skills (attribution) are obligated under law (liability) to follow orders (answerability) in accordance with their roles in fulfilling missions (blameworthiness). Violation of a set of expectations can lead to undesirable consequences, from professional embarrassment and stigmatization to courts martial and dishonorable discharge. Where dilemmas arise is in situations where the perceived expectations might conflict—for example, where the orders being issued might lead to mission failure—thereby putting the individual in a circumstance that calls for making ethical as well as strategic choices.

As civil servants and intelligence professionals, those who work for intelligence agencies face their own problematic configurations of accountability-based pressures. In part these are derived from the inherent conflict among the demands for deference of the civil service to the political will of elected officials and those standards of integrity and appropriate behavior associated with being a member of the community of intelligence professionals. The Hutton Inquiry was itself a direct consequence of the efforts of one particular individual—David Kelly—attempting to deal with these inherent conflicts. On the one hand, it was an investigation into the suicide of a member of the intelligence community who, at the time of his death, was under scrutiny for having violated civil service rules regarding unauthorized statements to the press. On the other hand, we can only speculate what motivated Kelly to assume such risks, but it is likely to have involved a sense that the norms of the profession had been violated by those who permitted the dossier to be manipulated for political purposes.

Despite its roots and focus in the actions of a single individual, David Kelly, the Hutton Inquiry also serves as a source of insight about the role of accountability and ethical choices within the intelligence community. For intelligence community professionals such as Scarlett and Jones, accountability mechanisms and the expectations they generate are not merely the source of dilemmas, they are also the starting points for coping strategies and actions used to deal with the resulting problems by allowing for some degree of freedom in selecting an approach to dilemmas. Our focus is on the normative frameworks that motivate them to make the choices they do in the face of the dilemmas that confront them.

Thick and Thin Accountability

The attribution thick and thin has been in vogue among social scientists for several decades, tracing back at least to its use by Clifford Geertz[20] who revolutionized (and, some would argue, saved) the study of cultures by establishing the methodological foundation for "thick description" (Geertz 1974; Shankman 1984). It was perhaps inevitable that the terms would be applied more substantively to social phenomena by attaching the adjectives to key concepts in ways that allow us to make meaningful differentiations to otherwise ambiguous ideas. It seemed most relevant in those cases where the distinctions of more or less would just not do. Rather, in each instance the somewhat fuzzy dichotomy of thick and thin is applied to the focal concept as a means of making distinctions that are simultaneously based on differences of degree as well as quality.

In many cases, thinness is related to the minimal or core conditions for the concept's realization. Jon Elster's "thin rationality" (1983), for example, represents the core process of making reasoned choices but does not address the reasons for those choices—which is the factor that leads to "thick rationality" (Yee 1996; Jones 2002). For Michael Walzer (1994, ch. 1), "thin morality" is "core" because it is universal rather than particular, broadly recognizable rather than specifically identified with the varied and distinct social circumstances from which it is drawn. In that sense, it is thin in the minimalist sense of being derived from various thick (maximalized) social, political, and economic conditions (cf. Habermas 1998). Benjamin Barber (1984) posits a view of electoral-based liberal democracy as thin in the sense of being a weak version of a more robust communitarian ideal based on active engagement and participation in local affairs.

An alternative perspective on the thick/thin distinction has emerged in applications where the intent is to differentiate between ideas associated with universalist, generalized, and abstracted principles (thin) and those emerging from local and particular relationships (thick). The distinction has been put to good use by Habermas and Rawls, and more recently by Avishai Margalit (2002), who posited thick relationships as the domain of ethics and thin relationships as the arena for morality. "Thick relations are grounded in attributes such as parent, friend, lover, fellow-countryman. . . . Thin relations, on the other hand, are backed by the attribute of being human" (pp. 7–8). Thick relationships are based on caring, while thin relations are based on rights (pp. 32–40).

The concept of accountability can also benefit from reflection on the thick/thin distinction. There is a need for caution, however, since the idea of accountability has become so distorted in recent years that one is likely to base the ideas of thick and thin accountability on incorrect grounds. The contemporary view of accountability has been narrowed to a point where it is regarded as synonymous with answerability; one result of this is that the expansion and extension of answerability is mistakenly regarded as an enhancement of accountability.

This cautionary point is critical to our distinction. It was articulated most recently by Michael Harmon in his critique of the major debates over administrative responsibility that has defined American public administrative thought in the twentieth century (Harmon 1995, 1996). Harmon contends that underlying the divisions represented by those debates—between Carl J. Friedrich and Herman Finer in the early 1940s (Friedrich 1940; Finer 1941), Herbert Simon and Dwight Waldo after World War II (Simon 1948; Simon, Drucker, and Waldo 1952; Waldo 1952), and most recently represented by the contrasting positions of John Burke and Terry Cooper (Burke 1986; Cooper 1998)—is a common rationalist perspective on administrative responsibility that assumes it is necessary to counter, deny, or suppress the personal responsibility of the public administrator in favor of deference to the authoritative priorities of the collective will. Harmon posits that the rationalist emphasis on answerability (to authority) and efforts to deny the human urge to engage in the making of responsible action results in the pathological behavior associated with modern bureaucracy and the administrative state.

Shifting the focus of discussion from the level of the individual administrator to systems of governance,[21] similar observations can be made for the concept of accountability. Most discussions of accountability have focused almost exclusively on a narrow ahistorical view that relies almost entirely on answerability. While answerability is an important aspect of accountability in its common, everyday use, it is a conceptually thin version of the term that reduces it to a form of generic behavior that is meaningless out of context. Accountability-as-answerability is merely (at its core) account-giving behavior (Mulgan 2000). As such, acts of accountability have been effectively articulated and scrutinized as linguistic performatives—that is, as statements that constitute actions in the form of reporting, making excuses, explaining, justifying acts, apologizing, and so on.

These performatives have no value unto themselves—they are merely the vehicles by which meaning is carried in a social relationship that demands or warrants account giving. They are functionally valuable but have no inherent content, and any meaningfulness they possess is derived from the context—the stage—in which they are performed.

It is this thin notion of accountability that dominates most discussions today, whatever the context or subject. In both the public and private sectors, the idea of being accountable is expressed almost exclusively in terms of being answerable or responsive to some entity—whether to specific officials, to stakeholders, or to the general population in the form of voters or consumers. The question of what one is answerable for now runs the range from justice and transparency to appropriate behavior and performance. Within this more general context, the key issue regarding accountability is expressed in terms of answerability as well—that is, whether the degree of answerability is sufficient. The typical assessment is usually negative, reflecting what seems to be an ever higher and broader set of expectations. As a consequence, there is a continuous and insatiable appetite for even more accountability. The result, however, is not a thickening of accountability, but an expansion and extension (a thickening, if you will) of answerability.

In the development of the dossier, and its role in the run-up to war, we regard Brian Jones as having made his decisions based upon thin principles, and we regard John Scarlett as having made his decisions based upon his relationships; thereby Scarlett's decisions were founded on a thick ethic.

The thick and thin distinction here reflects differing high-level ethical dispositions. These dispositions are, in part, rooted in the differing positions of players in the institutional framework. In our approach to conceptions of thick and thin in public administrators, we follow the definitions provided by Habermas, Rawls, and Margalit. That is, the distinction is between decisions and choices formed from thin, abstracted principles and those drawn from thick contexts and relationships. However, we also acknowledge, as Walzer makes explicit, that situation and context drive the thin as well as the thick normative dispositions.[22] This is most obvious within closed institutional frameworks, such as those to be found in the intelligence organizations. In these organizations, one's position and the peer group that one deals with can have a major influence on one's normative approach to work.

Normative dispositions are of course not without consequence. We suggest that the dispositions fundamentally shape the manner in which a person's expectations about accountability are shaped. The four categories of accountability we set out above—answerability, liability, blameworthiness, and attributions—must be defined and prioritized by the thinking agent. We suggest that the thick/thin distinction makes clear the different approaches that Jones and Scarlett took toward accountability. In short, the thick/thin distinction provides an instructive frame through which individual interpretations of accountability might be understood.

Let us return to Jones and Scarlett in more detail. In the following brief sections, we will describe the normative approaches that Jones and Scarlett took and then say how their decisions can be more clearly understood through the thick/thin frame.

Brian Jones

In the run-up to the dossier's publication, experts in Brian Jones's unit expressed concern about the language used in the drafts that they were reviewing. Jones called a meeting on September 19 with an intelligence operative, members of Jones's unit, and David Kelly. His aim was to reconcile concerns about elements of the dossier, including the 45–minute claim, with Kelly's general comments approving of it (Jones 2003, 73.12; 116.4–17). When Jones expressed concerns to his line manager, he was informed that "further intelligence" had been received. This intelligence corroborated the claims he was concerned about. However, he was not allowed to see this intelligence. His director had not seen it either. Jones emphasized the significance of this: "I would always have put a caveat on a conclusion which was based on something I had not seen" (Jones 2003, 82.10–84.10).

Given his concerns, Jones wrote to his manager and outlined his issues. He referred especially to the executive summary, which he argued was stronger than merited by intelligence.

> Although we have no problem with a judgement based on intelligence that Saddam attaches great importance to possessing WMD we have not seen the intelligence that "shows" this to be the case. Nor have we seen intelligence that "shows" he does not regard them only as a weapon of last resort, although our judgement is that it would be sensible to assume he might use them in a number of other scenarios. The intelligence we have seen indicates rather than "shows" that Iraq has been planning to conceal its WMD capabilities, and it would be a reasonable to assume that he would do this.[23]

His concerns, though raised with the JIC, were put aside because it was judged that the general context of the evidence, including the unseen "further evidence," merited these claims being placed in the executive summary (Hutton 2003, p. 121). At this point, it seems that John Scarlett, the head of the JIC, "was taking on-board the comment from Mr Campbell but not necessarily taking on-board the comment from the Defence Intelligence Staff" (Cragg 2003, 27.8–12).

The JIC approved the final draft of the dossier.[24] However, the importance of Brian Jones's memo cannot be underestimated. As Mary Dejevsky wrote in the *Independent*, "Jones gave the lie to the insistence of senior officials that there was no dissent in the ranks of the intelligence service" (2004). In an article he wrote for the *Independent*, Jones contended:

> It is clear from the evidence to the Hutton inquiry that the experts of the Defence Intelligence Staff (DIS) who dealt with chemical and biological warfare, including those working directly with me, had problems with some aspects of what was being said in various drafts of the Dossier that was published on 24 September 2002. (Jones 2004)

Dejevsky (2004) wrote, "The leading experts were in one department, their objections to the lack of caveats in the Dossier were widely shared, and they were overruled by those with less expertise and by the politicians."

Jones holds firmly to the view that considerations of political advantage—or even considerations of the pressure that politicians come under—should not have any bearing on the work of intelligence analysts. His formal expression of concern was undoubtedly motivated by a wish to see the DIS avoid criticism if no weapons were found. Not only did he regard himself as liable for sound intelligence analysis, he also attributed the characteristics of researchers both to himself and to his team. That is, his job was to provide the best analysis possible no matter what the policy consequences. In isolating himself from policy, Jones was also isolating himself from a narrow conception of answerability. His job was not to assist his superiors to achieve their aims; it was, in a sense, to be answerable to the truth.[25] He regarded himself as answerable for WMD intelligence analysis, and he made it clear that blame could not be attached to his department for any failure at a higher level to account for their judgments.

His testimony to the Hutton Inquiry reveals an attachment to thin principles of public-service work. This work is not mere function for Jones. In the course of one's work, one comes under an obligation to take responsibility for methods and means, even when the ends are justifiable. Jones's outlook was shaped by a thin set of norms. His self-perceived role centered on the provision of information; the circumstances under which the information was to be provided, or the consequences of the language used, were of minor, if any, relevance to his job. This should not be mistaken for mere pedantry. When Lord Hutton asked Jones if his concerns were "matters of language," Jones answered that "they were about language but language is the means by which we communicate an assessment so they were also about the assessment" (Jones 2003, 76.4–15).

Of course, Jones was, by some distance, isolated from political decision making, and even from the JIC. As a result, his attachment to strict factual accuracy, and the political checks that come along with that, was easier to achieve. For those who were closer to policy making, attachments seemed more complicated.

John Scarlett

In terms of relations with politicians, Scarlett was in a much more sensitive position than was Jones. His job was to assess intelligence information and then present it to the prime minister. The problem for a person in his position is that he is inherently at the mercy of politicians' policy agendas. He cannot avoid the tension between his professional responsibilities and answerabiliity to politicians, with whom he is in daily contact.

Formally, the JIC had ownership of the dossier. As Alastair Campbell wrote to Scarlett in a memo dated September 9, 2002, the dossier "must be, and be seen to be, the work of you and your team, and . . . its credibility depends fundamentally upon that."[26] Alastair Campbell denied that he had brought any undue influence to bear on Scarlett or the intelligence services over the dossier. However, a series of e-mails and memos from Campbell, chief of staff Jonathan Powell, and others did seem to bring pressure to bear on Scarlett regarding the presentational elements of the dossier. As we have noted, Lord Hutton expressed concern that the number of e-mails and memos on this issue "may have subconsciously influenced Mr. Scarlett and the other members of the JIC to make the wording of the dossier somewhat stronger than it would have been if it had been contained in a normal JIC assessment" (Hutton 2003, p. 320). Add this to the last-minute change prompted by Jonathan Powell's e-mail to Scarlett. A deadline for comments on the report had been set for 15:00 on September 19, but Powell's e-mail arrived forty-five minutes after this. In accepting the proposed change, Scarlett had accepted political advice without his colleagues' explicit say-so.

Regarding the 45–minute claim, Scarlett denied that its prominence was a result of pressure from Downing Street. Instead, it was based on reliable intelligence:

> In this particular case, it was judged straight away that the intelligence was consistent with established JIC judgments on the command, control and logistical arrangements and capabilities of the Iraqi armed forces and their experience and capabilities in the area of use of CP ammunitions. It brought an additional detail because for the first time in our reporting it gave a particular time, gave some precision. (Scarlett 2003b, 48.24–49.6)

Scarlett acknowledged that Brian Jones's department in DIS had expertise in this area, but he said that they were not the "lead branch" involved with the 45–minute assessment (Scarlett, 2003a, 109.1–8).

As we have noted, Scarlett's institutional position was far more complicated than that of Jones. Jones's task was simply to provide an analysis of intelligence material. Policy making lay outside his remit. Scarlett, on the other hand, was concerned with the presentation of the report to the public. Nevertheless, we should be clear that the JIC's task, as with the CIA analyst's insight quoted above, was to provide government with intelligence assessments that might assist it in formulating policies. Scarlett seems to have been walking on thin ice in assisting the government with presentation, swinging close to overstating the case for war.

Scarlett was, it seems, willing to accept that changes were required in order for the dossier to be presented to the public. We do not question that the JIC and drafters of the dossier took language seriously in the manner that Jones did. However, they may have sought to balance the precision that Jones sought with a willingness to "tighten" language. The boundary between a concern for presentation and making a case was extremely fine.

Scarlett's allegiance lay with ministers as well as with the principles of intelligence. Although Jones agreed with the war, he did not allow this to override his professional attachment to precision in the articulation of intelligence analysis. Scarlett's normative approach to the dossier was probably characterized by a thicker set of norms than those of Jones. They were rooted, to some extent, in specific relationships with policy makers, especially in the formation of judgments contained in the executive summary.

For Scarlett, accountability lay toward a simple conception of answerability. He regarded himself as being partly answerable to his superiors, rather than to thin principles. As such, he attributed a bridging role to himself, between the intelligence community and the prime minister. In the case of the dossier, the bridging role was between himself and the public. It is much more difficult to attach oneself to thin norms when the very substance of one's work involves a series of negotiations and compromises between various, differently motivated parties.

Conclusion

We do not claim that John Scarlett's decisions reflected weaker normative reasoning or a greater disregard for normative reason than did those of Brian Jones. Instead, we conclude that his thick conception of accountability in his role is a reasonable expression of the expectations that he worked under. Jones's community focused on a thin conception of allegiance to truth and reasonable analysis. For them, concrete relationships, political strategies, and even conceptions of the good should not have a bearing on information processing. Instead, their conclusions were simply a function of experience, good judgment and peer review.

Although we place a strong emphasis on environment, we do not deny that individual moral agency is a factor in the formation of normative dispositions and in perceptions of accountability. The extent to which autonomous agency was a factor in the decision-making processes of Jones and Scarlett is open to question. What is certainly the case is that they provide strong examples of the relationship between accountability, normative decision making, and institutional position.

The thick/thin distinction is important to setting out how these elements interact. Normative dispositions are apparent in public administration, as they are in all social interactions. When public administration is in direct contact with policy making, however, the various positions and dispositions can lead to the creation of profound tensions. The events leading up the war in Iraq are, of course, extreme examples of a general phenomenon. They are also a reminder that, no matter what formal structures are in place, success and failure rest with individual judgment. And individual judgment is a matter of ethical self-definition.

Epilogue

On the July 14, 2004, a committee of privy counsellors chaired by Lord Butler of Brockwell, published a report (*Butler Report* 2004) on WMD intelligence. The committee was charged by Parliament "to investigate the accuracy of intelligence on Iraqi WMD up to March 2003, and to examine any discrepancies between the intelligence gathered, evaluated and used by the Government before the conflict, and between that intelligence and what has been discovered by the Iraq survey group since the end of the conflict . . ." (Introduction, para. 1).

The *Butler Report* concluded that there had been serious failures in the methods of intelligence gathering and in the presentation of intelligence to the government and to Parliament. The report does not find fault with the JIC's integrity before the publication of the September 2002 dossier. The committee found that it was wrong for the JIC to have assumed "ownership" of the dossier, determining that it "was a mistaken judgement for the dossier to be so closely associated with the JIC." Nevertheless, they explicitly noted that the decision to do so was "collective" and "one for which the Chairman [John Scarlett] of the JIC should not bear personal responsibility" (ch. 5, para. 469).

Significantly, the *Butler Report* highlighted a major shortcoming in the way the September dossier was constructed. Comparing the dossier with the intelligence reports on which they were based, the committee determined that the JIC report had not reflected the uncertainties, caveats and other limitations of the available intelligence on Iraqi WMD (ch. 5, para. 333–41).

> . . . in translating material from JIC assessments into the dossier, warnings were lost about the limited intelligence base on which some aspects of these assessments were being made. The Government would have seen these warnings in the original JIC assessments and taken them into account in reading them. But the public, through reading the dossier, would not have known of them. (ch. 5, para. 464)

Given this, there are grounds for questioning John Scarlett's judgment in permitting the caveats of the intelligence assessment to be lost between drafts. However, as we explain above, the reasoning behind the JIC's doing this, despite objections from elsewhere in the intelligence community, may lie in thick moral judgments, rather than sinister motives. That Scarlett's moral judgments may have been mistaken should not lead us to conclude that he was self-consciously doing wrong.

Notes

[The authors' original citations to the website www.the-hutton-inquiry.org.uk were to individual url documents, which were subsequently placed under the Hearing Transcript page of the Hutton Inquiry Web Site. —Ed.]

1. The following terms apply in British parliamentary politics: the government is the majority party in Parliament; No. 10 Downing Street (Downing St.; No. 10) is the prime minister's office, though this term is sometimes employed to denote the informal executive power structures surrounding the prime minister; the cabinet is the council of ministers, from which policy is generally initiated; Parliament is the supreme power in Britain. It is divided between the lower and upper houses—the House of Commons and the House of Lords. Both houses work under a party-whip system, where party membership generally determines the voting records of members—this principle is highly regulated and rebellion is not taken lightly. The informal power structures of the Commons are in a constant tension between the ordinary members and the executive. MPs generally demand a greater say in policy formation, while (not least because internal division tends to be electorally damaging for a party) the executive tends to demand obedience to the whip system.

2. A second dossier was published in February 2003. It quickly came to light that parts of this dossier had been plagiarized from a twelve-year-old Ph.D. dissertation.

3. The Cabinet Office is the ministry that manages the relationship between the government of the day and the administrative arms of the state.

4. The dossier, "Iraq's Weapons of Mass Destruction," and all other material presented to the Hutton Inquiry, is openly available; see www.the-hutton-inquiry.org.uk; the dossier is available at www.the-hutton-inquiry.org.uk/content/evidence-lists/evidence-dos.htm.

5. The vote was not directly over whether or not Britain should go to war. However, the government presented a motion seeking power to deal with Iraq and rebel MPs moved to attach an amendment, seeking to commit the government to action only in the event of UN approval. This, in effect, set up a vote on the government's policy. There was a vote giving Blair power to invade on March 18, two days before the invasion took place.

6. Transcripts of this and other broadcasts relevant to the inquiry are available at www.the-hutton-inquiry.org.uk/content/evidence-lists/evidence-bbc.htm.

7. Notably one by Susan Watts on BBC television's *Newsnight* analysis program.

8. Letter from Kelly to his line manager, Bryan Wells, available at www.the-hutton-inquiry.org.uk/content/mod/mod_1_0019t00022.pdf. . It should be noted that Kelly was probably not being completely forthright. A transcript of a phone conversation he held with Susan Watts (available at www.the-hutton-inquiry.org.uk/content/bbc/bbc_1_0058t00063.pdf) reveals that he was willing to discuss the dossier. This confirms Gilligan's notes of the meeting, although Gilligan's notes were contradictory, and were judged unreliable by Lord Hutton

9. In his evidence to the FAC (entered in evidence to the Hutton Inquiry; available at www.the-hutton-inquiry.org.uk/content/fac/fac_2_0132t00167.pdf), Gilligan claimed that he had a primary source and had contacts with three others on the issue.

10. Alastair Campbell's diary, July 4, 2003, submitted in evidence to the Hutton Inquiry, available at www.the-hutton-inquiry.org.uk/content/cab/cab_39_0001t00002.pdf.

11. Reflecting general press and public cynicism about the Blair government, this was a concern despite the fact that news of Kelly's coming forward did not seem to reach the higher levels of government until after the FAC's inquiry had concluded its investigations.

12. It appears that the two meetings mentioned here, on July 7 and 8, were not minuted. The information is drawn from a note made for the record by Sir David Omand, the Security and Intelligence Officer in the Cabinet Office, on July 21, three days after Kelly's death (Hutton 2003, p. 38–39).

13. The report, "The Decision to Go to War in Iraq," was submitted as evidence in the Hutton Inquiry, available at www.the-hutton-inquiry.org.uk/content/fac/fac_3_0001t00104.pdf.

14. Revealed in e-mail from Andrew Gilligan to Greg Simpson, July 14, 2003, submitted into evidence to Hutton inquiry; available at www.the-hutton-inquiry.org.uk/content/fac/fac_6_0001t00003.pdf.

15. Transcript of Susan Watts's telephone conversation with David Kelly; available at www.the-hutton-inquiry.org.uk/content/sjw/sjw_1_0037t00043.pdf.

16. On the traditional and changing professional models for conducting intelligence, see Ward (2002) and Medina (2002).

17. Submitted into evidence to Hutton Inquiry, available at www.the-hutton-inquiry.org.uk/content/cab/cab_11_0070t00071.pdf.

18. E-mail from Jonathan Powell to John Scarlett, submitted in evidence to the Hutton Inquiry; available at www.the-hutton-inquiry.org.uk/content/cab/cab_11_0103.pdf. Don McIntyre, chief political correspondent of the *Independent*— he had argued that Saddam would only deploy WMD if attacked.

19. This perspective is expressed in a number of ways in studies of public administration norms and values; for example, see Denhardt and Denhardt (2000); Brewer, Selden, and Facer (2000); Pfiffner (1999); Crewson (1997); and Bouckaert (2001).

20. Geertz refers to an earlier use of thick and thin description by Gilbert Ryle; see http://www.geocities.com/comm6026/cult.html.

21. The relationship between responsibility and accountability is an ambiguous one in the literature. While some analysts treat the terms as synonymous, many more regard accountability as a component of responsibility or subordinated to responsibility. Dubnick's perspective, elaborated elsewhere, regards accountability as a central idea in defining modern governance, thus establishing it as the pinnacle (genus) for a class of subordinate concepts (species) of which responsibility is (an albeit important) one. See Dubnick (1998, 2002).

22. It should be noted that this was always implicit in the works of Rawls and Habermas, but has come increasingly to the fore over time.

23. Memo from Ministry of Defence official (Jones) to MA/DCDI, and so on, subnmitted as evidence to Hutton Inquiry; available at www.the-hutton-inquiry.org.uk/content/mod/mod_22_0001t00002.pdf.

24. It does seem, in actual fact, that John Scarlett had made amendments to the dossier after the final meeting of the JIC. We address this below.

25. Truth, that is, in the sense of an accurate appraisal of various facts about the object being studied.

26. Note of meeting from Campbell to Scarlett, September 9, 2002, submitted in evidence to Hutton Inquiry, available at www.the-hutton-inquiry.org.uk/content/cab/ cab_6_0002t00004.pdf.

References

Armstrong, Fulton T. 2002. "Sorting Out 'National Interests': Ways to Make Analysis Relevant but Not Prescriptive." *Studies in Intelligence* 46, no. 3. Unclassified edition. Available at http://www.odci.gov/csi/studies/vol46no3/article05.html.
Barber, Benjamin R. 1984. *Strong Democracy: Participatory Politics for a New Age.* Berkeley: University of California Press.
Bendor, Jonathan, and Moe, Terry M. 1985. "An Adaptive Model of Bureaucratic Politics." *American Political Science Review* 79, no. 3: 755–74.
Blair, Tony. 2002. Address to the House of Commons upon publication of the dossier, "Iraq's Weapons of Mass Destruction," September 24, 2002. *Hansard Debates,* 6th series, 21st volume of session 2001–2, column 3.
Blais, Andre, and Dion, Stephane, eds. 1991. *The Budget-Maximizing Bureaucrat.* Pittsburgh: University of Pittsburgh Press.
Bouckaert, Geert. 2001. "Pride and Performance in the Public Service: Some Patterns of Analysis." *International Review of Administrative Sciences* 67, no. 1: 15–27.
Brewer, Gene A.; Selden, Sally Coleman; and Facer, Rex L. II. 2000. "Individual Conceptions of Public Service Motivation." *Public Administration Review* 60, no. 3: 254–64.
Burke, John P. 1986. *Bureaucratic Responsibility.* Baltimore: Johns Hopkins University Press.
Butler Report. 2004. London: Stationery Office, 2004. Available at www.butlerreview.org.uk/report (accessed October 22, 2004).
Cabinet Office, United Kingdom. 2001. *National Intelligence Machinery,* 2d ed. Stationery Office (September).
Clark, John. 2003. *Testimony to the Hutton Inquiry.* Investigation into the Circumstances Surrounding the Death of Dr. David Kelly (Hutton Inquiry). August 27. 103:1–143:13. Available at www.the-hutton-inquiry.org.uk/content/transcripts/hearing-trans21.htm (accessed October 22, 2004).
Cooper, Terry L. 1998. *The Responsible Administrator: An Approach to Ethics for the Administrative Role,* 4th ed. San Francisco: Jossey-Bass.
Cragg, Anthony John. 2003. *Testimony to the Hutton Inquiry.* Investigation into the Circumstances Surrounding the Death of Dr. David Kelly (Hutton Inquiry). September 15. 11:11–57:4. Available at www.the-hutton-inquiry.org.uk/content/transcripts/hearing-trans31.htm (accessed October 22, 2004).
Crewson, Philip E. 1997. "Public-Service Motivation: Building Empirical Evidence of Incidence and Effect." *Journal of Public Administration and Theory* 7, no. 4: 499–519.
Dejevsky, Mary. 2004. "Dr Jones' Warning Memo May Well Turn Out to Have Been a Far-Sighted Move." *Independent,* February 4. p. 7.
Denhardt, Robert B., and Vinzant Denhardt, Janet. 2000. "The New Public Service: Serving Rather than Steering." *Public Administration Review* 60, no. 6: 549–59.
Dolan, Julie. 2002. "The Budget-Minimizing Bureaucrat? Empirical Evidence from the Senior Executive Service." *Public Administration Review* 62, no. 1: 42–50.
Dubnick, Melvin J. 1998. "Clarifying Accountability: An Ethical Theory Framework." In *Public Sector Ethics Finding and Implementing Values,* ed. Charles Sampford,

Noel Preston, and C-A Bois, pp. 68–81. Leichhardt, NSW, Australia: Federation Press/Routledge.

————. 2002. "Seeking Salvation for Accountability." Paper presented at American Political Science Association, August 29–September 1, Boston.

————. 2003. "Accountability and Ethics: Reconsidering the Relationships." *International Journal of Organization Theory and Behavior* 6, no. 3: 405–41.

Dubnick, Melvin J., and Romzek, Barbara S. 1993. "Accountability and the Centrality of Expectations in American Public Administration." In *Research in Public Administration*, ed. J. L. Perry, p. 37. Greenwich, CT: JAI Press.

Dyke, Gregory. 2003. *Testimony to the Hutton Inquiry.* Investigation into the Circumstances Surrounding the Death of Dr. David Kelly (Hutton Inquiry). September 15. 126:1–185:16. Available at www.the-hutton-inquiry.org.uk/content/transcripts/hearing-trans32.htm (accessed October 22, 2004).

Elster, Jon. 1983. *Sour Grapes: Studies in the Subversion of Rationality.* Cambridge: Cambridge University Press.

Festinger, Leon. 1957. *A Theory of Cognitive Dissonance.* Stanford, CA: Stanford University Press.

Finer, Herman. 1941. "Administrative Responsibility in Democratic Government." *Public Administration Review* 1, no. 4: 335–50.

Fountain, Nigel, and Smith, Sarah A. 2003. "Obituary. David Kelly: Biological Weapons Expert with a Reputation for Thoroughness." *Guardian*, July 19: 21.

Friedrich, Carl J. 1940. "Public Policy and the Nature of Administrative Responsibility." In *Public Policy: A Yearbook of the Graduate School of Public Administration*, ed. C.J. Friedrich and E.S. Mason, pp. 3–24. Cambridge, MA: Harvard University Press.

Gardner, Howard; Csikszentmihalyi, Mihaly; and Damon, William. 2001. *Good Work: When Excellence and Ethics Meet.* New York: Basic Books.

Geertz, Clifford. 1974. *The Interpretation of Cultures: Selected Essays.* New York: Basic Books.

Granovetter, Mark. 1985. "Economic Action and Social Structure: The Problem of Embeddedness." *American Journal of Sociology* 91, no. 3: 481–510.

Habermas, Jürgen. 1998. *The Inclusion of the Other: Studies in Political Theory*, trans. C. Cronin and P. De Greiff. Cambridge, MA: MIT Press.

Harmon, Michael M. 1995. *Responsibility as Paradox: A Critique of Rational Discourse on Government.* Thousand Oaks, CA: SAGE.

————. 1996. "Harmon Responds." *Public Administration Review* 556, no. 6: 604–10.

Hutton, Brian. 2003. "The Hutton Report: Return to an Address of the Honorable the House of Commons Dated 28th January 2004 for the Report of the Inquiry into the Circumstances Surrounding the Death of Dr. David Kelly C.M.G." London: Stationery Office. Available at www.the-hutton-inquiry.org.uk/content/report/index.htm (accessed October 22, 2004).

Janis, Irving L., and Mann, Leon. 1977. *Decision Making: A Psychological Analysis of Conflict, Choice, and Commitment.* New York: Free Press.

Jones, Brian F.G. 2003. *Testimony to the Hutton Inquiry.* Investigation into the Circumstances Surrounding the Death of Dr. David Kelly (Hutton Inquiry). September 3. 56:7–94:11; 115:1–139:2. Available at www.the-hutton-inquiry.org.uk/content/transcripts/hearing-trans28.htm (accessed October 22, 2004) and www.the-hutton-inquiry.org.uk/content/transcripts/hearing-trans29.htm (accessed October 22, 2004).

————. 2004. "There Was a Lack of Substantive Evidence. . . . We Were Told There Was Intelligence We Could Not See." *Independent*, February 4, p. 7.

Jones, Bryan D. 2002. "Bounded Rationality and Public Policy: Herbert A. Simon and the Decision Foundation of Collective Choice." *Policy Sciences* 35, no. 3: 269–84.

Klingner, Donald E.; Nalbandian, John; and Romzek, Barbara S. 2002. "Politics, Administration, and Markets: Conflicting Expectations and Accountability." *American Review of Public Administration* 32, no. 2: 117–44.

Margalit, Avishai. 2002. *The Ethics of Memory*. Cambridge, MA: Harvard University Press.

Medina, Carmen A. 2002. "The Coming Revolution in Intelligence Analysis: What to Do When Traditional Models Fail." *Studies in Intelligence* 46, no. 3. Unclassified edition. Available at http://www.odci.gov/csi/studies/vol46no3/article03.html.

Mulgan, Richard. 2000. "'Accountability': An Ever-Expanding Concept?" *Public Administration* 78, no. 3: 555–73.

Niskanen, William A. 1971. *Bureaucracy and Representative Government*. Chicago: Aldine Atherton.

Pfiffner, James P. 1999. "The Public Service Ethic in the New Public Personnel Systems." *Public Personnel Management* 28, no. 4: 541–55.

Scarlett, John McLeod. 2003a. *Testimony to the Hutton Inquiry*. Investigation into the Circumstances Surrounding the Death of Dr. David Kelly (Hutton Inquiry). September 23. 75:14–194:24. Available at www.the-hutton-inquiry.org.uk/content/transcripts/hearing-trans41.htm (accessed October 22, 2004).

————.2003b. *Testimony to the Hutton Inquiry*. Investigation into the Circumstances Surrounding the Death of Dr. David Kelly (Hutton Inquiry). August 26. 29:11–157:5. Available at www.the-hutton-inquiry.org.uk/content/transcripts/hearing-trans18.htm (accessed October 22, 2004) and www.the-hutton-inquiry.org.uk/content/transcripts/hearing-trans19.htm (accessed October 22, 2004).

Shankman, Paul. 1984. "The Thick and the Thin: On the Interpretive Program of Clifford Geertz." *Current Anthropology* 25, no. 3 (June): 261–80.

Simon, Herbert A. 1948. "The Administrative State"(a book review). *Journal of Politics* 10, no. 4 (November): 843–45.

Simon, Herbert A.; Drucker, Peter F.; and Waldo, Dwight. 1952. "'Development of Theory of Democratic Administration': Replies and Comments." *American Political Science Review* 46 (June 2): 494–503.

Stinchcombe, Arthur L. 2001. *When Formality Works: Authority and Abstraction in Law and Organizations*. Chicago: University of Chicago Press.

Sunstein, Cass R., and Ullmann-Margalit, Edna. 1999. "Second-Order Decisions." *Ethics* 110, no. 1: 5–31.

Waldo, Dwight. 1952. "Development of Theory of Democratic Administration." *American Political Science Review* 46, no. 1: 81–103.

Walzer, Michael. 1994. *Thick and Thin: Moral Argument at Home and Abroad*. Notre Dame, IN: University of Notre Dame Press.

Ward, Steven R. 2002. "Counterpoint to 'The Coming Revolution in Intelligence Analysis': Evolution Beats Revolution in Analysis." *Studies in Intelligence* 46, no. 3. Unclassified edition. Available at http://www.odci.gov/csi/studies/vol46no3/article04.html.

White, Michael; Watt, Nicholas; and Wintour, Patrick. 2002. "Blair Makes His Case as US Puts Squeeze on Iraq." *Guardian*, September 25: 1.

Yee, Albert S. 1996. "The Causal Effects of Ideas on Policies." *International Organization* 50, no. 1: 69–108.

_____ **Part 3**

Market Forces That Compromise
Administrative Ethics

_____ 8

Public Ethics and the New Managerialism:
An Axiomatic Theory

H. George Frederickson

Consider some of the primary characteristics of the new managerialism recipe:

- First, sharply reduce governmental regulations and red tape;
- then mix this with privatizing and contracting out many public functions thought heretofore to be primarily governmental;
- now reduce significantly the directly employed governmental workforce;
- do not train a cadre of government employees to be competent contract managers;
- now mix all of this with the widespread application of market logic, particularly the idea of institutional competition.

What would be the products of this recipe—its texture, flavor, smell? In the long run, will the recipe produce greater government efficiency? Will it produce governments more effective in global competition? Fairer government? More honest government? Will this recipe's finished product be a widespread increase in the legitimacy of government in the eyes of the people?

In the following pages I will consider the characteristics in the new public management or managerialism recipe with my eyes firmly fixed on issues of public-sector ethics and government corruption. It is popular to take the view that the new managerialism is here to stay and should be understood as the context within which we work. This leaves those of us interested in ethics in the position of determining how to make government as ethical as possible under the circumstances (Gilman 1997). From this position one would argue, for example, that an increased propensity for corruption associated with more contracting-out could be at least partially ameliorated by greater transparency in public affairs. From this practical position one accepts greater contracting-out as a political and administrative given and then suggests ways of getting the presumed benefits of contracting-out while reducing the risks of corruption. This is situational ethics.

Such a position is particularly useful for the ethicist who wishes to be part of modern trends and directions while still doing ethics. In this way the ethicist does not spoil the recipe for the managerialism reformers or spit into the managerialism reform wind. Ethicists, like most others, wish to be associated with the excitement and momentum of reform, and they dislike being regarded as retrograde defenders of the status quo—or worse, the shrill voice suggesting that we have failed to learn the lessons of history. If, for example, one argues the position that managerialism itself is inherently unethical and has a propensity for corruption regardless of the adoption of safeguards, it leaves the ethicist defending the status quo, including all the corruption that is part of it—a particularly vulnerable position to defend.

I shall take that position, nevertheless, following the dictum that it is always possible, particularly in the name of administrative reform, to make things worse. Furthermore, there are points at which it is the duty of the ethicist to spit into the wind, and I believe this to be one of those points.

Some Defining Assumptions

To consider the characteristics of the new public management project and to evaluate its likely results, I will make some defining assumptions upon which the arguments of this chapter rest. This is an axiomatic argument; the axioms (generalizations or modalities), I believe, are both empirically verifiable and deductively demonstrable. All axioms, like all generalizations or modalities, are subject to amelioration, to modification, or to adaptation; however, they are not subject to complete (or usually even significant) retraction, cancellation, or repudiation.

Axiom 1: Most forms of government corruption—conflicts of interest, bribery, fraud, kickbacks, skimming, trading on the prestige of office—occur at the point of transaction between officials who formally represent government authority and the use of public money, on the one hand, and individuals or organizations who seek money, favor, or influence, on the other hand. In this assumption the key is the point of transaction at the boundaries of a jurisdiction or agency between an agency official and a contractor, a client, a regulated firm, and so forth. The point of transaction can be relatively insignificant, as in the case of the police officer deciding whether to give a ticket, or the licensing officer deciding whether to grant a license. The point of the transaction can be significant, as in the case of the Defense Department procurement officer, or group of officers, deciding which defense contractor will get a multibillion-dollar contract.

Axiom 2: Absent laws, rules, social conventions, or social reciprocity, rational persons and firms will act on the basis of self-interest. Here I accept the rational, utilitarian assumption and argue that democratic laws, rules, and social conventions cause or influence both individuals and firms to adjust or adapt self-interested behavior in the direction of collective interests.

Axiom 3: Under democratic conditions, government institutions are more public-regarding than are either nongovernmental institutions or public firms. It follows, then, that the values of justice, equality, and equity are greater in governmental institutions than in nongovernmental institutions or private firms.

Prime Axiom: Over time, for every increase in jurisdiction boundary-spanning transactions there will be a corresponding increase in the probability of government corruption.

Although it is not an axiom, I am making a critical assumption about the ethics of public officials. Ethics is very much more than an attempt to combat corruption; it is also an attempt to do good. I accept the Joel Fleishman argument that in an imperfect world with imperfect men and women, government ethics will be found in a selfless public service (Fleishman 1981, pp. 82–83). The prospects for ethical government are greatest when there are selfless public officials. The prospects for ethical government are also greatest when there are rules, regulations, and systems of oversight that limit and carefully manage points of transaction. Both the logic and the effects of the new managerialism move democratic government further away from the prospect of an influential and selfless public service.

Cutting Red Tape

The first ingredient of the new public management recipe is to sharply reduce government regulations—red tape. I will use as an example the National Performance Review (NPR) process directed by Vice President Al Gore, which has led the process of slashing and simplifying the regulations in the Federal Register (Gore 1995). The logic is pure managerialism— results, not rules. In the words of the currently popular book *The Death of Common Sense,* "Decision making must be transferred from words on a page to people on the spot" (Howard 1994, p. 186). In many ways this is very good news for public administration. It conveys a much appreciated trust to maligned bureaucrats, an indication that they should have the discretion to use their expertise, professionalism, and common sense to be good managers and to be ethical. The NPR, in referring to public administrators, assumes "we're honest, not dishonest, intelligent, not stupid" (Gore 1995, p. 33). It also invites bureaucrats to find creative and simplified ways to solve problems and to be effectively regulatory without an excessive buildup of regulation sediment, recognizing that in that sediment are many obsolete regulations and much pointless paperwork. Finally, the NPR process calls for government reinventors to "get rid of bad rules and make good ones easier to understand" (p. 29).

In the enthusiasm for cutting red tape, it is useful to remember the reasons some of that red tape got there in the first place. I will deal here with just two.

First is the matter of due process and fairness. Simply put, the logic of due process and fairness "obliges officials to give people affected by governmental action a fair chance to get their views on official decisions registered so that their interests are not overlooked or arbitrarily overridden by those in power" (Kaufman 1977, p. 43). Due process is time consuming, cluttered with paperwork, and often expensive. The results were not always entirely fair, since persons and institutions of power and influence have their usual advantage. "To be sure, were there no Administrative Procedure Act, agencies would not cavalierly trample the rights of their clients; their statutes, judicial precedents, political pressures, and generally accepted standards of equity would keep them in check. But the act unquestionably compelled them to formalize and elaborate their procedures to a greater degree than they otherwise would" (Kaufman 1977, p. 45). In addition, there are special due process protocols that cover government employees; these provide protection from arbitrary dismissal and from political influence, and they guarantee fairness in hiring, promotion, assignments, and so forth.

How far is it possible to go in cutting red tape and streamlining government procedures without doing harm to our cherished rights and without doing some damage to fairness? At a minimum it is folly to imagine that there is no trade-off between a sharp reduction of the regulations that guarantee procedural due process and the substance of individual rights on the one hand, and the quality of governmental fairness on the other. Despite the political slogans of those who are reinventing government, they cannot have it both ways—to reduce procedural due process regulations yet to guarantee fairness for individuals and groups protected by regulations.

Second are the matters of compassion and protection. Much red tape can be traced to the wish to protect citizens in advance of possible harm by, for example, assuring the purity of food, the safety of flight, or the safety of drugs. Much of government red tape protects us on the highways (think of air bags, for example) and in the air. Hundreds of agencies at all levels of government are in the business of protecting us in advance, primarily through regulations and their enforcement—red tape. This regulation is often associated with the point of transaction—when the citizen buys a product or a service. This regulatory process puts a considerable burden both on those who make the products we buy and on those who sell the services we use. Because of federalism there is considerable duplication in the regulatory process, a further burden on producers.

A good bit of red tape also is designed to influence many forms of human association—schools on one hand, and students and parents on the other, labor and management, borrowers and lenders, brokers and investors, management and individual workers, researchers and their human subjects, husbands and wives, parents and children, and so forth. Laws and regulations associated with possible cases of sexual harassment, child abuse, and spouse abuse are excellent contemporary examples of red tape that would influence human association.

Red tape is a handmaiden to government programs of compassion, such as food stamps, aid to dependent children, Medicare, and Medicaid; after all, matters of eligibility and fairness are critically important. And, of course, there are many subsidy programs to farmers, small business owners, all families that own homes, and so on.

There can be little doubt that corruption has been associated with many of these programs, despite regulations and red tape. It is illogical to assume, however, that there would be less corruption in the absence of regulations and red tape.[1] More important, however, are the bigger policy issues associated with the protection of citizens and compassion toward citizens: Is it possible to achieve the results these programs have achieved without regulations and red tape? In the passion for deregulation is it possible that government will be less fair, the citizens will be less safe, and we will all be less compassionate?

Even if there were evidence that deregulation does not increase the propensity for government corruption, and there is no such evidence, debating the linkage between regulations and government corruption begs a bigger and more important question: Do government regulations make citizens safer and make life fairer and more compassionate? As axiom 1 indicates, I think the answer is yes. Public officials may be inclined, by education and disposition, to be compassionate, to protect us, and to be selfless, but laws and regulations codify those responsibilities.

Finally, I turn to Herbert Kaufman for his description of the importance of rules, regulations, and other forms of red tape:

The temptations facing the government work force are varied and enormous. They handle hundreds of billions of dollars in revenues (paychecks, retirement benefits, payments for supplies and services, rent, subsidies, tax refunds, etc.) and vast quantities of removable property, from postage stamps and office equipment to vehicles and electronic gear. Without exceedingly high controls, nobody would ever know if one government employee took a little here, and took a little there, and a third pocketed a bit somewhere else. . . . [It] is sometimes said the prevention costs more than the ailment. But, our attitude toward public property is typified by the comments of a famous economist ordinarily inclined to reject costs that exceed benefits in dollar terms: "The Office of Management and Budget should spend $20 to prevent the theft of $1 of public funds" (Okun 1975, p. 60). Not only are public property and public discretion held to have a special moral status, they occupy a special political position because abusing them eats away at the foundations of representative government. (Kaufman 1977, pp. 50–53)

Laws, regulations, and red tape set out the rules of behavior at the point of transaction. That these regulations are a drag on government efficiency is acknowledged. That these regulations can be duplicative, confusing, and too tightly drawn is also acknowledged. It is unquestionably helpful to administration to deregulate, particularly if effective administration is defined as efficiency. But regulations have always had more to do with ethics than with efficiency.

Increased Privatization and Contracting-Out

In government, few subjects are as politically fashionable as contracting-out and privatization. In view of the widely shared perception that contracting-out and privatization are good public administration, it is not surprising that few voices have been raised regarding the matter of ethics.[2]

In the United States privatization is almost always achieved by contracting-out, traditionally for capital projects such as buildings and roads or for goods such as defense machinery and weaponry. Contracting-out in this form is the virtual definition of the logic that point of transaction determines ethics. The long history of the private construction by contract of buildings, roads, prisons, military airplanes, and the like yields about the same set of conclusions. To ensure quality and to guarantee against kickbacks, skimming, and fraud it is essential to have very tightly drawn contracts and careful, close oversight, preferably by experienced government contract managers (Kettl 1993). This is the so-called *smart buyer* argument. When the government is not a smart buyer it will either get a shoddy product or it will be open to corruption. Given their long experience with construction companies and with vendors, most state and local governments are smart buyers most of the time. In some states and localities, however, a long tradition of graft and kickbacks is associated with contracting-out. Indeed, when former vice president Spiro Agnew was the elected executive of Baltimore County and later governor of Maryland, he engaged in so-called sand and gravel politics, a longstanding contracting kickback scheme. This was discovered after he was elected vice president, and he was forced to resign.

In the 1970s and 1980s, many cities and counties developed autonomous economic development authorities, freed of restrictions and regulations in their relationships with vendors and contractors. Several have been exposed as particularly corrupt (Henriques 1986).

> It is particularly fashionable these days to contract for social services at the state and local level. After he reviewed a host of such contract arrangements, Kettl found: (1) State and local governments tend not to know what results their social service contracts are buying. (2) Competition is low. (3) Contracts may degenerate into what are effective monopolies for the private vendors. He concluded that state and local governments are engaging in the equivalent of going on a shopping trip while blindfolded, making little effort to squeeze the tomatoes or thump the watermelon. (Kettl 1993, p. 175)

The 1980s saw three major corruption scandals in the U.S. national government. The biggest and most expensive was the savings and loan scandal, directly associated with a combination of deregulation, a diminished oversight capacity, and a promise of federal dollars to back up investments (savings) in savings and loan banks, should they fail. Fail they did, and in very large numbers at a cost of thousands of dollars to every American taxpaying family (Thompson 1993; Steinbach 1989; Rom 1996).

The largest single defense scandal in American history also occurred in the 1980s. In *When the Pentagon Was for Sale* (1995), a history of the so-called ill winds scandal, Andy Pasztor found that many of America's most respected defense corporations were systematically engaged in making payoffs to Defense Department procurement officers, setting up slush funds, rigging bids, and giving bribes. This entire scandal had to do, in one way or another, with contracting-out and with a lack of oversight.

To drive the point home, however, nothing can match the U.S. Department of Housing and Urban Development (HUD) scandal. In the early years of the Reagan administration, HUD was directed by Samuel Pierce and was led by a group of young political appointees from the private sector, none of whom had much experience in housing.[3]

From a rather early point in the HUD scandal it was well known that there

was widespread corruption at HUD. Several reports from the General Accounting Office (GAO) were strongly critical of HUD during this period (Kilpatrick
1989, p. A-25). HUD's own inspectors general during this period criticized the
agency, but softly, or as James Kilpatrick put it, "pianissimo" (p. A-25).

If the HUD scandal was generally known, why did the ordinary systems
of oversight fail? First, the HUD career civil service was evidently reluctant
to blow the whistle. Some claim that they did not know what was going on.
Others wished not to rock the boat or believed there was little they could do
about the corruption. Some had careerist excuses, worrying that they would
lose their jobs (McAllister and Spolar 1989, p. A-10). Whatever the rationale, it was not a shining moment for upper-level HUD civil servants.

Second, the Office of Management and Budget failed to act because it
"was preoccupied with trying to terminate some of the programs of HUD
rather than trying to police it "(McAllister and Spolar 1989, p. A-10).

Congress, controlled by Democrats, had direct institutional responsibility for
oversight. Hearings would come only after the end of the Reagan administration,
evidently because there was little political capital in hearings on HUD (Kobrak
1996). Key legislators claimed to have no knowledge of the corruption at HUD,
despite the inspectors general reports regarding GAO and HUD. Congress was
under little external pressure from local mayors, from developers, or from mort-
gage bankers, the traditional sources of HUD support, in part because much of
the "money had dried up" (McAllister and Spolar 1989, p. A-10).

Putting the HUD scandal in perspective, Peter Kobrak (1996) describes a
pervasive pattern of cozy politics. It must be understood that privatization via
contracting-out is particularly vulnerable to cozy politics. It is not difficult for
political actors or for contractors to turn privatization to their own purposes. In
cozy politics the contractor wins the contract, or retains the contract through
politics. Contractors, according to Smith and Lipsky (1993, p. 171), become
"players in the political process" rather than "sellers of services."

In his splendid treatment of privatization and contracting-out, Donald F.
Kettl reminds us that there are "common problems which afflict all contracting
relationships between buyers and sellers, in both public and private sectors.
Conflicts of interest and monitoring problems are endemic to all transactions
between principals and agents. The basic model underlying the competition
prescription itself suggests that agents (contractors) will have many goals besides those of the principal (government) and that principals will have difficulty detecting which missions their agents are carrying out" (1993, p. 201).

At the close of his presidency, Dwight Eisenhower warned against the
cozy politics of his day, the power of what he called the military-industrial
complex. Now we have many similar cozy relationships between government and private companies or nonprofits, particularly as contracting-out

has moved into the service side of government. There is the American county-mental health and drug rehabilitation nonprofit complex (Milward, Provan, and Else 1991), the U.S. cabinet department and Beltway bandit complex; the large American city-sports team owner demanding a new stadium to be paid for by the taxpayers (Rosentraub 1997), and many more. Corruption, such as fraud and kickbacks, has always been a problem in privatization by contracting-out, but these days it may be the growing political influence of contractors that presents the larger ethical question.

Downsizing

We turn now to the most politically popular characteristic of the new managerialism project—downsizing. Like deregulation and privatization, downsizing the bureaucracy is almost universally understood to be desirable. In the U.S. federal government's reinvention program, the directly employed civilian civil service has been reduced from more than 3 million to 2.7 million, or more than 10 percent, in less than six years.

It must be stated that bureaucratic downsizing is part of a more general move in the direction of smaller government. It turns out that downsizing bureaucracy is very much easier than simply cutting government. While both are politically popular, cutting government programs brings the problem of which programs to cut. Kettl and DiIulio put it this way:

> There can be absolutely no question that the general idea of cutting govern-ment is deeply popular with the American people and hence politically irre-sistible. But as congressional Republicans are now beginning to learn the hard way, that general support begins to evaporate as soon as cutting govern-ment means cutting specific middle-class entitlements and constituency-based programs. For example, when asked which federal programs "should be cut back in order to reduce the federal budget deficit," solid majorities of Ameri-cans say no to cuts in unemployment insurance (64 percent), environmental spending (67 percent), Medicaid (73 percent), Social Security (86 percent), and, last but by no means least, Medicare (88 percent). Likewise, while 65 percent of Americans favor cutting government and reducing the deficit if that means cutting welfare programs, majorities would vote to prevent cuts in federal programs that aid farmers (52 percent), provide loans to college students (65 percent), put more cops on the streets (68 percent), and fund school lunches (77 percent). (Kettl and DiIulio 1995, p. 2)

By comparison, downsizing the bureaucracy appears to be much easier, and the results appear to be clearer. In addition, cuts can be made across the bureaucracy, leaving programs in place but with smaller staff.

So we want it both ways—to have smaller government yet retain all the programs we cherish. The result has been that few programs have been discontinued. Defense spending and foreign aid have been cut, but most domestic programs and entitlements have proved to be very resilient. The issue, then, is not to cut government but to reduce the number of those who work for government (Kettl and DiIulio 1995, pp. 42–45).

The federal government had grown thick, particularly in the middle and upper ranks (Light 1995) and it appears that downsizing has reduced some of this thickening. Most of the critiques of federal bureaucratic downsizing are less positive. It is claimed that downsizing has sharply reduced worker morale, has resulted in a decline in institutional loyalty, and has impaired the institutional memory of many agencies (Jones 1998).

None of these points are profound or new. What is provocative is the assessment of downsizing as *hiding the bureaucracy*. In the hiding-the-bureaucracy argument it is claimed that the federal bureaucracy really has not been downsized, it has simply been relocated and hidden. Put differently, the only way bureaucracy could be saved was to hide it (Light 1998).

Although the data are very difficult to find, these estimates are thought to be approximately correct. First, the civilian federal civil service was just above 3 million in 1992 and is now just under 1.7 million, a drop of more than 45 percent in eleven years. But the funds for the paychecks of approximately 17 million workers in the states and in the nonprofit and corporate sectors can be traced directly to the federal government. For every one federal civil servant there are almost ten others in the hidden or shadow bureaucracy, working for government but not a part of government. These hidden bureaucrats are in the states, in defense contract companies, in the space contract companies, in the beltway bandits, and in the nonprofit and nongovernmental organizations with government contracts. We know a very great deal about the federal civil service. By comparison, we know very little about the hidden bureaucracy, which is much larger. We do not know the size and composition of the hidden bureaucracy because no agency or organization is charged with keeping track of it. We know little of the hiring practices and the diversity of the organizations where these bureaucrats are hidden. We do not know, but what we suspect is this: The hidden bureaucracy has grown at about the same rate as the civil service has been downsized (Light 1998).

In all the rhetoric and hyperbole of reinventing government, the Contract with America, and the claim that "the era of big government is over," it seems that our political leaders have found a way to save the bureaucracy by hiding it. Realistically, it can be claimed that the bureaucracy is able to provide more and better services for less, which supports the reinvention slogan, "a government that works better and costs less." Because there is little evidence that government costs less, we suspect that most of the work of those who once worked directly for government is now done by contract in the shadow bureaucracy.

If this is true, the federal government has managed to have it both ways—shrinking the formal bureaucracy and at the same time continuing the services provided by that bureaucracy. The hidden bureaucracy is exquisitely fragmented into dozens of agencies and thousands of contracts, and no agency or organization is keeping track of it. And the hidden bureaucracy is so complex and so far back in the shadows that it is unreasonable to expect the media to make it transparent.

For the new public service the central question is one of values (Frederickson 1997). It is clear that government employees are to pursue the public interest, as they see it, following axiom 3. The value question is how to achieve the public interest when power is shared with organizations that have other interests and values. "There is powerful pressure in contracted-out programs for the contractor's goals to become the government's goals. It is tempting for the government to buy what the contractor wants to sell. Indeed, the close relationship among contracting experts, both in and out of government, makes it even more difficult to make the government's goals paramount" (Kettl 1988, p. 42).

The pursuit of public policy usually means making difficult trade-offs between competing values such as equality and efficiency. When such policy choices are even partially delegated to or controlled by the hidden bureaucracy, we are face to face with the issue of accountability. In the new managerialism recipe, the answer to this dilemma is usually better or improved contract management, the subject to which we now turn.

Are We Training a Cadre of Government Employees to Be Competent Contract Managers?

When governmental activities are carried out by nongovernmental organizations, hierarchies are partially replaced by contracts between governments and contractors. "Instead of a chain of authority from policy to product, there is a negotiated document that separates policy makers from policy output. Top officials cannot give orders to contractors. They can only shape the incentives to which the contractors respond" (Kettl 1993, p. 22).

When contracts replace hierarchy, the logic of management changes from long-understood concepts or principles of administration, such as coordination and staffing, to different concepts, such as the formulation of requests for proposals or bids, the description and measurement of deliverables, systems of oversight, and the development of incentives and sanctions. Donald F. Kettl (1993, p. 205) suggests that this form of public management has the smart-buyer problem. To deal with the smart-buyer problem, it is essential that American government develop the capacity to be a smart buyer. If it does not, it will surrender authority and power to its private partners and "lose its ability to see the big picture and know how the pieces fit together."

Is American government developing the capacity to be a smart buyer? Kettl answers this way:

> Unfortunately, as government's reliance on contracting out has increased, so too has its disinvestment in its own capacity. At one time, scholars of public administration celebrated the fact that the government employed world-class experts on virtually every issue: mapmakers, chemists, engineers, attorneys, housing economists, librarians, agricultural analysts, food safety specialists. The government no longer has such a range of in-house expertise. In part, that is because of quantum leaps in the complexity of governmental programs. No organization, public or private, can hope to be master of all of the knowledge that lies behind society's major post–World War II innovations. In part, the government's expertise has dwindled because the demand for expertise has dwindled. In essence, the demand for expertise is far greater than the supply of experts, and private employers can almost always outbid the government, leaving the government no choice but to enlist private partners to help it in the day-to-day conduct of its work. In part, the loss of expertise has resulted from the enthusiasm of some elected officials, especially in the Reagan and Bush administrations, for shrinking the government. The bureaucrat-bashing campaign of the late 1970's and 1980's supported that movement. (Kettl 1993, p. 205)

If Kettl's observations about the loss of capacity in the federal government in the Reagan and Bush years are true, they would be doubly true of the Clinton years.

There is little evidence that the federal government or American state and local governments are engaged in widespread training of contract managers. We do know that contract management is a growing field of government employment. We know that few college degree programs include course work in contract administration, not even master's degree programs in public administration or public policy, the degrees most closely associated with government administration.

There has been a sharp increase in the number and quality of master's degrees that emphasize nonprofit organization and management. It appears that a whole generation of highly educated and motivated young people is prepared to work for the organizations that contract with government organizations. It is important to remember that most nonprofit organizations depend primarily on government funding. It is also likely that engineering, technical, consulting, and other firms and organizations that contract with government are stepping up their management competence primarily with persons who have studied engineering or business administration. This is happening at the same time that most governments are losing their management capacity. It appears, therefore, that we not only have a smart-buyer problem, we have a smart-seller problem.

Governments and Markets

If there is a fundamental ingredient in the new managerialism recipe, it is a belief in the supremacy of markets and competition over bureaucratic hierarchy as the way to organize and manage efficiently. This belief has one primary source in politics, the assumption among elected officials that businesses are better managed than governments because businesses must compete in the marketplace. This belief has another primary source in academe or in theory, the ascendancy of the logic of liberal economics and of the so-called public-choice perspective in public policy and administration. There is little doubt that the public-choice perspective is now dominant both in the study of public policy and in the study of public administration. The popular reinventing government movement and its application in the federal government, the National Performance Review (now known as the National Partnership for Reinventing Government), are a combination of business-oriented politics and public-choice theory.

At one level, the "competition prescription" argues that government agencies should be operated in businesslike ways, with efficiency as their objective (Kettl 1993). At another level, the competition ingredient argues that many governmental functions, such as public schools, would be more effective if they were, in fact, actual businesses.

For three reasons the capacity of market competition to increase efficiency is exaggerated. First, market competition assumes an open and even playing field in which government will buy the best product at the lowest price. In fact, most of the products and services bought by governments are purchased in highly imperfect markets, influenced by politics, the lack of competition, and serious information asymmetry that favors sellers. The logic of a genuine market seldom applies to the goods and services that government wishes to buy (Kettl 1003). Second, the logic of the market misrepresents the nature of competition even in the private marketplace. "Neither buyers nor sellers in private markets fully welcome competition because the uncertainty it produces complicates their lives. The lesson of complex private markets, Oliver Williamson [1985] observed, is that large organizations seek to reduce their uncertainty more than they seek low prices" (in Kettl 1993, p. 200). There would be no better example than the market antics of Microsoft in the 1990s.

Third, and most important to the argument here, is that contracting relationships between buyers and sellers "in both the public and private sectors" are fraught with conflict of interest and oversight or monitoring problems (Kettl 1993, p. 201). Buyers, particularly government buyers, simply cannot assume that sellers will have the same goals and values they have.

The biggest ethical issues associated with markets are not fraud, kickbacks, or bribery, although those can be big issues. The biggest issue is fairness. Fairness is not a concept or idea that fits into the logic of either perfect or imperfect markets. But fairness, both procedurally (as in due process) and in outcomes, is often the core issue in government. In the private market the question should be: Is this efficient? In the public sector the question is often: For whom is this efficient and for whom is it inefficient? The private market is designed to be efficient, not to be fair. Democratic self-government is designed to at least try to be fair, with a hope that it will also be efficient.

Conclusions: The Ethical Consequences of the New Managerialism

In order to bring together the features of the new managerialism recipe and to consider their long-range ethical consequences, let us fast forward to the year 2008. It is my prediction that in 2008 this ancient saying will have come to pass: Today's problems were caused by yesterday's solutions. The managerialism recipe—deregulation, privatizing, downsizing, and market competition—will make a dish that will spoil and become the problems of 2008, and these problems will be primarily ethical.

Some evidence is already coming in. It was about twenty-five years ago that the United States Congress voted to abolish the Civil Aeronautics Board, which regulated air routes, fares, and the like. Within a few years, a host of other regulated industries would be deregulated, for example, telephones, banking, trucking, cable television, and pharmaceuticals. The definitive study of the time concluded that deregulation was universally accepted as to be "espoused more or less automatically, by a wide range of office holders and their critics" (Derthick and Quirk 1985, p. 35). With the passage of time enough ordinary and ethical disasters have occurred to cause a rising cry of reconsideration. These ethical breaches include:

- The 130 billion dollar bailout of the savings and loans, which has cost each American family thousands of dollars—the direct cost of deregulation and corruption having been shifted to taxpayers.
- Individual large airlines virtually control travel at several major airports.

Long distance fares between major hubs are lower while service to smaller locations is less frequent and more expensive.

- Thus far it appears that the primary beneficiary of electric deregulation will be large industrial consumers, very likely at the expense of residential electric rate payers.
- Telephone deregulation has resulted in deteriorating service, and this service is becoming more expensive.
- The e-coli outbreaks are evidence that food inspection is woefully inadequate (Worth 1998).
- Jerry Mitchell's recent study (1999) of government corporations in America (remember that government corporations are virtual prototypes of the ingredients in the new managerialism recipe) concluded that the lack of governmental controls often results in corruption.
- After the spate of airline hijackings in the 1970s and early 1980s, the Federal Aviation Administration required airlines to screen passengers and luggage. Airlines controlled the cost of screening by hiring contractors that provided virtually no training, paid minimum wages, and gave their employees few if any benefits. It was these contract employees who allowed nineteen terrorists to board commercial airliners and use them as bombs to destroy the World Trade Center and part of the Pentagon (Frederickson and LaPorte 2002). It is notable in the response to the terrorism of September 11, 2001, the federal government established the Transportation Security Administration, a bureaucracy of about 50,000 directly employed civil servants, to manage passenger and baggage screening in American airports. This could be understood to be a response to the failures of the logic of managerialism, at least in the case of air travel security.
- For the past fifteen years it has been fashionable to eliminate traditional forms of government purchasing, particularly for relatively small items. Instead, jurisdictional credit cards are issued to employees, allowing them to purchase, within certain limits and standards, such things as office supplies. Certainly, almost all civil servants who have been issued such cards have used them correctly, but we regularly read of the abuse of this system. We can only conclude, therefore, that credit card abuse is a serious problem in some agencies of the federal government, in some state and local governments, and in some special districts and authorities. One wonders whether the misuse of credit cards and the attendant damage it does to both the public service and to public perceptions of government might more than offset the presumed benefits and efficiencies associated with the wide distribution of credit cards to civil servants.

Incidents and episodes such as this will increase over the coming decade and there will be a step-by-step process of reregulation. The primary impetus for this will be the issue of fairness. People have understood that government cannot always protect their food and their environment, but they have little tolerance for unfairness; deregulation is resulting in widespread unfairness.

Although there is little evidence thus far, it is safe to predict that the growth of noncapital contracting will slow and that there will be a combination of poor results (we are already seeing this in contracts for schooling) and scandals that will cause a drawing back from contracting. The issue here will be accountability. Who will be accountable when contractors fail to perform or when they steal or cheat?

It is also likely that the political rhetoric of smaller government, when it is evident that government is growing through the use of the contract bureaucracy, will start to ring hollow as people come to understand the dynamics of the shadow bureaucracy. We are making little progress in developing even a simple understanding of this new form of public service, let alone of designing ethical systems and standards for it. Following the logic of the prime axiom that was set out earlier in this chapter, the simple number of transactions between governments, contractors, and subcontractors will multiply the possibilities of corruption to the point that there will almost certainly be both large and small scandals. When that happens, the value and usefulness of a qualified professional public service will be very appealing to policy makers as a way to fix the problems of accountability and corruption.

Rewind to the present. If these predictions are accurate, what should we do now? Should we advise our leaders to stop mixing the new managerialism recipe because of a concern for our ethical future? Yes, at least to the extent that we make it clear to our leaders and to those who so strongly advocate the new managerialism that it is likely that the efficiencies it presumes are purchased at a dear price in corruption, unfairness, and governmental legitimacy.

Notes

1. There is a literature, particularly in economics, that suggests that regulations and red tape actually foster corruption (Slesinger and Isaacs 1968, p. 55; Rein 1983, p. 9; Jackson and Maughn 1978, p. 138). Standard regulatory tools such as licenses, permits, approvals, inspections, systems of oversight, fines, and prosecutions are major regulatory instruments. They all involve points of transaction, so it could be logically argued that the more regulation, the more points of transaction, and, therefore, the more opportunities for corruption. It appears in some cultures that elaborate regulatory processes are used by bureaucrats to extract bribes (Kim 1997). It is argued by Anechiarico and Jacobs (1996) that there have been so many cycles of corruption, lawmaking, and regulations in New York City that "the pursuit of absolute integrity" has rendered the city government ineffective. The challenge is to have enough regula-

tions to get the job done and an ethical public service carrying out or enforcing those regulations. Wholesale deregulation in the presence of a culture of administrative corruption will not help.

2. There is no small definition problem associated with privatization and contracting-out. In much of the world, privatization is understood to mean the selling of government programs (railroads, coal mines, airlines, businesses, utilities) to the private sector, which then owns and operates them for a profit. In the United States there are some examples of privatization of this sort, but not many. Virtually all the functions that are being privatized in Europe, particularly in the states of the former Soviet Union, were always private in the United States. There are exceptions, such as some commercially owned electric utilities, the Tennessee Valley Authority, and the Columbia Basin Project. There are lively discussions of the possible actual privatization of these and other government functions such as airports, but this type of privatization is rare. In the American context, then, privatization usually means contracting-out government activities to private (corporate), nonprofit, or nongovernmental organizations. Thus it is that the term privatization is used to describe contract prisons, certain welfare-to-work systems, and the management by contract of many public functions. (For a thoughtful consideration of some of these distinctions see Kobrak 1996.)

3. Because of the Civil Service Reform Act of 1978, President Reagan had many more high level political appointees than did his predecessors, and he used a political litmus test and a selection process that were primarily based on political support. This has come to be known in American public administration as "high level spoils" (Newland 1987). At a meeting of top political appointees and civil servants, Samuel Pierce pointed to the political appointees and said, "This is the board of directors. . . . We make all the policy decisions. . . . You are to carry out those orders and not ask questions" (McAllister and Spolar 1989, p. A-10).

References

Anechiarico, Frank, and Jacobs, James B. 1996. *The Pursuit of Absolute Integrity: How Corruption Control Makes Government Ineffective.* Chicago: University of Chicago Press.

Derthick, Martha, and Quirk, Paul. 1985. *The Politics of Deregulation.* Washington, DC: Brookings Institution.

Fleishman, Joel L. 1981. "Self-Interest and Political Integrity." In *Public Duties: The Moral Obligations of Government Officials,* ed. Joel L. Fleishman, Lance Lieberman, and Mark H. Moore, pp. 52–91. Cambridge, MA: Harvard University Press.

Frederickson, H. George. 1997. *The Spirit of Public Administration.* San Francisco: Jossey-Bass.

Frederickson, H. George, and LaPorte, Todd. 2002. "Airline Safety and the Problem of Rationality." *Public Adminstration Review* 62, S1:33–43.

Gilman, Stuart. 1997. "Realignment and Public Sector Ethics: The Neglected Management Problem in the New Public Administration." Paper presented at the Symposium on Public Sector Ethics, Organization for Economic and Community Development, Paris, November 1997.

Gore, Al. 1995. *Common Sense Government Works Better and Costs Less.* Third Report of the National Performance Review, Washington, DC: U.S. Government Printing Office.

Henriques, Diana B. 1986. *The Machinery of Greed: Public Authority Abuse and What to Do about It*. Lexington, MA: Lexington Books.

Howard, Philip K. 1994. *The Death of Common Sense: How Law Is Suffocating America*. New York: Warner Books.

Jackson, Donald W., and Maughn, Ralph B.1978. *Introduction to Political Analysis: The Theory and Practice of Allocation*. Santa Monica, CA: Goodyear.

Johnson, Haynes. 1991. *Sleepwalking through History*. New York: Anchor Books.

Jones, Vernon Dale. 1998. *Downsizing the Federal Government: The Management of Public Sector Workforce Reductions*. Armonk, NY: M.E. Sharpe.

Kaufman, Herbert. 1977. *Red Tape: Its Origins, Uses and Abuses*. Washington, DC: Brookings Institution.

Kettl, Donald F. 1988. *Government by Proxy: (Mis)Managing Federal Programs*. Washington, DC: Congressional Quarterly.

———. 1993. *Sharing Power: Public Governance and Private Markets*. Washington, DC: Brookings Institution.

Kettl, Donald F., and DiIulio, John J. Jr. 1995. *Cutting Government*. Report, Center for Public Management. Washington, DC: Brookings Institution.

Kilpatrick, James J. 1989. "It's Reagan's Mess at HUD." *Washington Post*, August 11: A-25.

Kim, Myoung-Soo. 1997. "Regulation and Corruption." In *The White House and the Blue House: Government Reform in the United States and Korea*, ed. H. George Frederickson and Youn-Hyo Cho, pp. 253–69. Lanham, MD: University Press of America.

Kobrak, Peter, 1996. "Privatization and Cozy Politics." *Public Integrity Annual* 1: 13–22.

Light, Paul A. 1995. *Thickening Government: Federal Hierarchy and the Diffusion of Accountability*. Washington, DC: Brookings Institution.

———. 1998. Comments at the Alan K. Campbell Institute Symposium, Maxwell School of Citizenship and Public Affairs, Syracuse University, May 19.

McAllister, Bill, and Chris Spolar. 1989. "The Transformation of HUD: 'Brat Pack' Filled Vacuum at Agency." *Washington Post*, August 6: A-1, A-10.

Milward, H. Brinton; Provan, Keith G.; and Else, Barbara A. 1991. "What Does the Hollow State Look Like?" In Public *Management*, ed. Barry Bozeman, pp. 309–22. San Francisco: Jossey-Bass.

Mitchell, Jerry. 1999. *The American Experiment with Government Corporations*. Armonk, NY: M.E. Sharpe.

Newland, Chester A. 1987. "Public Executives: Imperium, Sacerdotium, Colloquium? Bicentennial Leadership Challenges." *Public Administration Review* 47: 45–55.

Okun, Arthur M. 1975. *Equality and Efficiency: The Big Tradeoff*. Washington, DC: Brookings Institution.

Pasztor, Andy. 1995. *When the Pentagon Was for Sale: Inside America's Biggest Defense Scandal*. New York: Scribner.

Rein, Martin. 1983. *From Policy to Practice*. Armonk, NY: M.E. Sharpe.

Rom, Mark Carl. 1996. *Public Spirit in the Thrift Tragedy*. Pittsburgh: University of Pittsburgh Press.

Rosentraub, Mark S. 1997. *Major League Losers: The Real Cost of Sports and Who's Paying for It*. New York: HarperCollins.

Slesinger, Ruben, and Isaacs, Asher. 1968. *Business, Government and Public Policy*. Princeton, NJ: VonNostrand.

Smith, Steven, and Lipsky, Michael. 1993. *Non-Profits for Hire: The Welfare State in the Age of Contracting*. Cambridge, MA: Harvard University Press.

Steinbach, Carol. 1989. "Programmed for Plunder." *National Journal* (September): 259–62.

Thompson, Dennis F. 1993. "Mediated Corruption: The Case of the Keating Five." *American Political Science Review* 87, no. 2 (June): 369–81.

Williamson, Oliver E. 1985. *The Economic Institutions of Capitalism: Firms, Markets, Relational Contracting*. New York: Free Press.

Worth, Robert. 1998. "Why Deregulation Has Gone Too Far." *Washington Monthly* 30 (July/August): 10–16.

9

Ensuring Accountability in Human Services: The Dilemma of Measuring Moral and Ethical Performance

Lisa A. Dicke and Pitima Boonyarak

The search for better governmental organizations is a never-ending quest (Light 1998). Scholars, legislators, the media, public officials, and bureaucrats alike are not asking whether government bureaucracies should be reformed. The questions and the debates in recent years have centered on the relative advantages and limitations of two quite different basic approaches to public-sector reform. The first approach asks whether it is possible to reform existing bureaucratic structures and practices enough that we can indeed govern well through them (Ott and Goodman 1998; Peters 1996). The second approach assumes that existing structures and practices cannot be improved enough; instead, we should develop alternatives to bureaucratic organizational structures (Behn 1995; Kearney and Hays 1998). The question for proponents of the second approach is: Which of the many alternative reform models would serve as the best replacements for traditional bureaucracies, and under what circumstances? The first of these reform approaches—improving bureaucratic structures and practices—largely fell out of favor as the second approach moved to center stage during the decade of the 1990s (Peters 1996).

Reformers who favor alternatives to bureaucracy, and most particularly proponents of privatization, public-private partnerships, and the new public management argue that bureaucracy itself is a fundamental cause of government's problems. Any effective solution to government's problems thus must abandon the bureaucratic model (Ott and Goodman 1998). Four groupings of reform models have emerged from the myriad alternatives that have been proposed in recent years, each based on different perceptions of the root causes, values, and assumptions of government's problems: market government, participative government, flexible government, and deregulated government (Peters 1996). These reform models share a common, powerful, and widely accepted new public management reform ideology, which itself represents one of the greatest challenges today for government in and of the United States. The commentary in this chapter explores the essence and implications of this challenge.

Central Arguments of This Commentary

The central arguments proposed are listed below. Our intent is to convince the reader of the significance of the impact of each on efforts to ensure accountability in contracted human services in the United States.

1. Downsizing, devolution, diffusion, and empowerment are manifestations of a powerful and widely accepted political ideology.
2. Pressures for government to downsize, devolve, diffuse, and empower will not lessen in the foreseeable future despite a temporary rise in faith in government after September 11, 2001.
3. Accountability in government is a far more complex notion than simplistic legalistic adherence to the terms of a contract, protecting funds, or counting activities (Dicke and Ott 1999).
4. *Historically, and at least in theory, accountability in government has been achieved mostly upward through layers in hierarchies, from employees through supervisors and middle managers to elected officials and (again in theory) out to the public.*
5. *Downsizing, devolution, diffusion, and empowerment substantially diminish government's ability to achieve accountability through hierarchies.*
6. It has been widely but erroneously assumed that advances in performance measurement technology during the 1990s created the ability to ensure accountability for government services that are devolved, diffused, and entrusted to empowered employees.
7. Performance measurement technology is not yet able to provide the information that is needed for accountability in at least one major area of government activity, the human services.

Reform Ideology of the New Public Management: Decentralize and Let Go

During the decade of the 1990s, four principles evolved into truisms of new public management reform.

- *Downsize:* Government organizations are too large. Thus, government (and society) is improved by the mere act of shrinking it.
- *Devolve (or Decentralize):* Decisions should be made as close as possible to the people who are directly affected. One size does not fit all.
- *Diffuse:* Government should not engage in (or should withdraw from) the provision of any services that organizations in the private sector will provide.
- *Empower:* Free lower-level managers and employees from bureaucratic directives, rules, and policies, and give free rein to businesses and nonprofits that provide services to, or on behalf of, government.

These four truisms are manifestations of the powerful and widely accepted ideology of new public management that have not lessened in recent years: Higher levels (in organizations and of government) should relinquish power, control, authority, rule making, budget details, direct service provision, and close oversight—they should let go of many of their historic roles, responsibilities, and functions. Obviously, antigovernment ideology has not been the sole reason that the downsizing, devolution, diffusion, and empowerment movements have continued. The political ideology is also centered on the belief that the private sector can do a better job (Gibelman and Demone 2002). Thus the desire for innovation, efficiency, and flexibility that might be achievable through the adoption of business practices cannot be ignored. Antigovernment ideology is, however, one of the few explanations that can account for continued implementation of the movements despite the fact that cost savings have not been universally achieved and accountability is not always ensured.

The consequence has been widespread adoption of reform models that are consistent with and supportive of these truisms and the ideology of new public management. This was evident in essentially every new public management reform approach of the 1990s, including: Newt Gingrich's Contract with America; privatization (Savas 2000); the Sagebrush Revolution; quality or TQM (total quality management) (Alexander 1992; Bhote 1994; Deming 1986; GAO 1991, 1992; Joiner 1994; Juran 1992); National Productivity Review or NPR (Clinton and Gore 1995; Gore 1993; Kettl 1995); and self-directing work teams (Bowen and Lawler 1992; Orsburn et al. 1990; Weisbord 1991).

Support for the reform models has been fueled by the widely shared and frequently voiced public perception that government is incompetent. Government cannot be trusted to do anything right (Ott and Shafritz 1994, 1995; Peters 1996). Thus there is no reason to ask whether any particular decision should be made in Washington, DC, state houses, city halls, or contracted nongovernmental service providers and whether decisions should be made by higher-level public managers or employees who interact with recipients of services. The answer is known before the question is asked: One size does not fit all; make decisions as close as possible to the people who will be most directly affected; smaller is better. Under the new public management reform thinking, the choices are predetermined because they are based on the four truisms: downsize; decentralize or devolve; diffuse; empower.

Although the preceding paragraphs have probably led you to believe otherwise, there is reason to support many of the reform models that rest on these truisms but only when the assumptions upon which the reforms are based are warranted. Adoption of alternative models for delivering government services, however, poses serious challenges when we have not learned how to achieve fundamental responsibilities in and through them (Salamon 2002). And adoption of alternative models is widespread. Indeed, federal personnel implement few federal domestic programs (Radin 2000). Instead, the responsibility for allocation decisions and the actual delivery of services has been delegated to other entities including state and local governments, banks, other private businesses, and private nonprofit organizations (Salamon 1999). Across all levels of government in the United States, organizational reforms are being adopted because they "feel right." This adoption is occurring, however, before the technology is in place to administer them responsibly, and, surprisingly, with little thought or discussion about potentially dangerous consequences. One such responsibility that is endangered is accountability.

Accountability

In its simplest form, *accountability* is "answerability" for one's actions or behavior, "to higher authorities including elected and appointed officials who sit at the apex of institutional chains of command and to directly involved stakeholders, for performance that involves delegation of authority to act" (Kearns 1996, p.11). Accountability, however, is not a simple construct either in theory or in practice. It is a far more complex notion than simply legalistic adherence to the terms of a contract, protecting funds, and counting activities. Romzek and Dubnick (1994) identified four distinct dimensions of accountability: hierarchical, legal, professional, and political. Jabbra and Dwivedi (1988) raised another dimension: moral and ethical accountability.

Accountability as "answerability to higher authorities" (Kearns 1996) reflects the hierarchical and political dimensions of accountability. In this view, accountability in government is achieved mostly upward through layers in hierarchies, from employees through supervisors and middle managers to elected officials and (at least in concept) out to the sovereign public. Likewise, democratic loop theory (Fox and Miller 1995) posits that nonprofit organizations are accountable to the units of governments with which they contract. The contracting government employees and units are answerable (accountable) to elected officers in the executive branch, and "elected public officials are theoretically accountable to the political sovereignty of the voters" (Shafritz 1992, p. 4).

The meaning of accountability has been construed narrowly in government contract provisions and in common public use as answerability for adherence to the terms of contracts and for judicious use of public funds. A narrow construction has unfortunate consequences because accountability means far more than formal legal or fiscal control. Accountability is a concept steeped in longstanding notions of governmental responsibility and popular sovereignty. "The term [accountability] suggests the idea of taking 'into account' the consequences of one's actions for the welfare of others" (Donahue 1989, p. 10). Accountability is more than a set of legalistic obligations, however. It is also a moral, professional, and ethical construct that results when public officials and contractors serve with a commitment to do the right things.

Although a formal and legal concept of accountability is needed, it must be balanced with "a democratically grounded conception of responsibility" (Burke 1986, p. 39). Accountability must be an internal constraint or a sense of duty as well as an externally imposed set of requirements (Harmon 1995). "Organizational and professional behavior, political concerns, and the morality of administrative actions are equally important in the accountability domain" (Jabbra and Dwivedi 1988, p. 5). Professional codes of ethics are demonstrations of the belief that accountability can be instilled in public officials and contractors. Thus, for example, in many of the human services where the quality of programs and services is highly subjective (Dicke 2000), an adequate working definition of accountability must include at least five dimensions of accountability: legal, bureaucratic, political, professional, and moral (Dicke and Ott 1999). Without these five dimensions, accountability does not incorporate the full spectrum of government responsibilities for public resources (inputs), employee or contractor activities (performance), or outcomes of services (Suchman 1967)—including the highly desired but ultimately subjective construct, quality of life.

Without question, objective external controls, such as legally binding contractual obligations, are necessary for ensuring the full spectrum of government accountability. A belief in the law is essential to western notions of accountability, and the written contract is the symbol of this belief. Through legally binding contracts "the state is responsible for actions committed in its name, and those who exercise the power of the state are answerable for their actions" (Jabbra and Dwivedi 1988, p. 3). Contractors are answerable for the services they provide, and public officials are accountable for the use of public funds and for publicly funded services. In essence, we assume that when services are provided by nongovernmental organizations, or lower levels of government, government's accountability flows across the boundary via written contracts.

If, indeed, government has responsibilities in the moral, professional, and ethical dimensions of accountability, then public agencies and their contractors need to be answerable for the quality of services that are provided and the outcomes of services that are contracted out to private organizations—as well as for the prudent use of public funds. Unfortunately, downsizing, devolution, diffusion, and empowerment substantially diminish government's ability to achieve accountability through hierarchies. For example, in a study of organizational restructuring in the Ontario, Canada, hospital system that flattened organizational and professional hierarchies, Baumann and Silverman (1998) reported that 5,220 nurses were on unemployment insurance as the direct result of downsizing, and there was a corresponding rise in the number of unregulated workers. What aspects of accountability did Ontario's hospitals lose in the process? Since professionalism implies standardized knowledge, credentialing, and self-regulation, the losses included predictability, uniformity, and the positive client outcomes that flow from the "experience and knowledge [that professionals] bring to highly complex environments" (Baumann and Silverman 1998, p. 204). In addition, despite their flaws, bureaucratic hierarchies provide for continuity and structural accountabilities that are not found in highly devolved and decentralized systems.

Many performance measurement approaches and information system technologies that are used currently to achieve accountability erroneously equate accountability with control. When the quantity or quality of services falls below a predetermined level, the performance deficiency is measured and information is fed back through the information system to decision makers who initiate corrective actions—a classical application of a control system model (Donnelly, Gibson, and Ivancevich 1987). Control "derives from one basic property: the ability to determine events or outcomes" (Stout 1980, p. 6), a property of government services that unfortunately exists only rarely. The ability to control is a function of knowledge about the links between activities and results—about cause-effect relationships. With full knowledge a manager can control events and outcomes. In practice, managers often can have close to full knowledge about quantities of inputs and activities because these types of variables usually can be measured relatively easily. Examples might include the number of homeless people who secure employment while living in a homeless shelter, or the number of single mothers who are removed from a state's welfare rolls during a period of time. The same claim cannot be made about government's ability to measure the qualitative aspects of many of its functions and outcomes, most especially not in the human services. Outputs and outcomes in these types of programs can be extraordinarily difficult to measure. Consider, for example, the problems involved in measuring the quality of life for persons with mental retardation or the changes in beliefs, attitudes, and behaviors that are co-produced by service providers and aging clients with mental disabilities. Accountability seldom can be achieved by using control system approaches and technologies other than in the narrow contractual/legal/fiscal dimension of accountability. These approaches and technologies are far less effective in the moral, professional, and ethical dimensions.

Control systems require nearly full knowledge of the relationships between activities and outcomes, and only rarely is there full knowledge about these relationships in the moral, professional, and ethical dimensions of government accountability. Thus current performance measurement technology is not sufficiently well developed to permit government agencies to achieve accountability in important aspects of publicly supported services. The widely held assumption that advances in performance measurement technology during the 1990s created an ability to ensure accountability for government services that are being devolved, diffused, and entrusted to empowered employees (Halachmi 1999; Halachmi and Geri 1999; Ott, Boonyarak, and Dicke 2001) is well-intentioned, but erroneous, wishful thinking.

A Challenge for the New Public Management Reforms: Achieving Accountability Despite the Limitations of Performance Measurement Technology

The downsizing, devolution, diffusion, and empowerment movements that have been fueled by the new public management ideology (Ott and Dicke 2000) have been enabled by the assumption that performance measurement technology is well developed—it is up to the task. Accurate, objective, timely information about performance and outcomes can be available when they are needed to make corrections. Public administrators can know that things are not right and when interventions are warranted or needed—when they need to know (Stevens et al. 1995).

Although students and practitioners of public management began to take notice of performance measurement early in the 1980s (Epstein 1984; Morley 1986), it became one of the most popular topics in the literature during the 1990s (e.g., Ammons 1994; Behn 1995; Bouckaert 1993, 1995; Cohen 1993; Deller, Nelson, and Walzer 1992; Eccles 1991; Hedley 1998; Holzer and Callahan 1998; U.S. DOJ 1995; Kamensky 1993; Kaplan and Norton 1992, 1996; Nyhan and Marlowe 1995; Prager and Desai 1996; RAND 1990; Sorber 1993). Performance measurement had to take the center stage in the 1990s—it had to become a hot topic—because *it had to work.* Devolution, empowerment within government agencies, and diffusion through contracting-out and other varieties of "enterprise government" (Halachmi and Nichols 1997) could not be managed without valid, reliable, timely, and nontrivial measures of performance. Government accountability could not be achieved without it (Altshuler 1997; Rosen 1998). Measurement information had to be available to and accessible by higher-level managers, empowered work teams, and contracted organizations. Performance measurement was touted as not only doable but readily adaptable to the public sector. Today the use of performance measures is viewed as a way to develop consensus to guide policy, not just to manage. "Performance monitoring . . . [can] not only improve basic accountability, but [it] also [can] make government more responsive and more competitive" (Coplin, Merget, and Bourdeaux 2002, p. 699). "The measures you develop will guide your employees to deliver the results you desire" (Lisoski 2003, p.17).

Unfortunately, the task of measuring important aspects of performance in government systems with validity, reliability, and timeliness has proved to be far more difficult than many expected, particularly in the human services. Despite substantial advances in the past ten to fifteen years (Callahan and Holzer 1999; Warrian 1999), performance measurement technology cannot yet provide the information needed for upholding government's legal and bureaucratic accountability requirements, even within bureaucracies, and the problems are far more severe between organizations. Under reforms, the record is spottier still. A few of the accountability dilemmas associated with the use of current performance measurement technology under reformed conditions include: (1) falsification; (2) failure to adopt performance measurement technology; (3) information about performance and outcomes is gathered but not used; (4) performance measurement is not targeted to ensuring important dimensions of accountability; (5) operational measurement issues; and (6) politics.

Falsification

In no policy or program area are the accountability challenges associated with governmental reforms more acutely experienced than in human services contracting. In contracting, legal accountability is ensured through the provisions of the written contract, but quality and client outcomes are ensured through accountability mechanisms such as periodic auditing, monitoring, and provider self-reports. The validity of the data derived from these mechanisms is often questionable. In a study of human services contracting, for example, contracted provider employees reported pervasive falsifying of, and witnessing the falsification of, documents, including activity logs, reimbursement requests, and auditing reports (Dicke 2000). For example, state government case managers reported that contracted provider ratings on outcomes-based assessments (OBA) were suspect. Several case managers noted that "the OBA can be skewed." State government case managers also reported having been instructed to "back off" by higher-level administrators when duplicate payments were made to contractors. Blatant errors surfaced, and instances of substandard services were discovered (Dicke 2000). Monitoring of contracted providers was often hit-or-miss, or announced in advance, thus allowing the contractors to stage conditions to look better than they actually were at the program sites.

These findings are consistent with others. DeHoog (1984) found that two Michigan state departments charged with managing social service programs failed to conduct on-site inspections and instead "relied on self-reporting by contractors." Tate (2003, p. 6) reports, "It is not unusual to detect undercurrents of uncertainty about the accuracy, or even the truthfulness of reported performance measures."

Failure to Adopt Performance Measurement Technology

In addition to reliability problems, performance measurement technology has still not been implemented in many public agencies that contract with nongovernmental organizations (de Lancer Julnes and Holzer 2001). A survey conducted by the Governmental Accounting Standards Board in 1997, for example, found that although the number of organizations attempting to develop performance measurement systems was encouraging (53 percent), only 39 percent had actually developed output or outcome measures that could be used with any degree of effectiveness to help ensure accountability (GASB 1997). A study of public guardianship concluded that "highly individual and complex issues of public guardianship [were] addressed without the benefit of a clearly articulated approach to accountability" (Teaster 2003, p. 397).

The nearly unanimous finding of research on social services contracting in state and local government has been that oversight is virtually nonexistent due to a lack of time, resources, and political will (Kettl 1993; Rehfuss 1989).

In a study of social services in Arizona, Milward, Provan, and Smith (1994) found that the state department of health services had made no attempt to monitor the performance of local providers. The department stated that it did not have the administrative capacity to engage in performance evaluation. Although the studies cited in this paragraph are all at least ten years old, the problems they discuss remain timely. Posner's (2002) examination of accountability in third-party government, for example, identified administrative deficiencies at the Department of Housing and Urban Development, the Environmental Protection Agency, and the Department of Education that rendered each incapable of effectively monitoring its contractors.

Information About Performance and Outcomes Is Gathered but Not Used

"Leadership is the most critical element in whether or not performance [measurement] efforts, when initiated, are successful" (Enos 2000, p. 7). Even when performance technology is adopted and implemented, however, decision makers may still choose to ignore or bury the data. "Too many problems identified in audits are not resolved, but are identified as recurring problems in subsequent audits" (Russell and Regel 1996, p. 49). One possible explanation is the lack of resources or systems to process data. "Agencies may collect data that is, or could be, used for performance measurement; however, they do not always have system[s] in place in which those data are part of decision making processes" (Coplin, Merget, and Bourdeaux 2002, p. 700). Enos (2000, p. 9), however, found that although organizational leaders may review performance measurement data to identify performance deficiencies, "they almost never know how to improve them." And performance measurement may be intimidating to organizational leaders who are likely to bear the brunt of the blame when problems are discovered. Talking openly about the problems or deficiencies identified in a performance measurement audit involves risks. There are too many incentives "to protect an existing program rather than to open it up to criticism and a possible Pandora's box of changes" (Kingdon 1995, p. 310).

Performance Measurement Is Not Targeted to Ensuring Important Dimensions of Accountability

Many human services that are delivered through government-arranged contracts are targeted for extremely vulnerable groups of citizens who are at high risk of abuse, neglect, exploitation, and the possible erosion or violation of rights (Anetzberger 1996). If ethical accountability is to be achieved, performance measurement in human services must be tailored to validate that *conditions are right* for quality services to exist and to verify positive client outcomes. Measuring outcomes does little to *prevent* harm. Although after-the-fact accountability measures—such as recourse in the courts—are essential, ethical or moral accountability requires a more proactive approach.

The development of effective performance measurement technology for ensuring ethical accountability in contracted human services has been slow to develop, in part because it requires operationalizing definitions of ethics and what it means to provide quality care to human beings. Cragg (1998) identifies four obstacles that help to explain this delay as it relates to the development of ethical performance: the manipulation of ethical rhetoric to justify unethical, profit-motivated action; risks to managers in organizations that articulate ethical standards; the inappropriate promotion of ethics as a panacea for success; and finally, the belief that ethics should occupy only a peripheral place in guiding or structuring economic activity.

Establishing what constitutes ethical performance also requires a rather precise definition of morality and the instituting of organizational activities that promote and maintain right behavior. Conventionally, the definition and socialization of morality have been the responsibility of church or family. Thus managers in government organizations (who are constitutionally prohibited from preaching morality derived from any particular religious perspective) have been rightfully reluctant to intrude into this private realm. Besides, the reforms of the 1990s were implemented with an eye to the cost efficiencies and cost effectiveness that could be realized through market practices (Peters 1996). Under these competitive conditions, organizational ethics often become a luxury—something to be concerned about only when money is plentiful.

These factors discourage straightforward discussions of ethics: the development of ethical practices, the creation of accountability mechanisms that could verify ethical behaviors, and the adoption and utilization of performance measurement technology that addresses ethical concerns. For some, it may seem more prudent to avoid issues of ethics altogether, especially under devolved and diffused reform conditions when the likelihood of discovering ethical violations is limited in any case. The accountability question remains, however: easier and safer for whom?

Operational Measurement Issues

Measurement technology is most effective when the important aspects of a system's processes, outputs, or outcomes can be quantified or observed objectively. The number of pregnant women who attend prenatal classes or the number of contact hours between service providers and patients with Alzheimer's disease are not especially difficult to measure. Unfortunately, all too often that which can be measured easily is not very important (Gregory 1999; Halachmi 1999; Halachmi and Geri 1999), or measures are adopted without thought. "Too often, managers simply use the same measures their predecessor used. It's the easy way out . . . but it does not necessary reflect what is valued" (Lisoski 2003, p. 16). Does anyone truly care how thick the concrete is if freeways are hopelessly congested, how many pregnant mothers attend classes if they do not change their unhealthy lifestyles, or if the people who are removed from the welfare rolls have nowhere to live except on the streets? It is not difficult to measure the costs or quantities of many inputs, activities, and outputs. On the other hand, it is often very difficult to measure outcomes that are related to the moral and ethical dimension of accountability. Furthermore, it is difficult to measure the quality of many service-providing activities and outputs—counseling, for example. It is also difficult and expensive to measure and establish relationships between activities and outcomes (cause-effect relationships), in co-produced human services where activities can only influence the outcomes but cannot directly determine them.

When changes in behavior or lifestyle are the desired outcome, timeliness often becomes a serious problem for performance measurement technology. A few examples of problems with timeliness include outcomes of programs designed to improve the outcome of pregnancies and programs for people with chemical dependencies. Outcomes can take years or even decades to demonstrate except through indirect or proxy measures—a measurement approach that introduces goal displacement, which is another serious limitation of current performance measurement technology. "Organizational behavior reacts over time to maximize performance on those dimensions emphasized by the system at the expense of other equally or more important objectives" (Poister 1992, p. 201). Performance measures (and performance indicators) replace the true purposes that the indicators are employed to measure, or are given priority over other goals.

Politics

Citizens have the right to expect current, reliable information about the performance of their government. But identifying a single homogeneous public interest that could serve as an anchor for an assessment of the effectiveness of performance is a thorny, if not futile, task. In addition, although policy makers may enact laws and administrative regulations that require organizations to adopt performance measures, the organizational capacity or means for implementation may be lacking—"a process known as 'symbolic action'" (de Lancer Julnes and Holzer 2001, p. 696). Elected officials often give lip service to the rhetoric of reform but support decision processes and policies that provide them with political support and the ability to claim credit for whatever change matches their political agenda or supports their reelection campaign rhetoric (Radin 2000).

Accountability in government cannot exist without performance and outcome information. Any responsible attempt at reform that incorporates downsizing, devolution, diffusion, or empowerment requires solid performance measurement and the will to use information responsibly. Without accurate, meaningful, and timely information about measured performance, reforms amount to abdication of some of government's most basic responsibilities. We must not be deluded into expecting more from current performance measurement technology than it is able to deliver.

Why New Public Management Reform Models Continue to Be Adopted Despite the Limitations of Performance Measurement Technology

Reduced costs, increased responsiveness, and flexibility are the most commonly voiced rationales for downsizing, diffusion, devolution, and empowerment (Smith and Lipsky 1993). We argue, however, that ideology is the primary justification for national, state, and local governments to blindly continue to implement new public management-type reforms even when there are sound reasons to avoid doing so. Regarding *ideology*, we include:

- *Antigovernment political ideology.* Government is incompetent and cannot be trusted to do much of anything right (Ott and Shafritz 1994, 1995; Peters 1996).
- *Keep government out of business ideology.* Government's rules and requirements create unwanted bureaucratic interference (Ott and Dicke 2000).
- *Inaccurate assumptions about competition in the market and the dependence of contracting organizations.* The assumption of meaningful competition is not warranted in many of the human services markets (Saidel 1991; Smith and Lipsky 1993), an assumption that is necessary for markets to work. In reality, there are shortages of qualified contractors in the human services and long waiting lists to receive services.

Thus our central arguments are:

1. Downsizing, devolution, diffusion, and empowerment are manifestations of a powerful and widely accepted ideology.

2. Pressures for government to downsize, devolve, diffuse, and empower will not lessen in the foreseeable future.
3. Accountability in government is a far more complex notion than simply legalistic adherence to the terms of a contract, protecting funds, or counting activities.
4. Historically (and at least in theory), accountability in government has been achieved mostly upward through layers in hierarchies, from employees through supervisors and middle managers to elected officials and (again in theory) out to the public.
5. Downsizing, devolution, diffusion, and empowerment substantially diminish government's ability to achieve accountability through hierarchies.
6. It has been widely but erroneously assumed that advances in performance measurement technology during the 1990s created the ability to ensure accountability for government services that are devolved, diffused, and entrusted to empowered employees.
7. Performance measurement technology is not yet able to provide the information needed for accountability in at least one major area of government activity, the human services.

Downsizing, devolution, diffusion, and empowering offer exciting potential opportunities to improve the management of public organizations and services—and, thereby, governance in the United States. These approaches, however, also weaken or eliminate the historic notion of accountability upward through hierarchies to public officials who are accountable to the public, however imperfect such accountability may have been. We acknowledge that hierarchy never has been a highly successful approach to accountability, in theory or in practice. We cannot, however, blindly step away from hierarchical accountability before performance measurement technology is sufficiently well developed to replace it. Thus the search for better performance management technologies must be intensified. The interesting challenges for public administration as the "tide" (Light 1998) of new public management reform peaks are to

• align public-sector reform ideology, truths, and models more closely with operational realities;
• adopt reform models only if information technology is able to support the model's operational needs;
• continue to improve and refine the reform models, because some technologies may never be able to perform the tasks that existing models require of them; and

* accelerate efforts to improve the enabling technologies, particularly performance measurement.

Public officials cannot be permitted to simply assume that current performance measurement technology will take care of the accountability problem as public sector reform models are adopted. It is necessary to point out that the emperor is still not wearing any clothes. He may be pulling them on, but vital parts in the moral and ethical dimension remain uncovered.

References

Alexander, Phil. 1992. "Empowerment . . . Slogan or Operating Principle?" *Journal for Quality and Participation* 15: 26–28.
Altshuler, Alan A. 1997. "Bureaucratic Innovation, Democratic Accountability, and Political Incentives." In *Innovation in American Government*, ed. Alan A. Altshuler and Robert D. Behn, pp. 38–67. Washington, DC: Brookings Institution.
Ammons, David N. 1994. "The Role of Professional Associations in Establishing and Promoting Performance Standards for Local Government." *Public Productivity & Management Review* 17, no. 3 (Spring): 281–98.
Anetzberger, Georgia J. 1996. "Protective Services in the Context of Long-Term Care." In *Silent Suffering: Elder Abuse in America*, ed. Archstone Foundation, pp. 106–111. San Diego, CA: Professional Philanthropy Services.
Baumann, Andrea, and Silverman, Barbara. 1998. "De-professionalization in Health Care: Flattening the Hierarchy." In *The Ethics of the New Economy: Restructuring and Beyond*, ed. Leo Groarke, pp. 203–11. Waterloo, Ontario, Canada: Wilfrid Laurier University Press.
Behn, Robert D. 1995. "The Big Questions of Public Management." *Public Administration Review* 55, no. 4 (July/August): 313–24.
Bhote, Keki R. 1994. "Dr. W. Edwards Deming: A Prophet with Belated Honor in His Own Country." *National Productivity Review* 13 (Spring): 153–59.
Bouckaert, Geert. 1993. "Measurement and Meaningful Management." *Public Productivity & Management Review* 17, no. 1 (Spring): 31–43.
———. 1995. "Improving Performance Measurement." In *The Enduring Challenges in Public Management: Surviving and Excelling in a Changing World*, ed. Arie Halachmi and Geert Bouckaert, pp. 379–412. San Francisco: Jossey-Bass.
Bowen, David E., and Lawler, Edward E. III. 1992. "The Empowerment of Service Workers: What, Why, How, and When." *Sloan Management Review*: 31–39.
Burke, John P. 1986. *Bureaucratic Responsibility*. Baltimore, MD: Johns Hopkins University Press.
Callahan, Kathe, and Holzer, Marc. 1999. "Results-Oriented Government: Citizen Involvement in Performance Measurement." In *Performance & Quality Measurement in Government: Issues & Experiences*, ed. Arie Halachmi, pp. 51–64. Burke, VA: Chatelaine Press.
Clinton, William, and Gore, Albert. 1995. *Putting Customers First '95: Standards for Serving the American People*. Washington, DC: U.S. Government Printing Office.
Cohen, Steven. A. 1993. "Defining and Measuring Effectiveness in Public Management." *Public Productivity & Management Review* 17, no. 1 (Fall): 45–57.

Coplin, William D.; Merget, Astrid E.; and Bourdeaux, Carolyn. 2002. "The Professional Researcher as Change Agent in the Government-Performance Movement." *Public Administration Review* 62, no. 6 (November/December): 699–711.

Cragg, Wesley. 1998. "Ethics and Restructuring: Obstacles, Challenges, and Opportunities." In *The Ethics of the New Economy: Restructuring and Beyond*, ed. Leo Groarke, pp. 287–99. Waterloo, Ontario: Wilfrid Laurier University Press.

DeHoog, Ruth H. 1984. *Contracting Out for Human Services: Economic, Political and Organizational Perspectives*. Albany: State University of New York Press.

de Lancer Julnes, Patria, and Holzer, Marc. 2001. "Promoting the Utilization of Performance Measures in Public Organizations: An Empirical Study of Factors Affecting Adoption and Implementation." *Public Administration Review* 61, no. 6: 693–705.

Deller, Steven C.; Nelson, Carl H.; and Walzer, Norman. 1992. "Measuring Managerial Efficiency in Rural Government." *Public Productivity & Management Review* 15, no. 3: 355–70.

Deming, W. Edwards. 1986. *Out of the Crisis*. Cambridge, MA: MIT Press.

Dicke, Lisa A. 2000. "Accountability in Human Services Contracting: Stewardship Theory and the Internal Perspective." Ph.D. dissertation. University of Utah. *Dissertation Abstracts International* 61, 06A. UMI 9976119.

Dicke, Lisa, and Ott, J. Steven. 1999. "Public Agency Accountability in Human Services Contracting." *Public Productivity & Management Review* 22, no. 4: 502–16.

Donahue, John D. 1989. *The Privatization Decision: Public Ends, Private Means*. New York: Basic Books.

Donnelly, James H. Jr.; Gibson, James L.; and Ivancevich, John M. 1987. *Fundamentals of Management*, 6th ed. Plano, TX: Business Publications.

Eccles, Robert G. 1991. "The Performance Measurement Manifesto." *Harvard Business Review* (January–February): 131–37.

Enos, Darryl D. 2000. *Performance Improvement: Making It Happen*. New York: St. Lucie Press.

Epstein, Paul D. 1984. *Using Performance Measurement in Local Government: A Guide to Improving Decisions, Performance, and Accountability*. New York: Van Nostrand Reinhold.

Fox, Charles J., and Miller, Hugh T. 1995. *Postmodern Public Administration*. Thousand Oaks, CA: SAGE.

Government Accounting Office (GAO). 1991. *Management Practices: U.S. Companies Improve Performance through Quality Efforts*. GAO/NSIAD-91-190. Washington, DC.

———. 1992. *Quality Management: Survey of Federal Organizations*. GAO/GGD-93-9BR. Washington, DC.

Governmental Accounting Standards Board (GASB). 1997. *Report on Survey of State and Local Government's Use and Reporting of Performance Measures: First Questionnaire Results*. Norwalk, CT.

Gibelman, Margaret, and Demone, Harold W. Jr. 2002. "The Commercialization of Health and Human Services: Natural Phenomenon or Cause for Concern?" *Families in Society* 83, no. 4: 387–97.

Gore, Albert. 1993. *The Gore Report on Reinventing Government*. New York: Times Books.

Gregory, Robert J. 1999. "Social Capital Theory and Administrative Reform: Maintaining Ethical Probity in Public Service." *Public Administration Review* 59, no. 1: 63–75.

Halachmi, Arie. 1999. "Introduction: Performance and Quality Measurement in the Public Sector." In *Performance & Quality Measurement in Government: Issues & Experiences*, ed. Arie Halachmi, pp. 9–20. Burke, VA: Chatelaine Press.

Halachmi, Arie, and Geri, Laurance. 1999. "Service Quality and Stakeholders: The Case of the USDA's Animal and Plant Health Inspection Service." In *Performance & Quality Measurement in Government: Issues & Experiences*, ed. Arie Halachmi, pp. 83–100. Burke, VA: Chatelaine Press.

Halachmi, Arie, and Nichols, Kenneth L., eds. 1997. *Enterprise Government: Franchising and Cross-Servicing for Administrative Support*. Burke, VA: Chatelaine Press.

Harmon, Michael M. 1995. *Responsibility as Paradox*. Thousand Oaks, CA: SAGE.

Hedley, Timothy P. 1998, March. "Measuring Public Sector Effectiveness Using Private Sector Methods." *Public Productivity & Management Review* 21, no. 3: 251–58.

Holzer, Marc, and Callahan, Kathe. 1998. *Government at Work: Best Practices and Model Programs*. Thousand Oaks, CA: SAGE.

Jabbra, Joseph G., and Dwivedi, O.P., eds. 1988. *Public Service Accountability: A Comparative Perspective*. West Hartford, CT: Kumarian Press.

Joiner, Brian L. 1994. *Fourth Generation Management*. New York: McGraw-Hill.

Juran, Joseph M. 1992. *Juran on Quality by Design*. New York: Free Press.

Kamensky, John M. 1993. "Program Performance Measures: Designing a System to Manage for Results." *Public Productivity & Management Review* 16, no. 4: 395–402.

Kaplan, Robert S., and Norton, David P. 1992. "The Balanced Scorecard—Measures That Drive Performance." *Harvard Business Review*: 71–79.

———. 1996. "Using the Balanced Scorecard as a Strategic Management System." *Harvard Business Review*: 75–85.

Kearney, Richard C., and Hays, Steven W. 1998. "Reinventing Government: The New Public Management and Civil Service Systems in International Perspective." *Review of Public Personnel Administration* 18, 4:38–54.

Kearns, Kevin P. 1996. *Managing for Accountability: Preserving the Public Trust in Public and Nonprofit Organizations*. San Francisco: Jossey-Bass.

Kettl, Donald F. 1993. *Sharing Power*. Washington, DC: Brookings Institution.

———. 1995. "Building Lasting Reform: Enduring Questions, Missing Answers." In *Inside the Reinvention Machine: Appraising Governmental Reform*, ed. Donald F. Kettl and John J. DiIulio Jr., pp. 9–83. Washington, DC: Brookings Institution.

Kingdon, John. 1995. *Agendas, Alternatives, and Public Policies*, 2d ed. New York: HarperCollins.

Light, Paul C. 1998. *The Tides of Reform: Making Government Work 1945–1995*. New Haven, CT: Yale University Press.

Lisoski, Ed. 2003, January. "If You Can't Measure It You Can't Manage It." *Supervision* 64, no. 1: 16–19.

Milward, H. Brinton; Provan, Keith; and Smith, Lynne G. 1994. "Human Service Contracting and Coordination: The Market for Mental Health Services." In *Research in Public Administration*, vol. 3, ed. James Perry, pp. 231–79. Greenwich, CT: JAI Press.

Morley, Elaine. 1986. *A Practitioner's Guide to Public Sector Productivity Improvement*. New York: Van Nostrand Reinhold.

Nyhan, Ronald C., and Marlowe, Herbert A. Jr. 1995. "Performance Measurement In the Public Sector: Challenges and Opportunities." *Public Productivity & Management Review* 18, no. 4: 333–48.

Orsburn, Jack D.; Moran, Linda; Musselwhite, E.; and Zenger, John H. 1990. *Self-*

Directed Work Teams: The New American Challenge. Homewood, IL: Business One Irwin.

Ott, J. Steven, and Dicke, Lisa A. 2000. "Important but Largely Unanswered Questions about Accountability in Contracted Public Human Services." *International Journal of Organization Theory & Behavior* 3, nos. 3–4: 283–317.

Ott, J. Steven, and Goodman, Doug. 1998. "Government Reform or Alternatives to Bureaucracy? Thickening, Tides and the Future of Government." *Public Administration Review* 58, no. 6 (November/December): 540–45.

Ott, J. Steven, and Shafritz, Jay M. 1994. "Toward a Definition of Organizational Incompetence: A Neglected Variable in Organization Theory." *Public Administration Review* 54, no. 4 (July/August): 370–77.

———. 1995. "The Perception of Organizational Incompetence." In *The Enduring Challenges in Public Management,* ed. Arie Halachmi and Geert Bouckaert, pp. 27–46. San Francisco: Jossey-Bass.

Ott, J. Steven; Boonyarak, Pitima; and Dicke, Lisa A. 2001. "Public Sector Reform and Moral and Ethical Accountability." *Public Integrity* 3, no. 3: 277–89.

Peters, B. Guy. 1996. *The Future of Governing: Four Emerging Models.* Lawrence: University Press of Kansas.

Poister, Theodore H. 1992. "Productivity Monitoring: Systems, Indicators, and Analysis." In *Public Productivity Handbook,* ed. Marc Holzer, pp. 195–212. New York: Marcel Dekker.

Posner, Paul L. 2002. "Accountability Challenges of Third-Party Government." In *The Tools of Government: A Guide to the New Governance,* ed. Lester M. Salamon, pp. 523–28. New York: Oxford.

Prager, Jonas, and Desai, Swati. 1996. "Privatizing Local Government Operations: Lessons from Federal Contracting Out Methodology." *Public Productivity & Management Review* 20, no. 2 (December): 185–203.

Radin, Beryl A. 2000. "The Government Performance and Results Act and the Tradition of Federal Management Reform: Square Pegs in Round Holes?" *J-PART: Journal of Public Administration Research and Theory* 10, no. 1: 111–35.

RAND. 1990. *Pacer Share Demonstration Project: Preliminary Results.* June. Santa Monica, CA.

Rehfuss, John A. 1989. *Contracting Out in Government : A Guide to Working with Outside Contractors to Supply Public Services.* San Francisco: Jossey-Bass.

Romzek, Barbara S., and Dubnick, Melvin J. 1994. "Issues of Accountability in Flexible Personnel Systems." In *New Paradigms for Government,* ed. Patricia W. Ingraham and Barbara S. Romzek, pp. 263–94. San Francisco, CA: Jossey-Bass.

Rosen, Bernard. 1998. *Holding Government Bureaucracies Accountable,* 3d ed. Westport, CT: Praeger.

Russell, James P., and Regel, Terry. 1996. *After the Quality Audit: Closing the Loop on the Audit Process.* Milwaukee, WI: ASQC Quality Press.

Saidel, Judith R. 1991. "Resource Interdependence: The Relationship between State Agencies and Nonprofit Organizations." *Public Administration Review* 51, no. 6: 543–53.

Salamon, Lester M. 1999. *America's Nonprofit Sector: A Primer,* 2d ed. New York: Foundation Center.

———. 2002. *The Tools of Government: A Guide to the New Governance.* New York: Oxford University Press.

Savas, Emanuel. S. 2000. *Privatization and Public-Private Partnerships.* New York: Chatham House.

Shafritz, Jay M. 1992. *The HarperCollins Dictionary of American Government and Politics.* New York: HarperCollins.

Smith, Steven R., and Lipsky, Michael. 1993. *Nonprofits for Hire.* Cambridge, MA: Harvard University Press.

Sorber, Bram. Fall 1993. "Performance Measurement in the Central Government Departments of the Netherlands." *Public Productivity & Management Review* 17, no. 1: 59–68.

Stevens, John M.; Cahill, Anthony G.; Overman, E. Sam; and Frost-Kumpf, Lee. 1995. "The Role of Information Systems in Supporting Total Quality Management and Improved Productivity." In *The Enduring Challenges in Public Management: Surviving and Excelling in a Changing World,* ed. Arie Halachmi and Geert Bouckaert, pp. 119–49. San Francisco: Jossey-Bass.

Stout, Richard Jr. 1980. *Management or Control: The Organizational Challenge.* Bloomington: Indiana University Press.

Suchman, Edward A. 1967. *Evaluative Research: Principles and Practice in Public Service & Social Action Programs.* New York: Russell Sage Foundation.

Tate, Ross L. 2003. "Performance Measure Certification in Maricopa County." *Government Finance Review* 19, no. 1 (February): 6–9.

Teaster, Pamela B. 2003. "When the State Takes Over a Life: The Public Guardian as Public Administrator. *Public Administration Review* 63, no. 4: 396–404.

U.S. Department of Justice (DOJ). 1995. *DOJ Manager's Handbook on Developing Useful Performance Indicators,* Version 1.1. Washington, DC: U.S. DOJ, Justice Management Division, Management and Planning Staff.

Warrian, Peter. 1999. "Metrics for Metro: The Development of Performance Indicators for Social Service Delivery." In *Performance & Quality Measurement in Government: Issues & Experiences,* ed. Arie Halachmi, pp. 191–201. Burke, VA: Chatelaine Press.

Weisbord, Marvin R. 1991. *Productive Workplaces: Organizing and Managing for Dignity, Meaning, and Community.* San Francisco: Jossey-Bass.

10

Cowboys and the New Public Management: Political Corruption as a Harbinger

Peter deLeon

Introduction

Almost since the origins of recorded history, there have been instances of political corruption as chronicled by political scientists, sociologists, public officials, lawyers, and, of late, public-management scholars. Traditionally, political corruption has been viewed as aberrant political behavior by which the private gain triumphs over the public good, even if hard-and-fast definitions are difficult to agree upon.[1] The conventional wisdom, however, is generally more benign, holding that political corruption is simply a manifestation of relatively primitive economic/political cultures and that as sociopolitical maturation occurs, the old habits will naturally fall by the wayside (see Dobel 1978; Caiden and Caiden 1977). This hypothesis was implicitly confirmed by Almond and Verba in their classic *The Civic Culture* (1960), in which the nation-states with the highest presence of "civic culture" were seen to be less affected by political corruption.

Still, according to the reputational rating of Transparency International (TI), even today we find that leading nations in the world—for instance, France, Germany, and the United States—continue to be plagued by elements of political corruption. In the United States, deLeon (1993) drew up five unquestioned cases of political corruption that occurred during the 1980s: the devastating savings and loan (S&L) crisis, culminating in the U.S. Senate's public censuring of one of its members;[2] Operation Ill Wind, which plundered the Department of the Navy's procurement system; the Department of Housing and Urban Development (HUD) scandals, which brought a criminal indictment against that department's secretary; the Iran-Contra imbroglio, which came perilously close to possible charges for impeaching the president; and WEDTECH, in which two businessmen effectively fleeced the Small Business Administration (SBA), the Departments of the Navy and Army, and a few congressmen under the questionable guise of a minority business.[3]

The 1990s were not noticeably better. The Clinton administration repeatedly was charged with instances of political malfeasance. In the eight years of the Clinton presidency, no fewer than five special prosecutors were appointed to investigate Clinton's cabinet members (i.e., Secretaries Ron Brown of Commerce, Bruce Babbitt of Interior, Mike Espy of Agriculture, and Henry Cisneros of HUD), ultimately, of course, ending up with Judge Kenneth Starr and his lengthy (and very costly) investigation of President Clinton, leading to Clinton's subsequent impeachment (Baker 2000; Johnson 2001). To be fair, none of these principals were convicted (Secretary Brown died in an airplane crash during his investigation, and Secretary Cisneros's paramour, over whom he committed perjury, was sent to prison), but these examples do not constitute all the putative corruptions of the Clinton administration. For instance, the participation of the president and vice president in the unseemly world of campaign finances and in the events surrounding "travelgate" were held by many to reflect, if not corruption on the part of the Clintons (and their staff), at least a serious dereliction of executive authority (see Drew 1994). The relatively recent conviction of U.S. congressman James Trafficant (D-OH) and his subsequent removal from the House of Representatives richly illustrates the "bad apple" syndrome (Johnston 2001; Clines 2002).

These are examples that are drawn largely from instances of corruption on the federal level in the United States. If we include examples of municipal corruption (e.g., the 2001 conviction of Buddy Cianci, mayor of Providence, Rhode Island, on racketeering charges[4]), police transgressions (e.g., the Ramparts Division of the Los Angeles Police Department, which resulted in the voiding of hundreds of prosecutions), "victimless" crimes (e.g., prostitution), illicit gambling, and, of course, illegal drug trading, then the tales of political corruption in the United States are anything but trivial (see Anechiarico and Jacobs 1996, for elaboration). Thus it should come as no surprise that in the 2003 Transparency International rankings, the United States ranked no better than nineteenth, while Germany was tied for sixteenth, and France and Spain were twenty-third and twenty-fourth (TI 2003). It would seem that the economic and (more arguably) political trappings of modernity are little more than salves rather than remedies for political corruption.

For these reasons, scholars in public administration (e.g., Frederickson 1999), economics (Rose-Ackerman 1999), and political science (Heidenheimer and Johnston 2001) have once again entered the lists of those who wish to explain and minimize both political corruption and, just as important, the conditions that typically lead to political corruption. Proponents of the new public management (NPM) have likewise turned their attention to this condition, posing a series of structural and managerial reforms to address and, hopefully, to reduce the incidents and effects of corruption. Therefore, this chapter proposes the following: given that political corruption is generally considered to be a widely castigated and outlawed activity under almost any governmental regime, at least nominally, we can refer to its practitioners as analogous to *outliers*, or cowboys if you will. The question posed is: How can the NPM ride herd on these cowboys and minimize such activities? And, of equal importance to the understanding of political corruption and its possible alleviation, what shortcomings would NPM bring to these exercises and how might they be corrected?

This chapter will look closely at the mechanisms and suggestions offered by the NPM scholars in the service of two synergistic ends: first, to circulate their ideas to the wider public-affairs audience, and second, to suggest that NPM, taken verbatim, could benefit from the "friendly amendments" long offered by public administration scholars. This is, of course, another way of saying that there is no definitive answer to political corruption, short of implanting billions of electrodes into the greed cortex in billions of crania (i.e., that *both* institutional structures and administrative norms must be consistent and consonant to address the problems that result from political corruption). Indeed, we need to candidly admit, with, inter alia, Johnston (1982) and Rose-Ackerman (1978), that we do not suggest the elimination of political corruption (see Klitgaard 1988). This chapter is designed to present contemporary illustrations of corruption, primarily viewed through an NPM prism, as a means of constructively commenting more on NPM than on political corruption. By understanding this admittedly restricted phenomenon we can comment more knowingly on the strengths and weaknesses of NPM.

The discussion will begin with a brief overview of the theories that generally underlie the study of political corruption. It will move to an examination of NPM, specifically how its tenets seem particularly amenable to reducing corruption in the public sector. We then will consider some examples of corruption, particularly how they jibe with NPM principals and regimen. These will indicate possible NPM shortcomings and, finally, how these shortcomings might best be addressed by the traditional values espoused by public administration. Although it is easily argued that corruption knows no national boundaries, that it is as universal as social mischief, this chapter will focus on incidents in the United States.

An Overview of Political Corruption[5]

Let us first quickly review what it is we mean by *corruption*, specifically *political corruption*, as it occurs in democratic society. Corruption is almost always seen as a cooperative crime; whether it is bribery or nepotism or price fixing, two parties' collusion is necessary.[6] As in many other felonies, a unit of exchange—traditionally, money—must be involved; we shall return to this idea momentarily. Economist Susan Rose-Ackerman (1978) effectively argues that political corruption nearly always occurs at the nexus between the public and private sectors as a market exchange. It is rare, although not unheard of, for two public-sector agencies to plot to raid their respective public allocations. Sociologist Robert Merton (1968) strongly suggests that corruption is not necessarily mendacious, that its presence may indicate an alternative (or what Merton terms "latent") form of government, one incorporated into the everyday fabric of a society on a consistent, even functional, basis. In fact, it has been argued that, at least in the short run, corruption might actually be beneficial rather than deleterious.[7] Examples come easily to mind: If a zoning license or a building permit is holding up the development of a new office complex, then it should not be surprising to discover that other less-than-legal means of obtaining the zoning variance might be called into play (see Gardiner and Lyman 1978) and that builders, renters, and, ultimately, consumers will generally accept corruption as a legitimate means to counter bureaucratic inaction. The parallel to the Philippines, where such payoffs are referred to as *lagay*, or "speed money," is hardly far-fetched. Moreover, does anyone begrudge the cop on the beat an occasional doughnut from the local diner, a relationship in which the store owner might easily treat the doughnut as an irregular excise tax for services rendered? In short, no harm, no foul. This nonchalant attitude might explain why John Rohr's splendid *Ethics for Bureaucrats* (1989) fails to make even a single reference to corruption. By much the same token, Adam Bellow (2003) has written how familial associations serve valuable accountability functions—that is, a defense of nepotism.

The overall price tag, or ticket, for corruption is certainly not irrelevant, but it is hardly staggering. In 1993, deLeon "guesstimated" (since, in fact, we have no way of really knowing) that all forms of corruption in the United States—including so-called victimless crime, organized crime, and drug running—might very well cost tens of billions of dollars. Still, in an economy whose gross domestic product costs out into the *trillions* of dollars, perhaps we should not worry about corruption. In addition, the cost of capturing and prosecuting the culprits is hardly inexpensive.[8] Nevertheless, one might reasonably argue that "the financial costs of corruption are little more than fiscal friction, the sad but predictable 'costs of doing business' that can be as easily tolerated by the public as breakage or spoilage is by the merchant" (deLeon 1993, p. 33). This represents, then, a variant of the "no harm, no foul" syndrome.

But most observers agree that a strict cost-benefit accounting overlooks the symbolic effect of political corruption, implying, as it does, an inherent unfairness in a government's dealings with its citizens, resulting in a damaging lack of trust in the selfsame government. These perceptions represent the social capital "glue" that binds a society (Fukuyama 1995). James Q. Wilson recognizes a distinction here, when he indicates that "I am rather tolerant of some forms of civic corruption . . . but I am rather intolerant of those forms of corruption that debase the law-enforcement process, discredit its agents, or lead people to believe that equal justice is available only for a price" (1983, p. xxviii). Rose-Ackerman acknowledges that simple economics "cannot substitute for the personal integrity of political actors" (1978, p. 216). Furthermore, the abiding American faith in its democratic ideals—spanning two centuries and its political spectrum—is seemingly undermined by political corruption. Again, in Rose-Ackerman's words (1978, p. 10) "the case for corruption often presupposes a strikingly undemocratic standard for government action." John Girling (1997) observes that capitalism—surely the second of America's two great abiding orthodoxies (see Dahl 1998)—perhaps lies at the collusive heart of corruption and, therefore, its greatest deterrent is what he calls the nation's "normative strengths," its personal moral obligations and voluntary associations.

Finally, deLeon (1993) has pointed out the numerous forms of valued exchange (read "currencies") that motivate people to traffic in (and sometimes stand opposed to) political corruption. Money is the most fungible and commonplace unit of exchange, of course, but others might include public notoriety, familial or clan relations, social obligations, or even patriotism. Consequently, deLeon poses the following definition of corruption: "a cooperative form of unsanctioned, usually condemned policy influence for some type of significant personal gain, in which the currency could be economic, social, political, or ideological remuneration" (1993, p. 25).

The New Public Management

The new public management has been popularly depicted by a few key concepts, such as the decentralization of government and the importance of entrepreneurial activities (e.g., Barzelay and Armajani 1992; Osborne and Gaebler 1992). However, a closer look at this literature indicates a much richer tableau, with a theoretic base that draws on transaction cost analysis

(Coase 1937; Williamson and Masten1995) and principal-agent theory. The first suggests that all exchanges (or transactions) have a cost attached to them; in the words of Ferris and Graddy (1997, p. 91), these transaction costs are defined as "the costs (other than price) associated with carrying out two-sided transactions—that is, the exchange of goods or services from one individual to another with agreed-upon payment for performance." Basically, transaction cost analysis postulates that firms will actively try to minimize these costs, thus maximizing the firm's profits.

This form of analysis argues that the principal forms a hierarchical relationship with the agent to carry out the former's bidding, usually under a contractual basis. However, as Jones and Thompson (1999) have pointed out, this relationship is inherently problematic because the agendas of the pairing rarely agree; both pursue their own preferences or utilities, usually to the limits of what each perceives to be acceptable. Moreover, at least in theory, there are potentially debilitating information asymmetries: The principal has an overview of the firm's overall objective while the agent has a better view of day-to-day operation in the more immediate arena. Neither actor wishes to reveal information completely, for fear of surrendering comparative (bureaucratic) advantage. Therefore, the practical task of the principal-agent relationship is to reconcile the two perspectives.

To address the principal-agent problem, NPM suggests that end results—*not* process—provide clearer, more revealing information regarding the actors' (respective) preferences and thereby lead the principal to design better (more purposive) incentive systems in the context of the organization. By providing more accurate information to the principal, the agent's activities can be monitored and possibly corrected, resulting in what economists refer to as *transparency*. Furthermore, this information can counter the tendency by agents to serve their self-interests or, again in the language of the economist, the tendency to "shirk." These oversight capabilities are immensely enhanced by advances in modern management information systems and accounting (e.g., accrual) systems, which are integral components of the NPM system.

There are, of course, noted shortcomings to principal-agent theory when it is applied to the public sector. There is a growing awareness that principal-agent is a relatively unidirectional management procedure, in which the principal somehow manages to unilaterally control the agent (Fischer 1990). Alternative public-management protocols stress such ideas as a participatory managerial concept, in which agents and principals reach consensual agreements about goals and missions, which is a more democratic regimen (deLeon and deLeon 2002). In addition, the public sector is, in many ways, less focused than its private-sector counterpart and its product (and process) is more amorphous. For example, Moe (1984) has suggested that the public sector is directed by a multitude (or confusion) of principals such as elected representatives, elected executives, and a variety of superior-subordinate relationships (e.g., civil service) within the organization itself. In addition, the public and private sectors often are perceived as driven by differing sets of normative concerns. This distinction most readily can be viewed as their respective emphases on efficiency versus equity requirements (Okun 1975). The ultimate principals in the public organization are, of course, the citizens themselves and, depending on their own policy and program preferences, associated principals and agents can be sent (or can receive) a variety of conflicting signals (Ferris and Graddy 1997). All these conditions can result in obscured systems of managerial transparency and accountability in the public sector.

In summary, NPM offers several constructs and practices that would be useful in combating the excesses of political corruption; these include an emphasis on local, community-owned government, competitive government, mission-driven government, and results-oriented government that is both enterprising and decentralized. Modern accounting and management information systems are necessary adjuncts to these NPM principles. This brief review also indicates some potential oversights: While an appreciative nod has been given to the institutional features of an organization, there is little indication as to what key organizational variables would hinder/facilitate the introduction of NPM; that is, all organizations are treated by NPM as the same. Furthermore, even though democratic systems are seemingly inferred, there is no direct discussion of the values indicated by that political system; at its basis, NPM appears to be largely indifferent to political ideologies; it should produce laudatory managerial results regardless of its ideological bedrock.

With these overviews of both political corruption and NPM in hand, we can now turn to some recent incidents of political corruption to examine how NPM would have addressed them.

Political Corruption and the New Public Management

In many ways, NPM brings a raft of concepts and tools that should help to minimize corrupt activities. However, we need to vet these against the historical record that, too often, has shown that corruption remains an ungainly thread in the American political fabric. The scandals of the Reagan administration were mirrored by those of the Clinton administration. Without going into a series of case studies, let us draw upon these in a somewhat selective manner to suggest how the NPM might fare.

A priority concern in most recent administrations (at least since President Ford) has been the drive toward deregulation. Using Osborne and Gaebler (1992) as a beacon, Vice President Al Gore was aggressive in chairing the National Performance Review (Gore 1995). But before that, Congress had acted to decentralize and deregulate the savings and loan industry, arguably the most recognized arm of the financial industry (given that roughly two-thirds of Americans own their homes, almost all under the auspices of an S&L). Even in retrospect, it is difficult to imagine how much distress the S&L debacle caused. Some estimates are that the final, cumulative bailout cost to U.S. taxpayers was over $2 billion, or more than $2,000 for every man, woman, and child in the nation. L.J. Davis (1980, p. 51) commented that it was "not simply a debacle but a series of debacles that made a few people preposterously rich and will leave most of us significantly poorer." While the reasons are, of course, many and deal mostly with scurrilous activities on the part of the S&L industry (particularly bankers and real estate appraisers), the Reagan administration had acted to undercut the regulatory apparatus necessary to enforce federal oversight, and the state regulatory agencies were even less likely to pick up the regulatory slack. This neglect was furthered by compliant members of Congress (respondent to their S&L contributors) and even by secretary of the treasury Donald Regan, whose ideological stance was firmly bent toward deregulation.

The Department of Housing and Urban Affairs under Secretary Samuel Pierce was the scene of a number of indictments and convictions as Pierce and his chief lieutenants effectively gutted the Moderate [cost of housing] Rehabilitation Program (MRP), largely because, in Secretary Pierce's words, "I . . . considered the MRP to be an economically inefficient program, and during my last six years as Secretary . . . we tried to terminate it" (quoted in deLeon 1993, p. 53). What funds were left in MRP invariably found their way into the coffers of Republican businessmen, often with the assistance of consultants such as former secretary of the interior James Watt,[9] who claimed that HUD's bureaucratic quagmire forced them to circumvent the normal administrative processes. Finally, the Department of the Navy (in the Department of Defense) under the stewardship of Navy secretary John Lehman was tasked with building a 600–ship navy to confront the perceived Soviet threat. Secretary Lehman and Melvin Paisley, assistant secretary for research, engineering, and systems, realized that the Pentagon's massive procurement procedures would delay what they believed to be a national security priority. Not surprisingly, they moved to circumvent the regulations (see Pasztor 1995). Paisley testified to Congress on this matter: "We have brought the entire range of R&D functions within the direct management of the Navy Secretary. . . . My immediate staff and I will continue to develop appropriate policy and oversee its implementation" (quoted in deLeon 1993, p. 119). In a few cases, this meant that proprietary, even classified, information from one contract was shared with competitive bidders in order to assure that the winning contract would go to the second (i.e., preselected) bidder. When the improprieties were disclosed in 1986, Secretary of Defense Frank Carlucci suspended payment to the offending contractors, only (under congressional prompting) to restore all the contract payments ten days later for fear of affecting the companies' production lines and their promised delivery of weapons. Secretary Lehman was even less apologetic, as he reportedly "scoffed" when asked if his management style could have led to these problems. He was quoted as saying that he did not "see any possibility of any correlation between good, strong management and wrong doing" and, moreover, what blame could be affixed should be ascribed to the "bloated" Defense bureaucracy (quoted in Cushman 1988, p. 5).

In all these cases, the push for deregulation encouraged the unfiltered market forces into the government arena, quite consciously subverting the in-place regulations and causing numerous corrupt actions. In many ways, these actions represented entrepreneurial activities in which the boundary conditions between "entrepreneurial" and "illegal" were certainly stretched. Indeed, if criminal convictions are any indicator, the lines were not stretched, they were breached with hardly any acknowledgment of "wrong doing" (Cushman 1988). In reviewing the procedural carnage that Ill Wind brought to the Department of the Navy, a naval procurement expert commented: "Those layers of bureaucracy that prevent you from doing anything efficient are also what prevent the kinds of abuses that can come when a process is streamlined and placed primarily in the hands of political appointees" (quoted by Weintraub and Healy 1988, p.16).

Both George Frederickson (1999) and Herbert Kaufman (1977) make this point: Governmental regulation, or red tape, serves a valuable economic and social purpose in guaranteeing an equitable system, free and open to all actors. According to Frederickson, "At a minimum, it is folly to imagine that there is no trade-off between a sharp reduction in the regulations that guarantee procedural due process and the substance of individual rights and quality of government fairness" (Frederickson, p. 268).

Turning to the issue of NPM's reliance on principal-agent theory, we find that in the areas where corruption occurred, the culpable parties were typically the political appointees—the principals—rather than the in-place administrative staff—the agents. There was repeated congressional testimony on the HUD scandals to the effect that the reason underlying housing contractors' attempts to short-circuit the system was their perceived difficulty in working with the HUD administrative staff.[10] Time and again, HUD staff were overridden and ignored in Secretary Pierce's drive to politicize the office and its grant-allocation system. Similar arguments were couched by Lehman and his appointees against the Department of the Navy's procurement system: that it was unwieldy and took too much time, both fatal features considering the national security requirements of building a 600–ship navy. WEDTECH executives bribed a congressman to urge government bureaucracies, such as the SBA and Department of the Navy, to issue contracts to WEDTECH, even when auditors had been critical of its production capabilities (and, of course, its financial condition).

This observation—that political principals rather than administrative agents are more likely to engage in corrupt actions—is surely open to further investigation. But let us offer at least an initial proposition as to why principals would be more "morally challenged" than their agents. The former are generally and legitimately recruited from outside the civil service and are therefore possibly less likely to bring the necessary ethical training and standards to the administrative table. The large number of special prosecutors empanelled during the Clinton administration to investigate cabinet secretaries supports this possibility. On the other hand, the agents typically have spent much of their professional careers in the civil service; therefore, they would more likely have been exposed to (some would say socialized by) an ethical education proscribing political corruption.

This is not always the case, of course. The main culprits in the Reagan administration's Iran-Contra affair were three career naval officers sworn to uphold the very Constitution they consciously worked to subvert.[11] In addition, this insight can become quite murky as one quibbles over who is the principal and who is the agent as well as the state of their mutual contract. One point can be made: In a principal-agent orientation, the member more vulnerable to corrupting influence has generally been the principal.

The NPM philosophy and practice certainly accorded well with a reduction in corruption. More thorough accounting and budget procedures (read "transparency") would have uncovered the excesses perpetrated by the S&L executives and the HUD scandals. But it is important to note that information alone does not solve the ethical dilemmas that underlie corruption. In the HUD scandals, critical HUD inspector general reports detailed the managerial wrongdoings of the HUD secretary and his staff but—and this is hard to overemphasize—they were largely ignored. Former senator William Proxmire (who chaired the Senate's HUD oversight committee) was asked why he did not act to prevent this waste and fraud. His answer was simultaneously revealing and disturbing: "The answer is simple. We had no idea it was going on" (Proximire's testimony is quoted in deLeon 1993, p.78). Of what value, one needs to ask, is the accurate information provided by the

NPM if it is neither read nor acted upon? Moreover, a reliance on numerical controls confronts the old maxim: What is measured is what can most readily be measured. Thus what is difficult to measure—such as levels of probity or personal integrity—is undervalued (see Gregory 1999 for observations gleaned from the New Zealand NPM).

Another point must be made. The NPM orientation emphasizes efficiency, which implies a certain cost calculation. However, there are numerous examples of illegal actions where money was not the medium of exchange, where payoffs were in other currencies, such as patriotism (e.g., Iran-Contra), party ideology (HUD), or even peer group (what Janis [1980] called "groupthink") pressures (as was the case with "travelgate," an early flap in the Clinton administration in which the White House Travel Office staff was unceremoniously and illegally terminated because Clinton loyalists believed that the staff was not sufficiently solicitous to the new administration; see Drew 1994). And this says little about Merton's (1968) insight that corruption serves as an alternative form of government services that the existing government cannot provide on a timely basis. In short, NPM's clear focus on corruption as violating the efficiency (in the sense of cost) criterion overlooks a wide range of corruption for other currencies.

A final observation can be made. NPM, with its emphasis on organizational efficiencies and transaction cost analysis, brings a relatively new and key perspective to the study of corruption, perhaps replacing some antecedent views and surely supplementing others. Still, it is important to recognize that political corruption is the result of a symphony of conditions, some of which (personal greed and perceived financial means) are beyond the purview of legislation while others (organizational transparency) are more amenable. NPM is attuned to a limited set of transgressions, typically those that can be monitored—for instance, by the use of accrual accounting. Principal-agent theory has splendid capabilities (e.g., its attention to contractual terms) and some serious semantic problems (just who is the principal and who is the agent? or where does the citizen lie?). However, it does offer a valuable relationship tool. Basically, governing and politics are not always or exclusively about efficiency. Public administration scholars (e.g., Frederickson 1999) stress that equity and citizen access are the predominant criteria of democratic governance. Laurence Lynn (1998, p. 120) argues persuasively that "[t]o the extent that the problem of modern public administration is democratic accountability . . . then we must again focus attention on politics and the role of public law." Put another way: if NPM takes stock in the ends (results), what is its position on the means to achieve those ends? For instance: if the Bush administration's USA PATRIOT Act serves to thwart terrorism, is the citizen concerned that it might also undermine civil liberties to achieve that outcome? Of course, the final resolution is open to questions of priorities and risk analysis, but NPM to date has not effectively handled these issues.

Conclusions

The new public management proposes a relatively coherent, integrated package that combines both well-defined theory and practices. Taken as a whole, it has much to offer in terms of positively affecting the conditions that underlie political corruption. It is difficult to imagine that the S&L cowboys would have savaged their shareholders if they had been saddled with the instruments of transparency. A viable principal-agent construct would have prevented the Iran-Contra machinations. Moreover, there is no inherent reason that decentralized or community governments or policy entrepreneurism should be corrupt. And, to be honest, they usually are not corrupt; as we noted earlier, corruption might be persistent but it is not pervasive.

By the same token, myriad examples show where NPM would have been ineffectual in preventing corrupt actions. It could easily be argued that principal-agent theory led to Iran-Contra, which never would have occurred without the collusive (some would say conspiratorial) actions of the National Security Council members who, as Secretary of Defense Caspar Weinberger told the Tower Committee investigating the Iran-Contra affair, were "people with their own agenda," going so far as to keep their principal (the president) largely uninformed as to their actions. To be consistent, it was not surprising that they also kept the alternative principal, the Congress of the United States, completely uninformed (see deLeon 1993, ch. 7 and Draper 1991 for details).[12] Nor did modern accounting systems and one of the finest accounting firms in the world—to say nothing of a world of high-priced legal advice and investment bankers—prevent the bankruptcy and ignominy of Enron, which caused the layoff of more than 10,000 employees and destroyed their retirement system, a loss calculated to be over $1 billion. Indeed, there is some evidence that Enron was able to deceive its stockholders and various energy-consuming states (e.g., California) precisely *because* of its bookkeeping practices and in spite of internal alarms to that effect.[13] This leads us to a telling observation: The ability of corrupt perpetrators to succeed cannot be overlooked, even in the face of modern managerial systems, close cost accounting, and historical traditions.

These examples have a number of ramifications for NPM as it tries to corral the corruption cowboys. The primary observation is that while NPM does have a number of excellent ideas and practices, political corruption at its basis pivots on issues of ethical behavior, on both a personal and an institutional basis. A particular strength of NPM is that it is largely indifferent to personalities; one does one's assigned job, and, if the system is in place, the results are all but predictable. But, of course, people do make a difference— which brings us around to public administration scholars, who have repeatedly argued the centrality of ethics: George Frederickson (1999) is only the latest in a line of authors who indicate that good government demands good governmental ethics, not a system or structural "fix." He writes, "Both the logic and the effects of the new managerialism [NPR] move democratic government further away from the possibility of an influential and selfless public service" (p. 267).

No corrupt action reviewed here could have occurred, an ethicist would tell us, had the central governmental actors been of high moral fiber. No one would disagree, but there are a few additional thoughts to consider. First, of course, is that building redoubtable moral character has been the consensual advice for public administrators, at least since the days of Woodrow Wilson (and possibly going back to St. Augustine). Yet, even with this world of advice, corruption persists. Arguably, this is because ethical lapses will continue. Herein lies the difficulty with this contention: If it is true, do we have any reason to doubt which of the opposing scenarios will prevail—ethical lapses or moral probity—even leaving aside the ambiguities of ethical reasoning (e.g., which is preferred): constitutional processes or rescuing American hostages? And in the case of WEDTECH, which red tape did you want to support, government procurement regulations or affirmative action? History, alas, has sided with the former.

We need also to consider the effects of corruption on democracy. As Girling (1997) suggests, the symbolic nature of corruption is more damaging to the American body politic than are the accrued economic losses. As we have argued above, few would care if the diner's owner gave a doughnut to the cop on the beat unless it were somehow seen (e.g., the doughnut became a Corvette) as an inequitable means of gaining access, in which case it would be viewed as undermining the democratic heritage of the nation. This becomes an issue of accountability. The question of who is accountable to whom is impossible to ignore. NPM proponents would surely agree; the results of monitoring systems are naturally reported to someone. But this someone needs to be better defined in terms of democratic accountability. Accountability becomes even more crucial when the cowboy entrepreneurs are left to ride the administrative range. Who oversees their contractual arrangements or their implementation plans? This is only the first of many accountability questions.

This final observation has grave ramifications for the democratic society, as it speaks directly to the possible consequences if corruption were allowed to continue unchecked—not necessarily to flourish, just allowed to exist in a visible manner such that it can define a way of doing business in either the public or the private sector. For a society that lacks democratic accountability and ethical standing, Toobin's summary of the Enron investigation is ominous:

> In the end, prosecutors may be able to show only that [the principal Enron executives] presided over a culture where this kind of pervasive dishonesty flourished—which is not, in any legal sense, a crime. As the Enron investigations are coming to acknowledge, it may not be possible to divide up the systemic corruptions within the company into easily understood portions of wrongdoing. . . . All the people at Enron who played parts in these transactions pushed the company a little closer to ruin, and all of them could claim that they were only small cogs in a big machine. The sad truth of the criminal-justice system is that when everybody is guilty, no one is. (Toobin 2003, p. 55)

Admittedly, Enron is a privately held corporation and, as such, it might not be the perfect analogy for the public sector and political corruption. Still, Enron's demise should not be dismissed lightly, since in many ways its management operations were similar to NPM's principles and practices. What it and the other examples of political corruption we have reviewed do demonstrate is that NPM as a managerial philosophy must develop new means of corralling the mismanagement cowboys. Remedying its general neglect of administrative ethics is one place to begin.

Notes

1. As Michael Johnston (1986, p. 379) has commented, "We should not expect to find a sharp distinction between corruption and noncorrupt actions. Instead, we will find the gradations of judgment, reflecting a variety of equivocations, mitigating circumstances, and attributed motives."

2. Charles Keating was convicted (the conviction was later overturned on a legal technicality) on federal charges of financial mismanagement. He was later asked about his intentions when he contributed heavily to the political campaigns of five U.S. senators. In an era in which political statements are known for their waffling, Keating's answer speaks volumes to both corruption and campaign financing: "One question among the many raised in recent weeks had to do with whether my financial support in any way influenced several political figures to take up my cause. I want to say in the most forceful way I can: I certainly hope so" (quoted in deLeon 1993, p.153).

3. A few of these (such as Operation Ill Wind, HUD, and the S&L crises) were confirmed by Frederickson (1999).

4. According to Stanton (2003), one of the mayor's chosen contractors posed the rather plaintive question: "All I did was give kickbacks. Is that a crime or what?"

5. Much of the material in this and the following section is covered in greater detail in deLeon and Green (2001).

6. Professor Larry Johnson of the Naval Postgraduate School has kindly pointed out to me that embezzlement is one form of corruption that does not require an accomplice.

7. Merton (1968, p. 126) writes: "Proceeding from the functional view, therefore, that we should *ordinarily* (not invariably) expect persistent social patterns and social structures [involving political corruption] to perform positive functions *which are at the time not adequately fulfilled by other existing patterns and structures*, the thought occurs that perhaps this publicly maligned organization is, *under present conditions*, satisfying basic latent functions" (emphasis in original).

8. Kenneth Starr's costs as the special prosecutor investigating a number of charges against President Clinton were said to be approximately $40 million.

9. James Watt freely admitted to a House committee investigating the HUD allegations that he knew nothing about the MRP, but that was unimportant since he did have easy access to his former cabinet colleague, Samuel Pierce (see deLeon 1993).

10. One housing contractor testified before Congress: "It's a trickle-down theory. It's been a mess at the agency. . . . Mr. Chairman, I am sure you recognize that HUD is not an easy agency to deal with. It is an agency in disarray, with confused and conflicting policies, and we needed someone who could get it to respond. Mr. Watt played that important role, one that was, unfortunately, a necessity. In summary, do I think this selection process was good public policy? No. Do I think a more competitive process would have made better public policy? Of course, but the system was there. . . . Developers must not be blamed for the system they neither created nor administered (Judith Siegel, testifying before Congressman Thomas Lantos; quoted in deLeon 1993, p. 63).

11. Rear Admiral John Poindexter and Marine Colonel Robert McFarland were the National Security Advisors under President Reagan; Marine Lieutenant Colonel Oliver North was a principal desk officer under both. See Draper (1991) for complete details.

12. The question is left open as to whether the president would have objected if he had known; Lieutenant Colonel North and Admiral Poindexter both have implied that he would not have objected. Some credence to their argument was indicated at President Reagan's press conference in November 1986: "Because I don't think a mistake was made. It was a high-risk gamble, and it was a gamble, as I've said, I believe the circumstances warranted. And I don't see that it was a fiasco, or a great failure of any kind (Cannon 1991, p. 61).

13. Two recent works on Enron suggest that its principal executives may avoid criminal penalties, largely for two reasons: First, their financial manipulations in the energy market (such as "special purpose entities") were so complicated that they have claimed they did not understand what they were doing. One investigator has been quoted as saying "every other white-collar crime in history is arithmetic. Enron is calculus" (Toobin 2003, p. 50). Second—this defense is also known as the "lawyers and accountants never said no defense"—the claim has been made that the complicated investments were arguably not in technical violation of the law, although clearly in violation of its spirit. See McLean and Elkin (2003) and Toobin (2003).

References

Almond, Gabriel, and Verba, Sidney. 1960. *The Civic Culture*. Princeton, NJ: Princeton University Press.

Anechiarico, Frank, and Jacobs, James B. 1996. *The Pursuit of Absolute Integrity: How Corruption Control Makes Government Ineffective*. Chicago: University of Chicago Press.

Baker, Peter. 2000. *The Breach: Inside the Impeachment and Trial of William Jefferson Clinton*. New York: Scribner.

Barzelay, Michael, and Armajani, Babak J. 1992. *Breaking through Bureaucracy: A New Vision for Managing in Government*. Berkeley: University of California Press.

Bellow, Adam. 2003. *In Praise of Nepotism: A Natural History*. New York: Doubleday.

Caiden, Gerald E., and Caiden, Naomi J. 1977. "Administrative Corruption." *Public Administration Review* 37, no. 3 (May/June): 301–8.

Cannon, Lou. 1991. *Ronald Reagan: The Role of a Lifetime*: New York: Simon and Schuster.

Clines, Francis X. 2002. "Ohio Congressman Is Guilty in Bribery and Kickback Case." *New York Times*, April 12: A1, A22.

Coase, Ronald. 1937. "The Nature of the Firm." *Economica* 4: 386–405.

Cushman, John H. Jr. 1988. "Former Navy Chief Defends Policies." *New York Times*, September 17:5.

Dahl, Ronald. 1998. *On Democracy*. New Haven, CT. Yale University Press.

Davis, L.J. 1980. "Chronicle of a Debacle Foretold: How Deregulation Begat the S&L Scandal." *Harper's* 281, no. 1684 (September): 47–55.

deLeon, Peter. 1993. *Thinking about Political Corruption*. Armonk, NY: M.E. Sharpe.

deLeon, Linda, and deLeon, Peter. 2002. "The Democratic Ethos and Public Management." *Administration & Society* 34, no. 2 (May): 229–50.

deLeon, Peter, and Green, Mark. 2001. "Corruption and the New Public Management." In *Learning from International Public Management Reform*, ed. Lawrence Jones, James Guthrie, and Peter Steane, ch. 31. New York: JAI.

Dobel, J. Patrick. 1978. "The Corruption of a State." *American Political Science Review* 72, no. 3 (September): 958–73.

Draper, Theodore. 1991. *A Very Thin Line*. New York: Hill and Wang.

Drew, Elizabeth. 1994. *On the Edge: The Clinton Presidency*. New York: Simon and Schuster.

Ferris, James M., and Graddy, Elizabeth A. 1997. "New Public Management Theory: Lessons from the Institutional Economics." In *International Perspectives on the New Public Management*, ed. Lawrence R. Jones, Kuno Schedler, and Stephen W. Wade, pp. 225–40. Greenwich, CT: JAI.

Fischer, Frank. 1990. *Technology and the Politics of Expertise*. Newbury Park, CA: SAGE.

Frederickson, H. George. 1999. "Public Ethics and the New Managerialism." *Public Integrity* 1, no. 3 (Summer): 265–78.

Fukuyama, Francis. 1995. *Trust*. New York: Free Press.

Gardiner, John A. and Lyman Theodore R. 1978. *Decisions for Sale: Corruption and Reform in Land Use and Building Regulations*. New York: Praeger.

Girling, John. 1997. *Corruption, Capitalism, and Democracy*. London: Routledge.

Gore, Al. 1995. *Common Sense Government: Works Better and Costs Less*. Washington, DC: U.S. Government Printing Office.

Gregory, Robert J. 1999. "Social Capital Theory and Administrative Reform." *Public Administration Review* 59, no. 1 (January/February): 63–75.

Heidenheimer, Arnold J., and Johnston, Michael, eds. 2002. *Political Corruption: Concepts & Concepts*, 3d ed. New Brunswick, NJ: Transaction.

Janis, Irving. 1980. *Groupthink.* Boston: Houghton Mifflin.

Johnson, Haynes. 2001. *The Best of Times: America in the Clinton Years.* San Diego, CA: Harcourt.

Johnston, David. 2001. "U.S. Charges Colorful Ohio Congressman with Taking Bribes." *New York Times*, May 5: A1, A13.

Johnston, Michael. 1982. *Political Corruption and Public Policy in America.* Monterey, CA: Cole.

———. 1986. "Right and Wrong in American Politics: Popular Concepts of Corruption." *Polity* 18, no. 3 (Spring): 367–91.

Jones, Lawrence R., and Thompson, Fred. 1999. *Public Management : Institutional Renewal for the Twenty-First Century.* Stamford, CT: JAI Press.

Kaufman, Herbert. 1977. *Red Tape: Its Origins, Uses, and Abuses.* Washington, DC: Brookings Institution.

Klitgaard, Robert. 1988. *Controlling Corruption.* Berkeley: University of California Press.

Lynn, Laurence E. Jr. 1998. "A Critical Analysis of the New Public Management." *International Public Management Journal* 1, no. 2: 107–23.

McLean, Bethany, and Elkin, Peter. 2003. *The Smartest Guys in the Room.* New York: Portfolio/ Penguin.

Merton, Robert K. 1968. *Social Theory and Social Structure.* New York: Free Press.

Moe, Terry M. 1984. "The New Economics of Organization." *American Journal of Political Science* 28, no. 4: 739–77.

Okun, Arthur M. 1975. *Equality and Efficiency, the Big Tradeoff.* Washington, DC: Brookings Institution.

Osborne, David, and Gaebler, Ted. 1992. *Reinventing Government: How the Entrepreneurial Spirit Is Transforming the Public Sector.* Reading, MA: Addison-Wesley.

Pasztor, Andy. 1995. *When the Pentagon Was for Sale: Inside America's Biggest Defense Scandal.* New York: Scribner.

Rohr, John A. 1989. *Ethics for Bureaucrats.* New York: Marcel Dekker.

Rose-Ackerman, Susan. 1978. *Corruption: A Study in Political Economy.* New York: Academic Press.

———. 1999. *Corruption and Government.* New York: Cambridge University Press.

Stanton, Mike. 2003. *The Prince of Providence: The True Story of Buddy Cianci, America's Most Notorious Mayor, Some Wiseguys and the Feds.* New York: Random House.

Toobin, Jeffrey. "The Annals of Law: End Run at Enron." *New Yorker* 79, no. 32 (October 27): 48–55.

Transparency International (TI). 2003. Rankings. Available at http://transparency.org/cpi/2003/cpi2003.en.html (accessed October 25, 2004).

Weintraub, Daniel M., and Healy, Melissa. 1988. "Scandal's *Roots* Traced to Basic Reagan Policy Goals." *Los Angeles Times*, July 4: sect. 1, p. 16.

Williamson, Oliver E., and Masten, Scott E. 1995. *Transaction Cost Economics.* Aldershot, UK: Edward Elgar.

Wilson, James Q. 1983. *Thinking about Crime.* New York: Basic Books.

11

Public Ethics, Legal Accountability, and the New Governance

Laura S. Jensen and Sheila Suess Kennedy

During the past century, American governance has been transformed fundamentally. The scope of government action has increased at all levels of the federal system. Moreover, the means through which government addresses public problems have changed radically. Where public functions originally were performed primarily by state actors, and later delegated to closely related agents of the state, discretion over the day-to-day operation of public programs now routinely rests not with the responsible government agencies, but with a host of nongovernmental, third-party surrogates or proxies that provide programs under the aegis of loans, loan guarantees, grants, contracts, vouchers, and other new tools of public action. This exercise of core governmental authority by non- and quasi-governmental entities is perhaps the most distinctive feature of America's "new governance" (Salamon 2002, pp. 1–2; Kettl 1988, 1993).

Many observers are sanguine about this delegation of authority because they expect public problem solving to be enhanced by cross-sectoral partnerships. That private delegation does not comport with longstanding theories of public administration is not troubling, they suggest, for in the increasingly interdependent world of implementation networks, "no entity, including the state, is in a position to enforce its will on others" (Salamon 2002, p. 15). As Lester Salamon argues, the command and control of the sovereign, once the hallmark of democratic government, has become outmoded, and is being replaced by a new management paradigm that "makes collaboration and negotiation legitimate components of public administrative routine rather than regrettable departures from expected practice" (2002, p. 15).

We take issue with the notion that the transfer of sovereignty to nongovernmental agents is merely a management problem, because legal restrictions on the use and reach of public authority are fundamental to the United States's political and constitutional order. Explicit legal standards of right and wrong are a defining feature of American government (Frederickson 1993, p. 248; see also Rohr 1998). Substituting new forms of collaboration and management for hierarchical, bureaucratic chains of command cannot and should not mean abandoning traditional commitments to the public values of liberty, equality, and fairness. Nor should it obviate public actors' obligations to meet the standards for government behavior that stem from those values and are incorporated in public law. As Donald Kettl has observed (1993, p. 40), the government "is not just another principal dealing with another agent." The skepticism about government performance that has fostered the development of privatized governing arrangements in the United States has not yet been translated into lack of concern over how public authority is deployed.

Nowhere can this be seen more clearly than in the ongoing scandal over the abuse of prison inmates in Iraq, an international relations debacle of some magnitude. Before four contractors were killed in Falluja at the end of March 2004, few Americans were likely aware of the roles played by publicly paid, nongovernmental agents in the U.S. occupation. The April 2004 release of graphic photographs showing the sexual abuse of Iraqi prisoners incarcerated in the Abu Ghraib jail outside of Baghdad (a facility notorious for torture and execution under the rule of Saddam Hussein) has turned the expanding and largely unregulated role played by private contractors overseas into front-page news (Borger 2004; Miller and Miller 2004). It is now widely known that the U.S. government relies upon private contractors in Iraq not only for such tasks as mail delivery and foreign language interpretation, but also for intelligence gathering, the provision of security services, and the conduct of prison interrogations. As outrage over the events at Abu Ghraib escalates, questions of accountability are being raised in the United States and abroad. Who, precisely, is responsible for what happened? U.S. president George W. Bush? High-level Pentagon officials? The military personnel charged with running the prison? The nominally private employees still involved in operations at Abu Ghraib, who work for contracting U.S. firms CACI International and Titan Corporation?[1]

In our view, the incidents at Abu Ghraib and elsewhere demonstrate that the new governance's central challenge is not simply to enhance flexibility in governing partnerships so that innovation and performance may flourish, but to do so *while still assuring legal accountability for the means and ends of public action.* This is not an arcane legal problem, but a challenge that presents policy makers and citizens with a fundamental ethical dilemma. We rely upon our understanding of *the state* and *state action* in order to know when we may expect certain standards to apply to public programs and those who manage them, and when we may ask the courts to intervene and impose restraints upon misconduct or inappropriate uses of public authority. If we do not know what actions we may properly attribute to government, our constitutional rights and freedoms are undermined. Yet to subject every government vendor to constitutional constraints would effectively eviscerate the concept of *private* and weaken, not strengthen, liberty and creativity (Minow 2002, p. 30). If we are to maintain a vibrant, pluralistic polity that is governed effectively, efficiently, and accountably, we must be able to draw meaningful distinctions between private actions and actions taken on behalf of the state, and oversee the latter competently.

In this chapter, we will describe the principle of legal accountability that is at the heart of U.S. constitutional structure and demonstrate the difficulties involved in depending upon judicial review as an enforcement mechanism. We will do so by analyzing the federal judiciary's "state action" jurisprudence, which was neither consistent nor reliably protective of citizens' rights even before the advent of the highly privatized new governance. Next, we will review the record of the city of Indianapolis's privatization efforts to illustrate how the legitimacy of government depends upon our ability to distinguish public from private, and hold public actions and actors to account. We will conclude by calling for a refashioned law of state action applicable to the operational realities of contemporary "government by proxy" arrangements.

State Action in a Changing State

American governance fundamentally is premised upon the idea that the U.S. Constitution and public law more generally, places limits upon the actions that government may take. Adherence to the standards established in public law is essentially what transforms governmental rule from an exercise of raw power into a legitimate use of democratic authority. For governance to be accountable,[2] the limits imposed by public law must apply to all governmental action and be enforceable, whether the tasks of government are accomplished by actors who are officially public or nominally private. This poses major challenges in the United States's increasingly mixed regime, for the jurisprudence intended to keep exercises of government authority subject to public law's strictures has not kept pace with the ways in which privatization initiatives have been refashioning the nature of the state and state action (Gilmour and Jensen 1998; Kennedy 2001; Barak-Erez 1995; Metzger 2003).

The legal doctrine of *state action* was first defined by the U.S. Supreme Court shortly after the ratification of the Fourteenth Amendment, when the Court was called upon to define the extent to which that amendment protected the privileges and immunities of citizenship against inappropriate action by state government. In *Virginia v. Rives* (1879, p. 318), the Court declared that the Fourteenth Amendment applied "to State action exclusively, and not to any action of private individuals," adding that all state action counted, whether legislative, executive, or judicial. Similarly, in the landmark 1883 *Civil Rights Cases*, the Court held that the amendment's prohibitions applied to "all State legislation, and State action of every kind," including all "acts done under State authority" (pp. 11, 13). The "individual invasion of individual rights," by contrast, was "not the subject-matter of the amendment" (p. 11).

Over the past century, the Supreme Court repeatedly has reiterated that an "essential dichotomy" exists between state action and private conduct (see, e.g., *Shelley v. Kramer* 1948; *Jackson v. Metropolitan Edison Co.* 1978; *National Collegiate Athletic Association v. Tarkanian* 1988). State action is subject to judicial scrutiny for conformance with the numerous federal, state, and local rules that apply to government behavior, including the Bill of Rights and the Fourteenth Amendment; a host of general management statutes, such as the Administrative Procedure Act and the Freedom of Information Act; the terms of administrative regulations, executive orders, and budget circulars; antidiscrimination statutes, such as the Civil Rights Act of 1964 and the Americans with Disabilities Act; and importantly, at the state and local levels, Section 1983 of the Civil Rights Act of 1871. Private conduct, no matter how discriminatory, wrongful, or unfair, is not subject to scrutiny under these rules (though legal remedies may otherwise be sought through criminal prosecution, contract or regulatory enforcement, or common law actions).

However fundamental this dichotomy may be in principle, it has been difficult even for the courts asserting its existence to say what, precisely, separates *state* from *private* conduct in practice. Consider, for example, the disparate findings in two cases from the 1980s in which the Supreme Court reviewed the behavior of doctors treating dependent populations under the aegis of government funds and authority. In *West v. Atkins* (1988), an essentially unanimous Court decided that a private physician under contract to provide medical care to state prison inmates was a state actor. Although the doctor was not technically a government employee on the public payroll, the state's control over service delivery in the correctional context was held to render the doctor's conduct attributable to the state. In *Blum v. Yaretsky* (1982), by contrast, a divided Court allowed the state of New York summarily to reduce or eliminate the long-term care benefits of Medicaid patients upon the recommendation of private nursing home personnel. Although the nursing facilities received government funding and the benefit decisions in question were made pursuant to a state cost control policy, the Court held that the deprivation of patient benefits was not state action because ultimately it resulted from judgments made by private physicians and nursing home administrators "according to professional standards that [we]re not established by the State" (p. 1008).

The Supreme Court has reached similarly disparate conclusions in a set of decisions involving organizations that govern the conduct of amateur athletics. In *San Francisco Arts & Athletics, Inc. v. United States Olympic Committee* (1987), a divided Court upheld the U.S. Olympic Committee's (USOC) decision to exercise its authority under the Amateur Sports Act of 1978 to selectively ban a gay rights organization from using the word "Olympic" in the name of an event it sponsored. Despite USOC's status as a corporation created by federal law and its extensive authority over international athletic competition, the committee was not held to be a state actor; nor was the National Collegiate Athletic Association (NCAA), in a case in which its essential monopoly on rule making for college athletics forced a state university to impose disciplinary sanctions upon a tenured employee (*NCAA v. Tarkanian* 1988). Recently, however, in *Brentwood Academy v. Tennessee Secondary School Athletic Association* (2001), a five-member majority found that the Tennessee nonprofit organization that regulates high school interscholastic sports *was* a state actor, and it could be held accountable for violations of the Fourteenth Amendment.

As privately operated prisons and detention facilities have become more common, cases that challenge their management have begun to work their way through the judicial system. The lower federal courts recently have not hesitated to hold prison contractors accountable for their behavior as state actors, often noting that the power to deprive an individual of liberty is a quintessentially governmental power (*Plain v. Flicker* 1986). In *Skelton v. Pri-Cor, Inc.* (1991), for example, the U.S. Court of Appeals for the Sixth Circuit found that a private corporation operating a state corrections facility could be held liable as a state actor for violating the civil rights of an inmate. Similarly, in *Blumel v. Mylander* (1996), a U.S. District Court in Florida held that a private contractor that detained a man in a Florida jail for thirty days without a hearing was liable as a state actor for a due process violation. In *Giron v. Corrections Corporation of America* (1998), the New Mexico District Court decided that a private contractor's employee had engaged in state action when he raped an inmate in his capacity as a prison guard.

Even so, the federal courts do not speak with one voice in their decisions concerning the use of delegated authority in situations where plaintiffs are captives of the state, and thereby subject to whatever treatment is meted out in institutional settings. For example, a U.S. District Court in Texas held a private residential youth treatment facility liable as a state actor for the wrongful death of a twelve-year-old boy in *Lemoine v. New Horizons Ranch and Center, Inc.* (1998), but the U.S. Court of Appeals reversed (1999). In *Wade v. Byles* (1995), a U.S. district court in Illinois held that contractors that provide security at a public housing complex were not state actors, despite the fact that the security guards had the authority to carry guns, arrest people, and use deadly force. In a case involving alleged constitutional violations by privately employed prison guards in Tennessee, the U.S. Supreme Court declined to grant the guards qualified immunity, even though such immunity would clearly have been granted to guards employed directly by the state (*Richardson v. McKnight* 1997). These cases are difficult to reconcile.[3]

Little wonder that state action jurisprudence has been termed a "conceptual disaster area" (Black 1967, p. 95). As one commentator wryly has noted, the Supreme Court's "sifting" and "weighing" of the facts in state action cases differs from Justice Stewart's famous "I know it when I see it" standard for identifying obscenity "mainly in the comparative precision of the latter" (Brest 1982, p. 1325). According to Federal Judge Henry J. Friendly (1982, p. 1291), what we know about the distinction between public and private action is more "because the Court has pricked out more reference points than because it has elaborated any satisfying theory." The Court itself acknowledges that its state action decisions "have not been a model of consistency."[4]

The confusion is not due to lack of effort on the part of the justices. In the same year that Brest and Friendly issued their criticisms of the Court's state action jurisprudence, the Court articulated a two-pronged scheme for determining whether activities are attributable to government in *Lugar v. Edmondson Oil Co.* (1982, p. 937), a case that capped a series of legal challenges to the state-authorized debt collection procedures of private creditors.[5] For behavior to be considered attributable to the state, the *Lugar* majority wrote, it must both (1) "be caused by the exercise of some right or privilege created by the State or by a rule of conduct imposed by the State or by a person for whom the State is responsible," and (2) be undertaken by "a person who may fairly be said to be a state actor . . . because he is a state official, because he has acted together with or has obtained significant aid from state officials, or because his conduct is otherwise chargeable to the State" (see also *Rendell-Baker v. Kohn* 1982; *Blum v. Yaretsky* 1982).

The first prong of *Lugar*'s state action formula often may be easily satisfied, as when an individual simply acts "with knowledge of and pursuant to" a state statute (Metzger 2003, p. 1412, n. 149, citing *American Manufacturers Mutual Insurance Co. v. Sullivan* 1999). Note, however, that bona fide public employees are not automatically considered to be state actors even when they are performing their official duties. For example, public defenders are not state actors when they represent clients, despite their sources of income and official positions, because they act as adversaries of the state (*Polk County v. Dodson* 1982). "No one fact," not even actual public employment status, "can function as a necessary condition across the board for finding state action" (*Brentwood Academy v. Tennessee Secondary School Athletic Association* 2001).

Satisfying the second prong of *Lugar*'s scheme is also tricky, since asking whether a nominally private party "may fairly be said to be a state actor" effectively restates, rather than resolves, the problem of locating the hand of the state in legally suspect conduct. In its efforts to apply this part of the formula, the Court historically has considered three criteria: whether the party committing the conduct did so while performing a government or public function; whether the party's conduct was encouraged, facilitated, or compelled by the government; and whether a symbiotic relationship exists between the government and the party committing the challenged conduct. As Gillian Metzger has observed (2003, p. 1412), the Court sometimes has adopted a flexible, situational, pragmatic approach in identifying these criteria and applying them to reach an "overall gestalt sense" of whether questioned activities should be held to account under the rules that apply to state behavior. At other times, however, the Court has taken a rigid, restrictive, and highly formalistic stance in applying these criteria, treating them as distinct "tests" that represent exclusive grounds for finding state action and holding it accountable (see also Krotoszynski 1995, pp. 317–21; Gilmour and Jensen 1998, pp. 250–52).

The Public-Function Criterion

Decisions in many state action cases have hinged upon the *public-function* criterion, which asks whether private actors or organizations have exercised "powers traditionally exclusively reserved to the State" (*Jackson v. Metropolitan Edison Co.* 1978, p. 352) or "exclusive prerogatives of the sovereign" (*Flagg Brothers, Inc. v. Brooks* 1978, p. 160). Not surprisingly, the Supreme Court rarely has discerned state action when it has employed this standard. In *Flagg Brothers*, for example, the Court held that the seizure and sale of personal property by a private storage company was not state action, despite the fact that the procedures in question were both established by state law and enforced in state courts, because "the settlement of disputes between debtors and creditors" has not "traditionally [been] an exclusive public function" (p. 161). Similarly, the Medicaid benefits of elderly patients were terminated in *Blum*, the nursing home case discussed above, in part because the Court was "unable to conclude that nursing homes perform[ed] a function that has been 'traditionally the exclusive prerogative of the State'" (1982, citing *Jackson* 1978, p. 353). In *San Francisco Arts & Athletics*, the Court refused to find that the U.S. Olympic Committee had violated the Fifth Amendment due process clause because "[n]either the conduct nor the coordination of amateur sports has been a traditional governmental function" (1987, p. 545).

By contrast, the lower federal courts have recently found state action when applying the public-function criterion in cases that have involved the incarceration, residential treatment, and involuntary commitment of citizens and the detainment of aliens. Public functions served to identify state action in *Skelton*, *Blumel*, and *Giron* (the prison contractor cases discussed above), and in the district court opinion in *Lemoine* (the case involving the death of a young boy in a privately run, residential treatment facility). Similarly, in *Davenport v. Saint Mary Hospital* (1986), a U.S. District Court in Pennsylvania relied upon the public-function criterion to hold that the behavior of a private hospital was state action when it provided care to involuntarily committed patients. The U.S. District Court for the Southern District of Texas also decided in *Medina v. O'Neill* (1984, p. 1038) that the conduct of a private firm hired by the U.S. Immigration and Naturalization Service to detain aliens was state action, because "'the power to expel or exclude aliens' is a fundamental sovereign attribute exercised exclusively by the legislative and executive branches of the United States Government. . . . Likewise, detention is a power reserved to the government, and is an exclusive prerogative of the state."

The public-function criterion aims to ensure accountability by identifying private control over activities that are *essentially* governmental. Unfortunately, this emphasis on *essence* writes off the vast majority of the tasks performed by contemporary American government. Moreover, it offers no principled guidance on how to define those functions that are the exclusive prerogatives of government (Gilmour and Jensen 1998, p. 250). Looking to history and tradition is suggestive, but hardly dispositive. The Supreme Court has declared that elections, eminent domain, zoning, the exercise of preemptory challenges during jury selection, and municipal functions when private property "has taken on *all* the attributes of a town" are exclusive public functions. It also has asserted that certain functions, including education, fire and police protection, and tax collection, have been *more* exclusively administered by state and local governments than have other functions. Other authorities such as the National Academy of Public Administration and the U.S. General Accounting Office, however, have compiled different lists. It is not difficult to see why federal court decisions employing the public-function criterion have reached remarkably different results.

The Significant Government Encouragement (Close Nexus) Criterion

As we have noted, there are circumstances in which directly acting, bona fide government employees have not been regarded as state actors by the courts because of the jobs they perform in their official capacities. Yet, nominally private actors are sometimes so regarded, either because they have "acted together with or ha[ve] obtained significant aid from state officials, or because [their] conduct is otherwise chargeable to the State" (*Lugar* 1982, p. 937). In deciding whether government is ultimately responsible for inappropriate conduct, the judiciary must "assess the potential impact of official action [to] determine whether the State has significantly involved itself with invidious discriminations" (*Reitman v. Mulkey* 1967, p. 380). The *nexus* criterion asks "whether the government exercised coercive power or provided such significant encouragement that the complained-of misconduct . . . must be deemed to be the conduct of the government (*Barrios-Velazquez v. Asociacion de Empleados del Estado Libre Asociado de Puerto Rico* 1996).

Here again, the goal is to ensure accountability by recognizing control. The nexus criterion aims to identify situations in which such significant or elaborate links (financial, regulatory, administrative) exist between the government and a private party charged with misconduct that the former effectively controls the latter (*Logiodice v. Trustees of Maine Central Institute* 2002, p. 34). But what, precisely, constitutes a "significant" or "elaborate" link? The nexus criterion offers no principled guidance, and hence is no firmer as a standard for identifying state action than the public-function criterion. Courts applying it have sometimes found the government so implicated in misconduct of private actors that actions under challenge have been converted into state action for accountability purposes. This occurred in *Lugar*, where the Supreme Court held that a man's willful participation with state officials in the seizure of property under a defective state statute converted his conduct into state action. Yet in many cases, consideration of the nexus criterion has not led to judicial recognition of state action. In *Rendell-Baker v. Kohn* (1982), for example, the Supreme Court allowed a private high school summarily to terminate an employee without a hearing, even though the school was subject to extensive regulation, reporting requirements, and budget controls; received the vast majority of its operating budget from public sources;

and enrolled its pupils due to referrals from public-school officials and state drug rehabilitation agency personnel.

The Symbiotic Relationship Criterion

The *symbiotic relationship* criterion focuses upon the quality of the relationship between the government and the nominally private entity involved in an activity under challenge. State action is found when the degree of interaction between government and the private party renders them substantially inseparable and their relationship is interdependent or mutually beneficial in nature (symbiotic). As with the public function and close nexus criteria, applications of the symbiotic relationship criterion are inevitably fact-sensitive inquiries, and relatively minor factual distinctions have produced very different results.

The leading instance of public-private symbiosis constituting state action is found in *Burton v. Wilmington Parking Authority* (1961), in which the Supreme Court held that the refusal of a privately owned coffee shop to serve a black man was discriminatory state action, largely because the shop was a lessee in a publicly owned garage. An intricate financial and service relationship existed between the restaurant and the state. Moreover, the misconduct had taken place in a facility that flew both state and national flags on its roof, and bore official state signs that designated its public character. Accordingly, the Court declared that the state of Delaware "ha[d] so far insinuated itself into a position of interdependence" with the coffee shop that it had to "be recognized as a joint participant in the challenged activity." The state "ha[d] not only made itself a party to the refusal of service, but [also] elected to place its power, property and prestige behind the admitted discrimination" (p. 725).

A divided Court also converted nominally private behavior into discriminatory state action in *Edmonson v. Leesville Concrete Co.* (1991), a case that involved the race-based exclusion of potential jurors by private litigants exercising peremptory challenges. Noting the extent to which the nominally private actor had relied on governmental assistance and benefits to strike potential jurors—action that could not have occurred without the "direct and indispensable participation of the judge, who beyond all question [wa]s a state actor"—the *Edmonson* majority held that the state had not only made itself a party to racial bias in enforcing the peremptory challenge, but also "elected to place its power, property and prestige behind the [alleged] discrimination" (p. 624, citing *Burton* 1961, p. 725). The dissenting justices in the case failed to perceive the existence of a symbiotic relationship, and argued that "the government's involvement in the use of peremptory challenges falls far short of 'interdependence' or 'joint participation'" (pp. 636–37). "Whatever the continuing vitality of *Burton* beyond its facts," they wrote, "it does not support the Court's conclusion here" (p. 637).

The Supreme Court has not relied heavily upon the symbiotic relationship criterion in its decisions attributing state actor status to private parties. It may be that the Court is willing to recognize symbiosis only in instances when there is a perception that the state is involved in racial discrimination, however peripherally. Or it may be that the relationships between the state and private parties involved in challenged conduct have to involve reciprocity for state action to be identified (see Barak-Erez 1995, p. 1180). The nature and degree of interrelationship sufficient to establish a symbiotic relationship remains uncertain.[6]

In *Brentwood Academy*, the 2001 case involving the governance of Tennessee high school sports, a five-member majority of the Supreme Court articulated a fourth state action criterion: the "pervasive entwinement" of the government and the party committing the misconduct. Commentators have hailed the case as a "flexible, pragmatic, and situation-specific" inquiry that delved into "background connections" to locate state action (Metzger 2003, pp. 1414–15), but it is too early to tell whether entwinement will become a distinct test of state action in practice. Lower federal court judges are actively pondering the *Brentwood* majority's meaning, with some concluding that the entwinement criterion is either closely related to, or synonymous with, the symbiotic relationship criterion (see, e.g., *Johnson v. Rodrigues* 2002; *Logiodice v. Trustees of Maine Central Institute* 2002). Yet entwinement may set a lower bar than symbiosis, in that it seems to require a high degree of involvement or entanglement but *not* reciprocity or mutual *benefit*. The dissenters in *Brentwood* (Justices Thomas, Rehnquist, Scalia, and Kennedy) clearly saw entwinement as a new criterion by which misconduct can be attributed to the state. In their view, entwinement extends the state action doctrine "beyond its permissible limits" and "encroaches upon the realm of individual freedom that the doctrine was meant to protect" (p. 305).

A factor that complicates state action analysis still further is the tendency of reviewing courts to apply different standards of evaluation depending upon the nature of the constitutional right infringed by alleged misconduct, without articulating the basis for their use of different standards. In cases that involve deprivations of First Amendment religious liberties, for example, the Supreme Court has historically been much more willing to find—or even assume—the presence of state action. In a sense, reliance upon Establishment Clause doctrine allows the judiciary to evade state action inquiry by recasting the issues in terms of government support of religion. Yet, decisions that find a violation of the Establishment Clause hinge upon the presence of state action, whether that requirement is articulated or not. If certain liberties protected by establishment and equal protection doctrine are to be accorded greater importance than, say, due process guarantees, the courts arguably should say so explicitly, and explicitly justify such distinctions. But this has not occurred.

The principle at stake is simple: When government acts, mechanisms must be in place that allow us to hold government constitutionally, fiscally, and ethically accountable for that action, and it should not matter whether that action is taken by a public employee or by a contractor. If we cannot identify which actions are attributable to government, we cannot enforce that principle. Instead, we create areas of ambiguity within which unethical behavior—real or perceived—can further erode the public's trust in its governing institutions. That is precisely what occurred in the so-called Indianapolis Experiment.

The Indianapolis Experiment: A Cautionary Tale

From 1992 until 1999, the then-mayor of Indianapolis, Indiana, Stephen Goldsmith, was a leading proponent of privatization, which he preferred to call "marketization." His efforts were widely reported, in glowing terms, by the national media (*Washington Post* 1993; Stern 1994) and in somewhat less glowing terms by local commentators (Miller 2001a, 2001b, 2001c; Howey 1998, 1999).

The early days of the Goldsmith administration were marked by a series of press releases touting its efforts to cut middle management (almost invariably referred to as "fat") and replace "bloated bureaucracy" with "more efficient," private providers of goods and services (Remondini 1991). As with privatization initiatives elsewhere, the award of major contracts to manage operations that previously had been handled by municipal employees generated persistent allegations that political contributors were being rewarded with lucrative city business, and that privatization was simply another form of patronage (Ritchie and Kennedy 2001).[7] It can be argued that such suspicions are an inevitable outgrowth of the "government by expert" privatization model, which gives high priority to *product* or output, and short shrift to *process*. The problem is intimately connected to the issues of political and fiscal accountability that typically arise in the context of ambitious efforts at privatization.

Issues of legal accountability are inextricably intertwined with political and fiscal challenges. Because it is often unclear whether and when the activities of private entities operating under government contracts constitute state action, it is unclear whether and when they must obey laws intended to constrain state actors. Can a municipality avoid compliance with due process requirements, or intentionally infringe citizens' First Amendment rights, by the simple expedient of employing a nominally private company to provide public services? Are records that are maintained by city contractors subject to Freedom of Information inquiry? Must contractors comply with statutes that prescribe municipal processes? As the foregoing discussion of state action jurisprudence demonstrated, existing law is unclear, offering public officials opportunities to avoid limitations on government behavior by simply *calling* their actions or agents private (Gilmour and Jensen 1998). In Indianapolis, when the contractors who managed the city's wastewater treatment plant were charged with evasion of Indiana bid laws, Mayor Goldsmith claimed that compliance with those laws was unnecessary for a "private" actor (*Indianapolis Star* 1994).

Stability and predictability are vital elements of government legitimacy and a necessary condition of citizen trust. The move to privatization in the form of contracting out, however, is justified by the promise of finding a better deal, a cheaper supplier, or a different or more efficient way of delivering public goods and services. It invites—indeed, it celebrates—constant change. In Indianapolis under Goldsmith, change came to be seen as an end in itself, rather than as a side effect of necessary improvements; it was equated with progress and efficiency. The names of city departments were changed: the Department of Public Works, for example, became the Department of Capital Asset Management. Personnel changes were frequent: many employees were fired, and many others reassigned (Miller 2001a, 2001b, 2001c). Functions were relocated or contracted out with virtually no prior notice to affected agencies. In many courtrooms during the early months of the Goldsmith administration, court records piled up in boxes for months, awaiting the choice of a new, private microfilm company (Zore 2000). Not long after Goldsmith's election, his deputy mayor told previous mayor Bill Hudnut (1999) that the new administration's motto was "if it ain't broke, break it and then fix it." Not surprisingly, morale and employee turnover were persistent problems (O'Laughlin 2000). Moreover, race relations were affected. The local black community viewed privatization as a method of rewarding mostly white political contributors at the expense of blacks, who previously had been well represented in the city workforce (Ritchie and Kennedy 2001).

If careful consideration was given to the legal responsibilities attending these dislocations, it was not evident. Yet it was precisely the legal and fiscal accountability issues that gave rise to persistent charges of unethical behavior. Much of what pundits excoriate as bureaucratic and governmental inefficiency, or red tape, are really precautions against corruption. If trust in government requires accountability, lack of accountability contributes to distrust and even cynicism about government and those who are engaged in it (Hardin 1998). The political system requires structural safeguards that recognize the differences between government and private enterprise, and protect against abuse. When public and private are understood to be interchangeable, those safeguards are seen as expendable impediments to efficiency rather than as prudential mechanisms necessary to operational integrity.

The Indianapolis approach to privatization undercut legal and political accountability in several important ways:

- It had a marked and troubling effect on public criticism of the Goldsmith administration. Reporters who investigated allegations of misfeasance told similar stories of sources unwilling to be quoted or even to talk to the media (Krull 1999; Ullmann 1999). The implicit (and sometimes explicit) threat of losing business also quieted companies contracting with the city, and exerted a discernible chilling effect on relatives, business associates, and those who hoped to do business with the city in the future.
- Charges of misfeasance could be—and were—dismissed as unfounded complaints by disgruntled public employees. When an Indianapolis Parks Department engineer alleged improprieties by the contractor who had displaced him from his position, the administration dismissed his charges on precisely that basis. The city eventually settled the case for $300,000, after local media investigated and confirmed the allegations. The widely reported episode, together with a prolonged exposé by the *Indianapolis Star* of financial improprieties involving privatization of the city's golf courses and still other reports about irregularities involving the contract to manage the city's wastewater treatment plant, left many citizens uneasy and raised questions about the adequacy of the city's capacity to monitor contractors' performance (Howey 1998, 1999).
- Open books and records, regular audits, and other proofs of financial regularity are an essential element of accountability. In an increasingly privatized Indianapolis, it became more and more difficult to get a complete picture of city expenditures. As Kettl (1993) points out, a company doing business with the city does not thereby bargain to open its books to the world. If onerous reporting restrictions are imposed, the costs of complying with those restrictions will become part of the overhead charged against the contract—reducing the financial benefits privatization is supposed to provide. On the other hand, when public money is being spent, the public has a right to ensure that it is being spent in accordance with both the contract and the law.

The conflict between a private company's right to keep proprietary information private and the public's right to know where public funds are going was a subject of constant debate during the Goldsmith years. Midway through its administration, the city took a bill to the Indiana General Assembly aimed at "expediting" the contracting-out process. One of the changes it proposed would have removed from the definition of "public money" all sums paid to a private contractor pursuant to a legally binding and enforceable contract. Had that provision been enacted, no public audit of a contract could have occurred once payment to the private contractor had been made. Once the check had been written, the funds would be deemed private. Whatever the merits of this proposal, it generated quite a negative public reaction (Miller 2001a, 2001b, 2001c).

Unfortunately for the administration, as accusations mounted, most of the financial reports available to rebut the persistent charges of impropriety came from still other private contractors, who faced questions about their own independence. That the city's financial statements were prepared by a large accounting firm that had contributed over $30,000 to Goldsmith's political campaigns during the period in which it held the city contract raised conflict-of-interest charges (Howey 1999). Internal bookkeeping and audit capacities were contracted out, leaving the city without the management depth needed for good internal documentation and fiscal controls. At least partially as a result, nearly 30 percent of the contracts inherited by the subsequent administration were determined to be legally inadequate (Ritchie and Kennedy 2001). An audit by the State Board of Accounts in response to a taxpayer petition in 1999 found rampant and pervasive noncompliance with statutory requirements: lack of required documentation, acceptance of bids without statutorily required engineering estimates, incorrect cost codes, awards made to legally nonresponsive bidders, notices to proceed issued 100 days after the expiration of the allowable statutory period, change orders executed after the issuance of a certificate of substantial completion, contracts awarded despite the fact that fewer than the required three bids were received, and even mathematical errors in the computation of city payments due (State of Indiana 1999a, 1999b).

Indianapolis is certainly not the only city that has experienced irregularities of this sort, and not all of the problems of the Goldsmith administration can be attributed to privatization initiatives. However, the administration's failure to recognize the importance of the public-private distinction, and to address the vital issues of legal and constitutional accountability that depend upon that distinction, was a substantial contributor to its problems. Goldsmith and other administration officials apparently believed that once a contract had been executed with a private proxy to deliver a service on behalf of the city government, the service became "private" for most, if not all, legal purposes. By contrast, the public and the media took the view that if municipal government was paying for the service with tax dollars and choosing the provider, the service should be subject to the same rules that govern other public actions. This disconnect became increasingly obvious, as the administration and its critics essentially talked past each other.

Conclusion

There is nothing inherently wrong with the new governance's search for increased efficiency and cost effectiveness in the performance of public functions. However, it remains to be seen how the new governance can achieve efficiency and effectiveness without sacrificing the democratic norms of equity, accountability, and due process that are fundamental to our political order and constitutional culture. The muddied state of the law and jurisprudence related to state action enables and even encourages the kinds of abuses that have occurred in Indianapolis, Iraq, and a host of jurisdictions in between. Since we are unlikely to see the abandonment of government by proxy, the issue before us is what sort of new direction public law might provide so that governance can be simultaneously efficient, effective, equitable, and ethical.

A solution to this dilemma is beyond the scope of this chapter, but we can report that scholars are actively puzzling over ways to overcome the new governance–legal accountability impasse. Noting that an agency relationship is created whenever the government authorizes a private entity to act on its behalf, Sheila Kennedy (2001) has suggested that the laws of agency and partnership should apply, either directly or by analogy, and either prospectively (in contract negotiations) or retrospectively (in judicial review). Under the laws of agency, when government cloaks a contractor with real or apparent authority to act on its behalf, the ensuing action is deemed governmental. Widely utilized jury instructions, for example, define an *agent* as "a person who at a given time is authorized to act for or in place of another person," and specify that the conduct of the agent need not be expressly authorized by the principal for it to be "within the scope" of the agent's authority. If the conduct is "incidental to, customarily connected with or reasonably necessary for" the performance of an authorized act, it has occurred within the scope of authority and, if wrongful, can give rise to liability.

In a similar vein, Gillian Metzger (2003, p. 1456) has urged us to rethink state action in private delegation terms. Under such an approach, the key question would not be whether private entities wield government power but, rather, whether grants of government power to nominally private entities are adequately structured to preserve legal accountability. As in Kennedy's formulation, the central criterion for singling out particular private delegations for enhanced judicial scrutiny would be whether they authorize private entities to act on the government's behalf—that is, whether they meet the legal requirements of agency.

Finally, a more holistic approach has been proposed by Jody Freeman (2003), who somewhat counterintuitively suggests that privatization can serve as a means of "publicization," or a mechanism for expanding government's reach into realms traditionally thought to be private. Her point is not that we should use public law to force time-consuming and expensive standards and processes upon private entities (which contribute to some of the very problems of governance that efficiency-minded privatization advocates seek to solve). Rather, she argues, we might more creatively use vehicles such as conditional government spending, regulation, tort liability, and contract negotiation to motivate private actors to commit themselves to democratic norms of accountability, due process, and equality.

As Freeman has observed (2003, pp. 1329–30), and as the aforementioned events in Iraq and Indianapolis have demonstrated, citizens may be complacent when the privatized arrangements of the new governance run smoothly, but they expect government to step back in and "do something" when things go awry. Citizens rely on government to ensure accountability for action taken on behalf of the public, no matter who the state's agents might be. As privatization initiatives have begun to affect vital and politically contentious public goods, services, and activities, the public increasingly has appeared to be inclined to demand greater accountability from, and increased governmental supervision of, contractors. As we have noted, the private management of U.S. prisons has resulted in a steady stream of litigation in the federal courts, as well as a deluge of scholarly commentary. Reactions to voucher programs and the private management of public elementary and secondary schools also have generated a flood of studies, academic and popular commentary, and litigation. Citizen outrage over perceived abuses by health maintenance organizations (HMOs) has led to litigation and state and federal reform legislation (Freeman 2003, p. 1330). Most recently, the behavior of the public and private agents charged with conducting the "war on terrorism" has come under fire. Although it remains to be seen whether, and to what extent, private contractors employed at the Abu Ghraib prison will be held to account for the abuses that took place there, there can be no doubt that members of the media, government officials, and citizens alike are outraged by the unethical and inhumane acts that were enabled by, and committed under, the authority of the United States. The rise of the new governance has not lessened concern over how state power is deployed. The challenge at hand lies not in finding the will to ensure that privatized governing arrangements are appropriately accountable; the challenge lies in finding the way.

Notes

1. According to Brinkley and Glanz (2004a, 2004b), CACI had roughly 9,400 employees in 2003 and revenues of $843 million, some 92 percent of which came from contracts with the Department of Defense and other federal agencies. Titan has about 12,000 employees and earns approximately $2 billion per year, largely via contracts with federal defense and intelligence agencies. The companies claim that their contracts are classified. One of their employees stands accused of raping a young male inmate at Abu Ghraib but has not been charged, apparently because military law has no jurisdiction over him. Another employee involved in the extraction of sensitive information from prisoners via interrogation had no security clearance at all. Former CIA agent Robert Bair calls the free-ranging roles of the CACI and Titan employees at the Iraq facility insane. "These are rank amateurs and there is no legally binding law on these guys as far as I c[an] tell. Why did they let them in the prison" (Borger 2004)?

2. Our focus in this chapter is on legal accountability, or the means of ensuring that action taken by, or on behalf of, the state comports with the standards set for government behavior in public law. There are, of course, other forms of accountability, including political or electoral accountability; bureaucratic and professional accountability; and marketplace accountability (see Gilmour and Jensen 1998; Cooper 1995; Romzek and Dubnick 1987; Posner 2002).

3. Technically, the Court's decision in *Richardson* was limited to the immunity issue and did not explicitly address the issue of state action, but its implications for the differential treatment of public employees (ostensibly genuine state actors) and private contractors were clear. For a more thorough discussion of cases involving the privatization of corrections, see Trant (1999).

4. Justice Scalia, writing for the majority in *Lebron v. National Railroad Passenger Corporation* (1995, p. 378), citing *Edmonson v. Leesville Concrete Co.* (1991, p. 632), Justice O'Connor dissenting.

5. *Lugar*'s slim five-to-four majority held that a private party's participation with state officials in the seizure of disputed property was state action under Section 1983 of the Civil Rights Act of 1871 (42 U.S.C. §1983). Although state action inquiries technically involve constitutional questions, the federal courts typically have seen actions taken "under color of law" as synonymous with the constitutional concept of state action, and mixed constitutional and statutory liability and immunity precedents.

6. As the Third Circuit Court of Appeals recently wrote in *Crissman v. Dover Downs Entertainment Inc.* (2002, p. 242), "*Burton* has not been overruled, nor its reasoning discredited by the Supreme Court in the text of any opinion, despite numerous opportunities. . . . [W]e must conclude that, while *Burton* remains good law, it was crafted for the unique set of facts presented, and we will not expand its reach beyond facts that replicate what was before the Court in *Burton*."

7. Cutting middle management had consequences for Indianapolis party politics as well as for government. Howey and Schoeff (1998) have observed that when Goldsmith "sacked the mid-level bureaucracy that had accumulated during the Republican Lugar and Hudnut administrations, he essentially disemboweled one of the most pro-

lific and successful political machines of Midwest history." Afterward, the beleaguered Marion County GOP floundered as declining manpower and enthusiasm translated into an inability to get out the vote.

References

Barak-Erez, Daphne. 1995. "A State Action Doctrine for an Age of Privatization." *Syracuse Law Review* 45: 1169–92.

Black, Charles L. Jr. 1967. "The Supreme Court, 1966 Term—Forward: 'State Action,' Equal Protection, and California's Proposition 14." *Harvard Law Review* 81: 69–109.

Borger, Julian. 2004. "U.S. Military in Torture Scandal." *Guardian*, April 30. www.guardian.co.uk/Iraq/Story/0,2763,1206725,00.html (accessed October 26, 2004).

Brest, Paul. 1982. "State Action and Liberal Theory: A Casenote on *Flagg Brothers v. Brooks*." *University of Pennsylvania Law Review* 130: 1296–330.

Brinkley, Joel, and Glanz, James. 2004a. "Contractors Implicated in Prison Abuse Remain on the Job." *New York Times*, May 4. Available at www.nytimes.com/ 2004/05/04/international/middleeast/04CONT.html (accessed October 26, 2004).

———. 2004b. "Contractors in Sensitive Roles, Unchecked." *New York Times*, May 7. Available at www.nytimes.com/2004/05/07/politics/07CONT.html (accessed October 26, 2004).

Cooper, Phillip J. 1995. "Accountability and Administrative Reform: Toward Convergence and Beyond." In *Governance in a Changing Environment*, ed. B. Guy Peters and Donald J. Savoie, pp. 173–200. Montreal: McGill-Queen's University Press.

Frederickson, H. George. 1993. "Ethics and Public Administration: Some Assertions." In *Ethics and Public Administration*, ed. H. George Frederickson, pp. 243–61. Armonk, NY: M.E. Sharpe.

Freeman, Jody. 2003. "Symposium: Public Values in an Era of Privatization: Extending Public Law Norms through Privatization." *Harvard Law Review* 116: 1285–352.

Friendly, Henry J. 1982. "The Public-Private Penumbra—Fourteen Years Later." *University of Pennsylvania Law Review* 130: 1289–95.

Gilmour, Robert S., and Jensen, Laura S. 1998. "Reinventing Government Accountability: Public Functions, Privatization, and the Meaning of 'State Action.'" *Public Administration Review* 58: 247–58.

Hardin, Russell. 1998. "Trust in Government." In *Trust and Governance*, ed. Valerie Braithwaite and Margaret Levi, pp. 9–27. New York: Russell Sage Foundation.

Howey, Brian A. 1998. "Peeling the Goldsmith Onion: The Mayor Brought Dramatic Changes to City Government, But What It Cost and What We Got Is a Mystery." *Nuvo Newsweekly*, December 3.

———. 1999. "Goldsmith's Community Credit Card." *Nuvo Newsweekly*, May 20.

Howey, Brian A., and Schoeff, M. Jr. 1998. "Inside the Stunning '98 Indiana Election." *Howey Political Report*, November.

Hudnut, William H. 1999. Interview with Sheila Suess Kennedy, February 18.

Indianapolis Star. 1994. "Privatization Run Amuck." August 30: A06.

Kennedy, Sheila S. 2001. "When Is Private Public? State Action in the Era of Privatization and Public-Private Partnerships." *George Mason University Civil Rights Law Journal* 11: 203–23.

Kettl, Donald F. 1988. *Government by Proxy: (Mis)Managing Federal Programs.* Washington, DC: CQ Press.

———. 1993. *Sharing Power: Public Governance and Private Markets.* Washington, DC: Brookings Institution.

Krotoszynski, Ronald J. Jr.1995. "Back to the Briarpatch: An Argument in Favor of Constitutional Meta-Analysis in State Action Determinations." *Michigan Law Review* 94: 302–47.

Krull, John. 1999. Interview with Sheila Suess Kennedy, January 27.

Metzger, Gillian E. 2003. "Privatization as Delegation." *Columbia Law Review* 103: 1367–502.

Miller, Jack. 2001a. "Privatization in Indianapolis: Problems, 'Proximity Issues' and Oscar Robertson Smoot." In *To Market, To Market: Reinventing Indianapolis,* ed. Ingrid Ritchie and Sheila Suess Kennedy, pp. 347–90. Lanham, MD: University Press of America

———. 2001b. "Privatizing the City's Golf Courses." In *To Market, To Market: Reinventing Indianapolis,* ed. Ingrid Ritchie and Sheila Suess Kennedy, pp. 417–28. Lanham, MD: University Press of America.

———. 2001c. "Privatizing the City's Swimming Pools." In *To Market, To Market: Reinventing Indianapolis,* ed. Ingrid Ritchie and Sheila Suess Kennedy, pp. 429–42. Lanham, MD: University Press of America.

Miller, T. Christian, and Miller, Greg. 2004. "Iraq Prison Workers Questioned." *Los Angeles Times,* May 1: A7.

Minow, Martha. 2002. *Partners, Not Rivals: Privatization and the Public Good.* Boston: Beacon Press.

O'Laughlin, Beth. 2000. Interview with Sheila Suess Kennedy, June 28.

Posner, Paul L. 2002. "Accountability Challenges of Third-Party Government." In *The Tools of Government: A Guide to the New Governance,* ed. Lester M. Salamon, pp. 523–51. New York: Oxford University Press.

Remondini, David. 1991. "Goldsmith Looking to Cut City Force by Twenty-five Percent." *Indianapolis Star,* November 26: B01.

Ritchie, Ingrid, and Kennedy, Sheila Suess, eds. 2001. *To Market, To Market: Reinventing Indianapolis.* Lanham, MD: University Press of America.

Rohr, John A. 1998. *Public Service, Ethics, and Constitutional Practice.* Lawrence: University Press of Kansas.

Romzek, Barbara S., and Dubnick, Melvin J. 1987. "Accountability in the Public Sector: Lessons from the *Challenger* Tragedy." *Public Administration Review* 47: 227–38.

Salamon, Lester M., ed. 2002. *The Tools of Government: A Guide to the New Governance.* New York: Oxford University Press.

State of Indiana, Board of Accounts. 1999a. "Special Report of Construction Projects for Municipal Gardens Recreations Center and Carson Park Recreation Center," September 16.

———. 1999b. "Special Report of Construction Projects for Franklin-Edgewood Park, Krannert-King-Brookside Aquatic Centers, and Perry Park Ice Rink and Aquatic Facility," September 16.

Stern, William M. 1994. "We Got Real Efficient Real Quick." *Forbes,* June 20: 43–44.

Trant, Robert. 1999. "Comment: *Richardson v. McKnight:* Are Private Prison Operators Engaged in State Action for the Purposes of 42 U.S.C. §1983?" *New England Journal on Criminal and Civil Confinement* 25: 577–606.

Ullmann, Harrison. 1999. Interview with Sheila Suess Kennedy, January 23.
Washington Post. 1993. "A Mayor Shows Gore's Team the Way," August 25: A19.
Zore, Gerald. 2000. Interview with Sheila Suess Kennedy, June 20.

Cases Cited

American Manufacturers Mutual Insurance Co. v. Sullivan, 526 U.S. 40 (1999).
Barrios-Velazquez v. Asociacion de Empleados del Estado Libre Asociado de Puerto Rico, 84 F.3d 487 (1996).
Blum v. Yaretsky, 457 U.S. 991 (1982).
Blumel v. Mylander, 919 F. Supp. 423 (M.D. Fla. 1996).
Brentwood Academy v. Tennessee Secondary School Athletic Association, 531 U.S. 288 (2001).
Burton v. Wilmington Parking Authority, 365 U.S. 715 (1961).
Civil Rights Cases, 109 U.S. 3 (1883).
Crissman v. Dover Downs Entertainment Inc., 289 F.3d 231 (2002).
Davenport v. Saint Mary Hospital, 633 F. Supp. 1228 (E.D. Pa. 1986).
DeShaney v. Winnebago County Department of Social Services, 489 U.S. 189 (1989).
Edmonson v. Leesville Concrete Co., 500 U.S. 614 (1991).
Flagg Brothers, Inc. v. Brooks, 436 U.S. 149 (1978).
Giron v. Corrections Corporation of America, 14 F. Supp. 2d 1245 (D.N.M. 1998).
Jackson v. Metropolitan Edison Co., 419 U.S. 345 (1978).
Johnson v. Rodrigues, 293 F.3d 1196 (2002).
Lebron v. National Railroad Passenger Corporation, 513 U.S. 374 (1995).
Lemoine v. New Horizons Ranch and Center, Inc., 990 F. Supp. 498 (N.D. Tex. 1998); *reversed*, 174 F.3d 629 (1999).
Logiodice v. Trustees of Maine Central Institute, 296 F.3d 22 (2002).
Lugar v. Edmonson Oil Co., 457 U.S. 922 (1982).
Medina v. O'Neill, 589 F. Supp. 1028 (S.D. Tex. 1984), *vacated in part, rev'd in part*, 838 F.2d 800 (1988).
National Collegiate Athletics Association v. Tarkanian, 488 U.S. 179 (1988).
Plain v. Flicker, 645 F. Supp. 898 (1986).
Polk County v. Dodson, 454 U.S. 312 (1982).
Reitman v. Mulkey, 387 U.S. 369 (1967).
Rendell-Baker v. Kohn, 457 U.S. 830 (1982).
Richardson v. McKnight, 521 U.S. 399 (1997).
San Francisco Arts & Athletics, Inc. v. United States Olympic Committee, 483 U.S. 522 (1987).
Shelley v. Kramer, 334 U.S. 1 (1948).
Skelton v. Pri-Cor, Inc., 963 F.2d 100 (1991); *cert. denied*, 503 U.S. 989 (1992).
Virginia v. Rives, 100 U.S. 13 (1879).
Wade v. Byles, 886 F. Supp. 654 (N.D. Ill. 1995); *affirmed*, 83 F.3d 902 (1996); *cert. denied*, 519 U.S. 935 (1996).
West v. Atkins, 487 U.S. 42 (1988).

_____ **Part 4**

Unintended Outcomes of Anticorruption Reforms

12

The Cure for a Public Disease: The Foibles and Future of Corruption Control

Frank Anechiarico

Introduction

The irony of corruption control in the United States and elsewhere is that the more severe and more bureaucratic the controls, the less effective they prove to be. This is not to say that laxness or the absence of rules is preferable, but that a careful combination of strategies, excluding bureaucracy to the extent possible, has been considerably more effective in a number of settings. This chapter will first present the argument against bureaucratic controls (those in place around the United States). Second, several more effective strategies will be described by focusing on a key element of the anticorruption project: corruption control in public procurement. The chapter will conclude by examining the evolution of corruption control in the Netherlands and a proposed combination of elements that may be adopted by jurisdictions that have tried more traditional tactics with poor results.

The Traditional/Bureaucratic Anticorruption Project

The American Progressive Movement at the beginning of the twentieth century was, according to historians, the heir to the two great post-bellum nineteenth-century movements, abolition and the struggle for a professional civil service (Nelson 1982). Neither of the nineteenth-century movements was complete. Reconstruction collapsed, and large jurisdictions across the country ignored or perverted the merit ideal in public hiring—most prominently, New York City. But the fervor was still there. The destruction of the Tweed Ring and the election of a U.S president who had been the police commissioner of New York City, Theodore Roosevelt, spurred a nationwide movement to reorganize governance to replace self-serving, partisan fiscal priorities with public policy based on the sciences of public health, engineering, social service, economics, and a dozen others that had formed into professional organizations in the late nineteenth century (Wilson 1887). It is hard to fault these goals, given the inefficiency and/or corruption at every level of American government during this period. Wherever it might have led, it should be said that the road was paved with the best intentions.

As intentions take institutional form, however, goals often change. The sciences were to be deployed by individual professionals selected by a merit system based on written tests and oral examinations. *Politics*, meaning political party control, would be replaced with the "science of administration," as Professor Woodrow Wilson put it in his famous 1887 article (Nelson 1982, p. 121). William Nelson argues that the failure to use the moral crusade of abolition to transform society more generally resulted in a compromise.

If there could not be a moral community in the United States, based on a consensus about the rights of individuals of all races and on public recognition of the failure of governance by partisanship, the Progressives would have to use rules, laws, and new political structures to satisfy their ardor. These instruments were the institutional form of the Progressives' intentions, and it marked a fork in the road of their moral project.

It took nearly a century to enact into law the promise made to people of color by the post-bellum amendments to the Constitution. By contrast, the corruption control instruments or anticorruption project swept the nation in little more than a decade and continued to grow for a century (Anechiarico and Jacobs 1996).

The remarkable thing about the Progressive crusade is that its zeal and approach to corruption control remained unchanged generation after generation during the hundred years that it developed. Each scandal was followed by the outrage of elected executive and legislative officials, who might be held responsible for a lack of control. The response, which is illustrated in remarkable detail in the history of New York State and City, was and still is the institution of more rules, laws, and structures. This continued until, by the end of the twentieth century, the anticorruption project was a powerful, towering bureaucracy—a final fork in the road—that began to get in the way of public service delivery. The anticorruption project became such a dominant force that, as one former New York City agency commissioner put it,

"It's more important for the agency to look honest than to get anything done" (Anechiarico and Jacobs 1996, ch.11). The reach and authority of the anti-corruption bureaucracy has become remarkable. Of course, as new elements are added to the anticorruption project, the definition of corruption itself expands to encompass more and more official behavior. A brief review of its components begins to demonstrate the threat of this expansion to efficient, effective public service.

Components of the Anticorruption Project[1]

The Civil Service

The civil service is the sine qua non of the anticorruption project. It was the first piece to be put in place in the United States and elsewhere, and it caused an almost immediate power shift away from partisan authority in service delivery to the controls of nascent bureaucracy.

A study of the "constraints and opportunities" of the New York City civil service system by the Columbia University Program in Politics and Public Policy found that civil service reform had by the 1990s rendered city government ineffective and, ironically, subject to political manipulation—the worst of both worlds (Cohen and Eimicke 1993). The Columbia study surveyed managers of all ranks in three agencies and found uniform negativism about the personnel system. Criticism centered on five major problems: hiring takes too long; testing does not assess relevant abilities; promotion is not controlled at the agency level and deprives managers of a basic incentive; job descriptions are so technically and narrowly written that a minor internal transfer becomes a major bureaucratic issue; and discipline, punishment, and removal have been made all but impossible by civil service protections.

In response to some of these problems, Mayor Edward Koch created an office in 1983 to recruit minorities and women for administrative positions in New York City government. This office, the Talent Bank, came under blistering attack in a New York State anticorruption investigation because it accepted referrals from politicians (N.Y. State Commission on Government Integrity 1991a). The lack of "formal standards," in the view of investigators, tainted the employment of everyone hired through the Talent Bank. One long-serving administrator, whose name was included in the investigation and published by the New York Times simply because he had been referred to a deputy mayor by the Talent Bank, wrote a response to the Times: "By 1981 [when the Talent Bank forwarded his name], I had 12 years of public sector experience—federal, state, and city . . . I guess you have destroyed my credibility and that of others. Too bad for government, whose professionals and managers seem relentlessly and often inaccurately criticized by the news media, further discouraging talented people from entering its ranks and staying" (Trent 1989, A34). Although no legal violations were found, pressure from the media and the state commission forced the Talent Bank to close.

Conflicts of Interest and Financial Disclosure

Passage of the New York State ethics law in May 1991 precipitated a rash of resignations among local officials all over the state. The New York State Association of Counties reported over 100 resignations from county government positions, especially from county health boards, zoning and planning commissions, and community college boards (Sack 1991). But even if conflict of interest and financial disclosure laws do not deter people from seeking or accepting public office, public administration will suffer if ethics legislation negatively affects morale or if it makes decision making more defensive and slower.

According to the modern-day architects of the anticorruption project, financial disclosure by public officials must be exhaustive and ongoing. Review must be entrusted to an agency situated outside operational lines of authority. Rather than rely on credentials or professional norms, the crime-control strategy relies on deterrence, surveillance, and investigation.

Whistle-Blower Protection

The Federal Whistleblower Protection Act of 1989 strengthened the provisions of the 1978 act by making the Office of Special Counsel (OSC) independent of the umbrella Merit Systems Protection Board (MSPB) and allowing whistle-blowers to bypass the OSC and take complaints directly to the MSPB (Public Law 101–12, 103 Stat. 16, §2(a) 10 April 1989). The 1989 act also lowered the standard of proof necessary to make a case of protected whistle-blowing. The employee must show that his or her disclosure of information was a factor (rather than the *predominant or motivating factor*) in the subsequent negative personnel action or inaction.

The protection and encouragement of whistle-blowers enables all public employees to be investigators and activists in the anticorruption project. The whistle-blower machinery itself is a good example of the entrenchment of external control mechanisms. This machinery is predicated on the belief that the public service cannot effectively police itself. It assumes that anticorruption responsibility can be effectively discharged only by those who are either protected from or have no stake in the target agency's reputation. However, such people are likely to have little information about the agency's operations and little interest in whether the agency achieves its goals.

Internal Investigation

The presence of inspectors general and undercover field associates in various agencies created a system in New York City government that some employees describe as "big brother" and "like the old Soviet Union." No one knows whether a city employee is actually working for the Department of Investigation (DOI) as a field associate or whether an apparent member of the public is actually an undercover DOI investigator conducting a sting or an integrity test. A commissioner in the Koch administration, reflecting on her experience, commented that the worst part of the job was the fear that the DOI would one day summon her for questioning about a matter that had escaped her attention. "It's like living with the sword of Damocles perpetually threatening to drop." At one point, she found herself using pay phones because she worried DOI was wiretapping. "It seems funny now, but at the time it was frightening."[2]

The transformation of the DOI into a bona fide law enforcement agency has important implications for public administration. Agency heads operate by constantly looking over their shoulders, trying to anticipate how DOI investigators will perceive their decisions, and wondering which of their operations may be surreptitiously monitored.

State and Federal Prosecution

The biggest change in the law enforcement component of the anticorruption project is the aggressive role of federal law enforcement agencies in investigating and prosecuting corruption by high-level state and local officials, including governors and mayors (*United States Code* 18:§§1341 and 1343 [1988 and Supp. IV 1992]). The expansion of criminal law, especially regarding federal mail and wire fraud, has made it possible for the Federal Bureau of Investigation (FBI) to investigate and for the Department of Justice (DOJ) to prosecute just about any significant local corruption. Federal law enforcement officials may be more willing and able to prosecute local corruption than are their state and local counterparts. The federal prosecutors have more resources and are not as involved in local politics as local prosecutors (Maass 1989). Conversely, federal officials may be unfamiliar with the nuances of local politics, and, as a result, they have to rely on and work with local law enforcement. Since the mid-1970s, when the Department of Justice declared local corruption to be an enforcement priority, a number of governors, dozens of mayors, and hundreds of local public officials have been indicted and convicted for official corruption in federal court (*U.S. v. Margiotta* 1982).

Prosecutors are a greater presence in the daily lives of public administrators than they were a generation ago. Federal as well as local prosecutors' offices are likely to have specialized public corruption units, professionally committed to making cases. Prosecutors now expect public administrators to share the high priority that prosecutors have given to fighting corruption and racketeering.

Procurement Regulation

The reason Willie Sutton robbed banks is the same reason procurement systems are vulnerable to corruption: "That's where the money is." New York City's Parking Violations Bureau scandal, which reached two borough presidents among many others in the administration of Mayor Edward Koch, led to the establishment of the Procurement Policy Board (PPB) by way of the 1989 Charter revision. Within a year, the PPB issued several hundred pages of regulations covering every aspect of contracting (Procurement Policy Board Rules 1990).

The character and integrity of private contractors wishing to do business with New York City and other governments are now relevant. Would-be contractors must submit full disclosures about company and personal finances. Databases of background information on contractors are expanding. A negative determination by any government agency may eliminate opportunities to obtain city contracts because other agency heads will want to avoid criticism for doing business with racketeers. By 1990, a single agency's favorable finding, however, would not qualify a firm to do business with every other agency, because each agency had to make its own responsibility determination every time a contract was awarded.

Contracts were awarded according to lowest cost, not according to performance record. Even a contractor who previously had done shoddy work for an agency would be awarded a contract if his or hers was the lowest bid, unless the contractor was found nonresponsible (in terms of illegal activities). The result has been a race to the bottom, which many companies refuse to join. The Feerick Commission found that many contracts advertised by the New York City Human Resources Administration attracted very few bidders (N.Y. State Commission on Government Integrity, 1991a, ch.13). The field is further limited by the near obsession in New York City (and elsewhere) to avoid doing business with contractors who have even a tangential connection with racketeers. Examinations of family connections by the New York City comptroller have eliminated contractors who are related to reputed racketeers by marriage. Ironically, the higher the moral position that government takes, the higher the standard it will be held to, and the greater the criticism to which it will be subjected when it becomes known, as it will inevitably, that a particular contract is being performed by a firm associated with this or that gangster (Flynn 1994). Exaggerated ambition in procurement control causes unnecessary growth of the anticorruption project.

Auditing

Auditors have become influential actors in American government because of the numerous mandates and responsibilities they are assigned and because negative audits, particularly those that charge or intimate corruption, have the potential to undermine or destroy administrators. Scandal-sensitive politicians and bureaucrats implement financial controls, preaudits, and postaudits to protect themselves against the possibility of future charges that they ignored fraud and corruption.

Public administration reformers throughout the century have advocated the use of financial control in order to achieve corruption-free government. They have understood implicitly what Bentham (1995) and Foucault (1979) understood explicitly, that surveillance, monitoring, and control of information can produce conformity. Toward that end reformers have lobbied for more intensive and comprehensive financial controls, promising that such controls will contribute to governmental efficiency as well as honesty (U.S. General Accounting Office 1992).

The expansion of financial controls contributes to a steady shift in power from executive and legislative officials to comptrollers and other audit agencies. These information-gathering and monitoring agencies are becoming more important units of government. Their wide-ranging audits generate recommendations aimed at practically every aspect of agency organization, operation, and personnel policy. Because of the politics of corruption and reform, administrators ignore such recommendations at their peril. The auditing agencies have become key shapers of public administration.

The Routinization of Charisma

The struggle of the Progressives against corruption and its eventual transformation into the anticorruption project is a classic case of the routinization of charisma.[3] TR thumped the lectern and hundreds of clergy called for divine retribution on official peculation and theft of the public good. As has been noted, even though that fervor is now institutionalized, anticorruption rhetoric is relatively unchanged. Mayor Edward Koch inveighed against newly indicted members of his inner circle and exclaimed, according to Murray Kempton, "I am shocked!" so many times in one speech that Kempton suggested the phrase for the city motto (Newfield and Barrett 1989, p. 83). At the same time Koch was inveighing, U.S. Attorney for the Southern District of New York, Rudolph Giuliani, was raising the heat on circles much wider than Koch's intimates. Giuliani was most vociferous during the trials of officials that he prosecuted himself (Newfield and Barrett 1988, p. 488).

However, there is another side to Weber's story of the evolution of organization. It was Weber who not only described the ideal-type bureaucracy, but who provided the first, perhaps most devastating, critique of its influence on society. He argued that bureaucracy is destructive of personal freedom, and as it spreads it will splinter community (Weber 1978, p. 1449). Thus began the scholarly industry of identifying the pathologies of bureaucracy. Almost all of the classic pathologies apply to the anticorruption project: decision-making delay, overcentralization of rule administration, inadequate authority of middle management, defensive/uncreative administration, displacement of service goals with adherence to anticorruption rules, poor morale, barriers to interorganizatonal cooperation because of conflict of interest rules, and adaptive strategies that illegally circumvent anticorruption rules in order to return to the service mission. Each pathology by itself is enough to raise questions about the side effects of the anticorruption project. Together, they present a serious obstacle to the delivery of public services in a wide variety of jurisdictions across the United States and elsewhere. Again, it must be noted that the Progressives themselves cannot be held accountable for the failure of subsequent generations to "audit" reforms (Hofstader 1963).

Improved Corruption Control in Various (and Unexpected) Places[4]

Procurement is the second largest line in most public budgets, right after personnel costs. In New York City, for the past decade, it has hovered between $7 billion and $10 billion. This is an enormous amount of money and has engendered many fraudulent schemes: kickbacks to public officials, bid rigging, extortion from subcontractors and laborers, union extortion of contractors and public officials, false orders indicating the need for a change in work and an increase in cost, and lengthy and costly postcontract litigation from the winning (lowest) bidder seeking to increase the profit margin. Postcontract litigation may also be initiated by the contracting agency, due to poor performance and faulty products. To this list may be added the influence of organized crime in unions and contract/vendor organizations. While mob-influenced companies may produce acceptable or even superior work, they often inflate the price of public work by intimidating other bidders and arranging kickbacks with contracting officers. However, even if a mob-related company does nothing that is formally corrupt, many jurisdictions find it immoral and politically dangerous to do business with it.

The result of the corruption vulnerabilities surrounding procurement has been the heaviest accretion of bidding, auditing, and qualification rules in the anticorruption project. Revelations of shoddy work in the construction of schools and public housing or extortionate prices for basic materials like concrete have driven the creation of ever more stringent bureaucracy in this area. However, as indicated above, it is bureaucracy with perverse effects. The rules designed to protect the public from illicit, incompetent contractors end up attracting them. In order to win a contract with the lowest bid and still make a profit, the contractor or vendor has an incentive to cut corners, use poor quality materials and goods, and litigate for additional payments after the work is done. These "shortcut" companies do not have good reputations for performance, but past performance is seldom a criterion for bid acceptance.

Until very recently, New York City had the most baroque procurement system in the United States. The classic example of the problems it caused is that on average it took eight years to complete the construction of a school (Lehrer 2002). State and local rules, called the Wicks Law, required splitting the contract in four parts: electrical work, HVAC (heating, ventilating, and air conditioning), plumbing, and a fourth general contractor for other parts of the project (New York State, Division of the Budget 1987). This left the contracting agency with the general responsibility of coordinating the project. Delay was inevitable under this system. The building of the Woolman Skating Rink is a specific example of the costs of the anticorruption project in procurement. By the mid-1980s, during the administration of Mayor Edward Koch, the construction of the rink had become a national embarrassment. Construction had gone on for seven years and had cost $12.9 million. Cracks in the concrete that encased the cooling system required beginning again. At this point, developer Donald Trump, who was nursing electoral ambitions, offered to complete the rink in six months for a fraction of what had been spent so far. Mayor Koch agreed. The rink was completed for under $3 million and in five months, not six. Trump, of course, was able to use contractors with whom he had good relations and on whom he could count to do quality work, quickly. His business, developing residential and commercial property, depends on rapid, quality work in order to attract and keep tenants and establish an income stream to satisfy his bankers (Goldstock et al. 1990, p. 141).

With these and other examples in mind, Mayor Rudolph Giuliani (1984–2002) began his term determined to make city contracting more competitive by removing as many regulations as possible. His appointments to the Procurement Policy Board included contractors and others who shared his position. The Giuliani and (Mayor Michael) Bloomberg administrations' chair of the board, Brendan J. Sexton, and the executive director through 2002, Michael Stoller, also felt an urgency to stimulate competition and lower prices through deregulation. The city's procurement rules were completely overhauled under Sexton and Stoller, and competition for contracts began to expand.

One deregulation was crucial to the recovery and clearance effort at Ground Zero after September 11, 2001, particularly Title 9 of the Rules of the City of New York: Contracts and Procurement (1996–97) Section 3–06:

> 1–c: Authority to make emergency purchases [is possessed by] any agency . . . when an emergency arises and the agency's resulting need cannot be met through normal procurement methods. The agency shall obtain the proper approval of the Comptroller and the Corporation Counsel.

The city agency in charge of recovery and clearance at the World Trade Center (WTC) site, the Department of Design and Construction, got approval from the comptroller and corporation counsel and *selected* four contractors for each quadrant of what was called "the pile." These were contractors that had not done business with the city on a regular basis because of stifling regulations. They were chosen because they were among the most effective and best resourced for the work at the site: Tully Construction Company, AMEC Construction Management, Bovis Lend Lease, and Turner Construction Company. However, not all four companies, expert as they might be, were free of past corruption problems. Tully Construction Company had, in the decade before September 11, 2001, been found nonresponsible as a bidder on public agency contracts, which led Mayor Giuliani to refuse to allow Tully a contract with the City Department of General Services.

> Tully . . . has [also] been found non-responsible, by the [Department of] Sanitation. As with the earlier finding, the Commissioner's designee found that Tully neither provided information requested nor cooperated with a Comptroller's subpoena, failed to disclose required information on its [background information] form, and engaged in improper waste disposal in New Jersey. Sanitation also relied on the fact that Tully's president employed a known organized crime figure in one of his companies. ("Current Developments: City Contracts" 1995)

Another of the main WTC contractors, AMEC, had two fraud counts against it: one before 9/11 and one after.

> In November 2000, Morse Diesel, Inc. [which was shortly to become AMEC] pled guilty in federal court in the Eastern District of Missouri to one count of submitting a false claim to GSA concerning a contract for the

federal building in St. Louis, Missouri. . . . [T]he company submitted a
claim that the bond premium had been paid when in fact it had not. . . . the
company paid a fine of $500,000. In a more recent proceeding, AMEC, on
February 20, 2002 was placed on the list of Parties Excluded from Federal
Programs. . . . The cases were investigated by the Office of Inspector General, Office of Investigations, and the U.S. General Services Administration." (U.S. DOJ 2002)

What was needed was a way to monitor a company's ethical behavior on
the job, but at the same time to let it do what it does best. Luckily, the New
York City Department of Investigation had recently adopted a nonbureaucratic
technique for doing what was needed to ensure the integrity of Tully and
AMEC. The technique was a new part of the anticorruption project that managed to avoid bureaucracy and its pathologies. Its formal name was Independent Private Sector Inspector General (IPSIG). The idea behind IPSIG was to
allow high performance companies with ethical stains to continue working
for government—provided they accepted and paid for the continuous monitoring of a private-sector firm that would include attorneys with experience
prosecuting fraud, forensic accountants, and, often, double-check engineers.
The IPSIG would go over its reports with the company for comment before
presenting the reports and comments to the contracting agency. Any ethical
missteps would be noted that might result in fines or removal from the job.
The other role of IPSIG was as management consultant. An experienced IPSIG
could counsel a company on ways to save time and resources without sacrificing performance, thus providing a product ahead of schedule to the government and increasing its own profit margin.

The IPSIG idea (originally labeled Certified Investigative Auditing Firms)
was developed by Ronald Goldstock when he served as associate attorney
general of New York State and director of the state's Organized Crime Task
Force. It appears in a Task Force report on the construction industry in New
York City (Goldstock et al. 1990, ch. 8). Thomas Thatcher II, who also worked
on the Task Force, later became vice president and inspector general of the
New York State School Construction Authority and used IPSIG to monitor
companies that were building schools in New York City.

In New York City, specialty law firms and companies formed specifically
as IPSIGs are precleared for deployment by the Department of Investigation.
At Ground Zero, not just Tully and AMEC but all four contractors were assigned IPSIGs, which by the time they were deployed were referred to popularly as compliance monitors. Now that recovery and clearance are complete,
the job is recognized as one of the largest in recent city history, with none of
the usual taints of corruption and self-dealing. As Charlie LeDuff and Steven

Greenhouse put it in an influential article in *The New York Times*, the integrity and speed found at the WTC site was

> ... nothing short of a miracle, and with it, no small victory over cynicism about what labor can get done in New York ... if there is a downside, it is that this remarkable job might make people wonder long and hard about why deadlines cannot be met all the time. ... [As Kenneth Holden, the commissioner of the Department of Design and Construction put it,] there is a feeling among the workers to "show the world we know how to get back to work; let's move ahead to rebuild the greatest city in the world. This is a powerful motivator. (LeDuff and Greenhouse 2002, A-1)

The IPSIG model seems to be spreading. Miami-Dade County, Florida, government has adopted a version of the New York City model that it deploys on all large contracts. Miami-Dade IPSIGs are given authority to review all records and operations of the company they are given to monitor. However, in Miami-Dade, the company does not review and comment on IPSIGs' reports. The reports go directly to the relevant agency (www.miamidadeig.org).

The spread of IPSIGs is positive because it fits three of the four criteria— all but transparency—that are basic to a democratic (nonbureaucratic) and effective anticorruption project:

- *Transparency:* Public reports and Web sites should list all potential work, all bidders (if the job is bid, and an explanation if it is not bid), and track the amount of the winning bid so that interested parties and the public can see who is winning government contracts and whether patterns exist. Another purpose of increased transparency is to increase competition by making it easier for contractors and vendors to find information about the procurement process and its performance.
- *Clarification and simplification of rules and regulations:* The large number of rules that become a disincentive to bid on government work in many jurisdictions has been revisited. Rationalizing and clarifying rules and procedures increases competition and speeds the completion of contracts.
- *Involvement of public and private stakeholders:* Vendors, union lawyers, community groups, contractor associations, and others are interested in the outcome of the procurement policy process. Including them on oversight or advisory boards, rather than considering them opposition, can bring new perspectives to procurement officials and reduce the amount of animosity and litigation in procurement.
- *Involvement of middle management:* Agency contracting officers, who are

responsible for deploying the rules once a project is begun, can be given more authority to interpret the rules and make reviewable exceptions to the rules to assure fair, efficient bidding and work completion. Personnel policies to train and, if necessary, retrain personnel in key procurement positions must also be in place so that the new paradigm survives.

In deregulating procurement the Procurement Policy Board comes closest to fitting *all four* criteria. (Its rules are on its Web site.) It has created an oversight body, and its board includes former opponents. It has given agency chief contracting officers (ACCOs) a great deal more control of the procurement process. IPSIGs also empower middle management with a constant information flow from the job. IPSIGs are the product of rule simplification and, by their nature, they include public and private stakeholders. They do not yet include the wider public through publicizing their reports. IPSIGs should also be responsible to community boards in New York City and similar bodies elsewhere. The Procurement Policy Board puts all its rules and proposed changes on its Web site and sends them to its overseers. IPSIG reports should go on the Web site also, and there should be an oversight board in the Department of Investigation to review the IPSIG process as it develops.

Corruption and Cultural Change: The Case of the Netherlands

Although it is changing into a more bureaucratic administrative culture, corruption control in the Netherlands still fits the four criteria above because of the longstanding connection between an open administrative culture and an active and open civic culture. When a delegation from the New York State Organized Task Force visited the Dutch Ministry of Justice in the early 1990s, the task force's methods—wiretapping, stings, undercover agents, wired suspects, and surveillance—were broadly rejected by academics and ministry officials as antithetical to Dutch culture, inside and outside government. In the ten years since that meeting, there has been a great deal of publicity surrounding procurement scandals on national projects in the Netherlands. This publicity has shifted Dutch culture away from the laissez-faire approach of the 1990s to a more rule-oriented approach.

In anticipation of a record amount of national spending on railway tunnels in the next few years, governments at all levels in the Netherlands are building a more powerful and bureaucratic anticorruption project. There is now a national unit of the police, the Rijksrecherche, which is in charge of corruption investigation in public administration across the country. The National Audit Court, or Algemene Rekenkamer, has become far more concerned than it was in the past with reviewing the ethics rules that agencies have in place. The city of Amsterdam has a new corruption control office.

A good part of the change in Dutch administrative culture regarding corruption control is due to new and stringent anticorruption rules made by the European Union (EU) in Brussels. The Dutch have been more willing to adopt the EU's approach to public administration than has almost any other member of the Union. Corruption, the Dutch recognize, is a transnational problem in Europe.

The Dutch and Americans both may be approaching a more-or-less happy medium. They have widely different administrative and civic cultures, but the past decade has shown how quickly administrative culture will respond to shifts in civic culture. The broad academic and political critique of bureaucracy in the United States has persuaded, or in some cases forced, public administrators to find alternatives to large, rule-bound organizations in the delivery of services and in the regulation of civic activity. The discovery and wide media coverage of the long-term tradition of bid rigging in letting contracts in Amsterdam and around the country engendered local and national laws that create a more rule-bound and hierarchic anticorruption project than the Netherlands has ever had.

The key to a balanced system is to recognize that corruption, like most other crimes, is not completely eradicable. That is not to say that self-dealing, extortion, and bribery in government are acceptable. However, this practical recognition prevents the creation of a monolithic anticorruption project, such as the one that is being reassessed and, in many places, dismantled in the United States. It is vital that the accretion of rules and institutions does not become an obstacle to public service. Both the Netherlands and the United States are democratic systems that make it possible for public administration to adjust to shifting values in civic culture and enact sensible corruption controls.

Conclusion

During the early stages of the anticorruption project in America, there was little desire in civic culture for anything other than absolute integrity. Conversely, the civic values of moderation and self-regulation in the Netherlands did not recognize the corruption that moderation and self-regulation allowed. A balance is maintained by democratic communication between administrative and civic culture. Oversight boards and transparency, particularly, will sensitize an attentive public and the media to the extent and influence of the anticorruption project in a given polity. Sensitivity to the values and actions on both sides of the administrative/civic line will keep corruption control in balance.

Notes

1. This section is adapted from Anechiarico and Jacobs (1996); and Anechiarico and Jacobs (2002)

2. Inteview with former commissioner of a New York City Municipal Department, July 17, 1994.

3. This phrase is from Weber (1947, p. 364).

4. The parts of this section dealing with removal and clearance at Ground Zero as well as the criteria for reforming the anticorruption project appear in different form in a paper presented at the conference "Corruption—Private and Public" at John Jay College of the City University of New York, September 13–14, 2002.

References

Anechiarico, Frank, and Jacobs, James B. 2002. "Corruption Control in New York and Its Discontents." In *Political Corruption: Concepts and Contexts,* ed. Arnold J. Heidenheimer and Michael Johnston, pp. 665–76, New Brunswick NJ: Transaction Publishers.

———. 1996. *The Pursuit of Absolute Integrity: How Corruption Control Makes Government Ineffective.* Chicago: University of Chicago Press.

Bentham, Jeremy. 1995 [1791]. *The Panopticon Writings,* ed. Miran Bozovic, pp. 29–95. London: Verso.

Cohen, Steven, and Eimicke, William B., eds. 1993. *New York City Solutions II: Transforming the Public Personnel System.* New York: Columbia University Program in Politics and Public Policy.

"Current Developments: City Contracts." 1995. *City Law* 1 (December):3.

Flynn, Kevin. 1994. "Plow Now Anyhow, Buried City Hired Tainted Contractors." *Newsday,* February 28: 7.

Foucault, Michel. 1979. *Discipline and Punish: The Birth of the Prison.* New York: Vintage.

Goldstock, Ronald; Marcus, Martin; Thatcher, Thomas D. II; and Jacobs, James B. 1990. *Corruption and Racketeering in the New York City Construction Industry.* New York: New York University Press.

Hofstadter, Richard, ed. 1963. *The Progressive Movement, 1900–1915.* New York: Simon and Schuster.

LeDuff, Charlie, and Greenhouse, Steven. 2002. "Far from Business as Usual: A Quick Job at Ground Zero." *New York Times,* January 21: A-1.

Lehrer, Peter M. 2002. *Report of the Chancellor's Commission on the Capital Plan.* New York: New York City Board of Education.

Maass, Arthur. 1987. "Public Prosecution." *Public Interest* 89 (Fall): 107–27.

Miami-Dade County Code. 2003. Available at www.miamidadeig.org (September 7).

Nelson, William E. 1982. *The Roots of American Bureaucracy 1830–1900.* Cambridge MA: Harvard University Press.

New York City Code. 1996–97. *Rules: Title 9, Contracts and Procurement, Section 3–06.*

New York State Commission on Government Integrity (Feerick Commission). 1991a. "Playing Ball with City Hall: A Case Study of Political Patronage in New York City." New York State Commission on Government Integrity: *Government Ethics Reform for the 1990s,* pp. 498–99. New York: Fordham University Press.

———. 1991b. "A Ship without a Captain: The Contracting Process in New York City." *Government Ethics Reform for the 1990s*, p. 471. New York: Fordham University Press.

New York State Division of the Budget. 1987. *Fiscal Implications of the Wicks Law Mandate* (May).

Newfield, Jack, and Barrett, Wayne. 1989. *City for Sale: Ed Koch and the Betrayal of New York*. New York: Harper and Row.

Procurement Policy Board Rules. 1990. (August 1). http://www.ci.nyc.ny.us/html/selltonyc/html/ppbrules.html

Sack, Kevin. 1991. "New York Ethics Law Leads Local Officials to Quit Posts." *New York Times*, May 18: 26.

Trent, Brooke. 1989. "Letter to the Editor." *New York Times*, February 10: A 34.

U.S. Department of Justice (DOJ). 2002. Available at www.usdoj.gov/usai/cae/home (Accessed June 14. Not currently available).

U.S. General Accounting Office. 1992. *Report to Selected Members of Congress: Mass Transit Grants, Noncompliance, and Misspent Funds by Two Grantees in UMTA's New York Region* (January).

United States Code. 18:§§1341 and 1343 (1988 and Supp. IV 1992).

United States Code. Public Law 101–12, 103 Stat. 16, §2(a) (April 10, 1989).

U.S. v. Margiotta. 688F.2d 108 (2d Cir. 1982).

Weber, Max. 1947. *The Theory of Social and Economic Organization*, trans. A.M. Henderson and Talcott Parsons, intro. Talcott Parsons. New York: Free Press.

———. 1978. *Economy and Society: An Outline of Interpretive Sociology*, ed. Guenther Roth and Claus Wittich, trans. Ephraim Fischoff. Berkeley: University of California Press.

Wilson, Woodrow. 1887. "The Study of Administration." *Political Science Quarterly*, vol. 2, pp. 197–222.

13

In Search of Virtue: Why Ethics Policies Spawn Unintended Consequences

Kathryn G. Denhardt and Stuart C. Gilman

Public trust in government depends on a robust perception that public employees are acting in the public interest and not for private gain. However, public trust also depends on a perception that government employees are able to make good judgments based on standards of reasonableness. While a zero-gift policy (according to which a public official may receive absolutely nothing of value from vendors, clients, or the general public) leaves no room for doubt about expectations, it also leaves no room for participating in basic social graces because situations like the following become problematic:

- An employee at the Social Security Administration (SSA) helps an elderly woman settle her husband's death claims. The woman sends the SSA employee flowers.
- An Agriculture Department employee ensures that a farmer gets crop damage payments that are due the farmer. In the fall, the farmer sends the employee a basket of apples.

Accepting the flowers violates a zero-gift policy, but how does one return them? The basket of apples might be donated to a charity or put out for all to eat, but accepting it would still have violated a zero-gift policy. In one extreme example, a government official received written advice from an ethics officer suggesting that the use of tissue paper and water (i.e., use of restroom facilities) in a private contractor's facility might be construed as a gift. If all these situations constitute violations of an ethics policy intended to prevent corruption of government officials, then it comes as no surprise that government employees as well as clients and contractors might view the ethics policy as extreme bureaucratic rigidity to be mocked rather than honored.

It is necessary to construct ethics policies in ways that promote trust in government and yet are reasonable in application. Our first question should be: Do gift policies address a real concern that the public has about government? And the answer would be: Yes. Confidence in government is eroded when there is any appearance that a public servant's actions are influenced by a gift of any sort. In *Deconstructing Distrust*, the Pew Research Center for the People and the Press found that "[d]iscontent with political leaders and lack of faith in the political system are principal factors that stand behind public distrust of government. Much of that criticism involves the honesty and ethics of government leaders" (Pew, p. 4).

Specific statements from respondents in the Pew research fell into categories like "politicians are dishonest/crooks" and "only out for themselves/for own personal gain." Without a doubt, distrust in government is fed by revelations that personal gain in the form of gifts or other benefits might have influenced a public official's actions. A gift policy is essential, therefore, and as important for elected officials as it is for civil servants. However, our experience in observing the implementation of zero-gift policies at all levels of government in the United States leads us to conclude that enforcing such rigid policies is as likely to cause cynicism among government employees as it is to inspire the highest standards of ethical conduct. Moreover, it places unnecessary barriers between government employees and those they serve when public servants are required to refuse and return even token gifts of appreciation.

If gift policies are needed as an integral part of assuring ethical government practice—and we believe they are—how should governments construct policies that will both provide appropriate guidance for ethical conduct and enhance public trust in government? How do we avoid constructing policies that are so restrictive that large numbers of government employees would find it difficult to do their jobs *and* stay in compliance with the ethics policy? Answering these questions depends on understanding precisely what ethical standards or virtues we intend to address by creating the policies.

Gift policies are intended to avoid *corruption* of government officials and employees by prohibiting the exchange of anything of value, thus prohibiting bribes (whether blatant or in the guise of a gift) that would influence actions of government employees and officials. It is also understood that gifts might create a *conflict of interest* for the public servant by pitting private gain against public duty. *Transparency* is another ethical standard that comes into play when we consider that the gift exchange might raise questions in the minds of observers about how government really operates, whether or not any such influence actually exists. For example, when other clients observe the delivery of flowers or apples, do they perceive that a gift might be required in order to assure speedy resolution of a problem? Do competing vendors perceive that contractors who have given gifts are more likely to win a contract?

Each factor—corruption, conflict of interest, and transparency—contributes something to our understanding of why gift policies are necessary; they will be explored in turn.

Corruption

In both politics and business, corruption is one of the premier policy issues of the twenty-first century. A number of forces have caused the dramatic rise of corruption as a worldwide issue. As globalization has encouraged foreign investment, many opportunities are presented for corruption of public servants, often to speed along what could be a very slow approval process for new investments and businesses in an old and traditional system. The spread of democracy in nations that have had a different form of government almost inevitably leads to some traditional practices being redefined as corruption. The varied and uneven infusion of development funds in developing economies also presents opportunities for corruption, as those seeking funds have no established systems to apply for and receive the funds.

Admittedly, some discussions of corruption can have cultural overtones. Although in some societies family obligations are paramount—it is not uncommon in the Middle East for individuals to take government jobs in order to benefit their families—many others actually have criminal restrictions on nepotism. However, the global push of modern economies is moving toward common views on the necessity of viewing government employment as acting on behalf of some sort of public interest and of viewing bias in favor of family or tribe as inappropriate.

Dennis Thompson described the three basic elements of corruption as when "a public official gains, a private citizen receives a benefit, and the connection between the gain and the benefit is improper" (1993, p. 369). But it is not always clear what constitutes an improper connection between the gain and the benefit and what differentiates corruption from legitimate ways of conducting business. Among the most interesting aspects of the fight against corruption are the ongoing attempts to define the conceptual elements that are generally agreed to comprise it. Certain events (frequently a high-profile scandal) can result in a shift of ethical standards to define behaviors as "corrupt" that might have been considered proper before the event. In analyzing the case of the Keating Five,[1] Dennis Thompson suggests that what might once have been called legitimate "constituent service" must now be viewed as a form of corruption because it makes use of public offices for private purposes even though the elected officials received only political benefit (via campaign contributions) rather than direct personal benefit. Thompson refers to this as *mediated corruption* (1993).

> . . . . [M]ediated corruption differs from conventional corruption with respect to . . . these three elements: (1) the gain that the politician receives is political, not personal and is not illegitimate in itself, as in conventional corruption; (2) how the public official provides the benefit is improper, not necessarily the benefit itself, or the fact that the particular citizen receives the benefit; (3) the connection between the gain and the benefit is improper because it damages the democratic process, not because the public official provides the benefit with a corrupt motive. (1993, p. 369)

As Dennis Thompson has written: "What exactly the principle [against private gain from public office] prohibits is not so clear, and its ambiguities are the source of many of the problems in implementing ethics in our time" (1995, p. 49). This problem extends to the very heart of the notion of conflict of interest. Andrew Stark in a complex analysis of this problem contends that "pure private gain from public office . . . takes place in a realm beyond even the twilight zone of quid pro quo, where the official is neither capable of affecting the interests of the concerned nor beholden to them, and where the official's in-role judgment is thus in no way compromised" (1997, p. 119).

Therefore, issues that are general policy matters (e.g., tax increases) are not considered conflicting by Stark because they affect an entire class of people. A policy maker who would be affected by taxes would not be conflicted in providing expert testimony against a tax increase. Another example in the United States is the part-time legislator at the state level who votes on a policy issue involving his or her profession. So a part-time legislator, who also is a practicing lawyer, would not be conflicted if she killed a bill in committee that would have limited legal fees in liability cases. Yet another recent example is former president Bill Clinton's pardons at the end of his presidency; questions arose about whether one pardon was "bought" through gifts and campaign contributions. A further example is the accusation against a recent Canadian prime minister for improper use of position in order to affect a golf course decision.

The major point of these examples is not their illegality (as many were not deemed to have involved illegal acts), but rather the public perception of the acts. In looking at ethics issues we often dwell on whether or not the act was legal. This can be only part of the equation. Our concern about these issues must focus not only on preventing criminal (or administrative) wrongdoing, but also on the impact of certain actions on the trust of a people in their government. The end output of government ethics programs is not to put people in jail but to maintain the confidence of people in their government. Parenthetically, the main purpose of private-sector ethics programs should be to maintain the confidence of stakeholders, stockholders, and employees in the integrity of the corporation.

Conflicts of Interest

In late 2003 the Organization for Economic Cooperation and Development (OECD) approved guidelines for managing conflicts of interest. This guidance will impact public services in most developed countries and in many developing countries as well. This official agreement defines a conflict of interest as a "conflict between the public duty and the private interests of a public official, in which the public official has private-capacity interests which could improperly influence the performance of their official duties and responsibilities" (OECD 2004, p. 4). Categories or types of conflicts of interest include representing private parties (with or without compensation), receiving pay from two different sources that conflict, and taking actions upon leaving a position that could be construed as exploiting one's former position.

Although it might seem obvious, it is necessary to have at least two interests in order to have a conflict of interest. In an often used example, one might have a personal financial investment that could be impacted by decisions one makes as a part of one's official role or job, producing a conflict of interest for the individual. But what does that really mean? How large an investment is enough to create a real conflict? Frequently, absent a legal definition, any investment could conflict with one's job.

Often, legal interpretations of conflicts of interest lag behind significant changes in the economy or society. For example, in the 1960s, the U.S. Department of Housing and Urban Development prohibited many of its employees from having personal credit cards. Several classes of employees still have that prohibition. In the banking economy of the 1960s, perhaps a personal credit card could produce a conflict of interest, but it is hard to imagine that the same could be said in today's economy, with credit cards arriving unsolicited in the mail.

Conflicts of interest are often viewed as solely the province of the government, but such conflicts can occur in any setting. A common example would be an employee who arranged for her spouse to secure a contract with her company. The company would have a right to expect that she would act in their interest, not for her personal or family gain. Another private-sector example would be an employee who, in seeking another job, would offer "insider" information about the company he is leaving in order to impress the person interviewing him.

However, it is also true that public servants, especially in democracies, are generally held to higher standards than their private sector counterparts. This is what philosophers call "supererogatory" responsibilities.

Perhaps the earliest and most famous extended treatment of conflicts of interest is in Plato's *Republic*.[2] In Plato's classic attempt to describe the "ideal" republic he created several classes of citizens—to be described in the myth of the metals. The average citizen was "of copper," the guardian, equivalent to a bureaucrat, was to be of silver, while the Philosopher-King would be made of gold.

In order to eliminate the potential of conflicts of interest in the Republic, Plato first argued that men and women are equally capable of being guardians—both logically and to eliminate any potential that men would act in a biased manner to protect women. Second, Plato argued that the guardians must be "lied to" and convinced that they are above the need to own private property. Instead they would live together in barracks provided by the city-state. Having men and women live together would produce children, and—again to eliminate conflict of interest—Plato had the children taken away from their parents and raised by the state.

The education of the guardian class would be carefully regulated so that "they are gentle to their own people, and dangerous to enemies, not unlike well bred dogs"(1950, p. 69). This idealized vision of a society that tries to eliminate all conflicts of interests helps focus on the dilemmas inherent in addressing conflicts of interest. There are elements of individual freedom that most societies would not be willing to sacrifice, and yet without some controls all positions would be conflicted. This is why modern societies struggle to regulate conflicts of interest, and have such a difficult time in striking a reasonable balance.

The nature and dynamics of organizations can shape conflicts of interest. In Britain and France, relatively few civil servant positions change when there is a change of political leadership. The emphasis is on the professionalism, dependability, and independence of their civil service. In contrast, the United States (and most presidential-modeled governments) has a greater degree of conflicts of interest because of the immense size of its politically appointed bureaucracy. Every executive branch election results in literally tens of thousands of government positions turning over at the federal, state, and local levels. Edmund Beard has argued that this is the Faustian bargain that the United States has made in order to have greater democratic accountability (1978, pp. 244–45). Nonetheless, the cost of maintaining oversight of such a large system would give many less-wealthy nations pause. The oversight is necessary in order to assure that new entrants into the government service following an election understand and abide by ethics laws with which they may not be familiar, and which might require them to divest of certain financial holdings in order to avoid conflicts of interest in their new duties in the government. When large numbers of government positions are filled with political appointees, such oversight is costly and time consuming, but essential to maintain public trust in government.

Transparency

The value of *transparency* in government addresses issues of corruption and/ or conflicts of interest through mechanisms that make the actions of government, and the interests of government officials, open to inspection. Open meetings laws allow the public to observe firsthand the deliberations of government entities. Having government employees and officials file personal financial disclosure forms allows the public to discover potential conflicts of interest between the officials' personal finances and the decisions they make as part of their government roles.

Assuming that one could identify conflicts of interest through these methods of transparency, it does not necessarily follow that one would know how to cure them. Typically, specific remedies might entail ridding oneself of the interest (divestiture), excusing the interest (waiver), or ensuring that the individual make no decision that could be influenced by the interest (recusal). Many of these require complex administrative systems to make them work effectively. However, in some cases, they either cannot work at all or they place an incredible burden on the individual or the organization.

An example of such a "hard case" is a government official's spouse who works for a private company that does business with her agency. (In the private sector, this same problem can exist for spouses who work for competing companies.) This has become a more and more common problem. One remedy might be to move the individual into a nonvolatile position. However, if the individual's expertise is needed or the agency simply cannot afford this solution (or this is a key person in the corporation), there is no easy solution.

The same problems exist for recusal and waiver. In the case of recusal, one might find that the employee cannot carry out the duties of the job at all, or that the interest is so deeply buried (e.g., the employee owns stock in a holding company that has no direct influence on decisions in the company, which does business with the government) that no obvious problem presents itself. In the case of waiver, the question revolves around the standards one uses and the independence of the individual making the decision. The corporate compliance (or ethics) officer plays this role more effectively than most government ethics officers because revealing the conflict to the compliance officer usually is enough. Bringing the issue to the attention of an objective third party who can take any action deemed appropriate is generally viewed as enough to remedy the situation. In government, however, ethics officials rarely have the authority to make a judgment that a particular conflict of interest poses no real threat to the public interest.

This is the most basic level of transparency. And it is true that in some issues transparency is the only salutary action that can be taken. Most often, transparency systems are used to prevent conflicts of interest beforehand by identifying them and eliminating them as problems. Yet when no solution to a conflict exists, transparency can have a moderating impact by assuring that the potential conflict is revealed and inviting scrutiny of the actions of those involved.

As an example of such scrutiny, when U.S. president Bill Clinton left office he had to declare all of the gifts he wanted to take with him on his financial disclosure form. In the United States, only the president and the vice president are exempt from the administrative limitations on gifts; nevertheless, they are required to disclose gifts. Because the press had access to the financial disclosure forms, they could write articles about what they viewed as his excesses. The result was that President Clinton returned the majority of his gifts, and at least in one case, actually returned something he had brought into the White House with him!

Gift Policies Are Essential, but Also Problematic

Clearly, it is important in government to prevent the appearance (and reality) of impropriety by having good policies about the acceptance of gifts from those who do business with government. A code enforcement administrator should not accept a gift of travel to a sign vendors' convention, and there should be a policy that makes this impropriety clear to the administrator and to vendors, as well as providing sanctions for any violations that might occur. Government employees should not seek or expect gifts from anyone for doing their jobs, and no client or vendor should be given the impression that they will get better service or more consideration if they offer government employees some type of gift.

Zero-gift policies are well intentioned and grounded in important values, but the enforcement of such policies too often results in situations that defy commonsense standards of reasonableness and propriety. In one case, a major procurement process had to be voided after a losing bidder reported that the procurement official had accepted a Big Mac and fries from the winning vendor at the local McDonald's. This violation of a strict no-gift policy cost taxpayers hundreds of thousands of dollars and the procurement officer's job, even though there was general agreement that the lunch did not influence the official's decision.

Until 1993 the U.S. federal government used the model ethics code contained in Executive Order 11222, which specified that no gifts of any value could be accepted. At that time there was no *de minimus* provision allowing gifts of minimal value to be accepted within the standard. In order to enforce this policy, agencies such as the Internal Revenue Service and the Department of Defense imposed administrative sanctions on employees for accepting anything of value from a client, vendor, or member of the public. The largest number of administrative actions taken by the inspector general at Defense between 1985 and 1992 was for accepting free coffee and refreshments from contractors. Almost 1,000 official reprimands were issued per year for such offenses, often preventing or delaying promotions of the employees who received the reprimands. The combined total of all other administrative violations (e.g., misuse of government property) was no more than 100 in any year (Office of Government Ethics 1992, p. 75). Enforcing this zero-gift policy required ethics officials to spend an inordinate amount of time, and enforcement authorities to squander precious resources, often to the detriment of other significant ethics considerations.

The policies can impact relationships between government and clients in other ways as well, such as the creation of unnecessarily awkward situations. In local government, zero-gift policies can mean that government employees may not accept social invitations from neighbors because this would mean receiving something of value (e.g., dinner or refreshments) from someone who might at some future date do business with the local government. Should public employees interact with the public with such a degree of detachment that they ensure no expression of appreciation would ever be offered by those they encounter? Surely this would feed the stereotype of the rigid, uncaring bureaucrat, when we know that such "uncaring" behavior is one cause of the deteriorating trust in government (Pew 1999). We believe that by modifying gift policies to permit gifts of minimal value (*de minimus*), many such unintended quandaries can be avoided, while at the same time assuring adherence to the values intended to be achieved by the policies.

A "Bright Line" De Minimus *Policy Is Preferable to a Zero-Gift Policy*

The zero-gift policy enforced by the federal government before1993 was intended to raise ethical standards of all federal employees and to increase public trust in government. Those who enforced the policies came to believe that the opposite was occurring. Federal employees were offended by the notion that they "could be bought for the price of a cup of coffee" and developed a jaundiced view of ethics policies in general. Ethics training and guidelines began to be a target of ridicule rather than a call to a higher standard of public service. Enforcement of the zero-gift policy actually undermined respect for other, critical ethics rules.

The federal government's response was to publish a new set of government-wide standards of conduct in 1993, which specifically eliminated a number of things from the definition of a gift—for example, coffee, doughnuts, greeting cards, plaques and certificates intended solely for presentation (Standards of Ethical Conduct). In addition, these guidelines instituted an exception for unsolicited gifts with a market value of $20 or less per source per occasion, not to exceed an aggregate value of $50 in a calendar year. Thus, the federal government abandoned a zero-gift policy in favor of building in enough "breathing room" to allow for common social courtesies such as small gifts of appreciation. These changes were based in part on recommendations of the Federal Commission on Ethics Law Reform in which the commission states:

> [O]ur analysis also incorporates the four key principles noted by the President when he signed Executive Order 12668 creating this Commission. One, ethical standards for public servants must be exacting enough to ensure that the officials act with the utmost integrity and live up to the public's confidence in them. Two, standards must be fair; they must be objective and consistent with common sense. Three, the standards must be equitable across the three branches of the Federal Government. Finally, we cannot afford to have unreasonably restrictive requirements that discourage able citizens from entering public service. (1989, p. 2)

One indication that respect for federal ethics rules has rebounded is found in the *Executive Branch Employee Ethics Survey 2000*. The survey shows that in the year 2000, "the frequency of ethics training is directly related to employees' positive perception of an ethical culture and ethical employee behavior in their agencies" (*Executive Branch Employee Ethics Survey*, p. 8). In addition, the study findings show that "significant relationships exist between program awareness (i.e., familiarity with the ethics program and the Rules of Ethical Conduct), program usefulness (i.e., in making employees more aware of issues, and in guiding decisions and conduct), and ethics outcomes" (*Executive Branch Employee Ethics Survey*, p. 10).

Within the private sector there has been a growth of conflict of interest concerns, expressed as company policy.[3] Although not having the weight of government administrative rules, or their complex interpretations, the private sector has had a great deal of success in disciplining employees for what some have considered "abstract" violations. Some of this is no doubt due to the lack of the enormous protections of civil service rules, but a great deal relies on expecting employees to be able to interpret commonsense application of the policies. Company codes in corporations as varied as Merck Pharmaceuticals, Shell Oil Corporation, and Lockheed Martin Corporation have been very successful in articulating clear standards and enforcing them through a variety of disciplinary actions. These private-sector disciplinary actions have generally been upheld in most courts in OECD countries.

A *de minimus* gift policy is also the approach taken in many local governments. In 1990 the city of Los Angeles enacted a gift policy that creates a "bright line" rather than a zero-gift policy for gifts of minimal value. Los Angeles city officials may not accept a gift or combination of gifts within a calendar year from one source that exceeds the following values: $25 from registered lobbyists and lobbying firms; $100 from other "restricted sources" as defined by law, such as persons who have matters pending before the official; and $320 from any other source. Exceptions to the gift limits include gifts from family members—spouse, child, parent, grandparent, grandchild, sibling, niece, nephew, in-laws, aunt, uncle, first cousin (Los Angeles City Ethics Commission).[4] It is worthy of note that a *de minimus* gift policy should specify (1) a maximum value for any single gift, (2) a maximum aggregate value for all gifts from a single source in a given time period, and (3) provisions that allow for personal gifts from family members. If a provision for a maximum aggregate value for all gifts is missing, for example, a government entity might encounter a situation in which the spirit of the law is circumvented by someone giving a public official a set of golf clubs—one at a time—as occurred in Florida.

While prohibitions related to gifts, bribery, corruption, and conflicts of interest are necessary, there are good arguments that such policies are not sufficient. Our efforts to enhance public trust in government and avoid corruption and conflicts of interest would benefit greatly from solutions that give greater attention to transparency.

Provisions for Public Disclosure of Gifts and Independent Third-Party Review

Another strategy for avoiding rigidity while promoting public confidence in government is to utilize the mechanisms of public disclosure and/or approval by an independent third party. On some occasions government employees are offered something of value that would be of significant benefit to the government while not posing a conflict of interest. For example, after Hurricane Andrew some emergency management professionals who had managed the crisis in Florida were asked to share their knowledge and experiences with other emergency managers and consultants at meetings around the country. The invitations were often accompanied by an offer to pay travel expenses. These managers were being offered something of significant value (travel expenses) for sharing what they had learned with the profession. It is likely that the emergency manager would also learn things at the meetings that would benefit the employing government. Reasonable people might agree that this would be a worthwhile exchange, but a strictly enforced gift policy would probably prohibit it. An alternative would be to have a policy requiring the approval of an independent third party in such cases. This third party would have no conflict of interest and could make a reasonable judgment regarding the situation.

Andrew Stark's article "Beyond Quid Pro Quo: What's Wrong with Private Gain from Public Office?" (1997) offers a discussion of a similar case in which William Sanjour, an employee of the Environmental Protection Agency (EPA), was invited (expenses paid) by a North Carolina environmental group to speak to them about the dangers involved in locating a hazardous-waste incinerator in Northampton County. According to the policy at the time, if this were a part of Sanjour's official public role he could not accept the invitation unless the EPA was willing to pay for the trip, because accepting the travel expenses constituted receiving outside compensation for an official act. The EPA was put in the bind of either paying for the trip (for which it had not budgeted), or preventing Sanjour from making the trip to share his expertise with the public. Provisions for an independent third-party review might have allowed the environmental group to pick up travel expenses. The third party might have acknowledged that Sanjour did receive something of value but also that no improper influence would be exerted in the situation. This outside review and approval could permit a "cleansing" of the appearance of impropriety.

Such third-party review can also be helpful when there is genuine disagreement among the parties about whether a conflict of interest exists. For example, in the aftermath of his exemplary response to the Washington, DC, area sniper attacks that killed ten people and severely injured three others in the fall of 2002, Police Chief Charles Moose was offered a lucrative contract for writing a book about the events of that period. There was serious disagreement among parties involved about whether Moose would have a conflict of interest if he accepted the book contract while he continued to function as police chief in Montgomery County, Maryland. An independent review by the Montgomery County Ethics Commission was important in finding resolution of this contentious situation. Although the decision that the contract violated the county ethics code was controversial, most did view the decision as legitimate and objective.

Another option is to require public disclosure of all gifts as a way to detect and deal with any potential conflicts of interest that could erode public trust. Such a provision puts the emphasis on transparency rather than on rigid rules, and it allows for public dialogue about what constitutes a reasonable gift. Although many such systems have an agency responsible for reviewing and advising public officials about potential problems, the primary purpose is the transparency of interests. Openness is critical for maintaining the confidence of citizens in the integrity of their government.

Public servants are citizens and members of their communities as well as employees of government. Zero-gift policies tend to make an employee's private activities more awkward and troubling. One example of this was presented in an issue of *Public Management* (February 2000) by the International City/County Management Association (ICMA). A city manager had been involved in volunteer activities related to multiple sclerosis (MS) for over ten years. He was selected as "volunteer of the year" and would be receiving the award at an upcoming MS-sponsored race. A sports-apparel company had donated a pair of running shoes, socks, a jacket, a hat, and a racing uniform (all with their logo) to be presented to the volunteer of the year. The city manager sought advice of both his city attorney and the ICMA about the propriety of accepting the gifts. The ICMA and the city attorney advised that the manager's volunteer activities were separate from his official duties and thus acceptance of the gift was permissible. This advice is consistent with the ICMA's ethics guideline that states: "It is important that the prohibition of unsolicited gifts be limited to circumstances related to improper influence. In *de minimus* situations, such as meal checks, some modest maximum dollar value should be determined by the member as a guideline. The guideline is not intended to isolate members from normal social practices where gifts among friends, associates, and relatives are appropriate for certain occasions" (ICMA, *Code of Ethics*). Such a case shows how difficult it is to draw the line between what is job related and what is private, as well as the importance of seeking independent third-party review when questions arise.

Requiring the government employee to publicly disclose the gift through financial disclosure forms or other gift reporting mechanisms maximizes transparency. Public trust tends to erode most when it appears that public officials are trying to hide the gifts or when there is no mechanism for making the circumstances of the gift public. By having in place a mechanism for such disclosure, the reasonableness of the gift can be assessed not only by the individual and the government but also by the public.

In basketball, referees are allowed to exercise judgment as to whether contact with another ballplayer interfered with play. The notion here is that if there is no interference, it is incidental contact. In other words: no harm, no foul. In much the same way, there are many potential conflicts of interest that seem to have no consequence or harm. For example, it is clear that private gain from public office seems, on its face, to be a profound example of conflict of interest. Yet as Jane Ley, of the U.S. Office of Government Ethics (OGE), has reminded OGE staff more than once, when employees accept their salaries for doing their government jobs they are privately gaining from their public offices. Suddenly, what was first perceived to be a profound evil is actually benign.

Conclusion

The efforts in recent years to rebuild trust in government by encouraging civic engagement are based in part on building bonds and partnerships between communities, governments, businesses and nonprofits. If those interactions are successful, there are likely to be more, rather than fewer, opportunities for government employees to receive "something of value" from these other entities (e.g., meals or trips associated with board of directors meetings on which a public official might sit because of his/her government position). A zero-gift policy may discourage government employees from interacting with nonprofits, businesses, and the public, during a time when we are trying to encourage greater interaction and partnerships through other initiatives. A more reasonable and workable solution would be a *de minimus* gift policy allowing the acceptance of gifts of a specified minimum value, along with mechanisms for independent third-party review and disclosure of all gifts received.

What is most important when considering government ethics policies is that there be a clear understanding of what values are at stake. How is public trust affected (positively or negatively) by the action or policy in question? Would reasonable people agree that the situation presents a conflict of interest or an opportunity for corruption? Can transparency strategies (e.g., disclosure) and independent third-party review provide democratic accountability without undue rigidity? These questions and others explored in this chapter suggest that while ethics policies are of great importance, we must also be cognizant of unintended negative consequences.

Notes

1. Five U.S. senators accepted political contributions from savings and loan executive Keating who was under investigation for fraudulent bank practices. The five senators met with federal bank examiners and urged them to end their "harassment" of Keating. Keating was later found guilty of fraud, and imprisoned.

2. It is important to note that there was no meaningful distinction between the

public and private sectors in ancient Greece. The Greek polis expected citizens to have both public and private roles (see John Wild, *Plato and His Modern Enemies*).

3. For almost two decades the classic way of defining conflicts of interest was to distinguish between the economic and political spheres. Not only is this overly simplistic, it actually avoids the obvious problem of personal conflicts and the possibility of conflicts of interest between private-sector entities. For an example of this argument see Andrew Kneier (1976).

4. We appreciate the help of Barbara Freeman, director of communications, Los Angeles City Ethics Commission, in summarizing the gift policy of the City of Los Angeles.

References

Beard, Edmund. 1978. "Conflict of Interest in Public Service." In *Ethics, Free Enterprise and Public Policy*, ed. Richard DeGeorge and Joseph Pichler, pp. 232–47. New York: Oxford University Press.

Executive Branch Employee Ethics Survey 2000: Final Report. 2000. Prepared by Arthur Andersen for the U.S. Office of Government Ethics. Available at www.usoge.gov/pages/forms_pubs_otherdocs/fpo_files/surveys_ques/srvyemp_rpt_00.pdf.

Federal Commission on Ethics Law Reform. 1989. *To Serve with Honor. Report of the Federal Commission on Ethics Law Reform*.

International City/County Management Association. Code of Ethics. Available at www.icma.org/go.cfm?cid=1&gid=2&sid=3 (accessed October 27, 2004).

International City/County Management Association. 2000. "Running for a Cause." *Public Management* (February): 4.

Kneier, Andrew. 1976. "Ethics in Government Service." In *The Ethical Basis of Economic Freedom*, ed. Ivan Hill, pp. 215–32. Chapel Hill, NC: American Viewpoint.

Los Angeles City Ethics Commission. Available at http://ethics.lacity.org/pdf/oldsite/GiftGuide.pdf (accessed October 27, 2004).

Office of Government Ethics. 1992. *Second Biennial Report to Congress* (March).

Organization for Economic Cooperation and Development (OECD). 2004. *Recommendations of the Council on Guidelines for Managing Conflict of Interest in the Public Service*. Available at www.oecd.org/dataoecd/13/22/2957360.pdf (accessed October 27, 2004).

Pew Research Center for the People and the Press. *Deconstructing Distrust: How Americans View Government*. Available at http://people-press.org/reports/display.php3?ReportID=95 (accessed October 27, 2004).

Plato. 1950. *The Republic*, trans. A. D. Lindsay. New York: E. P. Dutton and Company.

Standards of Ethical Conduct for Employees of the Executive Branch. Available at www.usoge.gov/pages/laws_regs_fedreg_stats/oge_regs/5cfr2635.html (accessed October 27, 2004).

Stark, Andrew. 1997. "Beyond Quid Pro Quo: What's Wrong with Private Gain from Public Office?" *American Political Science Review* 91, no. 1: 108–20.

Thompson, Dennis F. 1995. *Congressional Ethics: From Individual to Institutional Corruption*. Washington, DC: Brookings Institution.

———. 1993. "Mediated Corruption: The Case of the Keating Five." *American Political Science Review* 87, no. 2: 369–81.

Wild, John. 1953. *Plato and His Modern Enemies*. Chicago: University of Chicago Press.

Part 5

Administrative Ethics in Global Perspective

14

An Anatomy of Official Corruption

Gerald E. Caiden

In studying public ethics, the concern is about what *should* be done, what *should* be the correct behavior expected of public officials, what acknowledged code of ethics *should* be followed, what public officials *should* know instinctively is right or wrong. What now passes as acceptable conduct can be judged or measured against an ideal, an absolute good, or against what experts profess are best practices based on such criteria as public interest, universal good, beneficial outcome, absence of harm, social equity, communal welfare, future good, minimal evil, promotion of civic order, lack of resentment—singularly or in any combination. Subjectivity is unavoidable as the choice depends on personal values and priorities.

Another, possibly less controversial, approach is the exact opposite: to study that which should *not* be; that which should *not* prevail; that which commonly is felt instinctively to be wrong, hateful, unjust, unacceptable; that which should not be practiced, taught, or held up to be a guide. Instead of looking at the good, one looks at the bad. Maybe there is more universal agreement as to what ought to be avoided, condemned, scorned, even unmentionable in polite society, just as people may not agree on what is fair but can agree on what is unfair. As for corruption, this is the dark side of human conduct—unethical behavior, religiously branded as sin. For all intents and purposes, the term *corruption* covers most conduct unbecoming public officials. It connotes standards, norms concerning how those in public office should behave but from which they have departed, have abused, have fallen short, or have let everybody down. What follows is a bird's-eye view of corruption, a generalized account of the anatomy

278 GERALD E. CAIDEN

and physiology of improper official conduct, as it pertains to commonly occurring examples. Are there standards, norms, common expectations that define the use of the term *corruption*? Clearly there are, and, what is more, there seems to be a remarkable degree of agreement in time and place. Ever since written records have survived, the same kinds of objectionable behavior have been identified, irrespective of language, religion, culture, ethnicity, governance, location, philosophy, or social values. These have always been considered unworthy and their practitioners considered villains. In exercising their public power they have departed from what has been expected of them, accurately expressed in Lord Acton's famous dictum, "Power corrupts and absolute power corrupts absolutely," simply because they have been tempted. They have disappointed those over whom they have exercised their public power whenever their departure has become public knowledge.

Bribery is a good illustration. The act of giving (or promising to give) or accepting any consideration with a view to persuading or inducing or influencing any official decision has always been considered wrongful behavior, obviously corrupt. It is morally unacceptable whether or not a decision was so affected. Those found guilty are socially disgraced for their reprehensible conduct. Yet bribery has been and remains ubiquitous whenever the prospective rewards prove too tempting to susceptible individuals willing to risk the chance of being caught. The question is not whether bribery exists (it does) or is suspected, but to what extent, by whom, with what harm inflicted on the innocent. Who is most susceptible? What organizations are prone? Where does bribery prevail? The answers are of use to criminals seeking to evade discovery and punishment, to businesses seeking valuable public contracts, to parents seeking unfair advantages for their children, to job seekers, to free riders, to anybody who wants to know how governance really is being conducted.

Researchers for the Berlin-based Transparency International (TI) who investigate corruption in general and bribery in particular have in recent years tried to document how much bribery exists and who are the main offenders. They collect information from some ninety countries where TI has branches, and they conduct surveys of public opinion about the propensity to commit and accept bribes. They have devised a table of comparative bribery, TI Bribe Payers Index, which lists countries in which bribery is least or most suspected. But how reliable are TI's findings? Is it really true that males are more prone to bribery than are females or does such a finding merely reflect how few females have ever been in an official position or had access to public office? What happens where the respectable term *economic rent* replaces bribery? Or when "one person's bribe is another person's gift" (Rose-

Ackerman 1999, p. 5)? Or when legal donations to party election funds assure special access to key policy makers?

Transparency International, after just a short life span of some ten years, has become a major research body regarding corruption. It was founded in 1993 by a former World Bank official, Peter Eigen, who grew impatient with attempts to persuade that organization to take more interest in corruption. It has since become a major contractor to international organizations, including the World Bank, and to national governments that are now willing to fight corruption. Despite its methodological flaws, interested parties look forward to the annual release of the TI Corruption Perceptions Index, which is composed of fourteen different polls from seven institutions and measures perceptions of business people, the general public, and country analysts about levels of corruption. It is embarrassing for countries that are ranked near the bottom, but it highlights how widespread corruption is even among the high-scoring countries of North America, Europe, and the Commonwealth, let alone among the poor developing countries in Africa and Asia. But how clean is clean and how dirty is dirty? Perceptions may bear little relation to the facts. So many variables go into the responses of those asked and so much depends on their circumstances and environment that not too much reliance can be placed on such surveys. Unless one appreciates the complexities of the whole subject, it is perilous to take the findings at face value. Nevertheless, if there is a high degree of agreement people cannot be that far off the mark—at least for comparative purposes.

That there is consensus has been demonstrated in the run-up to the first global, tough anticorruption convention, condemning corruption in both public and private sectors, which was approved by a special ministerial meeting of the General Assembly of the United Nations and signed in Mérida, Mexico, in December of 2003. This was the culmination of a long process, going back at least a decade, when the subject was first brought to the attention of the world body. Drafts of the convention were challenged by three permanent members of the Security Council: China, which has been experiencing growing troubles with corruption within the Chinese Communist Party; Russia, which has been facing problems caused by the penetration of organized crime into its public sector; and the United States, which has seen a decline in the credibility of its public institutions following revelations of business wrongdoing, professional fraud, political spoils, and other examples of misdeeds at every level of its government. Not that the other two members have exactly been clean. France has been coping with revelations of top-level corruption in its state-owned oil companies and political party financing, and the United Kingdom has been incensed by official deception. Few remember the fate of the Bank of Credit and Commerce International, one of the world's chief banks for laundering the ill-gotten gains of the corrupt in the early 1990s, which has not seemed to have dented the international money laundering business or to have prevented its use by international terrorists. Where once corruption used violence as an ultimate or final instrument of enforcement only, it now adds indiscriminate violence to its other dysfunctions.

The United Nations convention joins previous international resolutions against specific aspects of corruption, such as bribery and embezzlement, and international action to combat the spread of corruption. Thus, Switzerland, the former haven for the ill-gotten gains of corruption, has reversed itself and is cooperating with looted countries to recover lost public funds. Besides arranging regular international anticorruption meetings and assisting its country branch members to intensify their anticorruption campaigns, TI aids in the establishment of effective independent anticorruption commissions. Several notoriously corrupt regimes, as in Nigeria and Kenya, have been replaced by newcomers intent upon cleansing governance. The definition of corruption has been extended to include trading in narcotics, weapons, prostitutes, orphans, and children; exchanges in logging and oil rights or endangered species; computer and information technology crime; tax evasion; nonenforcement of the rule of law or professional ethics; statistical fraud; fraudulent political party funding; trading in influence; banking secrecy; and accountancy fraud. It has also been extended to include business, nongovernmental organizations (NGOs), quasi-autonomous public bodies (QUANGOs), government-organized NGOs (GONGOs), and mafia-organized NGOs (MONGOs).

As are murderers and rapists, the scoundrels involved in corruption scandals are always newsworthy because they offend common decency. People want to see that justice is done, by which they mean that wrongdoers are not allowed to get away scot-free. They are appropriately punished for their misconduct as a warning to anyone who thinks of repeating what they did. All corruption, that bundle of misconduct that betrays public trust, falls into much the same category. Alas, corruption is not so easy to identify. Murder is murder. Rape is rape. Stealing is stealing. Corruption, including bribery, is more ambiguous because it shades off from gross impropriety to gray areas that, while still morally offensive, are perfectly legitimate, not subject to prosecution, and may be excusable—even justifiable—in pursuit of acceptable ends. Corrupt acts may be reprehensible but they may be quite innocent in themselves. Indeed, many people caught up in a corrupt venture may be unaware that they were so used; they protest that they too were victims of the corrupt and that they are guiltless. They may have been too naive, unsuspecting, ignorant, blind, even incompetent and stupid, but they were (and are) not corrupt.

The Essence of Corruption

The starting point in determining what constitutes corrupt practice is with the *act* itself, that specific form of behavior that is considered wrong and offensive. Those who behave in such a way must know that what they are doing is morally wrong, clearly out of line, and unacceptable. They knowingly steal. They perjure themselves. They bribe or accept bribes or pass on bribes or record bribes or disguise bribes. They interfere where they have no business interfering. Their acts are deliberate, not accidental or incidental. They are flagrant and, worse still, done without any pangs of conscience or shred of guilt. In short, they do know right from wrong but venture on regardless. But what is considered right or wrong varies from place to place and from one time to another. What at one time was once considered natural, acceptable, and even necessary, such as cannibalism or infanticide, is later seen as wrong. What was seen as wrong, unconscionable and unnatural in the past becomes more acceptable and tolerated. What is seen as right or wrong in one culture, or religion, or ideology is not seen that way in another. Fortunately, in the case of corruption, there has been remarkable universal agreement over the centuries as to which specific acts fall within its rubric. Any differences have been marginal, not central.

This convergence has been made possible by looking at the *motivations* of the actors. Why were the acts done? They may protest otherwise but it seems fairly clear to others that they benefited in some way that would not otherwise have occurred. They had themselves or their nearest and dearest in mind. They knew what they were doing and how advantaged they would be. Their actions were premeditated. They had thought things out, or thought they had, and had known what they were getting themselves into. They had been deliberate and must have felt that, if discovered, what they were doing would not be approved but would be seen as conduct unbecoming, wrong, unjust, and immoral. Because they suspected that their acts would be resented, they tried to hide what they were about. They acted in the dark, confided only in a select group or inner circle that they thought they could trust not to reveal anything; they intimidated anyone who might spill the beans, silenced suspected whistle-blowers, preyed on the gullible, and took advantage of the trust and goodwill vested in them. When discovered, they tried to brazen things out, destroyed any incriminating evidence, used their positions to hush up any incidents, and turned the tables on their accusers. Clearly, they knew they were up to no good.

Again, attitudes are not necessarily consistent or absolute. Much depends on who it is that is being accused. Allowances are given for quite different reasons. On the one hand, the corrupt act is so grave that if it is exposed,

282 GERALD E. CAIDEN

public trust in public institutions or anyone with authority might collapse into chaos, anarchy, violence, and revolution, disasters that might very well damage the social fabric irreparably. Better then if such corruption is covered up and knowledge of it is kept to a very few trusted insiders. On the other hand, the corrupt act might be considered so trivial and minor that it can be overlooked or forgiven because of its far greater good for the community. It can be excused as long as the wrongdoer is contrite or remorseful or ashamed on discovery, promises to refrain in the future, and makes amends by offering compensation or doing penance. This is in contrast to the obvious guilty and unapologetic person who exposes and testifies against others in the inner circle upon the promise of receiving a lighter punishment for informing, thereby entrapping others.

None of these cases fall into the exceptional category of heroic corruption in which the actors gain nothing for themselves but risk much by acting for what they believe to be in the best interests of the community. They act selflessly and their motivation is idealistic on behalf of some justifiable, legitimate, and harmless cause. Of course, they may be mistaken and their actions may be reprehensible, but they may claim that they had no other option and their cause was, in their eyes, truly noble and deserving. They can be compared with whistle-blowers, who make much the same case when they are accused of being self-promoting, or vengeful, or otherwise less nobly motivated. Some of them are and others are not, but every so often there are indeed individuals who act righteously without thinking of themselves.

Judgment depends much on what were the actual outcomes or results or *consequences* of the alleged corrupt act. Who benefited and who suffered? Apart from rare heroic corruption, the actors benefited or gained something they would not have gained otherwise, that is, if they had not acted as they did. Their intervention altered or changed outcomes. Resources were improperly redistributed. Some people gained unfairly at the expense of others, whether or not the latter were aware of their loss. By not playing by the commonly accepted rules, the outcomes were deliberately changed in some predetermined fashion. Harm came to innocent, trusting, honest, moral folk who were kept in the dark. An inner circle manipulated things for some secret agenda and made sure its members were not injured. Others outside the circle suffered the consequences despite claims that nobody lost and nobody was a victim. Only in the case of heroic corruption can it be said that the winners deserved to win. Corruption distorts in favor of the undeserving and penalizes the truly deserving. The corrupt cheat the underprivileged by taking away what is rightfully theirs. This is the injustice and immorality of corruption: When it is revealed and understood by the deprived, it reminds them of their powerlessness and inferiority, and it may goad them to seek revenge.

Corruption is the antithesis of morality, which may be a better way of defining it than the tortuous and fruitless search for a description that is more inclusive. Jim Wesberry has probably provided one of the best descriptions, capturing the essence of corruption:

> Corruption thrives on darkness and invisibility. It is anonymous and unmeasurable. It is rooted in the very human vices of greed and lust for power. . . . [It] is colorless, shapeless, odorless, collusive, secret, stealthy, shameless. . . . It often leaves no trail but that impressed in human minds, memories and perceptions. (Caiden, Dwivedi, and Jabbra 2001, p. 1)

In recent years, this will-o'-the-wisp has been imprinted on people's minds by such concrete examples as the attempts of the Italian government to rein in the mafia; the brutality of the Russian mafia; the decline in Japan's economic fortunes; the 1990s recession in Southeast Asia; political upheavals in the Philippines, Pakistan, Venezuela, and Mexico; the hollow governments in much of Southern Africa; the forced resignations of the European Commissioners; political party financial scandals in Western Europe and North America; the operations of the narco-democracies in Latin America and the offshore banks in the Caribbean; the inside looting of some major American business corporations; manipulated trading on world stock exchanges; and global trading in illegal goods and services, international smuggling, and money laundering that is actually encouraged by rogue governments and weakly combated by other governments and international agencies.

All these are unmistakable illustrations of corruption at work around the globe, with serious repercussions for all. This obvious presence of corruption gave birth in the early 1990s to Transparency International, which publicizes this menace and records actions to combat it. As a result, the international community could no longer ignore corruption and reversed course by acknowledging it, promoting measures to combat it, and employing TI to expose and contain it. The taboos that once shielded corruption have fallen. Corruption is acknowledged to be an obstacle to world development because it discourages investment, undermines stability, destroys effective governance, and demoralizes people. The societal price that is paid is too high and needs to be reduced. It is now internationally acknowledged that

> [a] decade ago, corruption—especially in developing countries—was considered relatively harmless and even beneficial in instances where "grease" was needed to accelerate legal government actions. Corruption was a taboo topic in discussions among governments and between international agencies and governments. In contrast, corruption is now widely viewed

as very harmful (especially to the poor), a legitimate subject in international dialogues, and a concern worthy of frontal attention from international institutions such as the World Bank, the regional development banks, the IMF [International Monetary Fund] and the United Nations Development Program.

Aside from its out-of-pocket cost to bribers and its cost to non-bribers in lost business or delayed or non-performance by government, corruption has numerous indirect costs. Especially where it is pervasive, corruption can deter honest people from entering government service (which tends to make the corruption self-sustaining), provides incentives to create a planning and budgeting bias in favor of large capital-intensive projects at the expense of work in the social sectors (where the opportunities for grand corruption are less), reduces tax revenues thereby requiring higher tax rates, undercuts necessary regulations (including environmental ones and building ones), facilitates crime, and can erode political stability and respect for law. (Richardson 2001, p. 3)

Tackling Corruption

The international concern with corruption has been accompanied by a burst of studies, many of them repetitive and rather short on practicalities. This should not surprise, as the subject is rather messy and fuzzy. Moral indignation is all very well, but it does not necessarily translate into operational details. Corruption (or rather corrupt practices), like sin, takes so many forms, covers such a range of activities, and takes place in so many contexts that generalizations may be very wise and good but they give little guidance as to which remedies best suit which particular circumstances. For instance, the open giving and taking of bribes, clearly corrupt activity, is different from the secretive falsification of accounts and receipts, also clearly corrupt activity. But the giving and taking of bribes may be the expected price of doing business and outsmarting competitors, or it may be a quite exceptional, cleverly disguised practice known to few. It may take a crude form, such as the flagrant transfer of cash, or a sophisticated form, such as prearranged betting odds where the fixed outcome equals the negotiated bribe paid in untraceable property or personal favors. Likewise, the falsification of financial records can be the work of individuals who believe they cannot be caught, as they have sole charge and nobody else ever checks; or it can be part of sophisticated, professional accounting practices based on acceptable guesstimates, wishful projections, questionable depreciations, and permitted allowances where proof is not required or is very difficult to obtain. Figures can be massaged (not faked) sufficiently to hide more than they reveal, thereby distorting the true financial picture and deceiving those who take the figures at face value. Tackling corruption takes a large cast of specialists, many of whom work in isolation, using quite dissimilar tools.

Before tackling corruption, certain crucial questions have to be answered step by step, just as the medical profession has to do in treating patients who complain of being unwell. What exactly is wrong? Is the complaint real or imaginary? If it remains untreated is it likely to become severe or even life threatening, or is it just a minor nuisance or inconvenience? What technical aids can be employed to assist in locating and assessing the extent of the disorder? Is any treatment possible, available, and affordable? Is the selected treatment new and experimental or tried and proven? Does the patient understand what is involved in the possible treatment, and is the patient prepared and willing to undergo the course of treatment? If the treatment does not go as planned, what can be done? At what point does the treatment have to be discontinued, or repeated at a later time? Who should be involved in making these decisions?

Though the societal sickness of corruption may be as old as human disease, when these questions are applied to corruption, the answers are not as clear and certain as those developed by the medical profession for personal illness. What is the truth behind people's complaints of corruption? How serious is the corruption? If there are multiple corrupt practices, which one should be tackled first or given priority treatment? How accurate is the diagnosis? Are the symptoms confused with the underlying causes? Why does something need to be done? What can be done? What is required for effective and lasting treatment? Does the necessary support exist? Can that support be so institutionalized as to keep up the pressure for effective action? What constitutes success, and how is success to be measured? At what point does treatment need to be changed because it is not working, or not working well enough?

As in medicine, the literature about and practice of combating corruption provides many answers and much food for thought. But when it comes to actually doing it in a particular situation, corruption fighters are very much on their own. No case is exactly the same as another. There are always variations, unknowns, and risks. Exploratory investigation may reveal no reason for concern, or it may uncover something much worse than has been suspected. The diagnosis may be incorrect. The wrong treatment may be recommended. The expected backing evaporates; people run for cover, no longer willing to be associated with combating corruption. The corrupt may turn the tables and outwit any attempt to confine their activities, just as whistle-blowers find themselves being investigated and victimized by the real villains. The analogy to medicine stops here. One assumes that anything that cures human ailments is welcomed and those who cure are ennobled and blessed for their good work. When it comes to corruption, the corrupt may hold all the cards, defy investigation, accuse the investigators, plot to eliminate accusers (and succeed), and teach a new generation to be even more corrupt. Corruption has so far proved to be highly elusive to effective treatment and reappears in so many guises that constant vigilance has to be maintained.

Take a specific example: Some police officers expect and receive gratuities, a practice that may or may not be banned. The practice may be quite exceptional or may be common. People know this. They may resent having to give police officers anything at all above their official compensation, but for the sake of a quiet life they go along with police requests for what seems to be quite small (although to the poor even small is costly). Why do these police officers expect, or ask for, or take gratuities? Are they inadequately compensated, ill paid, poverty stricken, unfairly treated? Are they just plain greedy? Can they be compensated or rewarded in less beggarly fashion? Are they just proving their power, or showing off, or suffering from some undetected mental illness? Why do people give them gratuities? Do they fear what might happen if they do not? Do they expect to be remembered in return and get special favors, priority service, or favorable treatment? Is there any way people can show their appreciation to police officers without having to give individual gratuities? What do the police think about the practice? What influence does the practice have on police behavior, performance, discipline, and administration? And so the questions mount.

In order to tackle this practice, the organizational culture of police services may have to be transformed so as to minimize the practice and to discipline any officer who takes gratuities. The general public has to be educated not to give gratuities and not to expect favors in return. Alternatives have to be provided whereby people can express their gratitude for police services. The police have to be rewarded for their performance in such a way that both police esteem and public attitudes are enhanced. As long as the practice continues, police officers will be tempted to favor the highest givers, who in turn will expect special service from police. The general public's view is distorted when they see police on the take; they wonder what else police are up to when they are not seen. The police give the appearance of being bribable, self-debasing, and exploitive; for these reasons truly professional police will not accept gratuities.

Police gratuities may be a minor problem compared to other things that trouble the public about police conduct and performance. Other forms of police corruption may grate on the public much more, and these other forms may be much more serious. The practice of accepting gratuities may look innocent and victimless, but it is probably indicative of far worse police lawlessness, indifference, or contempt for the public at large. It may even be an outward sign of police conspiracy. If the police are that bad, there will be ample indications that they are out of control, a law to themselves.

This illustration is not meant to single out police as more corrupt than other public organizations, although they are likely to have greater opportunities than others to transgress professional norms. If the police are corrupt it is likely that much else is corrupt. Police corruption is as good a place to begin as any, because a trustworthy, fearless, and incorruptible police force can soon sort out corruption elsewhere: in governance, in other professions, and among the general public. This illustration is intended to show how difficult it is to decide what to tackle first, where to start with some reasonable expectation of initial success to spur continued efforts, how large the task is likely to be, and how one set of problems is mixed up with so many others.

Distinguishing Individual from Systemic Corruption

Police gratuities illustrate one feature about official corruption that has been inadequately considered: the distinction between individual and systemic corruption. Put more colloquially, when does a rotten apple contaminate others in the barrel and when does a defective barrel contaminate its contents? Few organizations confess to corruption or to retaining employees with dirty hands. On the contrary, most are indignant about any suspicion that they act immorally or employ anybody guilty of immoral practices. They profess innocence even though they know that not all their employees are blameless. In fact employee theft is common, so taken for granted and unpreventable that little is done about it. In practice, all organizations try to prevent even the appearance of corruption and try to rid themselves of anyone with dirty hands. This is especially true of police services, which again may be illustrative of how organizations try to avoid individual corruption.

Before police services select anyone, they do what they can to spot and weed out undesirables. They insist on references, do background checks, refer to criminal records, give aptitude tests, insist on competitive professional examinations that include psychological and moral questioning, and do what they can to exclude applicants who are suspected of not being fit for police work. Once applicants are accepted they must go through a probationary period, during which background checks are completed and the newcomers are observed on the job. Even before new recruits are put out on the street, they receive training and instruction on what should be done in various circumstances and what is the expected performance. The newcomers are provided with exceptionally qualified instructors, and they are assigned to specially prepared supervisors who are expected to set a model example, to correct deficiencies in practice, and to make regular progress reports on their charges.

These supervisors are watched in turn by the hierarchy above them. In addition, a special unit (the internal affairs division) usually exists to investigate any complaints or suspicions of corrupt practices or wrongdoing. Public police organizations are subject to all the outside controls exercised over all other public agencies, and they have their own professional bodies that jealously guard police reputation. Theoretically, all these safeguards should suffice to minimize police corruption by pinpointing individual wrongdoing.

No system is perfect, however, as the continuing incidents of police corruption show. It is unrealistic to believe that corruption does not exist. Of the millions of people employed, a certain percentage of undesirables will be selected and recruited and abuse the position. They find ways to help themselves, and they hide their deviations. When this occurs, their workmates may not know because the dishonest ones are simply too clever, or isolated, or trusted, or creative to be exposed, and any solid evidence is in their own hands. No one else can possibly know unless the victims speak out, which is not easy to do because in the case of police services, police officers are intimidating; they represent legitimate authority; they often have special powers and privileges; they are supported and given the benefit of any doubt by the community; and it is one person's word against another's. Sooner or later, the corrupt make mistakes, and for those who know what to look for the evidence is plain. Even employees who work alone must make reports that can be checked; must mix eventually with others whose suspicious can be aroused by unusual, odd, or defensive behavior; must be evaluated by supervisors using procedures designed to uncover misconduct; must be wary lest their victims blow the whistle on them; and must fear that collaborators might turn against them. In short, they have to remind themselves that they work in a glass bowl and cannot expect indefinitely to escape suspicion, surreptitious investigation, and eventual exposure, unless they are protected.

Wrongdoers in organizations can depend on some initial protection. Suspicions are one thing; definite proof is another. Since corruption is furtive, obtaining the evidence without revealing the search and forewarning the participants is difficult. Without sufficient conclusive evidence, deviants are usually given the benefit of any doubt. Collaborators who suspect that they too will be caught can be relied on to cover up. Innocent colleagues feel obliged to protect one another, because that is what they would expect others to do in a similar situation. They all feel threatened or under suspicion, and they rally around one another. Peer protection is useful in confining knowledge to the in-group in the hope that it will go no further and that everyone is not blamed for the misconduct of a few. Nobody likes to reveal dirty hands to the outside, and nobody likes the scrutiny of suspicion.

All groups protect themselves. In police services, this comes under the rubric of "the vow of silence"; other comradely groups have similar self-protective devices. The corrupt believe, rightly or wrongly, that they will receive a fairer hearing from their peers than from outsiders, and the facts seem to bear this out. Peers seem to be more lenient than authority figures and the legal system in cases of individual corruption. Finally, no organization likes to wash its dirty linen in public. It prefers to handle such things in its own way and hide its scandals from the wider public arena. It wants to avoid any unwelcome publicity.

Institutionalized Corruption

Institutionalized or systemic corruption is different. It should neither be confused with nor treated as if it were individual corruption. Systemic corruption occurs when the whole organization, its culture, leadership, management, and staff knowingly indulge in corrupt practices, turn a blind eye to wrongdoing, or, alas, even encourage such inappropriate behavior. How can this occur? Again examples are drawn from police services, in this case from local police services in the United States (Caiden 1977). Some police departments in the past broke the law or refused to enforce laws that police officers disliked. They rioted instead of maintaining the peace. They employed secret, unconstitutional, and illegal methods. They colluded with criminals and organized crime organizations. They stole, and they protected burglar rings. They transported stolen goods in police cars, and when they were called to investigate they destroyed incriminating evidence. They falsified evidence, and they trumped up charges against innocent people. They perjured themselves. They consorted with prostitutes and narcotics dealers. They held back seized goods to use to bribe informants or to infiltrate closed criminal gangs. Again, these examples are not meant to show police in a bad light, but merely to show the possibilities that are available to police and not available to other organizations. Other organizations have their own potential avenues for corruption.

In systemic corruption, somebody within knows about and indulges in regular corrupt practices and expects others to do the same as they do, or at least to remain neutral, passive, or indifferent to what goes on around them at work. On an even larger scale are the kleptocracies, where virtually all public organizations are corrupt. The whole governance system and everyone who comes into contact with it is corrupted and loots whatever is accessible. Transparency International has published lists of countries where such systemic corruption is reputed to prevail. What characterizes systemic corruption?

1. The organization parades for external consumption a code of ethics that is contradicted by internal practices.
2. Internal pressures, mostly informal so that there is no written record, encourage, abet, and hide violations of the external code.
3. Nonviolators are excluded from the inner circle and any benefits emanating out of violations.
4. Violators are protected and when discovered treated leniently, whereas their accusers are victimized for revealing hypocrisy.
5. Nonviolators suffocate in the venal atmosphere and their consciences trouble them thereafter.
6. Prospective whistle-blowers are terrorized and forever discredited; they need to be permanently protected from retaliation.
7. Violators become so accustomed to their wrongdoing that they begin to think of themselves as invincible; they feel when they have been exposed that they have been unfairly picked out.
8. Collective guilt finds expression in rationalizations of the internal violations, which no one intends to discontinue without strong external pressure.
9. Internal investigators rarely act and find ready excuses to discontinue investigation.
10. Internal authorities maintain that any incidents are isolated, rare occurrences. (Caiden and Caiden 1977)

These characteristics have been amply demonstrated in the recent Enron-Andersen scandal (Caiden 2002) and the much wider, ongoing business and accounting investigations in the United States. They point to collusion at the highest levels of government and business and the problems of organizational self-policing (Caiden 1992).

Individual corruption can be rooted out by organizational sanctions buttressed by the legal system, which can impose much harsher penalties. Individual wrongdoers are confronted with the evidence and disciplined for minor offenses. They stay, but under a black cloud that never fully dissipates and may follow them wherever they go. Major offenses warrant immediate exit—dismissal, possible professional discipline, and possible prosecution that may result in life imprisonment or worse (death in China and Iran). The scandal is localized, steps are taken to prevent any repetition, and the incident is soon forgotten.

Systemic corruption cannot be dealt with so easily. There is no guarantee that even if all the offenders are dismissed and others are reallocated the corruption will not continue virtually uninterrupted, merely with a different cast of characters. For external consumption, formal investigations are held and some low-level offenders may be charged, but insiders know that things will continue much unchanged. There might be one significant difference. Successors, mindful of possible individual repercussions, might make sure that they will not be exposed in the same way by reorganizing to make exposure more difficult. In short, the people may change but the corrupt practices persist. Institutionalized corruption requires major reforms in business law, professional practice, organizational and professional culture, ethics and education, public accountability, and political finance. All of these will be opposed by vested interests who are reluctant to admit liability.

The existence of widespread systemic corruption adversely affects the whole society and corrupts all those who come into contact with it, both insiders and outsiders.

1. It perpetuates closed politics and restricts access to decision making, thereby impeding the reflection of social change in political arrangements.
2. It suppresses opposition, thereby building up public resentment that needs only a flashpoint to erupt into violence.
3. It perpetuates and widens social divisions, further dividing the haves from the have-nots.
4. It obstructs policy change, thereby sacrificing the public interest to narrow, partial, and select interests.
5. It blocks much needed reforms and perpetuates poor administrative practices that give offense and reduce performance.
6. It diverts scarce resources away from public amenities and services to private affluence amid general squalor.
7. It contributes to social anomie by shoring up inappropriate arrangements.
8. It undermines trust in public institutions and alienates people.
9. It is dysfunctional to globalization, modernization, and effective governance.
10. It entrenches an international political-criminal network that undermines global security.

This is so strong a charge sheet that it can no longer be ignored by public leaders. Unfortunately, too many leaders got where they are by way of systemic corruption, and too many international and national organizations themselves suffer from systemic corruption that is so habitual that insiders no longer recognize it for what it is. Too few realize that such systemic corruption cannot be tackled as if it were just individual corruption. Something more drastic is required, but the leaders lack the will, time, patience, and expertise to make much progress, and some may be too compromised to change the very system that brought them to the top. It is easier and more comforting to agree to nonbinding resolutions, hold conferences in pleasant spots, sponsor erudite studies, distribute high-minded reports, and generally go through the motions of correcting wrongdoing rather than taking actions that might implicate and embarrass colleagues. If greed is suspected to be behind so much systemic corruption, then money laundering should be the prime target. However, despite the talk, little has been done to curb dirty money and the dirty hands that launder it.

Remedies

The current noise about corruption, a distinct change from the past, indicates that there is genuine interest in curbing corrupt practices. Fortunately, the state of the art has now progressed to the point that experts know what needs to be done. They just await a green light to get to work. They sense that world leaders are not yet fully committed to unite their efforts, and they are hesitant to plunge without further evidence that corruption can indeed be reduced. All need or await more forceful action from civil society to overcome their qualms. Help is readily at hand once leaders give the go-ahead.

In addition to the accumulating abundance of expert advice on what needs to be done about corrupt practices, a new industry has emerged that deals only with providing education and training regarding public ethics and with the investigation of wrongdoing. Governments and businesses with problems have been more prepared to accept advice and research. They are not ashamed to sponsor conferences and meetings on ethics and corruption. The international community, as well, echoes this new frankness, as is evidenced by the passage of international resolutions condemning bad practices; statements by world leaders, in which they promise action against the corruption menace; the success of Transparency International; increased technical assistance in dealing with corruption; the publicity given to anticorruption assemblies; and the increasing concern by international business leaders about venality and the unfavorable image generated by the too-frequent exposure of scandal.

No place is entirely free of corruption, and even the most venerated institutions are contaminated by scandal. Everywhere, the powerful abuse their positions, maybe just to show that they possess power. In any event, corruption has to be tackled wherever it exists. Although immediate attention should be given to those corrupt practices that are judged to do the most harm, it may be easier to begin with or concentrate on the forms that can be tackled with a fair prior assessment of success so that momentum can build for campaigns to deal with more difficult forms. A choice has to be made about where to place emphasis: on legal reforms and law enforcement; on independent investigation and embarrassing publicity; on personal morality and individual integrity; on organizational safeguards; on public education; on example and leadership; on anticorruption campaigns that are focused on selected targets; or on any combination of these and other instruments for tackling corrupt practices.

Unfortunately, one form of corruption is likely to feed on another. It would help if public tolerance of corruption were to be reduced, if people were less passive, and if less reliance were placed on wrongdoers to clean their own hands. Dirty hands do not clean themselves; they besmirch all they touch. So, in preparation, the public has to stiffen up, protest, and back anticorruption efforts. Everybody involved has to refrain from using position and office for private advantage, to impose the same discipline on others, and to remove the guilty from all positions of public trust. All this presupposes freedom of information and free mass media willing to investigate complaints of wrongdoing and expose corruption without fear or favor. Alas, this remains a tall order for most countries where, until this happens, corruption will continue to present serious challenges to integrity, well-being, and stability. In these circumstances, anyone can become a victim of the distortion of power, governance, incentives, and desserts. Transparency International and its country chapters provide an alternative and a conduit.

While the cynics will continue to scorn anticorruption efforts, history shows that corruption can be curbed. More countries are discovering that corrupt practices can be managed and brought under control, although constant vigilance will be necessary to prevent deterioration. The following factors seem to be crucial (Caiden 2001):

- *Moral and trustworthy leaders (and their close relations).* Able and virtuous people have to be attracted to public service and retained without great personal sacrifice. They have to be carefully selected, screened, and monitored to see that their hands (and those of their close relatives) remain clean. There has to be instant removal from office of anyone with dirty hands and immediate disciplinary action against anyone who condones corruption.
- *Appropriate social regulation.* A root cause of corruption is social controls for which there is virtually no support. Outward conformity is only achieved at the cost of sullen resentment and common cause to evade such controls. Governance intervenes where it is unwelcome, which merely results in evasion and lack of enforcement.
- *Regular law revision.* Repeal is needed of vague, anachronistic, and

internally contradictory laws and regulations that prevent the law-abiding from conducting their business in a lawful manner. In every jurisdiction there are probably orders that have outlived their usefulness but remain on the books because no regular review and revision is instituted.

- *Reduction of monopolies.* Inevitably and almost unconsciously, monopolies exploit their position. Where competition cannot be introduced, they have to be carefully monitored and subject to transparency and full accountability to ensure their actions are legal, moral, productive, sensitive, and effective.
- *Open democratic governance.* Clearly, autocracies have a higher propensity to corruption. Every effort has to be made to ensure government in the sunshine. This is very difficult to obtain in private organizations and in public organizations that have been exempted for good reason from democratic norms, procedures, and controls. At the very least, redress and compensation should be provided when wrongdoing occurs.
- *Professionalism.* Amateurism has its place in democratic governance but democratic administration requires professionals who adhere to professional ethics and standards, avoid harm, keep abreast of the state of the art, and are so jealous of their reputations that they ensure competent performance, discipline, and reliable self-policing.
- *Competence.* Wherever there is incompetence, corruption creeps in. System, order, and regularity are essential for the detection of abuses. Competent administration in itself is a major deterrent to corruption as irregularities are likely to be spotted quickly, long before they can be routinized.
- *Personal integrity.* When all is said and done, there is no substitute for individual integrity and the unwillingness of people to compromise with corruption. People who know right from wrong rarely depart from norms and prefer exit to participation in wrongdoing. Ethics education is imperative and cannot be taken for granted.

None of these measures is easy to translate into specific conditions. Robert Klitgaard (1988) has probably been closest. He provided a general framework for anticorruption efforts much along these lines but was more specific and practical, including taking the profits out of corruption and frying the "big fish" in public. He also emphasized tackling weak cultures of public accountability, fostering the democratic ethos, strengthening the appeal of public service, improving capacity building, and inculcating a culture of public accountability and transparency.

The Bottom Line

As has been emphasized elsewhere (Caiden 2001, p. 451), corruption is a particularly viral form of bureau pathology. Once it enters the life stream of any system, it quickly spreads. If it is left untreated, it will eventually destroy the effectiveness of the infected area. Even if it is caught quickly and treated in time, there is no guarantee that it will have been eliminated altogether. Current strategies aim only at containment and minimization, not eradication. The ingenious are always one step ahead, and they will remain so as long as personal integrity is lacking in individuals.

References

Caiden, G.E. 1977. *Police Revitalization.* Lexington, MA: Lexington Books/D.C. Heath.

———. 1992. "Public Disillusion and Organizational Self-Policing." Paper presented at the fifth International Anti-Corruption Conference, Amsterdam, March.

———. 2001. "Dealing with Administrative Corruption." In *Handbook of Administrative Ethics,* 2d ed., ed. Terry L. Cooper, pp. 429–55. New York: Marcel Dekker.

———. 2002. "Enron, Accountancy, and Professional Ethics," *Public Integrity* 4, no. 4 (Fall): 321–32.

Caiden, G.E,. and Caiden, N.J. 1977. "Administrative Corruption." *Public Administration Review* 37, no. 3 (May/June): 301–9.

Caiden, G.E;. Dwivedi, O.P.; and Jabbra J., eds. 2001. *Where Corruption Lives.* Bloomfield, CT: Kumarian Press.

Klitgaard, R. 1988. *Controlling Corruption.* Berkeley: University of California Press.

Richardson, P. 2001. "The Global Assault on Corruption." *Journal of Public Inquiry* (Fall/Winter): 3–7.

Rose-Ackerman, S. 1999. *Corruption and Government: Causes, Consequences and Reform.* Cambridge: Cambridge University Press.

Additional Reading

Anechiarico, F., and Jacobs, J.B. 1996. *The Pursuit of Absolute Integrity: How Corruption Control Makes Government Ineffective.* Chicago: University of Chicago Press.

Centro de Investigacion y Docencia Economicas. 2001. *Gestion y Politica Publica* 10, no. 2: entire issue.

Chand, S.K., and Moene, K.O. 1999. "Controlling Fiscal Corruption." *World Development* 27, no. 7: 1129–40.

Chand, S.K; Moene, K.O.; and Mookherjee, D. 2003. "Fiscal Corruption: A Vice or a Virtue? A Comment." *World Development* 31, no. 8: 1469–72.

Chapman, R.A., ed. 1993. *Ethics in Public Service.* Edinburgh: University of Edinburgh Press.

———. 2000. *Ethics in the Public Service for the New Millennium.* Aldershot, UK: Ashgate.

Coronel, S.S., ed. 1998. *Pork and Other Perks: Corruption and Governance in the Philippines.* Metro Manila, Philippine Center for Investigative Journalism.

Dobel, J.P. 1999. *Public Integrity.* Baltimore: Johns Hopkins University Press.
Fjeldstad, O.-H., and Tungodden, B. 2003. "Fiscal Corruption: A Vice or a Virtue?" *World Development* 31, no. 8: 1459–67.
Girling, J.C. 1997. *Corruption, Capitalism and Democracy.* London: Routledge.
Godson, R., ed. 2003. *Menace to Society: Political-Criminal Collaboration Around the World.* New Brunswick, NJ: Transaction.
Gray, C.W., and Kaufman, D. 1998. "Corruption and Development." *Finance & Development* 35, no. 1: 7–10.
Heidenheimer, A., and Johnston, M., eds. 2001. *Political Corruption,* 3d ed. New Brunswick, NJ: Transaction.
Hellman, J., and Kaufman, D. 2001. "Confronting the Challenge of State Capture in Transition Economies." *Finance & Development* 38, no. 3 (September): 31–35.
Inspectors General of the United States. 2001. "The War on Corruption." *Journal of Public Inquiry* (Fall/Winter).
Jamieson, A. 2000. *The Antimafia: Italy's Fight against Organized Crime.* Basingstoke, UK: Macmillan.
Kang, D.C. 2002. *Crony Capitalism.* Cambridge: Cambridge University Press.
Kettl, D.F. 2000. *The Global Public Management Revolution: A Report on the Transformation of Governance.* Washington, DC: Brookings Institution.
Klitgaard, R. 1998. "International Cooperation against Corruption." *Finance & Development* 35, no. 1: 3–6.
Langseth, P. 1998. *Building Integrity: What Is to Be Done?* Economic Development Institute. Washington, DC: World Bank.
Maor, M. 2004. "Feeling the Heat? Anti-Corruption Agencies in Comparative Perspective." *Governance* 17, no. 1: 1–28.
Mauro, P. 1998. "Corruption: Causes, Consequences, and Agenda for Further Research." *Finance & Development* 35, no. 1: 11–14.
Mbaku, J.M. 1999. "Corruption Cleanups in Developing Societies: The Public Choice Perspective." *International Journal of Public Administration* 22, no. 2: 309–45.
Mitra, C. 1998. *The Corrupt Society: The Criminalization of India from Independence to the 1990s.* New Delhi: Penguin Books India.
Neild, R. 2002. *Public Corruption: The Dark Side of Social Evolution.* Oxford: Anthem Press.
Noonan, J.T. 1984. *Bribes.* New York: Macmillan.
Organization for Economic Cooperation and Development (OECD). 1999. *Public Sector Corruption: An International Survey of Prevention Measures.* Paris.
———. 2000. *Trust in Government: Ethics in OECD Countries.* Paris.
———. 2001. *No Longer Business as Usual: Fighting Bribery and Corruption.* Paris.
Potts, M.; Kochan, N.; and Whittington, R. 1992. *Dirty Money.* Washington, DC: National Press Books.
Qhah, J.S.T. 2001. "Globalization and Corruption Control in Asian Countries." *Public Management Review* 3, no. 4: 453–70.
———. 2003. *Curbing Corruption in Asian Countries: A Comparative Analysis.* Singapore: Times Media Academic.
Schacter, M., and Shah, A. 2001. *Look Before You Leap: Notes for Corruption Fighters.* Policy brief, no. 11. Ottawa: Institute on Governance.
Siddiqui, T.A. 2001. *Towards Good Governance.* Oxford: Oxford University Press.

15

Public-Service Ethics in a Transnational World

Diane E. Yoder and Terry L. Cooper

Corruption and bribery permeate state boundaries and they are temptations to public administrators and managers in every country. Many countries have recognized this and instituted comprehensive ethics policies and programs to combat such hazards. In addition, however, many international organizations have begun to establish international standards for public ethical conduct, common standards that can be implemented in several countries for more consistent public-management ethics. In this chapter, we begin to investigate these emerging global standards. Our purpose is not to provide an empirical look at existing standards and their implementation; rather, we offer an introduction to the regional and international efforts to establish ethics frameworks that go beyond singular efforts by countries to combat corruption.[1]

We begin by looking at the confluence of reasons for the emerging global ethical standards. Following that, we examine some of the global and regional initiatives to create a convergence of ethical standards for public managers. We also examine the work of Transparency International, a nongovernmental effort to promote ethical conduct in government and business. Next, we identify and discuss the emerging global values that appear to underlie the current collaborative efforts. Finally, we offer some preliminary observations about these emerging standards, the social construction process that guides this phenomenon in the absence of shared foundational beliefs derived from culture and religion, and future prospects. We caution readers that our work, while it begins to fill a gap in the literature, is preliminary and evolving. Our hope is to begin a dialogue about these international efforts that may lead to more comprehensive study of them and their effectiveness.

Behind the Emerging Global Standards

The past ten years have witnessed the creation of international and regional efforts to standardize ethics frameworks for public administrators, in addition to efforts by individual countries to combat corruption and bribery. Several reasons explain the emergence of global ethics standards. First, governments and international organizations find themselves in an increasingly interdependent world. We have argued elsewhere (Cooper and Yoder 1999) that at some point in the conceivable future the nation-state may no longer be the locus of governance for collective life, owing to increasing migration, the demise of the former Soviet Union and Eastern bloc, and regional political upheavals in Africa and the Middle East. Such events have fueled a global connectedness or interdependence that transcends national boundaries and is manifested in financial, political, environmental, technological, and cultural ways. For example, our global economy is driven by 300 multinational corporations, which control one-quarter of the world's total productive assets, and a network of international financial conglomerates, which manage daily financial transactions. In the political arena, supranational organizations like the United Nations (UN) have created international military, environmental, and humanitarian alliances. Technologically, we have witnessed cooperative efforts among nations in space exploration and satellite technology, air transportation, and electronic communications.

This increasingly interdependent and interconnected world creates a need for government structures that transcend individual nation-states. Soysal describes this move toward global interdependence as "an increasing interdependence and connectedness, intensified world-level interaction and organizing, and the emergence of transnational political structures, which altogether confound and complicate nation-state sovereignty and jurisdiction" (1998, p. 195). Likewise, Keohane and Nye describe the current period of globalism as "thick" (versus "thin") globalism. "Globalization is the process by which globalism becomes increasingly thick" (Keohane and Nye 2000, p. 108). According to their argument, this period is characterized by a growing "density of networks," in which interdependent organizations grow in numbers "intersect more deeply at more points" (p. 112). Change is rapid in thick globalism, and we see an increase in "transnational participation" or an increase in the number of participants that span national boundaries.

This transnational participation involving global and regional cooperatives may improve governance in an interdependent world. As Waltz argues, "The more interdependent the system, the more a surrogate for government is needed" (1999, p. 699). Farazmand echoes that sentiment, "globalization has facilitated connection and coordination among peoples, governments, and nongovernmental organizations" (1999, p. 514). However, Farazmand points out that the increasing interdependence and globalization does not mean that nation-states and state administration are doomed. In fact, he argues that "globalization has not brought about the end of the state and its bureaucracy; nor will it result in the decline of the state in the future" (p. 514). This does not mean that the nation-state is not threatened by increasing supranational governance by "global" groups like the World Bank, the International Monetary Fund, and various UN groups. One such threat, argues Farazmand, is the possibility of increased corruption, and he reminds public administrators that they "have a global responsibility to act ethically and morally in a coordinated manner. They must expose and fight corruption at any level and at any time" (p. 519).

Some may argue that the rise in international ethics initiatives is no different from the rise in international organizations in general, which stems from globalization. As O'Toole and Hanf argue, "A vast array of regimes and organizations has been established to manage whole fields of activity and collective policy problems" (2003, p. 159). However, we discovered other reasons in addition to globalization that may explain the emergence of international ethics efforts. First, many countries throughout Europe, as well as the United States, Canada, Australia, and New Zealand, spent the past decade beginning to reform their public-management structures. For example, the 1990s witnessed a major rethinking of the public bureaucracy in the United States and an effort to improve government performance under the rubric of "reinventing government." These reforms include efforts to privatize public services, devolve administrative decisions to more local levels, and increase the amount of discretion available to individual bureaucrats. Declining citizen confidence in government performance has also prompted these reforms. In addition, many countries experienced budgetary pressures in the 1990s, creating expectations to provide more services with fewer financial and labor resources. Another reason for the emerging standards is one many scholars have long recognized: the threat to developing countries from internal corruption and bribery. Collingwood examines the practice of "conditionality," which in effect ties international financial assistance to policy reforms and "good governance" in recipient states, and emerged in the late 1980s. Good governance is defined as: "Transparency and accountability in government, economic liberalization and privatization, civil society participation, and respect for human rights, democracy and the rule of law" (2003, p. 55). And

Seligson writes, "There is growing belief in the corrosive effects of corruption in retarding economic development and undermining the consolidation of democratic governance" (2001, p. 221).

Another reason for the emerging standards is, as Rose-Ackerman argues, that the end of the Cold War changed the international administrative landscape. "The end of the Cold War has changed the balance of forces and removed any compelling need to support corrupt regimes for national security reasons. The widespread corruption and organized crime influence in the former Eastern bloc have made the problem difficult to ignore" (1999, p. 177). Rose-Ackerman also notes the increasing move toward privatization and deregulation and the rethinking of the relationship between the market and the state as reasons for the emergence of global ethical standards.

Finally, a growth in globalized organized crime is another reason for increasing international ethics initiatives. Stanislawski argues that in the wake of the Cold War, the real threat to governments and to the democratic process comes from, "rogue non-state actors in the form of transnational organized crime or terrorism" (2004, p. 155). He continues, "Corruption, intimidation, and the unhesitant use of force brought a growing number of influential authority figures, state agencies, and institutions under the control of wealthy criminal organizations, weakening public administration and poisoning the social fabric of transitioning societies" (2004, pp. 155–66). He suspects that the nonstate actors seek cover from their state governments and within their boundaries, which is why efforts to combat such actions and government protection must span international borders.

One might think that the increase in attention to international ethics standards and fighting corruption and bribery may be best explained in terms of increasing terrorism worldwide, and, certainly, the attacks of September 11, 2001. Our research efforts began prior to the September 11 attacks and we found that the international initiatives discussed herein predated the September 11 attacks. In fact, to date, we find little mention of terrorism or combating state-sponsored terrorism within these initiatives. In one case, we found just the opposite to be true. Transparency International, a leading nongovernmental ethics initiative, forewarned of a possible decrease in attention to corruption and bribery as governments struggled in the war on terrorism. They noted that the increase in attention to corruption and bribery of the past decade is "likely to be counterbalanced by increased emphasis in certain governments on antiterrorism agendas that downgrade the corruption issue" (Transparency International 2004a).

Certainly, this new era of international and regional cooperation to fight corruption and promote integrity and transparency in public administration and management stems from reasons that are more complex than simply wanting to clean up governance, and thus require more sophisticated ideas and strategies. As Gilman writes: "This new environment is one in which preventive measures are particularly important. Certainly, the enforcement side of the equation must also be strong. But in this new era of heightened expectations, we must go beyond investigation, prosecution, and punishment of misconduct" (2000, p. 136). We now turn to some of the more significant international organizational ethics cooperatives.

Organizational Efforts to Create Global Ethics Standards

In this section, we begin to explore some of the major governmental initiatives to create global standards for public-management ethics. The UN takes the lead in these global efforts, although corruption and similar terms are not listed as among the "global issues on the UN agenda" (www.un.org/issues). Our treatment of these international efforts will be introductory and brief; our intention is to give the reader a broad-brush look at the emerging initiatives. Future research will examine each initiative more in depth and begin to look at implementation and effectiveness of global ethics standards. As stated, although we recognize the efforts of many private-sector organizations to focus attention on ethics in business and financial transactions, in this chapter, we are mainly interested in ethics initiatives that speak directly to public administrators. We also note that the member nations of the various initiatives are listed in the Appendix.

Global Initiatives

We begin by looking at several "global" initiatives undertaken by the United Nations to create international ethics standards. In the 1970s, the UN began to address ethics standards by establishing an Ad Hoc Intergovernmental Working Group on the Problem of Corrupt Practices. General Assembly Resolution 3514 (December 15, 1975) authorized the ad hoc group, whose purpose was to issue statements on corruption and bribery, and guidelines for how member states should punish various transgressions of public officials. The UN defined public officials as elected or appointed public servants at the national, regional, or local level. The group also argued for member states to cooperate in the investigation and prosecution of corruption. The group's work culminated in a draft agreement that was never formally adopted. The principles of that agreement, however, laid the foundation for the UN's anti-corruption efforts two decades later.

In 1996, the UN spoke firmly on corruption through its General Assembly on a Declaration against Corruption and Bribery and its attendant International Code of Conduct for Public Officials adopted at the eighty-second plenary session (A/RES/51/59). The Declaration is nonbinding, but it echoed the body's earlier efforts to suggest punishments for corruption and bribery, cooperation among member states, and the disclosure of information to expose corrupt practices. The Code of Conduct argued that a public office was "a position of trust, implying a duty to act in the public interest. Therefore, the ultimate loyalty of public officials shall be to the public interests of their country" (UN 1996). The Code of Conduct further specifies: "Public officials shall ensure that they perform their duties and functions efficiently, effectively, and with integrity, in accordance with laws or administrative practices. They shall at all times seek to ensure that public resources for which they are responsible are administered in the most effective and efficient manner" (UN 1996). The Code of Conduct calls for fairness and impartiality among public officials, offers guidelines on conflict of interest and disqualification, promotes disclosure of assets, recommends against the acceptance of gifts to curry favors, and notes that at times, public officials must maintain the confidentiality requirements of their governments. Although these UN documents highlight the importance of international standards for ethical behavior, they are nonbinding and lack specificity. They offer a more general guide and may help to set the tone for regional initiatives, which we examine in the next section.

Many UN efforts to combat corruption are organized under the UN Office on Drugs and Crime, which focuses on transnational organized crime, corruption, and trafficking in human beings. Many efforts began within this office, which was at one time the UN's Centre for International Crime Prevention's (CICP) Office for Drug Control and Crime Prevention. That office created a Global Programme against Corruption to assist member states in their efforts to fight corruption in 1999. The impetus for this initiative was pervasive corruption in both the public and the private sectors. The program consists of a research component and a technical assistance component. Specific measures were proposed for implementation at the international level. First, a "pool of high-level international experts" should be established to focus the research and training of the program (UN Centre for International Crime Prevention 2000). Next, the program calls for transparency and accountability in government transactions, and the "need for the creation of internationally recognized mechanisms of transparency and accountability." The programme also suggests the creation of international legal instruments that focus on bribery and corruption. Finally, the program calls for the creation of an international database and an international forum to help fight corruption and share information among member states.

In December 2000, the UN directed the CICP to begin to draft an international convention to fight corruption (General Assembly Resolution 55/61). Between January 2002 and October 2003, an ad hoc committee met seven times to negotiate the convention. The committee's work was adopted by the General Assembly in October 2003 and opened for signing in December 2003 in Mérida, Mexico. The convention will stay open for signing until December 2005, and must be ratified by thirty nations to be enacted. The convention is a promising step in the global fight against corruption. It specifies prevention activities, criminalization of a broad range of corrupt acts, international cooperation, and recovery of assets taken through corrupt practices (UN General Assembly 2003). It includes mandatory criminal sanctions for certain acts of corruption and even speaks to related acts like obstruction of justice. However, the convention does not require protection for whistle-blowers. As of this writing, of the 111 signatories (with reservations from Iran, Tunisia, and Viet Nam), only Kenya and Sri Lanka had ratified the convention. When the convention is ratified and enacted, it will be "the first global instrument embracing a comprehensive range of anti-corruption measures to be taken at the national level" (Transparency International 2004b, p. 111).

One other "global" initiative merits attention. In September 1997, 1,000 delegates from ninety-three nations met in Lima, Peru, for the eighth International Anti-Corruption Conference. The resulting document represents a key global effort to speak against corruption. The conference was sponsored in part by Transparency International, the UN, the World Bank, and the International Development Bank. The declaration urges international and regional efforts to ratify and implement codes of conduct, statements against corruption, and to cooperate in the prevention and punishment of corrupt practices. The declaration also recommends that individual nations "should operate in a transparent and accountable manner at all levels, with the public having access to information to the maximum extent possible" (Lima Declaration 1997, p. 4). The signatories also call on nations to "assure the independence, integrity and de-politicisation of the judicial system as the cornerstone of the rule of law on which the effectiveness of all efforts to combat corruption depends" (Lima Declaration 1997, p. 4). The declaration notes that civil society must agree to the same ethical standards, and that schools and religious institutions should raise awareness about corruption and bribery. Although the declaration is simply a statement of principles, it shows that corruption is a global concern and requires efforts on all levels of society to combat it.

The Global Forum on Fighting Corruption represents another international effort that merits mention. The first forum was held in 1999 in Washington, DC, and hosted by then vice president Al Gore. The meeting of representatives from ninety countries promoted "Guiding Principles for Fighting Corruption and Safeguarding Integrity among Justice and Security Officials." These principles focus on hiring, management practices, codes of conduct, criminal sanctions, auditing, autonomy, fairness, deterrence, disclosure, cooperation, and research to prevent corruption. The second forum, held in May 2001 in the Hague and hosting representatives from more than 100 countries, continued the work of the first forum. The third forum was held in Seoul in May 2003, and focused on legal enforcement of anticorruption measures and ongoing challenges.

We also note the United States Office of Government Ethics (OGE). As part of the OGE, the Office of Government Relations and Special Projects offers technical assistance to foreign countries that are working to prevent corruption. The OGE is a separate agency within the executive branch of the U.S. government and although it is a unilateral ethics initiative that "helps to prevent not to detect, investigate or prosecute corruption" (USOGE 2004), it does promote cooperation programs in an advisory capacity with the UN and several regional ethics initiatives. As stated on their Web site: "OGE . . . shares its ideas and experiences with foreign governments directly and within multilateral processes" (USOGE 2004). It also offers technical assistance to U.S. government agencies that work with foreign governments on anticorruption issues.

These global efforts to create international standards for public-management ethics are broad and still emerging. These initiatives speak to the desire to promote consistent messages and develop management tools to fight corruption. They also foster cooperation among diverse nations, but due to their nonbinding nature, they may not have much effect on global corruption overall.

Regional Initiatives[2]

Organization for Economic Cooperation and Development

Perhaps the most-developed regional initiative to fight corruption is that of the Organization for Economic Cooperation and Development (OECD), which boasts thirty member nations and relationships with dozens more. The reasons for OECD's push into the public-ethics field are summed up in its survey of public-sector corruption: "Corruption in government and public administration is a complex and pervasive phenomenon. It is a concern of OECD member countries because, among other things, it is believed to distort the operation of economic activity and weaken political stability. In governance terms, corruption threatens democratic public institutions by permitting the influence of improper interests on the use of public resources and power by undermining the confidence of citizens in the legitimate activities of state" (OECD 1999).

The OECD first began discussing corruption in 1989. However, it ramped up its anticorruption efforts in 1997, when the member nations agreed to the Convention on Combating Bribery of Foreign Public Officials in International Business Transactions (reaffirmed in February 1999). The convention called for cooperation among member states to fight corruption, but also noted the importance of the individual member countries to strengthen their national efforts and mechanisms to prevent corruption. The convention was precipitated by a paper published by OECD's Public Management Committee (PUMA) called "Ethics in the Public Service" (OECD 1996). This document was based on a survey of nine OECD countries to discover their national mechanisms for fighting corruption. The report called for far-reaching efforts to control corruption and bribery: "By definition, the management of ethics and conduct is not just about monitoring and policing behaviour. It is also about promoting integrity and good conduct. It is about seeking some consensus on what is good behaviour and giving public servants some guidance as to how they should act, make decisions, and use discretion in their everyday work" (p. 11). As of spring 2004, however, thirty-five nations had ratified the convention, but several nations were slow to ratify and begin implementing legislation. Monitoring and enforcing the convention have proved difficult, and critics argue that the convention has several loopholes that need to be closed (Transparency International 2004b). Currently, OECD is working on draft guidelines on conflicts of interest for public officials. OECD also offers guidelines for combating corruption in multinational corporations.

OECD recognizes that public-service ethics are based on values that may be culturally specific, but that different governments "often confront similar ethical challenges" (OECD 1998a). However, core fundamental values can drive multinational efforts to establish public conduct standards. Based on that argument, OECD promotes what it calls an Ethics Infrastructure, which consists of eight elements that lead to control, guidance, and management. The exact manifestation and balance of these elements is left to individual countries to create based on their cultural specifics. Briefly, the eight elements include:

- Political Commitment (e.g., clear anticorruption messages and actions from government leaders);
- Effective Legal Framework (e.g., enforceable laws and regulations defining conduct standards);
- Efficient Accountability Mechanisms (e.g., monitoring and evaluation procedures);
- Workable Codes of Conduct (e.g., statements on obligations, roles, values);

- Professional Socialization Mechanisms (e.g., education and training);
- Supportive Public Service Conditions (e.g., equity and fairness, appropriate salaries);
- Coordinating Ethics Bodies (e.g., specially created agencies or committees to coordinate and monitor efforts); and
- Public Involvement and Scrutiny (e.g., an active civil society with access to information).

What these eight elements translate into for individual OECD members depends upon each country. Overall, OECD recommends: the development and regular review of ethics policies and procedures; the promotion of government action to impose ethical standards; the incorporation of ethics into administrative reforms and management practices; and the integration of procedural rules and ethical values (OECD 1998b).

Finally, OECD conducts research on various anticorruption efforts around the world. For example, in 2000 the OECD published *Trust in Government,* a study of anticorruption measures in twenty-nine nations that represents one of the first international documents on ethics standards (OECD 2000c). In one of their policy briefs supporting the idea of trust in government, OECD argued that "citizens trust public institutions if they know that public offices are used for the public good" (2000a, p. 5). Based on this premise, the group advocated that standards of conduct or behavior with criminal laws and attendant punishments be legislated by member nations.

Anti-Corruption Network for Transition Economies

The OECD works with other international groups to combat corruption. For example, OECD recognizes the unique situation that "transition economies" or former communist-controlled countries may face. Thus, OECD works with the Anti-Corruption Network for Transition Economies (ACN), which was created in 1998. This group consists of former Soviet Union and Eastern bloc countries, civic associations, and international donor agencies, and is more of "a forum for the exchange of concrete, action-oriented information between anti-corruption practitioners and analysts in Eastern Europe and Former Soviet Union" (ACN 2000). This public-private collaboration offers member nations information on how to fight corruption and bribery and links them with other organizations fighting corruption. It maintains an Internet Web site, hold annual meetings and Steering Group meetings, promote coalitions among government agencies and civic associations, and sponsor regional workshops. OECD notes that transition economies have in common certain legacies of their former communist administrations. These include:

(a) a lack of coordination with no clear delegation and accountability systems; (b) a lack of coordinated personnel management; and (c) a lack of a common state administration profession (Synnerstrom 1998).[3]

Council of Europe

In 1949, ten countries in Europe founded the Council of Europe (COE), the purpose of which was to "strengthen democracy, human rights, and the rule of law throughout its member states" (Council of Europe 2000). Now boasting forty-five members,[4] the Council developed the Multidisciplinary Group on Corruption in 1994, which recognizes the importance of multinational efforts to fight organized crime and corruption. In 1996, the member Council adopted the Programme of Action against Corruption and agreed to implement it before the end of 2000. The program was to create international instruments to prevent corruption, establish a code of conduct for public officials, and elaborate a convention on civil remedies for damages stemming from corruption. Called "a public document and a message addressed to every individual public official," the Model Code of Conduct emphasizes the importance of diligence, effectiveness, confidentiality, impartiality, fairness, and personal and administrative integrity. In January 1999, the COE formally wrote CETS No. 173, Criminal Law Convention on Corruption. The convention specified that member nations must enact legislative efforts to prevent corruption, bribery of national and international officials, corporate bribery, and money laundering. It also specified that member nations must establish international cooperative efforts to battle corruption. Finally acquiring the necessary fourteen ratifications a full three years later, the convention went into effect in 2002. In spring 2003, the council established the Additional Protocol to the Criminal Law Convention on Corruption. This protocol, which has not been ratified by all COE members as of this writing, mandates that member nations implement individual anticorruption and bribery prevention programs and begins to lay the foundation for monitoring and enforcement by appointing a subgroup to evaluate implementation.[5]

That subgroup is a regional coalition that COE also sponsors. GRECO, the Group of States against Corruption, was formed in May 1998, although the groundwork for the group began as early as 1994. GRECO is responsible for monitoring the Criminal Law Convention on Corruption and the Additional Protocol. The group was formed in response to corruption that was seen as "a major threat to the rule of law, democracy, human rights, fairness and social justice" (Directorate of Legal Affairs 1999, p. 6). The group also argues that corruption "hinders economic development, and endangers the stability of democratic institutions and the moral foundations of society"

(Directorate of Legal Affairs 1999, p. 6). GRECO bills itself "as a flexible and efficient follow-up mechanism, called to monitor, through a process of mutual evaluation and peer pressure, the observance of the Guiding Principles in the Fight against Corruption" (GRECO 2001, p. 1). Perhaps most notably, GRECO developed the Model Code of Conduct for Public Officials, which applies to all public officials, and "fills the gap between on the one hand often abstract legal regulations as to the principles of behaviour and, on the other hand the requirement of guidance in numerous difficult situations of an employed person's day-to-day life" (GRECO 2000, p. 7). The code deals with specific issues like reporting, conflict of interest, declaration of interests, political activity, privacy, gifts, bribery, abuse of authority, information, integrity, and use of resources.

Stability Pact for South Eastern Europe

With the European Union's prompt, several nations of South Eastern Europe joined together in late 1998 (prior to the war in Kosovo). Their mission was to "achieve the objective of lasting peace, prosperity, and stability" (Stability Pact for South Eastern Europe 1999 p. 1). Interestingly, in their founding document, the countries wrote that they "recognize their responsibility to work within the international community to develop a shared strategy for stability and growth of the region" (Stability Pact for South Eastern Europe 1999, p. 1). Although ethics is not their primary mission, the Stability Pact seeks to promote citizen participation, combat corruption and illegal activities, and promote human rights policies. This group works with major international organizations (e.g., COE, NATO, UN), and recognizes the need to focus "on the development and the strengthening of administrative and institutional capacity as well as civil society . . . to reinforce the consolidation of democratic structures" (Stability Pact for South Eastern Europe 1999, p. 8). Their work spans three broad areas: creating a "secure environment," promoting "sustainable democratic systems," and furthering "economic and social well-being" (www.stabilitypact.org/about/default.asp). The program is built on four key principles: institutional mechanisms (e.g., an Anti-Corruption Steering Group), assessments, country-by-country monitoring, and technical assistance.

Organization of American States

The Organization of American States (OAS) boasts the mission of "unequivocal commitment to democracy," and in keeping with that mission, the OAS has made corruption a key issue. In 1996, in Caracas, Venezuela, twenty-one

Latin American countries, along with the United States and Canada, signed the Inter-American Convention against Corruption. Since then, other OAS members have signed the convention, which defines corruption broadly to include soliciting, offering, or accepting a bribe, acting or failing to discharge duties for personal gain, fraudulently using or concealing property, and aiding or abetting any corruption (OAS 1996). This agreement is part of the 1997 Inter-American Program to Fight Corruption. This program focuses on comparative studies of states' anticorruption efforts, conducts legal research, drafts codes of conduct for member nations' consideration, disseminates information, and supports consultations with other international organizations about their anticorruption efforts. OAS also works with the Trust for the Americas under the rubric "Transparency and Governance." This effort thus far has sponsored summits on corruption and training, and is the first to implement evaluation mechanisms to monitor the implementation of the Inter-American Convention (Gilman 2000).

One important effort of OAS is its continuing attention to corruption in its Summit of the Americas program. Important declarations and initiatives result from these summits. For example, in the third summit held in 2001 in Canada, the group established the Network of Government Institutions of Public Ethics in the Americas. This group acts as a facilitator and locus of exchange for ideas and tools to fight corruption among OAS member nations. They also sponsor videoconferences, workshops, and joint research efforts. In January 2004, in Mexico, the OAS sponsored a Special Summit of the Americas acknowledging that OAS had fourteen new heads of state since the 2001 summit. This special summit resulted in the Declaration of Nuevo León. The declaration eschews corruption and bribery and affirms the OAS member states' commitment to democracy and transparency in governance. The declaration is especially interesting because it (a) mentions the need to combat terrorism as part of its commitment to democratic governance and (b) specifically acknowledges the UN Convention against Corruption as "a valuable instrument to confront this scourge, and therefore we commit to consider signing and promoting its ratification" (OAS 2004).

ADB-OECD Anti-Corruption Initiative for Asia-Pacific

In 1999, the Asian Development Bank (ADB) and the OECD organized a workshop on corruption with public officials and business officials from over thirty nations "to counter the malign influence of corruption" (ADB/OECD 2001, p. 1). The group concluded that "corruption erodes confidence in political institutions and endangers public sector reforms; exacts a disproportionate cost on the poor who may be deprived of basic public services; distorts the allocation of resources and undermines competition in the market place" (ADB/OECD 2001, pp. 1–2). As such, in 2000, the group held a conference in Seoul and developed its Anti-Corruption Action Plan for Asia and the Pacific. The goal of the group is to develop anticorruption strategies, enhance law enforcement and protect whistle-blowers, promote transparency and accountability, build a merit-based civil society, increase disclosure, and strengthen evaluation and oversight. The group sponsors an annual conference, supports country teams responsible for policy implementation, and has a secretariat and managing committee for general policy review. The action plan acknowledges that regional cooperation "is critical to the effective fight against corruption" (ADB/OECD 2004) and identifies three "pillars of action" upon which anticorruption efforts should be based. These pillars include:

- Developing effective and transparent systems for public service,
- Strengthening anti-bribery actions and promoting integrity in business operations, and
- Supporting active public involvement (ADB/OECD 2004).

The plan has been endorsed by twenty Asian and Pacific countries, including Hong Kong and China, which endorsed the plan in April 2003.

Global Coalition for Africa

The Global Coalition for Africa (GCA) was created in 1990 to serve as a forum on issues relating to development in African nations. In 1997, the GCA formally addressed the issue of corruption in a policy forum and launched an initiative to combat bribery in procurement. The GCA defined corruption as "the abuse of official position for private gain," and cited the level of corruption in some African countries as "endemic" (GCA 1997). The group noted the importance of addressing corruption in ways specific to the individual country's experience, but argued that anticorruption strategies must include: public-sector measures, watchdog agencies, public awareness, civic participation, an accountable judiciary, and the involvement of the media and private business. In 1999, the GCA held a Global Forum on Fighting Corruption, from which a declaration on collaboration evolved. This document contained much more direct language and principles for controlling corruption in African countries. Among other things, the eleven signatories agreed to:

- Demonstrate leadership and political will;
- Create budgetary and financial transparency, accountability, and integrity;
- Eliminate conflicts of interest through effective laws and procedures;

- Implement reforms that would restore integrity and morale to the public service;
- Promote transparency in public procurement;
- Establish and enforce self-regulating codes of conduct;
- Establish autonomous, independent anticorruption agencies; and
- Facilitate cooperation in investigating and prosecuting corruption (GCA 1999).

At the same time, the GCA adopted a declaration on promoting integrity among justice and security personnel. In 2001, the coalition sponsored the Global Forum II, where good governance and fighting corruption were the focal points for the twenty-two African countries that were represented.

United Nations' Charter for the Public Service in Africa

In 2000, the UN's Division for Public Economies and Public Administration assisted the African Training and Research Center in Administration for Development in drafting a public-service charter and code of conduct for public officials in the region. The purpose of the charter was to increase awareness about public-service ethics, promote strategies for increasing transparency and professionalism in public service, and create behavior-changing tools for African countries to implement (UN 2000). The Charter, officially published at the Third Pan-African Conference of the Ministers of Civil Service in Namibia, listed the fundamental principles of public service as: equality of treatment, neutrality, legality, and continuity (UN Department of Economic and Social Affairs 2001). The charter also cited the fundamental values of professionalism and ethics for public servants and noted rules of conduct on integrity, conflict of interest, disclosure, and political neutrality. Representatives from thirty-eight African nations endorsed the charter and the African Training and Research Centre in Administration for Development works with the nations and the UN to implement the charter. In support of the charter, the UN Department of Economic and Social Affairs also sponsors the Project on Public Service Ethics in Africa, whose mission is to provide information on management standards, ethics initiatives, and anticorruption tools to help charter nations. The project also tracks anticorruption efforts in charter nations.

African Union

The Organization of African Unity (OAU) was established decades ago to assist African nations in their efforts to drive out colonialists and apartheid, to develop their economies, to nurture their sovereignty, and to promote cooperation. In September 1999, the OAU became the African Union and the efforts to establish a convention of anticorruption ensued. After several meetings and drafts, the African Convention on Preventing and Combating Corruption was finalized at the Maputo Summit in Mozambique. The convention needs fifteen member nations to ratify it before it takes effect. As of this writing, only Comoros had ratified the convention, although twenty-nine of the fifty-three member nations had signed it. The four-pronged approach of the convention seeks to prevent, detect, punish, and eradicate corruption (African Union 2004). In doing so, the convention is founded on the principles of democracy and participation, respect for human rights, transparency, accountability, and social justice, and directs governments to adopt, implement, and enforce tough legislation to fight corruption and money-laundering.

The Middle East

The foregoing examples of international initiatives on public-service ethics and behavior involve governmental efforts. When we first began this research in 2000, most of the regions in the world were represented by these agreements, with the exception of the Middle East.[6] We investigated the League of Arab States and the Organization of Petroleum Exporting Countries (OPEC) and did not find collaborative agreements or statements on public-service ethics. We continued to investigate regional anticorruption coalitions that include the Middle East and as of this writing, we still cannot find governmental coalitions. In fact, in sifting through materials from OPEC and the League of Arab States, we did not find references to corruption or bribery. A search of nongovernmental organizations like the Arab Organization for Human Rights and the Arab Administrative Development Organization also proved fruitless. However, the Arab Business Council offers standards of behavior and codes of conduct for Arab business officials, and several civic organizations in the Middle East sponsored a conference in spring 2004 that acknowledges the importance of democratic values.[7]

In Transparency International's Global Report on Corruption 2004, Reinoud Leenders and John Sfakianakis wrote of the Arab region: "Corruption continued to thrive in virtually all domains of economic, administrative, and political activity across the region [from 2001 to 2002]" (Transparency International 2004b, p. 205). The authors argue that the continued corruption stems from "the lack of institutional reforms accompanying economic liberalization programmes [that] has created new opportunities for rent seeking" and "the prevalence of authoritarian rule in the region [that] constitutes a major hindrance to transparency and accountability at both state and private sector levels" (p. 205). They report that individual governments "acknowledge that corruption is an impediment to good governance" (p. 208), but see little effort on the part of individual nations or coalitions in the Middle East to take action. We add that some individual nations are beginning to join international efforts like Transparency International (see below) and are trying to work with international agencies. For example, Gilman (2000) reports that Egypt has strong ties to the U.S. Office of Government Ethics.

Nongovernmental Initiatives

Our purpose here is not to address the financial or business initiatives to combat corruption. However, we must note the efforts of the World Bank, the Asian Development Bank, and the Asia-Pacific Economic Cooperation in promoting transparency, accountability, and fair dealing in business and financial practices. Each of these organizations has statements or nonbinding principles on combating corruption and bribery.

One of the most noteworthy nongovernmental initiatives to combat corruption is Transparency International (TI), which bills itself as "the only international non-governmental organization devoted to combating corruption [that] brings civil society, business, and governments together in a powerful global coalition" (Transparency International 2004c). Working to establish chapters in 120 countries,[8] TI aims to promote cooperation in fighting corruption, safeguard public procurement, and disseminate information on how to fight corruption and bribery, with an emphasis on empowering local efforts to prevent corruption. TI advocates public deliberation, disclosure of information, whistle-blowing, administrative reform, and forming an "integrity circle," in which a small group of colleagues agrees not to engage in corruption. The national chapters are campaigning for national anticorruption strategies through lobbying, working with the media, and facilitating working groups. As we mentioned above, some countries we did not find represented in the governmental initiatives (e.g., India, Israel) are represented within TI. In addition, this is one initiative we found that listed a number of countries from the Middle East among its members, although several countries were in the process of establishing chapters and several countries listed the International Secretariat of Transparency International as their contact.[9]

Transparency International seeks to raise awareness of its core values: transparency, accountability, integrity, solidarity, courage, justice, and democracy. Every two years, the group sponsors the International Anti-Corruption Conference, the most recent of which was held in Seoul, Korea, in May 2003. According to the group, 900 people came from 108 countries to discuss corruption and share anticorruption strategies. Transparency International also works to institute multinational conventions and to monitor compliance, but is quick to say that it "does not expose individual cases" of bribery or corruption (Transparency International 2004b). As with many of the initiatives mentioned here, the focus is on the prevention of corruption, not the policing of infractions. As part of their efforts to raise awareness and to facilitate the development of anticorruption policies and procedures in member countries, TI also collects information on anticorruption efforts and publishes a wide variety of documents, including an annual report on anti-corruption efforts. Its Global Corruption Report 2004 is a comprehensive look at types of corruption, efforts in thirty-four individual countries to combat corruption, and global initiatives.

Clearly, the international community has recognized the importance of banding together to combat corruption and bribery. As Gilman and Lewis note, these initiatives "appear to undermine the 'cultural determinism' thesis which has heretofore dominated ethics discussion in public administration" (1996, p. 523). Others are not so optimistic about the efforts. Rose-Ackerman notes: "Some observers question this new interest by international organizations. They view corruption as a domestic political problem that should be left to individual countries. To these critics, outsiders' reform efforts represent an unacceptable attempt to impose 'Western' values" (1999, p. 177). She suggests that some countries will resist attempts to curb corruption because of the benefits to their economies. She also warns that this push to standardize ethical behavior "may be just a temporary fad. The international community is at the point where rhetoric must be translated into concrete programs" (1999, p. 178). We would agree. However, we recognize that these fledgling efforts need time to blossom into fully elaborated, concrete mechanisms to prevent corruption. Furthermore, these systems need time to establish accountability and enforcement mechanisms that are binding. At this point, it seems premature to judge the effectiveness of such initiatives or predict their doom. Rather, we think it is crucial to begin to identify the common values behind such initiatives, which we do below.

Emerging Global Values

Most of the more significant efforts by international organizations to establish common standards for public ethical conduct have focused largely on creating the components of an ethics infrastructure to prevent corruption, protect human rights, and, in some cases, support democratization. Parallel to these government-oriented activities, more broadly focused deliberation is under way in several arenas such as the Institute for Global Ethics, the Center for Global Ethics, and the Caux Round Table concerning a global ethic that includes business and civil society. As we mentioned, such efforts are important, but lie beyond the scope of this work. The specific values and ethical principles underlying these structural projects remain to be identified, explained, and qualified; thus, we begin this section by identifying the values and ethical principles more implicit in the former and explicit in the latter. We conclude with a comparison of these two streams of thought and discourse.

We urge the reader to keep in mind an important distinction drawn by Gilman and Lewis (1996) throughout this discussion. They maintain that one must differentiate the particularities of specific cultures around the globe from public administrative ethical standards that are beginning to be shared internationally. Gilman and Lewis present a frontal challenge to the conventional wisdom that administrative ethics must vary widely just because the norms and values of national cultures do so. They argue, "there are fundamental values—treated at a higher level of abstraction— that are closely associated with democracy, market economy, and professional bureaucracy" (1996, p. 518). In their judgment, these shared values, which transcend the cultural diversity of societies, are emerging as global ethical standards for public administration. Not everyone agrees that an increasingly interdependent world translates into shared values. Kettl argues that today's interdependence has created "an emerging system of governance without government, management or control. Shared values, which shaped governmental policies in the past, have yet to emerge" (2000 p. 492). We agree with Gilman and Lewis, however, and have found that an emergent base of shared values is present in these anticorruption initiatives. In other words, we may be seeing a generic orientation to public administration coming into being, not around scientific principles, as the American Progressive Movement advocated in the early twentieth century, but rooted in common ethical principles on an international scale. It is the evidence for these shared ethical perspectives that we propose to examine.

Before we discuss specific values, we highlight the importance of trust in the emerging global initiatives. As we have argued elsewhere (Cooper and Yoder 1999), the regional communities and institutional innovations like those discussed above, are, and will continue to be, founded on social trust, which undergirds social capital. Two types of trust promote social connections: "thick" and "thin" (Newton 1997). The former is based on regular interaction among members of a community who share common backgrounds (e.g., religious, ethnic), while the latter is based on loose, weak, heterogeneous, social relations among people in a community. Newton writes, "Modern society is based on the 'thin' trust, which tends to be associated with the organic solidarity or gesellschaft of looser, more amorphous, secondary relations,"

(1997, p. 578). We argue that the international ethics innovations are communities built on thin trust because they do not involve the "intensive, daily contact between people, often of the same tribe, class, or ethnic background," in thick trust societies (Newton 1997, p. 578). Rather, we see the global ethics initiatives as more loosely organized across national boundaries and yet not beholden to a central government. Perhaps this is why the emerging initiatives have "no teeth" when it comes to enforcing their standards of conduct. We suspect that their continued existence and growth will parallel an increase in their collective "muscle."

Putnam notes that "social trust in complex modern settings can arise from two related sources—norms of reciprocity and networks of civic engagement" (1993, p. 171). It follows, then, that social trust both fuels and is enlarged by these global anticorruption initiatives. Putnam points to norms of reciprocity as another basis of social trust. As these emerging initiatives continue to grow, we believe that norms of ethical conduct will flourish in reciprocal agreements and that trust will continue to grow. Trust must be bolstered, however, by credible commitment (Shepsle 1991). A commitment is a bond, covenant, or promise to act in a prescribed manner. A commitment can be made credible in one of two ways. First, individuals may be intrinsically motivated to uphold their commitments—this is known as "motivational credible commitment." When formal laws or conventions must be instituted for individuals to uphold their commitments, "imperative credible commitment" is created. In the absence of an international tribunal to monitor international ethics violations, collaboratives must rely on both imperative and motivational credible commitment. Indeed, the latter may be more important at this juncture than the former.

Ethics and International Organizations

The central thrust of the international efforts discussed above appear to be accountability, regulatory structures, and monitoring processes to prevent corruption and provide "transparency." In advocating these characteristics of government, these organizations assume that democracy and market economics are objective phenomena that are spreading throughout the world, and that anticorruption efforts and human rights initiatives are critical components of democracy and market economies. Passing references are made to the importance of public confidence and mutual trust as essential for the effective functioning of international agreements, democratic governments, and markets, but little substantive treatment of how these concepts are ethically grounded exists. An OECD "Issues Paper" summarizes this level of understanding global ethics as follows:

While democratic governance is common to all OECD Member countries
it is, naturally, mediated through local administrative institutions, community values and historical traditions. Each of these provides a possible source
of basic ethical values for public officials. The failure of public officials to
uphold the basic ethics expected of them could be labeled breach of public
trust, abuse of power or corruption. Evident breaches of this kind lead to a
decline in public confidence in democratic governance. The essence of any
ethics system is that it serves to assure the public that its government is
working only in the public interest. (OECD 2000b)

Our observation is that three things may be driving the global anticorruption efforts. First, economic interdependence continues to grow and solidify
a truly global economy. Second, in addition to the expanding global economy,
many countries continue to develop their domestic economic infrastructure.
Third, many countries are creating or strengthening their democratic governance structures. We suggest that the growing worldwide concern for corruption prevention and transparency in governance stems from a realization
that underlying the effective operation of market economies and democratic
government must be commitment to several requisite values: the right to
self-determination, freedom, honesty, trust, and stability. We wish to make it
clear that we are not suggesting that these are the only ethical values important for markets and democratic governance, but the ones we see implied in
the newly emerging institutions around the world.

Self-determination is the foundational right upon which both the democratic and market paradigms rest. Eighteenth-century thinkers such as Thomas Jefferson viewed this right as anchored in natural law and ordained by
God. The United States Declaration of Independence exemplifies this perspective with its dual assertions about the rights of individuals to pursue life,
liberty, and happiness, and the right of free people to pursue their own des-
tiny. Although some adherents to natural law may still ground the right of
self-determination in that way, most claims for such rights are made on the
basis of taken-for-granted consensus or conventions such as the United Nations Declaration of Human Rights. Transparency, then, appears to be viewed
as a requisite for people to secure this right individually and collectively.

In the emerging global initiatives, freedom in several forms is viewed as
essential for self-determination, including freedom of information, autonomy
of economic choice, and autonomy of political choice. Without transparency
in government operations, two of these—freedom of information and political choice—are not possible. More precisely, to the extent that one cannot
see into the workings of government, these freedoms are more or less constrained. These two freedoms are linked; without freedom of information

about governance one cannot freely make informed political choices intended to achieve some balance of one's own individual interests and the public interest. Without information, one cannot act freely. Corruption and secrecy in governmental decision making and action, both of which conceal the actual operations of government, deprive citizens of necessary information and constrain freedom and autonomy.

This proposition not only applies to government, but, for example, is also a basic principle in other professional fields. For example, in medical ethics it is referred to as "informed consent." Patients cannot exercise their right to autonomy concerning treatment of their own bodies unless their physician's diagnosis, the evidence on which it is based, the available range of options, the risks involved, and the probable consequences of any therapeutic course of action are provided in understandable language.[10] Patient autonomy requires transparency. Similarly, citizen autonomy necessitates transparency.

The emphasis on transparency assumes a more general freedom of information and its dissemination throughout a society to be requisite for market economies. A free market assumes access to the necessary information about corporations, conditions of domestic and international trade, changing preferences of consumers, and actions of government that affect economic outcomes. To the extent that information asymmetries exist due to a lack of transparency, one cannot enter the marketplace and engage in informed transactions.

Among the international organizations we examined, especially within OECD, participants are concerned that the new roles of public managers may result in corruption of government that reduces transparency and distorts the functioning of both governments and markets. The worry is that traditional public-service values are increasingly displaced by business values as governments enter into partnerships and contracts with businesses. As the lines between government and business are increasingly blurred, public managers are encouraged to think and act more like private-sector entrepreneurs than trustees of the public good. Corporations inclined to use bribery and other forms of illegal influence in their relations with government may find these new public entrepreneurs more susceptible to "back room" deals that are not transparent to the public in either their political or their economic roles. Hence, strong emphasis on the centrality of transparency to preserve both political and economic freedom prevails.

Honesty is implied as essential if access to the operations of government and the economy and freedom of information are to be meaningful. The importance attributed so widely to transparency assumes that what citizens are allowed to observe must be actual governance and not a facade of symbolic politics intended to mislead. Citizens need to be able to expect and receive an honest representation of what government has done, is doing, and is proposing to do if they are to be able to exercise political freedom. Only to the extent that honesty characterizes the functions of government do citizens have any opportunity to hold officials accountable. Accountability is an essential ingredient in exercising free political choice. Honesty includes the intent to maintain the veracity of government documents, official statistics, budgets, policy decisions, investigations, financial dealings, and agency performance. Deception, the intentional substitution of untruth and misinformation, limits the freedom of citizens in their political choices and decisions. It is intended to manipulate rather than liberate.[11]

Similarly, a market economy requires honesty as a requisite element of transparency for effective functioning. Transactions are the central mechanism for markets. Honesty in transactions includes the intention to keep one's promises. Free competition among buyers and sellers in the marketplace is dependent on access to honest economic information. These, in turn, depend on veracity of documents concerning economic performance, forecasts, and regulations. As market economies become increasingly interdependent on a global scale, honesty becomes of greater and greater importance.

Trust is viewed as the essential glue that holds both democratic governance and market economies together in the emerging global standards for ethics. In a sense, it is the product of freedom and honesty as described above. Trust is largely confidence in the predictability of behavior, and that confidence may come from either motivational or imperative credible commitment. Citizens trust government when they have sufficient honest information about how it actually functions to anticipate what it will do under varying circumstances, and the freedom to act on that information—to hold it accountable and to effect change. Economic actors in the marketplace trust the institutions within which financial transactions are made when they can predict bargains being kept, money being transferred, and contracts being honored. Consequently, trust is the ultimate object of transparency. Trust enables commitment to work for the common good in governance and the building of wealth in the market. Distrust causes citizens to retreat from engagement in collective problem solving and electoral decisions. Distrust evokes economic self-protection, reluctance to risk capital, and fear of buying and selling. In a world of increasingly interdependent governments and economies, trust rises to paramount importance.

Stability is a by-product of freedom, honesty, and trust in both governance and economics. Every government and every business values stability. Neither set of institutions can function well in a turbulent environment in which predictability is lacking and trust is weakened. Sometimes stability is sought directly by imposing order and attempting to coerce conduct.

Control becomes the paramount value rather than trust. Those who advocate transparency and the values that undergird it appear to have recognized that governmental and economic stability are achieved indirectly through providing freedom of political and economic choice, honesty in economic and governmental affairs, and thereby cultivating trust. When people trust their institutions, they support them rather than trying to overthrow them. Necessary and desired change can be accomplished in an ongoing fashion within fundamentally stable institutions. In the language of systems thinking this is "dynamic equilibrium," change within a self-adaptive and self-regulating environment, homeostasis of the human body being one of the most visible examples.

Our reflections on the values implicit in preventing corruption and providing transparency, as reflected in the documents of international organizations seeking to establish global ethical standards, have led us to some inferences. We believe that the logical underpinnings for these emphases are self-determination, freedom, honesty, trust, and stability. Our inferences are an attempt to provide an ethical analysis to explain and ground the calls for transparency and the prevention of corruption. Given the institutional support for these efforts and their attendant values, we conclude that they may well reflect an emerging global standard for public ethics. However, one caveat is that this agenda is being pushed by the major economic powers. Although similar efforts are afoot in developing countries, it remains to be seen whether they will join in adopting the institutional enforcement mechanisms being put in place by organizations such as the OECD.

Conclusions

In this section, we offer some preliminary conclusions about the global ethics initiatives and offer suggestions for further research. When we first began this research, our most general observation was that these various regional and global declarations, agreements, and organizations can be understood as elements in a process of socially constructing a new international reality. That remains our conclusion now. In the absence of absolute foundational values and principles for public management conduct that are shared globally, consensus must be developed around those values necessary for increasingly interdependent world economy and political institutions. Agreements must be worked out and conventions developed through dialogue and deliberation, much like the work of the UN to develop the Convention against Corruption. This is an exceedingly complex and difficult process involving a lot of transnational communication that may take decades and develop very unevenly around the world, but we are highly encouraged by the intensity of work by various initiatives to develop further and to implement regional and global ethics standards. More important, if ratified, the UN Convention against Corruption will be a valuable and global instrument in the fight against corruption. Until then, the most aggressive and structured efforts are those being undertaken by the OECD, which represents the stronger economic and political world powers. Having developed market economies and democratic governments together, OECD countries are much further along in the social construction process of identifying shared values and principles than many others. For those who view the plethora of conferences, statements, and declarations as empty rhetoric, we would suggest that not all rhetoric is empty, but sometimes a necessary part of weaving together shared foundations for trust, collective decision making, and action. Patience is required, but the power of modern electronic communication, including television and the Internet, may drive this process along more rapidly than anyone expects.

A more problematic concern we share is that the social construction process we see under way is largely driven by commitment to market economies and democratization. While these powerful phenomena seem to be ascending in the wake of the collapse of the Soviet Union and former Eastern bloc countries, it is not at all clear that they will become universal. Nations less able to compete in a market-oriented world, or in which less support for that economic perspective exists, may not smoothly engage the process of creating global ethical standards. The same may be true where support for democratic government is lacking or weak. The initial blush of enthusiasm for capitalism and democracy could wane or go sour, resulting in a similar loss of commitment to the consensus that seems to be emerging. In other words, the future is uncertain.

The role of public administration researchers is a complex one. Gilman argues that the role of the research community "has been a negative role" (2000, p. 147). We do not necessarily share that summary judgment; rather, we argue that the positive role for future research should be one of examining more closely the extent to which convergence around international ethical standards continues and implementation mechanisms are adopted. After all, the rhetoric could turn out to be empty. It also will be important to examine the extent to which efforts to create an ethics infrastructure that transcends national cultural diversity also includes discussion of the values and principles that undergird the structural arrangements. Is real ethical consensus spreading around the world or is it just structures to punish and prevent corrupt behavior?

Appendix

Following is a list of countries belonging to the ethics initiatives and groups mentioned. The listings are taken from group documents and Web sites. We listed countries as they appear in that documentation, hence some differences in country names will appear (e.g., Kyrgyz Republic versus Kyrgyzstan).

African Union

Algeria, Angola, Benin, Botswana, Burkina Faso, Burundi, Cameroon, Cape Verde, Central African Republic, Chad, Comoros, Congo, Côte d'Ivoire, Democratic Republic of Congo, Djibouti, Egypt, Equatorial Guinea, Eritrea, Ethiopia, Gabon, the Gambia, Ghana, Guinea Conakry, Guinea-Bissau, Kenya, Kingdom of Lesotho, Kingdom of Swaziland, Liberia, Libya, Madagascar, Malawi, Mali, Mauritania, Mauritius, Mozambique, Namibia, Niger, Rwanda, São Tomé and Principe, Sawrawi Arab Democratic Republic, Senegal, Seychelles, Sierra Leone, Somalia, South Africa, Sudan, Tanzania, Togo, Tunisia, Uganda, Zambia, Zimbabwe

Anti-Corruption Network for Transition Economies

Albania, Armenia, Azerbaijan, Belarus, Bosnia and Herzegovina, Bulgaria, Croatia, Estonia, Former Yugoslav Republic of Macedonia, Federal Republic of Yugoslavia, Georgia, Kazakhstan, Kyrgyzstan, Latvia, Lithuania, Moldova, Romania, Russian Federation, Slovenia, Tajikistan, Turkmenistan, Ukraine, Uzbekistan

Council of Europe

Albania, Andorra, Armenia, Austria, Azerbaijan, Belgium, Bosnia and Herzegovina, Bulgaria, Croatia, Cyprus, Czech Republic, Denmark, Estonia, Finland, France, Georgia, Germany, Greece, Hungary, Iceland, Ireland, Italy, Latvia, Liechtenstein, Lithuania, Luxembourg, Malta, Moldova, Netherlands, Norway, Poland, Portugal, Romania, Russian Federation, San Marino, Serbia and Montenegro, Slovakia, Slovenia, Spain, Sweden, Switzerland, Former Yugoslav Republic of Macedonia, Turkey, Ukraine, United Kingdom

Global Coalition for Africa

The Global Coalition for Africa (GCA) works with the forty-nine countries in Sub-Sahara and Africa and does not have member nations per se. The cochairs of the GCA board are from:

Botswana, Ethiopia, Mali, South Africa, Canada, Norway, United Kingdom

Group of States against Corruption (GRECO)

Albania, Armenia, Azerbaijan, Belgium, Bosnia and Hersegovina, Bulgaria, Croatia, Cyprus, Denmark, Estonia, Finland, France, Former Yugoslav Republic of Macedonia, Georgia, Germany, Greece, Hungary, Iceland, Ireland, Latvia, Lithuania, Luxembourg, Malta, Netherlands, Norway, Poland, Portugal, Romania, Serbia and Montenegro, Slovakia, Slovenia, Spain, Sweden, Turkey, United Kingdom, United States of America

Organization of American States (OAS)

Antigua and Barbuda, Argentina, the Bahamas, Barbados, Belize, Bolivia, Brazil, Canada, Chile, Colombia, Costa Rica, Cuba (suspended), Dominica, Dominican Republic, Ecuador, El Salvador, Grenada, Guatemala, Guyana, Haiti, Honduras, Jamaica, Mexico, Nicaragua, Panama, Paraguay, Peru, Saint Kitts & Nevis, Saint Lucia, Saint Vincent and the Grenadines, Suriname, Trinidad and Tobago, United States, Uruguay, Venezuela

Organization for Economic Cooperation and Development (OECD)

Australia, Austria, Belgium, Canada, Czech Republic, Denmark, Finland, France, Germany, Greece, Hungary, Iceland, Ireland, Italy, Japan, Korea, Luxembourg, Mexico, Netherlands, New Zealand, Norway, Poland, Portugal, Slovak Republic, Spain, Sweden, Switzerland, Turkey, United Kingdom, United States

Stability Pact for South Eastern Europe

Members: Albania, Bosnia and Herzegovina, Bulgaria, Croatia, Former Yugoslav Republic of Macedonia, Moldova, Romania, Serbia and Montenegro. Partners: European Union, Canada, Japan, Norway, Russia, Switzerland, Turkey, United States

United Nations Charter for the Public Service in Africa

Angola, Algeria, Benin, Burkina Faso, Burundi, Cameroon, Central African Republic, Chad, Congo, Côte d'Ivoire, Democratic Republic of the Congo, Djibouti, Ethiopia, Gabon, the Gambia, Ghana, Guinea, Lesotho, Libya,

Madagascar, Malawi, Mali, Morocco, Mauritius, Mozambique, Namibia, Niger, Nigeria, Rwanda, São Tomé and Principe, Senegal, Seychelles, South Africa, Sudan, Swaziland, Uganda, Zambia, Zimbabwe

ADB-OECD Anti-Corruption Initiative for Asia-Pacific

Australia, Bangladesh, Cambodia, Cook Islands, Fiji Islands, Hong Kong (China), India, Indonesia, Japan, Kazakhstan, Republic of Korea, Republic of Kyrgyz, Malaysia, Mongolia, Nepal, Pakistan, Papua New Guinea, Philippines, Samoa, Singapore, Vanuatu

Transparency International

*Contact is listed as International Secretariat of Transparency International
**Chapter in Formation
Algeria, Argentina, Armenia, Australia, Austria*, Azerbaijan, Bahrain, Bangladesh, Belgium, Benin, Bolivia*, Bosnia & Herzegovina, Botswana, Brazil, Bulgaria, Burkina Faso*, Burundi, Cambodia**, Cameroon**, Canada, Chad, Chile, China, Colombia, Costa Rica**, Côte d'Ivoire*, Croatia**, Czech Republic, Denmark, Dominican Republic*, Ecuador, Egypt, El Salvador*, Estonia, Ethiopia, Fiji, Finland**, France, Gabon*, the Gambia, Georgia, Germany, Ghana, Greece, Guatemala, Guinea*, Haiti**, Honduras*, Hungary, India, Indonesia, Iran*, Iraq*, Republic of Ireland*, Israel, Italy, Jamaica*, Japan**, Jordan** Kazakhstan, Kenya, Korea (South), Kuwait*, Kyrgyz Republic, Latvia, Lebanon, Lithuania, Republic of Macedonia**, Madagascar, Malawi*, Malaysia, Mali*, Mauritania*, Mauritius, Mexico, Moldova, Mongolia, Montenegro*, Morocco, Mozambique*, Namibia*, Nepal, Netherlands**, New Zealand, Nicaragua, Niger**, Nigeria, Norway, Palestine, Pakistan**, Panama, Papua New Guinea, Paraguay, Peru, Philippines, Poland, Romania, Russia, Samoa, Senegal, Serbia**, Sierra Leone, Singapore*, Slovak Republic, Slovenia**, Solomon Islands, South Africa, Spain**, Sri Lanka, Sweden*, Switzerland, Taiwan**, Tanzania*, Thailand, Togo*, Trinidad and Tobago, Turkey, Uganda, Ukraine, United Kingdom, Uruguay, United States of America, Vanuatu**, Venezuela*, Yemen**, Zambia, Zimbabwe

Notes

   Portions of this chapter were reprinted from "Public Management Ethics Standards in a Transnational World," *Public Integrity* 4, no. 4 (Fall 2002). Copyright © 2002 American Society for Public Administration (ASPA), and used by permission of M.E. Sharpe, Inc.

1. We do not address the efforts of multinational corporations or business associations to establish ethical standards for financial transactions; although efforts are numerous and important, they are beyond the scope of this chapter.

2. The Appendix lists the member nations of the regional initiatives.

3. We found a listing for the Baltic Anti-Corruption Initiative on the ACN Web site as well as on the OECD Web site. The listing refers to the initiative as a workshop, but it does not offer details. Subsequent research turned up no information. We think it is important to mention this, because it speaks to the efforts of the Baltic states to battle corruption.

4. At this writing, Monaco is applying for membership, and observer status has been granted to the United States, Canada, Japan, Mexico, and the Holy See.

5. This protocol also makes a statement against terrorism.

6. We also note the absence of some major nations from these agreements, including the People's Republic of China, Israel, and India. This is not to say that these countries do not have individual or national anticorruption initiatives. India, for example, has a Cultural Vigilance Commission, an independent government body with representatives in each state in India, which monitors and investigates bribery and corruption complaints.

7. See www.weforum.org/pdf/ABC/Jordan_code.pdf (accessed October 28, 2004) and www.arabreformforum.com (accessed October 28, 2004) for more information.

8. Transparency International has fully established independent chapters in eighty-five countries.

9. In February 2004, Transparency International worked with anticorruption advocates from twenty countries to develop the *Source Book on Fighting Corruption in North Africa and the Middle East.*

10. These patient rights are ultimately grounded in a belief in the individual dignity of human beings. Considerable attention is paid to the concept of human dignity, its meaning and requirements, in the nongovernmental deliberation about global ethics, but little is said about it in the governmentally oriented discussions.

11. In some instances, official deception can be justified, such as in police undercover work, in times of emergency when telling the full truth might create unavoidable panic, or during conditions of war when complete honesty might make a nation vulnerable. However, these instances, which Bok (1979) has called "lies for the public good," should be agreed to and set in policy in advance.

References

African Union. 2004. "Press Releases." http://www.africa-union.org/News_Events/Press_Releases.htm.

Anti-Corruption Network for Transition Economies (CAN). 2000. General information. Available at www.nobribes.org (accessed October 28, 2004).

Asian Development Bank/Organization for Economic Cooperation and Development (ADB/OECD). 2001. ADB/OECD workshop on combating corruption in Asia/Pacific Economies. Available at www.oecd.org/daf/Asiacom/initiative.htm (accessed October 28, 2004).

———. 2004. Anti-Corruption Action Plan for Asia and the Pacific. Available at: http://www1.oecd.org/daf/ASIAcom/ActionPlan.htm.

Bok, S. 1979. *Lying: Moral Choice in Public and Private Life.* New York: Vintage.

Collingwood, V. 2003. "Assistance with Fewer Strings Attached." *Ethics and International Affairs* 17, no. 1: 55–68.

Cooper, T.L., and Yoder, D.E. 1999. "The Meaning and Significance of Citizenship in a Transnational World: The Implications for Public Administration." *Journal of Administrative Theory and Praxis* 21, no. 2: 195–204.

Council of Europe (COE). 2000. General information. Available at http://www.coe.int/T/e/Com/about_coe/default.asp

Directorate of Legal Affairs. 1999. *Agreement Establishing the Group of States against Corruption*. Strasbourg: Council of Europe.

Farazmand, A. 1999. "Globalization and Public Administration." *Public Administration Review* 59, no. 6 (November/December): 509–22.

Fox, C.J., and Miller, H.T. 1996. *Postmodern Public Administration: Toward Discourse*. Thousand Oaks, CA: SAGE.

Global Coalition for Africa (GCA). 1997. "Corruption and Development in Africa" (Technical Report: GCA/PF/N.2/11/1997). Washington, DC.

———. 1999. *Collaborative Frameworks to Address Corruption: Summary Report*. Washington, DC.

Gilman, S.C. 2000. "An Idea Whose Time Has Come: The International Experience of the U.S. Office of Government Ethics in Developing Anticorruption Systems." *Public Integrity* 2, no. 2: 135–55.

Gilman, S.C., and Lewis, C.W. 1999. "Public Service Ethics: A Global Dialogue." *Public Administration Review* 56, no. 6: 517–24.

Group of States against Corruption (GRECO). 2000. Recommendation 10 on Codes of Conduct for Public Officials. Available at http://www.greco.coe.int/docs/RecCM(2000)10E.htm.

———. 2001. What's the GRECO? Available at http://www.greco.coe.int/web/Default.htm.

Keohane, R.O., and Nye, J.S. Jr. 2000. "Globalization: What's New? What's Not? (And so What?)." *Foreign Policy* 118 (Spring): 104–19.

Kettl, D.E. 2000. "The Transformation of Governance: Globalization, Devolution, and the Role of Government." *Public Administration Review* 60, no. 6 (November/December): 488–97.

Lima Declaration. 1997. Eighth International Anti-Corruption Conference. Available at http://www.transparency.org/iacc/lima/limadecl.html .

Newton, K. 1997. "Social Capital and Democracy." *American Behavioral Scientist* 40, no. 5: 575–86.

Organization of American States (OAS). 1996. Inter-American Convention against Corruption. Available at http://www.oas.org/juridico/english/Treaties/b-58.html.

———. 2004. Declaration of Nuevo León. Available at www.summit-americas.org (accessed October 28, 2004).

Organization for Economic Cooperation and Development (OECD). 1996. *Ethics in the Public Service: Current Issues and Practice*. Paris. Available at http://www1.oecd.org/puma/ethics/pubs/eip96/op14.pdf (accessed December 22, 2004).

———. 1998a. *Improving Ethical Conduct in the Public Service*. Paris. Available at www.oecd.org/puma/ethics/pubs/rec98/rec98.htm (accessed October 28, 2004).

———. 1998b. *Principles for Managing Ethics in the Public Service*. Paris. Available at http://www.oecd.org/dataoecd/60/13/1899138.pdf (accessed December 22, 2004).

———. 1999. *Public Sector Corruption: An International Survey of Prevention Measures*. Paris.

———. 2000a. *Building Public Trust: Ethics Measures in OECD Countries*. PUMA Policy Brief no. 7. Paris.

PUBLIC-SERVICE ETHICS IN A TRANSNATIONAL WORLD 327

———. 2000b. "Issues Paper: Symposium on Ethics in the Public Sector: Challenges and Opportunities for OECD Countries." Available at www.oecd.org/puma/ethics/symposium/issues.htm (accessed October 28, 2004).
———. 2000c. *Trust in Government: Ethics Measures in OECD Countries*, no. 8. Paris. Available at http://lysander.sourceoecd.org/vl=8085245/cl=47/nw=1/rpsv/~6677/v2000n8/s1/p1 (Accessed December 2004).
O'Toole, L.J. Jr., and Hanf, K.I. 2003. "American Public Administration and Impacts on International Governance." *Public Administration Review* 62, special issue (September): 158–69.
Putnam, R.D. 1993. *Making Democracy Work: Civic Traditions in Modern Italy.* Princeton, NJ: Princeton University Press.
Rose-Ackerman, S. 1999. *Corruption and Government: Causes, Consequences, and Reform.* New York: Cambridge University Press.
Seligson, M.A. 2001. "Corruption and Democratization: What Is to Be Done." *Public Integrity* 3, no. 3 (Summer): 221–41.
Shepsle, K.A. 1991. "Discretion, Institutions, and the Problem of Government Commitment." In *Social Theory for a Changing Society*, ed. P. Bourdieu and J.S. Coleman, pp. 245–65. Boulder, CO: Westview Press.
Soysal, Y.N. 1998. "Toward a Postnational Model of Membership." In *The Citizenship Debates: A Reader*, ed. G. Shafir, pp. 189–220. Minneapolis: University of Minnesota Press.
Stability Pact for South Eastern Europe. 1999. Stability Pact for South Eastern Europe. Available at www.stabilitypact.org/pact.htm.
Stanislawski, B.H. 2004. "Transitional 'Bads' in the Globalized World: The Case of Transnational Organized Crime." *Public Integrity* 6, no. 2 (Spring): 155–70.
Synnerstrom, S. 1998. "Professionalism in Public Service Management: The Making of Highly Qualified Efficient and Effective Public Managers." Paper presented at the OECD National and International Approaches to Improving Integrity and Transparency in Government Conference, Paris.
Transparency International. 2004a. *Transparency International Strategic Framework.* Berlin.
———. 2004b. *Global Corruption Report 2004.* London: Pluto Press.
———. 2004c. About TI. www.transparency.org/about_ti/index.html (accessed October 28, 2004).
United Nations. 1996. *International Code of Conduct for Public Officials.* New York.
———. 2000. *Background and Synopsis of the Draft Charter for the Public Service in Africa* (Report no. ST/SG/AC.6/2000/L.3). New York.
United Nations Centre for International Crime Prevention. 2000. Programme information. Available at www.unicri.it (accessed October 28, 2004).
United Nations Department of Economic and Social Affairs. 2001. Charter for the Public Service in Africa. Available at http://unpan1.un.org/intradoc/groups/public/documents/un/unpan001906.pdf (accessed October 28, 2004).
United Nations General Assembly. 2003. UN Convention against Corruption. A/RES/58/4. New York.
U.S. Office of Government Ethics. 2004. Agency information. Available at www.usoge.gov/pages/international/inernat_page.html
Waltz, K.N. 1999. "Globalization and Governance." *PS: Political Science and Politics* 32, no. 4: 693–700.

16

Globalization and Public-Service Ethics: Some Directions for Inquiry

Richard K. Ghere

Dialogue began in late spring 2001 about a convergence of two topics seldom conjoined: globalization and public-sector ethics. The former is typically an external matter of international economics and trade policy, quite distant from the moral tenor of public service within the boundaries of the United States. Yet in their conversations, published to elicit wider discussion, Donald Menzel and Willa Bruce recognize globalization as an identity-changing force. Specifically, these two scholars perceive it as the compelling of citizens—and public servants in particular—to reconsider who we are and what we will become in terms of an international breadth of moral obligation. Although they foresee profound impacts of global forces on public administration, both professors are candid about their own difficulties in grasping the totality of globalization, much less its ramifications for public-service ethics. Bruce writes to Menzel:

> Globalization is so overwhelming to me. I've had a hard time deciding how to respond to the questions you raise. Partly, I think that's because globalization speaks of subjects so vast and complex that I cannot encompass them, much less see them or touch them. I can't help but wonder how any of us can talk about the large issues affecting humankind, when we seem unable to deal with the ones in our own country and neighborhood. How can I love humankind, but ignore my neighbor? (May 6, 2001)

Since Professors Menzel and Bruce initiated this dialogue, much has happened in the world that even further confounds our understanding of globalization and its implications for public service. Although some might claim that the era of globalization ended on September 11, 2001, others assess those tragic events as dramatically illustrating its turbulent nature—indeed, testimony to the need "to make sense out of the ups and downs of globalization" (as Menzel writes to Bruce on June 3, 2001). My task in this chapter is to advance the baton in this second, but still preliminary, leg of inquiry about globalization and public-service ethics. The first section presents a framework that lends focus to the overwhelming nature and reach of globalization, particularly as it pertains to public management in the United States. The second section charts some direction for those who might contribute further to this dialogue. Specifically, it supports eight recommendations for research (four normative and four empirical) that can guide those so motivated to explore how global forces affect the present character of public-service ethics.

Globalization and Public-Service Ethics

This section will examine whether and how the forces of globalization affect public-service ethics as a professional pursuit and academic study. Specifically, we first look to a recent United Nations (UN) document (1998) that establishes an ecological model for analyzing public administration within the global setting. The ecology outlined in this document assumes significance in comparison to earlier perspectives characterized in three predecessor (1951, 1961, and 1975) UN publications. The second task here is to characterize if and how the U.S. administrative experience—together with its ethical grounding—fits within the broader, generalized ecology presented in the 1998 UN document. Clearly, the terrorist events of September 11, 2001, raise troubling questions about how globalization will affect public administration in the future. Given this uncertainty, it is helpful to compare pertinent statements that two leading theorists (Donald Kettl and George Frederickson) made before the tragedies, with their corresponding commentaries after. Ostensibly, the temporal comparisons of each scholar's viewpoint can offer insight regarding the relationship between globalization and public-service values in the wake of these momentous events.

Connecting Globalization and Ethics upon "Ground in Motion"

Determining whether and how public-service ethics relate to global forces requires an apt characterization of the canvas—and particularly, the texture of that canvas—that expresses that relationship. Use of the term *texture* here is deliberate in reference to an essay published nearly forty years ago, "The Causal Texture of Organizational Environments," by theorists Emery and Trist (1965). Although conventionally interpreted in the sociotechnical context of work, this essay also supports a more recent transformational leadership literature by tapping literature as it relates to large-scale societal challenges for public leaders (for example, see Hickman 1998). Emery and Trist's beginning sentence characterizes efforts to assess globalization's impact on public-service ethics in an increasingly uncertain yet interconnected international system: "A main problem in the study of organizational change is that the environmental contexts in which organizations exist are themselves changing at an increasing rate, and toward increasing complexity" (1965, p. 21). In the context of profound societal forces, this suggests that the very public administration that stewards core public-service values is subject to forces that redefine it.

In their essay, Emery and Trist differentiate among four types of causally textured environments presented sequentially in terms of increasing systems of complexity and uncertainty. Especially when compared to its predecessor documents (UN 1951, 1961, and 1975), *Rethinking Public Administration* (hereafter *Rethinking PA*) (UN 1998) sets forth an ecology with some characteristics of Emery and Trist's fourth texture of causal connectedness:

- Not only the organizational components (for example, administrative systems and variables within) are dynamic and changing, but the field itself (for example, international setting) is turbulent—the "ground is in motion" (1965, p. 26).
- Interdependencies increase between economic concerns and other facets of society—most notably, its governance, ". . . economic organizations are increasingly meshed in legislation and public regulation" (1965, p. 26).
- The consequences of trends increase unpredictably at an exponential rate—and at any point may become "amplified beyond all expectations" (1965, p. 26).

Specifically, *Rethinking PA* places a governance focus on public administration as an ecology of multiple systems and trends—frequently in tension with each other—that is driven by a politic focused on national interest. In this regard, the preface to chapter 1 speaks to this envelopment of public administration *within governance*[1] as common among nations: "Above all, public administration is part of the web of governance, deriving its form and substance from public policy. Thus, the most important attribute of public administration is its place in the political system" (UN 1998, p. 4).

Table 16.1

Emery and Trist's Stages of Causal Texture (1965) as Related to Global Ecologies of Public Administration

Stage of causality	Description	Organization response	Value implication
Type I Placid, as randomized	"Goods" and "bads" (stable in themselves) are randomly distributed—no competition	No distinction between tactic and strategy	Best practices values
Type II Placid, clustered	"Goods" and "bads" are hung together in certain ways; no competition	Strategy apart from tactic	Situational contingencies for best practices
Type III Disturbed, reactive	"Goods" and "bads" are hung together in certain ways; competition exists among organizations	Operations as strategic response in anticipating competitors	
Type IV Turbulent Fields	Change occurs not only from competing organizations, but from the field itself	More intense operations, meshing of economy in laws and regulation	Values to cope with relative uncertainty; to achieve social stability

Source: Adapted from Emery and Trist (1965).

Figure 16.1 offers diagrammatic representation of the ecology presented in the beginning of *Rethinking PA* (UN 1998, pp. 1–18). This diagram depicts an administrative ecology of five interacting components that are *shaped by*, and that in turn *shape*, five global trends—operative within particular nations (as designated by subscripts a, b, and n). By inference, I locate *public-service ethics* as a subcomponent of civil society that is directly influenced by ideology. Especially important here is the sense of change interacting with change as five major trends of globalization—themselves undergoing transition—affect how subsystems of governance interact. Indeed, the messiness of Figure 16.1 aptly depicts the current ecology as "ground in motion" turbulence of Emery and Trist's fourth stage of causal texture. Referring again to their essay, it is instructive to note how these theorists treat the issues of *organization response* and of *values* in relation to increasing complexity. These ideas in turn invite speculation about the roles values play amid the

332

Figure 16.1 **Public Administration from a Global Governance Perspective**

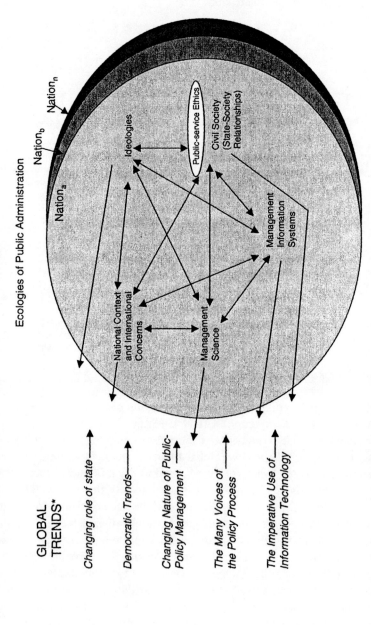

Source: Adapted from United Nations, *Rethinking Public Administration: An Overview* (New York, 1998).
*Interacting arrows among the trends omitted.

current complexities of global governance. Along these lines, Table 16.1 shows how organization responses range from forthright tactics (type 1), to basic strategies (type 2), and then to more intense strategic program operations and policies (types 3 and 4). Yet interestingly, Emery and Trist suggest that, although basic values may become more complicated in view of necessary contingencies (say, in type-2 environments), they again become more generalized (and ostensibly simpler) symbols for coping with relevant uncertainty.[2] As such, "they have the conceptual character of 'power fields' and act as injunctions" to achieve stability (Emery and Trist 1965, p. 28).

A pair of observations directed at the U.S experience seems appropriate here. Figure 16.1 shows emergent global trends (most notably, "the changing role of the state" and "the changing nature of public-policy management") intruding on governance subsystems that are tightly packed with cultural tradition and prevailing norms. Stated in the vernacular, the question becomes "*what* will give, and *how*?" when global realities clash with ingrained, fundamental values. Further, Emery and Trist's notion that values are enjoined as coping mechanisms against uncertainty offers an institutional glimpse of public-service ethics as an instrument in maintaining social stability. Ethics, if valid in application to global governance—functioning to preserve prevailing ideologies and state-society relationships—could hide important, emerging patterns of global complexity.

The Imprint of the September 11, 2001, Tragedies on the Ecology

From a perspective of global governance (such as that depicted in Figure 16.1), the terrorist events appear to underscore the salience of "the many voices of the policy process"—including those alienated by globalization—who seek to impact economic agendas within and among nations. This suggests that globalization bears the seeds of its own vulnerability—that is, it offers the voices it alienates an opportunity to subvert international economic agendas (see Dyer 2001). Thomas Barnett of the U.S. Naval War College told a National Public Radio (NPR) news analyst that this *connectivity* (obvious in Figure 16.1) exerts a strong, alienating counterforce:

> If you look around the world and ask yourself who's doing OK with globalization . . . that part of the world should not be considered a potential enemy. . . . There *is* a big chunk of the world where there's a lot of fear and dread with regard to growing connectivity and cultural content associated with it. That part of the world is where you find ideologies that not only fear globalization but want to reject it. (NPR 2001)

Barnett's observations are reinforced by those of Strobe Talbott, who served as a deputy secretary of state in the Clinton administration: "We're moving into an era where the great divide . . . is between those who feel like winners in the process of globalization and those who feel like losers. People like Osama Bin Laden and forces like al-Qaeda play upon the resentments of those who feel like losers" (NPR 2001).

With respect to the global ecology, the September 11 tragedies signify how fragmented, diverse interests can alter the policy directions of adversaries. Jeffery Garten of the Yale School of Management (and former undersecretary of commerce) stresses how these terrorist events have shifted the fundamental theme (changed the agenda) of globalization: "In the 1990s, the watchword was 'opportunity'—new opportunities for producers and consumers around the world. Now the watchword is 'vulnerability'—how do we protect ourselves against this global, open society where virtually anything can be transmitted, both good and bad, very quickly?" (NPR 2001). He goes on to associate this agenda shift with a reemerging role of the state in relation to markets:

> There was an underlying mindset that globalization really translated into more openness in the world economy: the lowering of trade barriers, the expansion of deregulation everywhere, a decline in the role of the state, and a vast increase in the power of free markets. And I think a lot of that now has to be reexamined, because the fundamental role of the state is coming back very strong. (NPR 2001)

One take on these observations is that the resurrection of the state signals the waning of globalization as a significant organizing force. An alternative view (advanced here) maintains that the same globalization that had *marginalized* the state and its public service currently *elevates* them. Yet the uncertainty and complexity in discerning what the tragedies mean for government and public service give credence to Emery and Trist's description of turbulent environments where "the ground is in motion." To an extent, commentaries by two leading scholars in the field of public administration (before and after September 11, 2001) offer insight regarding the implications of the tragedies for public service.

Kettl Commentaries Before/After September 11, 2001

Published nine months before the terrorist attacks, Donald Kettl's statement on the transformation of governance linked globalization—both as a set of intertwined forces and as an ideology—with a devolution of governmental authority in U.S. polity (2000). The implications of these simultaneous but contradictory trends focus upon the need for new administrative capacity in a transformed environment. In effect, new strategies must replace conventional management styles of hierarchical structures and traditional lines of jurisdictional authority. Not surprisingly, many of Kettl's comments on globalization stress the pertinence on "national context and international concerns" as a component of the public administration ecology shown in Figure 16.1:

- Globalization (combined with devolution) marginalizes institutions and processes in ways that strain traditional governmental actors (pp. 491–92).
- Globalization erodes national sovereignty and in turn obstructs economic policy making (p. 490).

Although Kettl's pre–September 11 statement does not explicitly hone in on ethics, it does address the changing nature of "civil society (or state-society relations)" as depicted in Figure 16.1. Early in his article, Kettl speaks to citizen expectations amid globalization as a major conundrum for those in public service: "[D]espite these transformations, the *expectations* on government . . . remain rooted in a past that no longer exists. Citizens expect their problems will be solved and tend not to care who solves them" (2000, p. 488). While citizens may share traditional expectations notwithstanding a world transformed, they are less likely to share values in the face of "galloping globalization" (Kettl's term) and market autonomy:

> In many ways, globalization has sparked an emerging system of governance without government, management, or control. Shared values, which shaped government policies in the past, have yet to emerge. National sovereignty has shrunk along with government's capacity to understand and shape the emerging issues and the conflicts that underlie them. (Kettl 2000, p. 492)

Editors of the *PA Times* asked Donald Kettl, among others, to contribute to the October 2001 edition in reaction to the September 11 tragedies. In his essay, "The Next Public Administration Revolution," Kettl predicts resurgence in government and public service as *people* who are vital to the critical needs of civil society. Most significant in this post–September 11 commentary is Kettl's elaboration on the need for a place-based coordinative capability that can surmount the interjurisdictional rivalries among traditional bureaucracies—citing problems between the Federal Bureau of Investigation and Central Intelligence Agency in response to the tragedies (2001, p. 3). Rather than suggesting the scrapping of functionally arranged bureaucracy altogether, Kettl underscores the importance of developing strategic-thinking capability for effective responses to chaotic situations. Thus, he discusses the need for human capital in these terms:

> The fundamental nut to crack now is this: We manage our organizations along functional lines—such as fire, police, intelligence, and defense. However, the problems we need to solve are increasingly place-based. . . . We shouldn't move away from public administration's traditional foundation of functionally-structured organizations. But we need to get much smarter, much faster, in how to match functional organization with place-based problems. (Kettl 2001, p. 3)

In reference to the global ecology in Figure 16.1, Kettl's first commentary observed a "civil society"—along with globalization priorities (on free trade) as "national context vis-à-vis inter-national concerns"—that had marginalized government and public service. This in turn severely limited policy effectiveness in responding to critical situations, including those arising from global connectivity. His *PA Times* response to the tragedies observed a "civil society," transformed by the tumultuous events, that support the coordinative authority of government. Now citizens appear more apt to care about *who* (government vis-à-vis the public sector) solves their problems and about *how* they are addressed.

Frederickson Commentaries Before/After September 11, 2001

In contrast to those of Donald Kettl, the Frederickson commentaries are more heavily weighted toward public-service ethics in civil society than toward globalization. Selected sections in George Frederickson's influential book, *The Spirit of Public Administration* (1997), reflect his thinking about ethics and public-service values against a backdrop of global governance prior to 2001.[3] As they are related to the ecological components shown in Figure 16.1, Frederickson's pre–September 11 observations largely focus on linkages between "ideology" and "state-society relationships." He laments the tenacity of a utilitarian philosophy in U.S. political culture that, in championing individualism, significantly narrows the definition of *public* and *public interest*. In concluding his first chapter, Frederickson also argues that "in our culture, thinking has never been as important as doing." Although he does not mention globalization per se, Frederickson devotes an entire chapter to a critique of governance, an outcome of the free-trade policies of the 1990s on public management. There he argued that the rhetoric associated with governance has threatened both the core values of public administration and the leadership capabilities of its institutions.

Like Kettl, Frederickson spoke to the emerging status of public service in the aftermath of the tragic events in the October 2001 *PA Times*. In particular, he addressed changes in citizen attitudes and perceptions that are pertinent to the global ecology in Figure 16.1: Global terrorism in this case impacted "civil society (state/society relations)" in a way that connects the disconnection from public institutions. This newly found connectedness, according to Frederickson, has restored honor in public life. He extends his discussion to other components of the ecological model in reference to the managerial implications of addressing terrorism:

> Terrorism, like environmental pollution, nuclear proliferation, and organized crimes, has little respect for borders. Combating such enemies will require the United States to be both sovereign and carefully networked. We are in a high state of interdependence, and as such the state of our networks are as important as our sovereignty. The diminished capacity of borders to contain problems calls for highly developed forms of interjurisdictional cooperation and coordination. While some of this cooperation and coordination is political, much of it is administrative. . . . The skilled practice of multijurisdictional administrative coalition building and maintenance is part of the job description of the 21st century public administrator. (Frederickson 2001, p. 11)

Comparisons of both scholars' statements—both before and after the events of September 11—reveal similar patterns of assessment. Before these events, both spoke of dysfunctional society-state relationships in which the diminished status of public institutions seriously impeded governmental capability. Frederickson focused upon the utilitarian ideological roots of citizen indifference to public life, and Kettl elaborated upon the demands that an entrepreneurial globalization places upon government—despite its diminished status. In the aftermath of September 11, both experts observe how citizens have turned to revere their public service in a time of threatened security. Each points to similar administrative needs in an era of global vulnerability: a place-based coordinative capability (Kettl) and multijurisdictional administrative coalition building (Frederickson). Both scholars characterize these critical competencies explicitly as long-term needs.

Viable Avenues for Ethics Research

Guided by the global ecology presented above as impacted by the terrorist events of September 11, this preliminary study of globalization's effect on public-service ethics identifies four fruitful areas for inquiry. First, the sense of change interacting with change—as evidenced by the dense causal interactivity shown in Figure 16.1—questions whether the character of public-service ethics can withstand and adapt to prolonged instability. Second, the formidable complexity of globalization critically challenges the capability for sustaining reasoned public dialogue in a utilitarian culture that is unaccustomed to reflection beyond its immediate and tangible needs. Third, global trends related to "many voices of the policy process" afforded greater access to governance by information technology raise the issue of transparency as it may impinge upon local accountability in public stewardship. And finally, globally focused initiatives on behalf of humanitarian interests contend with professional ethics that are steeped in the principles of public law premised upon a constant national sovereignty—a premise that warrants reconsideration in reference to the dynamics of the global ecology.

Public-Service Ethics amid Globally Induced Instability

Initially, it can be said that forces of globalization—as they affect the context of public service in the United States and elsewhere—tend to disturb both the civil and the institutional stability that typically ground the ethical enterprise. As they are related to the ecology shown in Figure 16.1, issues of government ethics and public trust serve to bond (or sever) "state-society relationships" in civil society. At a general level, ethical pursuits function to stabilize society in preserving "morality as a social institution" (see Frankena 1963, pp. 5–6). More specifically, public-service ethics need to reflect and champion particular public-service values that rest upon longstanding ideological assumptions (such as suspicion of government power, biases for efficiency, and others outlined by Van Wart 1998, pp.144–51)—hence the linkage with "civil society" depicted in Figure 16.1. Simply put, stability and continuity, as aligned with ideological expectations, are typically mainstays of the public trust.

Instability, on the other hand, may elevate particular collective needs for security at the expense of other public-interest values (say, individual liberty or efficiency; see Stone 2002, pp. 37–130) that are more customarily revered in civil society. Stone has observed that during times of instability, security imperatives assume symbolic power in unifying a society beset with chaos (pp. 90–91). This corresponds to Emery and Trist's contention that values "have the conceptual character of 'power fields' and act as injunctions" (Emery and Trist 1965, p. 28) to achieve, or at least portray, stability and clarity amid extreme complexity. As such, security-oriented needs (or perhaps values and injunctions) give elected policy makers unusual latitude in times of instability, which may in turn pose ethical dilemmas for public administrators who grope to (re)assess the essence of public interest in these circumstances.

In reference to the September 11 tragedies, attention to *insecurity* logically raises questions regarding its duration and the restoration of normalcy (or in systems terminology, equilibrium). Some could dismiss the instability problem merely as a temporary reshuffling of values attributed to fighting terrorism—as during other wars—until a return to the status quo. Yet the global dynamic in Figure 16.1 projects an inherently unstable international environment well into the future. This environment subjects societies to the agendas of a varied array of non- (or anti-) institutional actors empowered by the resources (such as information technology and international patterns of finance) that globalization offers. What particularly stands out here is the abrupt shift, noted earlier, from a globalization of (free-market) opportunity to one of vulnerability, which in turn rearranges perceptions of public needs and elevates the stature of public service, at least for a while. If globalization in fact bears the seeds of its own vulnerability, it is reasonable to ask "what next?"

Normative Inquiry

In the aftermath of September 11, 2001, national-level policy makers spoke often of "the new normalcy," which, in appealing for continued vigilance, suggests prolonged instability. Such an environment impacts squarely on the public administrator as a crucial linchpin between civil society and the state. Essentially, a presumption of instability challenges the public servant's obligation to pursue recognized public problems consistent with established public-interest values (see Van Wart 1998, pp. 83–85). It may, for example, ask much to expect public managers to design contingencies for a broad array of improbable possibilities associated with terrorism. Or administrative executives may experience severe problems in the implementing of human-service programs, given budgets that are skewed heavily toward security needs yet far short of what is needed to allay citizen anxieties. Given these unusual circumstances, we can learn more about the character of public-service ethics by assessing it *absent* the implicit expectation of normalcy—as stated in the first agenda item:

(1) Normative research might consider whether/how a presumptive shift from stability to instability affects the substance and character of public-service ethics.

Research in this direction could seek modification in how ethical responsibilities are understood in light of this different societal condition that places unprecedented demands on the public sector. Is it justifiable, for example, to compromise usual standards of accountability and openness in pursuit of sensitive public-security goals? If not, research could identify new forms of responsibility conundrums that might arise and then recommend strategies to reason through those dilemmas. Further, ethics research could be more receptive to system theories and organization theories that find the function and character of values dependent upon context—such as environmental complexity. Emery and Trist's provocative discussion of the symbolic power of values to clarify the inherently complex appears to be especially pertinent: Could the invocation of traditional public-service values amount to oversimplifying complex reality? If so, it becomes important to study how this symbolic power is wielded—by professional administrators and policy makers alike.

Empirical Inquiry

Starting with the unique role of Tom Ridge—the first director of the newly formed Office of Homeland Security—and including numerous other administrative situations, opportunities arise for case studies of public managers who confront critical problems related to destabilizing circumstances. In particular, empirical case study research could focus on the ethical implications of how administrators structure critical, but necessarily messy and ill-defined, problems in the midst of a tense citizenry expecting results (see Ackoff 1974; Pavlek 1988).

(2) Empirical research could pursue case-study analyses that probe the ethical implications of administrative roles addressing ill-structured problems related to globally induced social instability.

Prompted by the magnificent dedication of emergency personnel in response to the terrorist tragedies, citizens across the United States recognized these public servants as heroes. Given some existing literature that probes the heroic nature of ethical public managers (see Bellavita 1991; Hubbell 1991), it is logical to attempt to determine whether excellence in these critical situations requires extraordinary levels of wisdom and commitment. Or could the appropriate mental attitudes and moral qualities that Stephen Bailey identified (1965) sufficiently prepare those of normal professional competence to address these challenges in an admirable fashion?

Content of Public Dialogue vis-à-vis Complexity
of Globalization

The quip "complexity is hard to understand" raises serious issues about the capability of public dialogue to comprehend the essence of globalization and to support reasoned public responses. Specifically, the tone of societal discussion sets constraints in which public officials reason through tough dilemmas that often have moral implications. Indeed, Frederickson's observation that September 11 "connected the disconnection" between people and government speaks to current unity in public dialogue. Yet more ethically significant is whether it rises to the level of reason needed to grasp the intricate dynamics of globalization.

In *The Nexus and the Olive Tree*, Thomas Friedman elaborates on the instability caused by globalization's propensity to incite "backlash against the system" (1999, pp. 263–94). As the above comments of experts in international economics (Barnett, Talbott, Reich, and Garten on NPR 2001) indicate, globalization affords any number of international factions the power to "play upon the intentions of those who feel like losers" (Talbott on NPR). The horrendous exercise of that power on September 11 in turn fueled another backlash of U.S. public opinion that, although unified, has shifted toward stridency on behalf of nationalism and security, while perhaps compromising traditional commitments to liberty and individualism. An NPR/ Kaiser/Kennedy School Poll on Civil Liberties in late November 2001 indicated that 58 percent of respondents trust national government to combat terrorism and 56 percent believe that even *legal* noncitizens should not enjoy the same rights as citizens. And of the 59 percent in that survey who favor a required national identification card, more than half believe that such a document should contain information specifying (non)citizenship (96 percent), fingerprints (88 percent), DNA makeup (64 percent), criminal record (73 percent), and religion (59 percent).[4]

Yet there is evidence that this post–September 11 stridency has waned as global events—most notably, the Iraq War—have unfolded since the tragedy. Two years after 9/11, the Program on International Policy Attitudes (PIPA) at the University of Maryland published survey results that indicate considerable support for diplomatic, cooperative approaches to fighting terrorism in preference to the unilateral, preemptive policies of the Bush administration. When they were asked about the more important lesson of September 11, 2001, 81 percent endorsed the statement "the U.S. needs to work more closely with other countries to fight terrorism" as compared to only 16 percent who supported unilateral approaches. The PIPA survey also reflected the public's opinion that governmental actions detaining those who are suspected of terrorist activities (permitted by the U.S. PATRIOT Act adopted six weeks after 9/11) were excessive. In reference to the Act's removing government limits in detaining these suspects, 52 percent of those surveyed endorsed the view that "government has already gone too far."[5] Clearly, this reversal of public opinion invites varying interpretations—as a collective lack of will, as a predictable tempering of the extreme reaction to horrendous events, or as a growing real-ization of contemporary global affairs. Yet it is uncertain whether this redi-rected opinion represents a stable pattern of reasoned discourse or merely an interlude awaiting reactions to subsequent global backlashes.

Normative Inquiry

George Frederickson stresses how entrenched utilitarianism leads citizens toward moral ambiguity that defines *public good* as protecting the status quo of the present moment:

> We pursue efficiency, economy, order, and predictability. Like good utilitar-ians, we tend toward a high regard for moral ambiguity. We stress operating efficiency and procedural due process, protecting the boundaries and lon-gevity of each bureau and agency, and reducing all big issues to questions of means and short-run benefits. We avoid policy discussions that tend to focus on purposeful long-range ends. Louis Gawthrop (1984) refers to this as an "ethics of civility" in which we function under the rule of law, based on written codes and standards, rather than of a people. We seek to do good by not doing evil. Because we cannot define what is good, it is simply easier to find what is wrong and try to fix it. (Frederickson 1997, p. 29)

Clearly, these utilitarian justifications point inward rather than outward beyond our geographic and cultural boundaries. Fox and Miller emphasize that, in essence, utilitarian notions of public good lack substance. Instead, they take form as calculation of majoritarian interests: "'Good' will be what we decide democratically to do in order to promote happiness. This view can generate considerable rhetorical power" (1995, p. 22).

The logic of a utilitarian public good takes on profound ethical signifi-cance amid unstable global forces—especially with regard to external events that infuse emotion in public dialogue. Fox and Miller's reference to the rhetorical power of majoritarian passions underscores the power and latitude of elected policy makers in interpreting the ambiguities of globalization in the context of public values. Although citizen reactions to the September 11, 2001, tragedies elevate public service and strengthen a sense of national sov-ereignty, they pose significant questions regarding how to reconcile endur-ing public-service values with the passions of public dialogue in reaction to global turbulence.

(3) Normative inquiry could trace the meaning of public good—for whom?—in reaction to the complexities of globalization.

That research possibility provokes another opportunity for normative explorations with respect to likely conflicts that pit imperatives for action in response to global adversities against longstanding values of public stewardship:

(4) Normative inquiry might consider what (if any) roles public servants ought to assume in redirecting the passions of public dialogue in reaction to stressful global circumstances.

In essence, this inquiry could consider whether public administrators (either individually or collectively) should speak out when they recognize that the passion of public dialogue unduly is usurping important values such as equality of liberty—especially on behalf of noncitizens. Frederickson's account (taken from Arendt 1963) of Danish bureaucrats' heroism on behalf of Jews during German occupation appears instructive here (1997, pp. 197–200). Nonetheless, this Danish situation focused specifically upon resistance against a foreign, occupying force. Yet perhaps these Danish bureaucrats pursued a fundamentally different public good than is found in U.S. society: In explaining this bureaucratic compassion, Arendt reported that "it was the result of an authentically political sense, an inbred comprehension of the requirements and responsibilities of citizenship and independence" (1963, p.179). This "authentically political sense" appears to be the substance that is lacking in a utilitarian culture that reacts to the exigencies of the moment.

Empirical Inquiry

Again, the case study offers a logical method for assessing how public administrators confront conflicts between fundamental values and passions of public opinion in reaction to adverse global issues.

(5) Empirical inquiry can analyze whether and how imperative notions of the public good that arise in reaction to global issues can prompt public officials to depart from more traditional public-service values.

It is reasonable to look to those public administrators who interact directly with noncitizens to face these conundrums. Yet the passions of a tense public dialogue may have widespread implications for how public administrators treat individuals—as consumers, as citizens, or as subjects (that is, potential terrorists). A variant from this stream of inquiry could extend to a reconfigured public service, as Kettl recommends, organized strategically around place rather than around central hierarchy. Ethics researchers who would opt to analyze the behavior and actions of those who occupy place-based roles could do much to scrutinize if and how ethical values are inculcated in administrative efforts that react to global uncertainties.

Transparency and Its Public-Service Implications

Journalist Thomas Friedman coins the term *globulation* in reference to how globalization imposes democratic ideas on disparate national cultures. He relates the following:

> *The Wall Street Journal* reported that when senior finance officials from the United States, Japan, China, and eleven other Asian countries gathered for a meeting in Malaysia in November 1997, they found that the Malaysian Central Bank had put up an electronic scoreboard, the sort you usually find at an NBA basketball game, which displayed a running tally of Malaysia's currency reserves to reassure visitors about the soundness of the country's economy. (1999, p. 145)

Friedman uses this illustration to introduce *transparency*, a condition vital for success in a global economy. At first glance, the notion of a transparent society appears congruent with fundamental public-service values such as openness, disclosure, and accountability. German-based Transparency International (a nongovernmental organization) characterizes *non*-transparency as "corruption," a more accommodating term than "bribery" (given the inability of the United States to enact campaign finance reform; see Pope 2000).

Yet a closer look at presumed connections between transparency and government ethics leads to murky, sometimes provocative, waters. For example, some critics charge that the causality that links transparency reform to legitimacy merely stamps a capitalist ideology of liberalism on societies that are inherently legitimate *within* (see Rajagopal 2000, pp. 495–507). Friedman's scoreboard analogy offers a perspective that is helpful here. He argues that transparency keeps "the electronic herd" (that is, international investors in an age of information technology) from stampeding out of a given country at the sniff of economic ills: "They stampede to the next country and crush everything in their path. So how do you protect your country from this? Answer: You cut the grass, and clear away the brush, so that the next time the wildebeest sees something rustle in the grass it thinks, 'No problem, I see what it is. It's just a bunny rabbit'" (1999, pp.145–46). In that Friedman's wildebeest explanation smacks more of trade contingency than of principled legitimacy, it becomes easier to understand (without necessarily accepting) the charge that transparency advances the economic ideology of the West.

The counterclaim is that transparency measures indeed *strengthen* national systems and, in so doing, enable them to have more viable economic participation in a global economy (see Unzicker 2000). Thus most nations currently seek to adopt these reforms (Wallace-Bruce 2000). Yet either way, antagonisms that arise from transparency reforms imposed on other cultures (or even on factions therein) can trigger backlashes—again calling attention to system instability in the global ecology.

How transparency affects public service depends upon whether one looks from the inside out or from the outside in. As to the first, more scrutiny on the outside, foreign investors and business ventures within the United States clearly enhance the public sector and its accountability—provided that appropriate legislation is feasible. In passing the Foreign Corrupt Practices Act of 1977, the U.S. Congress placed the onus of preventing criminality on businesses, rather than on governments, in matters that involve bribery of public officials. Twenty years later, a like measure was adopted by the Organization for Economic Cooperation and Development (OECD), an alliance of twenty-nine industrialized nations (Unzicker 2000). Hypothetically extending this, local and state governments in the United States enter into service provision partnerships with private firms active on international fronts in pursuing overseas ventures and capital acquisition (Ghere 2001). The remoteness of a private partner in other business ventures (perhaps competing bottom lines) as well as in seeking foreign capital to underwrite local service delivery creates accountability blind spots that transparency could address—in the form of legislation, agency rule making (such as in the Securities and Exchange Commission), or international treaties.

Yet the view from the outside in raises more ominous questions for public policy and governmental operations in the United States. Specifically, some transparency provisions in international trade treaties—most notably, Chapter 11 of the North American Free Trade Agreement (NAFTA)—hold signatory nations accountable for fair treatment of foreign businesses and investors against discrimination of a protectionist or an exclusionary nature. In the case of NAFTA, injured parties can seek compensatory redress through international tribunals as arbiters. At present, legal scholars disagree as to whether this Chapter 11-imposed transparency substantially erodes (U.S.) national sovereignty or merely reaffirms long-accepted principles of international trade. At issue is how particular wording in Chapter 11—"tantamount to expropriation"—is to be applied and interpreted in cases of state actions that encumber foreign business and investment. Yet at least at some level, these NAFTA provisions *do* hold national government liable for the actions of its subjurisdictions as well as the public service. It is unclear whether nondiscriminatory regulations (particularly environmental protection measures) of state and local governments can by definition stand above discrimi-

natory intent in tribunal arbitration. Some argue that such worries are unfounded given NAFTA's environmental awareness (see Gudofsky 2000; Laird
2001). Others, however, perceive "tantamount to expropriation" to be a reliable business strategy for circumventing public actions in host countries,
regardless of purpose (see Ferguson 2000).

But how, if at all, do these international transparency issues affect public
administrators? Indirectly, the NAFTA case *The Loewen Group Inc. v. United
States* is instructive. Invoking Chapter 11's "tantamount to expropriation," a
Canadian funeral home conglomerate successfully sued the national government for a discriminatory verdict in a state civil court. In essence, a Mississippi
jury awarded punitive damages to a prominent local undertaker (also mayor of
Biloxi) in a breech-of-contract dispute.[6] The Canadian claimant's case for compensatory damage through the NAFTA process appears warranted, since the
trial judge let an excessive judgment stand (see Krauss 2000). In effect, the
state court endorsed a local jury that, perhaps in an effort to uphold "local
community values," rendered a discriminatory outcome (much like a partisan
referee on a basketball court). By analogy, the ethical paradox for the local
public official arises: how to be accountable and responsive to the values of the
local community (see Kirlin 1996) yet still act within the boundaries of international transparency provisions (such as NAFTA Chapter 11)—*recognizing* that
those provisions could be manipulated as contingent legal maneuvers in tribunals outside the United States. Such a dilemma appears pertinent to a range of
public issues that involve industrial property and business practices, including
land use, taxation, economic development, and environmental protection.

Empirical Inquiry

Clearly, efforts to curb corruption and bribery are hallmarks of government
ethics reform in the United States. Nonetheless, the transparency provisions
of international trade treaties can hold public-sector actions accountable for
injurious actions through legal forums outside the United States in a manner
that at least potentially compromises national sovereignty. For ethics researchers, the crosscurrents between externally imposed fair treatment of global
investment and accountability to local sentiments could spur dilemmas for
public officials, whether they are public managers, legislators, or jurists. Specifically, this avenue of study might focus on dilemmas that pit international
transparency against local accountability.

(6) Empirical analysis might explore how international transparency provisions affect government's capability to sustain responsive and accountable public service.

Prudent empirical inquiry would resist overstatements regarding (1) the authority and scope of external forums in arbitrating transparency disputes and (2) presumed indifference toward regulatory purposes in host nations, especially those that promote public health. Instead, research that selects the "hard cases" (see Laird 2001)—wherein the exercise of public powers could be construed as protectionist—would offer more useful and robust findings than would a sensationalized exposé of clearly abusive business strategies that use transparency as a ruse.

Globalization, Public Law, and Regime Values

"Think globally, act locally." Exactly what this catchy slogan entails leaves much to the imagination. Perhaps for the citizen, it suggests that actions in the normal course of living take on moral significance in a global setting— for example, a global awareness might oblige a consumer to resist purchasing furniture constructed of rain forest mahogany. Yet for the public servant, thinking globally while acting locally implies various situations and actions, some that clearly align with the public interest, while others stray from it. On one hand, Donald Kettl's call for a place-based strategic capacity in the wake of the September 11 tragedies underscores an obligation to strengthen local security in anticipation of threatening international circumstances. On the other hand, the moral disposition to think globally, although viable for the consumer, can land the public purchasing agent or trust fund manager in trouble—especially if it impinges upon bureaucratic values that are reinforced by legal precedents.

John Rohr argues convincingly that these regime values entrenched in the law rise above other commendable moral rationales (such as "high road" decency or political philosophy) as the appropriate means for bureaucrats to understand ethical obligation. Specifically, his method for discerning professional ethics from regime values rests upon these considerations:

- Ethical norms should be derived from the salient values of the regime.
- These values are normative for bureaucrats by virtue of oath to the regime.
- These values can be discovered in the public laws of the regime—particularly those amplified by Supreme Court decisions and opinions (Rohr 1989, pp. 60–84).

Rohr's approach seeks out professional ethics that fall short of the broader, normative questions of justice per se but that instead focus on a pragmatic responsibility to uphold the essential values of the polity. Thus the question is "How can I reinforce the values of the regime?" rather than "Is the regime value just?" (1989, pp. 69–71). Nonetheless, the bureaucrat's task of ethical discernment often plods through ambiguities surrounding both the legal basis of the value and the nuances of the particular administrative situation. These ambiguities may require the pertinent question to be reformulated as "If I do X, do I expressly interfere with (regime value) Y?" Rohr's reliance on (implicit or explicit) oath-taking as a support for regime values prompts a comment especially germane to public-service ethics in a global era: "Pluralism . . . makes it impossible to hope for an operational understanding of the public interest derived from some common metaphysical premise. Despite that pluralism, however, it is safe to say that most of us would agree that one should adhere steadfastly to the oaths one has taken"—to the Constitution of the United States as the "preeminent symbol of our political values" (1989, p.70).

How regime values play out amid questions of morality and fairness on a global scale should prove interesting. When President Clinton remarked that "Americans had a lot to do with the ending of apartheid," he essentially affirmed that state and local governments indeed assume roles as global actors (see Fitzgerald 2001)—perhaps implementing divestiture and selective purchasing actions that express the moral outlooks of (at least some) constituents as global citizens. As early as 1976, Madison, Wisconsin, adapted a selective purchasing law that targeted companies transacting business in South Africa, and at least eleven other state/local entities have since then aimed measures against various nations charged with human rights abuses (Fitzgerald 2001, pp. 6–16). In what Fitzgerald calls "a new federalism in a global era," such state-local global activity contends with two countervailing legal principles—the Dormant Foreign Affairs Power (presumably a regime value derived from extraconstitutional interpretation) and international trade treaty nondiscriminatory (as opposed to selective) language. While the Dormant Foreign Affairs Power reserves authority to the federal level, it is unclear whether state and local actions that take global views of portfolio management or purchasing interfere with foreign affairs. In related court disputes, public body defendants stress the exercise of their proprietary rather than their regulatory intents (such as the enacting by the Commonwealth of Massachusetts of its Burma Law, targeting Myanmar's [Burma's] forced labor practices—see Fitzgerald 2000; Head 2000) as fiduciary stewardship. And nondiscriminatory language in international trade treaties muddies the water insofar as it strengthens the political clout of private-sector trade organizations in Congress and the federal courts.

The legal uncertainty that surrounds globally focused purchasing and trust fund actions exemplifies Rohr's assertion that ethical enterprise sometimes requires bureaucrats to navigate ambiguous territory. Yet even more clear-cut determinations of ethical (non)responsibility may bode problematic in the global context. On the surface, attention to regime values would appear to prompt public servants to dismiss pangs of moral responsibility stemming from international accords *not* ratified by the United States. Ostensibly then, administrators in the Immigration and Naturalization Service, public schools, and local social service agencies are bound by no obligation toward the children of aliens (particularly those most affected by government actions in the wake of September 11) on the humanitarian and compassionate grounds of the International Convention on the Rights of the Child—not ratified by the United States. The issue appears to be open and shut as a matter of law. (In fact, some could interpret nonratification as an overt *rejection* of convention principles that establish an ethical prohibition *against* special accommodation for such children.) Yet suppose that the United States *had* ratified the convention, but Congress did not adopt specific legislation that enabled treaty provisions in particular agency venues (as in the case of the Canadian government; see Knop 2000). Even in such a circumstance, one might find difficulty discerning regime values that direct ethical obligation toward children of the world, without U.S. citizenship, who are affected by the agencies of U.S. government.

Normative Inquiry

In explicating regime values as the preferred approach to bureaucratic ethics, John Rohr offers elegant justification for a legally oriented obligation that is widely accepted as mainstream government ethics. Indeed, prominent textbooks characterize *legality* as the preeminent managerial decision criterion (Lewis 1991, pp. 46–92) and emphasize the "responsibility to elected officials through support for the law" (Cooper 1990, pp. 62–63). Yet Rohr's discussion is especially helpful here in taking us directly to the fundamental predicament in discerning public service obligation toward a global morality. In essence, how can a particular "high road" concern for humanitarianism and compassion calculate into the common denominator of a pluralist public interest? Although Massachusetts's Burma Law was subsequently found to be unconstitutional, its origins are instructive. Legal scholar Peter Fitzgerald reports that Seattle World Trade Organization protestor Simon Billenness succeeded in persuading one state representative to adapt apartheid sanctions to target Burma by "literally substituting one country's name for another in a new bill" (2001, pp. 2–3). Did these stratagems build on regime values (in view of existing apartheid measures) or subvert them? How many of the state's citizens knew or cared about Myanmar's labor practices? To paraphrase Solon (see Rohr 1989, p. 6), is worry about such injustice (and the prevalence of it elsewhere) simply more morality than the nation can possibly bear—especially as it girds against terrorism after September 11, 2001? Thus research efforts that would extend the ethical enterprise in public service to international humanitarian issues will contend with a strong inertia of legal constraints that point inward rather than outward.

(7) Normative inquiry could assess how/whether public-service ethics that are grounded in regime values can effectively incorporate humanitarian obligations to particular groups (usually of noncitizens) most affected by agency actions.

Empirical Inquiry

Understandably, regime values protect a pluralist public interest from the whims of splinter factions purporting to save the world. Although it may suffice to a point, such a stand-pat justification may prove unsettling for some as a notion of professional responsibility that is insensitive to large numbers of children, workers, and so forth in the world. The issue of global consciousness forces the identity question (that Professor Bruce asked), "Who are we?" in moral problems that pit a legally constrained professional responsibility against humanitarian obligations. In *The Spirit of Public Administration*, George Frederickson and David K. Hart reformulate the question as "the bureaucrat: careerist or moral hero?" (1997, p. 197) and then refer to "the patriotism of benevolence" exhibited by Danish bureaucrats on behalf of Jews during Nazi occupation (pp. 200-1). At one point, these authors comment,

> "It was therefore the Founders' intent that all public servants should view the process of government as a moral endeavor; theirs is not just to administer, but to assist in bringing the ideals of democracy into existence. . . . For that reason, public servants must be both moral philosophers and moral activists, which would require (1) an understanding of and belief in the American regime values; and (2) a sense of the primary duty of public servants to act as guardians and guarantors of the regime values for the American public. (Frederickson 1997, p. 205)

For the public servant, the rubber hits the road in understanding how to reconcile regime values with moral activism and philosophy. This task becomes all the more difficult but no less critical in administrative settings responding to security threats from the backlashes that globalization fosters. Perhaps public administrators can learn from the judicial dilemmas that the domestic courts face in ruling on the provisions of international treaty law.

Karen Knop relates that the courts—in the pursuit of neutrality—frequently "structure themselves" into binary, "all or nothing" decisions. The alternative may be to establish dialogue within networks (of domestic and international court officials) that can legitimate the international norm (Knop 2000, pp. 531–35). In like fashion, the ethical public manager who can restructure issues pertaining to global humanitarianism away from binary choices against legal constraints would benefit from the moral courage to surmount ambiguities in situations and values. These problem-structuring issues bear special significance for those who assume positions of reconfigured agency authority—in line with Kettl's "place-based" and Frederickson's "coalition-maintaining" recommendations. Empirical research that may emerge in analyzing administrative responses to the September 11 tragedy or other global backlashes could thus focus on the linkage between how problems are structured—in relation to the law (or the nonexistence of it) and the capability to extend compassion or accommodation.

(8) Empirical research could determine how problem structuring in response to pertinent global situations affects moral obligations to accommodate groups affected by related administrative actions.

It is worth noting that this final suggestion for ethics research relates also to the preceding themes—systems instability, quality of public dialogue, and transparency.

Conclusion

It is fitting that closing observations from this preliminary study respond to the original dialogue initiated by Professors Menzel and Bruce to stimulate discussion about globalization and public-service ethics. To an extent, the work herein sheds light on two of the three identity questions these scholars pose: "Who are we"—as a public? We are utilitarians, riveted on the here and now, who resist abstract thinking about things public. We are independent, perhaps by principle but *most certainly* by virtue (or accident) of geopolitical buffers from dependency and instability, and our expectations on government have (at least up until the present) reflected those presumptions of independence and continuity. The utter complexity of globalization and the threatening instability of its backlashes now blindside us and threaten to undermine our cultural identity. As the two professors imply, our collective potential for compassion on an international scale appears to be no greater than our uneven track record for discerning public good in how we treat neighbors within local and national communities.

"Who are we"—as public administrators? We are principled in service, yet practical and resourceful in approach. We can be morally courageous in pursuit of just causes, but clearly those inclinations are checked by sovereign law as reflected in our professional values and by the tenor of public voices—understandably more shrill in the aftermath of September 11, 2001. Of the two, the latter appears to be the more formidable constraint, due in part to our skills in working through the moral ambiguities of the latter in application to particular situations. And ironically, some of the international trade implications of globalization *itself* may obstruct our motivations for compassionate action on a global scale.

Efforts in this chapter cannot meaningfully respond to the "what will we become" question. Yet they do suggest that the prospect of adopting a global ethic—"a framework for defining right and wrong that knows no social, economic, or political borders" (Menzel to Bruce May 18, 2002)—remains far in the future. In the meantime, public administrators can *re*professionalize, rather than *de*professionalize, their ethics in a manner that incorporates global humanitarian concern on a roughly equal footing with the more traditional claims on administrative obligation. To do so, practitioners need researchers to map globalization's ethical terrain and to recommend approaches for globally pertinent actions that are just, prudent, and feasible.

Notes

1. Such envelopment of public administration within governance and national interest marks a striking departure from the three earlier UN documents. Generally reflecting the traditional dichotomy between politics and administration, both *Standards and Techniques of Public Administration* (1951) and *A Handbook of Public Administration* (1961) characterized public administration as a compendium of good practices—independent from policy concerns. From this stance, the former (1951) assessed administrative deficits in developing areas according to these standards, and the latter (1961) assisted government officials and area specialists to solve such problems. In terms of ethics, both reports (at least implicitly) characterized the establishment of career systems based upon merit as appropriately finding the meritorious and liberating them from corrosive regime values (UN 1951, pp. 20–24; 1961, pp. 34–46). To a degree, the 1975 report *Development Administration* represented a departure as it embraced a program-budget-systems logic that cast public administration as an open and dynamic system in pursuit of national (that is, *economic*) development. This systems approach to public administration across nations—recast as development administration—said little if anything about ethical values (beyond brief references to the significance of the informal organization). In comparing these four UN documents, it becomes apparent that thinking about the field of public administration in a global (or international) context has changed dramatically over the past half-century. Specifically, the current ecology (at least as depicted in *Rethinking PA* 1998) encapsulates administrative experience within competing subsystems of globally directed

governance and, as such, resembles Emery and Trist's description of complexly textured causality—their fourth type of environment.

2. To some extent, the successive public administration ecologies in the four UN documents appear aligned with Emery and Trist's treatment of responses and values (shown in Table 16.1): *Standards and Techniques of PA* (1951) articulates managerial best practices (tactics) to identify administrative deficits (*bads*), and *A Handbook of PA* (1961) is contingency focused in terms of (strategically) implementing best practices in particular developing areas. Both appear to be congruent with Fox and Miller's notion of "the ethics of authoritative command" in classical public administration (1995, p. 21). How *Development Administration* (1975) fits is less clear—perhaps its Program Planning Budget Systems (PPBS) logic constitutes a set of operations in the race for economic development, but values (apart from faith in rational systems) are not stressed. And it is indeed the values/ethics dimension of the current (*Rethinking PA* 1998) ecology that is under examination in this chapter.

3. Primarily, this (combined) commentary is drawn from three chapters of Frederickson's book, *The Spirit of Public Administration* (1997): "Finding the 'Public' in Public Administration" (ch. 1); "Public Administration as Governance" (ch. 3); and "Ethics and Public Administration" (ch. 7). The title of chapter 7 can be misleading because most of this book appears to be devoted to public-service ethics and values at various levels of specificity.

4. See the NPR/Kaiser Family Foundation/Kennedy School of Government Civil Liberties poll at www.npr.org/programs/specials/poll/civil_liberties/civil_liberties_static_results_2.html (accessed October 28, 2004).

5. See the PIPA Poll, "Americans on Terrorism: Two Years After 9/11" at www.pipa.org/OnlineReports/Terrorism/FindingsTerr9.03.pdf (accessed October 28, 2004).

6. Specifically, plaintiff O'Keefe's original breech-of-contract claim stemmed from the Loewen Group's acquisition of funeral homes in local competition with O'Keefe's operation. After this, the Loewen Group discontinued selling burial policies of the Gulf National Insurance Company, owned by O'Keefe, in those competing funeral homes (see Krauss 2000).

References

Ackoff, Russell L. 1974. *Redesigning the Future.* New York: John Wiley.

Arendt, Hannah. 1963. *Eichmann in Jerusalem: A Report on the Banality of Evil.* New York: Viking Press.

Bailey, Stephen K. 1965. "Ethics in the Public Service." In *Public Administration,* ed. Roscoe C. Martin, pp. 283–98. Syracuse, NY: Syracuse University Press:

Bellavita, Christopher. 1991. "The Public Administrator as Hero." *Administration and Society* 23, no.2: 155–85.

Cooper, Terry L. 1990. *The Responsible Administrator: An Approach to Ethics for the Administrative Role.* San Francisco: Jossey-Bass.

Dyer, Gwynne. 2001. "U.S. Must Understand Conspiracy." *Dayton Daily News,* December 19: 7A.

Emery, Fred E., and Trist, Eric L. 1965. "The Causal Texture of Organizational Environments." *Human Relations* 18, no.1: 21–32.

Ferguson, Julia. 2000. "California's MTBE Contaminated Water." *Colorado Journal of International Law and Policy* 11, no. 2: 499–561.

Fitzgerald, Peter L. 2001. "Massachusetts, Burma, and the World Trade Organization." *Cornell International Law Journal* 34, no. 1: 1–54.

Fox, Charles J., and Miller, Hugh T. 1995. *Postmodern Public Administration.* Thousand Oaks, CA: SAGE.

Frankena, William K. 1963. *Ethics.* Englewood Cliffs, NJ: Prentice Hall.

Frederickson, H. George. 1998. *The Spirit of Public Administration.* San Francisco: Jossey-Bass.

———. 2001. "Honor in the Public Life." *PA Times* 24, no. 10: 11.

Friedman, Thomas L. 1999. *The Lexus and the Olive Tree.* New York: Farrar, Straus and Giroux.

Ghere, Richard K. 2001. "Ethical Futures of Public-Private Partnerships: Peering Far Down the Track." *Public Organization Review: A Global Journal* 1, no. 3: 303–20.

Gudofsky, Jason L. 2000. "Shedding Light on Article 1110 of the North American Free Trade Agreement (NAFTA) Concerning Expropriations." *Northwestern Journal of International Law and Business* 21, no. 1: 243–315.

Head, Carol E. 2000. "The Dormant Foreign Affairs Power: Constitutional Implications for State and Local Investment Restrictions Impacting Foreign Countries." *Boston College Law Review* 42, no. 1: 123–72.

Hickman, Gill Robinson. 1998. "Leadership and the Social Imperative of Organizations in the 21st Century." In *Leading Organizations*, ed. Hickman, pp. 559–71. Newbury Park, CA: SAGE.

Hubbell, Larry. 1991. "Heroes in the Public Service: A Rejoinder." *Administration and Society* 23, no. 2: 194–200.

Kettl, Donald F. 2000. "The Transformation of Governance: Globalization, Devolution, and the Role of Government." *Public Administration Review* 60, no. 2: 488–97.

———. 2001. "The Next Public Administration Revolution." *PA Times* 24, no. 10: 3.

Kirlin, John J. 1996. "What Government Must Do Well: Creating Value for Society." *Journal of Public Administration Research and Theory* 6, no. 1: 161–85.

Knop, Karen. 2000. "Here and There: International Law in Domestic Courts." *New York University Journal of International Law and Politics* 32, no. 2: 501–36.

Krauss, Michael I. 2000. "NAFTA Meets the American Torts Process: *O'Keefe v. Loewen.*" *George Mason Law Review* 9, no. 1: 69.

Laird, Ian A. 2001. "NAFTA Chapter 11 Meets Chicken Little." *Chicago Journal of International Law* 2, no. 1: 223–30.

Lewis, Carol W. 1991. *The Ethics Challenge in Public Service.* San Francisco: Jossey-Bass.

Menzel, Donald C., and Bruce, Willa. 2001. "Globalization and Ethics: A Dialogue to Start a Dialogue." *PA Times* 24, no. 9: 3–4.

National Public Radio (NPR). 2001. "Globalization and Terrorism." *All Things Considered*, December 14. Available at http://www.npr.org/ramfiles/atc/20011214.atc.06.ram (accessed October 28, 2004).

Pavlek, Thomas J. 1988. "Structuring Problems for Policy Action." In *Managing Disaster: Strategies and Policy Perspectives*, ed. Louise K. Comfort, pp. 22–38. Durham NC: Duke University Press.

Pope, Jeremy. 2000. *TI Source Book 2000.* Berlin: Transparency International.

Rajagopal, Balakrishnan. 2000. "From Resistance to Renewal: The Third World, Social Movements, and the Expansion of International Institutions." *Harvard International Law Journal* 41, no. 2: 529–78.

Rohr, John A. 1989. *Ethics for Bureaucrats: An Essay on Law and Values*. New York: Marcel Dekker.

Stone, Deborah. 2002. *Policy Paradox: The Art of Political Decision Making*. New York: Norton.

UN Department of Economic and Social Affairs. 1961. *A Handbook of Public Administration*. New York.

———. 1975. *Development Administration: Current Approaches and Trends*. New York.

UN Division of Public Administration and Development Management, Department of Economic and Social Affairs. 1998. *Rethinking Public Administration: An Overview*. New York.

UN Technical Assistance Administration. 1951. *Standards and Techniques of Public Administration*. New York.

Unzicker, Andrea D. B. 2000. "From Corruption to Cooperation: Globalization Brings a Multilateral Agreement against Foreign Bribery." *Indiana Journal of Global Legal Studies* 7, no. 2: 655.

Van Wart, Montgomery. 1998. *Changing Public Sector Values*. New York: Garland Publishers.

Wallace-Bruce, Nii Lante. 2000. "Corruption and Competitiveness in Global Business—The Dawn of a New Era." *Melbourne University Law Review* 24, no. 2: 349–78.

17

Conclusion: Ethics and Public Management— Answers and Questions

Richard K. Ghere

Introduction

This conclusion is a synthesis of the preceding chapters within some broader research topics in the maturing subfield of government ethics. Some thirty years after the coalescence of government-ethics research as a self-conscious concerted effort, it is appropriate to ask "What longstanding questions have now been answered?" and "How well have they been answered?" We recognize that, over time, some persisting questions shift in context and new ones arise in response to changing public events and expectations. Thus, the categories used here are framed more broadly than those George Frederickson used in concluding *Ethics and Public Administration* in 1993. A first concern focuses, for example, on the ethical character of *people* in public administration (as good or bad) but with greater attention to *context* (or situation—a troublesome word in some ethical conversations). This is followed by attention to the array of behavioral attributes that affect the ethical quality of decisions made in public-sector settings. A third discussion considers the theoretical nature of public-management ethics in relation to issues raised by contributors to this volume. Finally, this chapter comments on the research implications of concerns arising from each of these integrative discussions.

Nature of Persons: The Contextual Dimension

In the first instance, it is logical to recognize *context* as key in scrutinizing the ethical actions of individuals (or for that matter, groups), whether in personal life or in professional settings. However, this leads to some approach-avoidance—on one hand, context implies that actions respond to situations, but "situation-talk" casts a chill over ethics conversation since it is frequently associated with an undisciplined relativism that ignores principle (see Ruggiero 2004). The challenge at hand is how to treat context more aggressively as an essential and productive dimension in the study of government ethics.

It is helpful to distinguish between references to specific contexts (such as the strength of "pro-business" ideology in U.S. society) from a more generalized meaning related to the immediate circumstances of an action. Regarding the former, Donald Menzel recognizes "community, culture, and the ethical environment" as one of five topical categories of recent government ethics research in chapter 2 of this volume. Here the focus is on particular factors that impinge upon both the (non)recognition of ethical salience and subsequent action. Specific context in turn focuses on the constellation of influences pressing upon the particular decision setting. For example, in *Public Integrity*, Patrick Dobel describes the strong pressures to evoke conformance among cabinet-level actors in the Johnson administration to support the escalation of bombing in the Vietnam conflict. Specifically, Dobel illustrates how Johnson stigmatized dissenters (particularly, Bill Moyers who was cast as "the house moralist" and "Mr. Stop-the-Bombing") and how others positioned themselves to advantage if this dissenter fell from presidential grace (Dobel 1999, pp. 99–105). Here the emphasis is on the particulars of the situation.

Further consideration of this distinction between specific and generalized meanings of contexts aligns with some "big ideas" articulated over the years concerning the nature and practice of public administration. First, in regard to specific environmental contexts, Stephen Bailey's efforts to circumscribe the moral thinking of Paul Appleby offer a fertile perspective. Bailey understood Appleby's assumptions about the moral ambiguity of persons, who are in the shifting sands of context—"the contextual forces that condition moral priorities in the public service" (Bailey 1965, pp. 289–92). Taken a bit further, the inference is threefold: (1) that even among more forthright circumstances, the ethical character of the person may be unpredictable and inaptly dichotomized as "good" or "bad" but (2) takes on meaning within a particular setting wherein competing forces and rationales converge. And (3) the effective public servant needs to recognize not only the moral ambiguities of persons, but the moral ambiguity of situations, as well as policies and procedures.

It is intriguing to bring forward Bailey's admonitions from Appleby's writings of the 1940s to the Abu Ghraib prison scandal arising from the Iraq war and occupation of 2003–4. Here, low-ranking reservists with very limited military training and experience were thrust into roles of considerable responsibility in prison supervision, presumably within the parameters of universal principles of humane treatment found in the Geneva Convention. An extensive photographic record documented patterns of prisoner abuse within the Abu Ghraib facility that reportedly occurred within other prisons under U.S. occupation as well. Currently, military judicial proceedings are under way to sort through the factors that drove defendants to engage in these immoral behaviors and to determine if actions of a few enlisted persons were in fact prompted by the directives of military superiors or government contractors. In this specific context, it appears that reservists, detached from rather ordinary civilian backgrounds (one defendant worked as an assistant manager of a pizza shop and another as a part-time state prison guard) lost a sense of ethical direction in a new and unfamiliar setting. Time will tell if higher-ranking personnel, trained and experienced careerists in public (military) service, were as prone to losing their moral bearings in the context of a military occupational experience stemming from a preemptive policy rationale to eradicate global terrorism.

Abu Ghraib presents an example of contextual ambiguity brought on by a confluence of events that eclipses the moral contours of conventional public settings and, in so doing, gives rise to ethical blind spots. Blind spots may affect individuals differently. For some, they may be the source of profound frustration and confusion, leading to discomforting cognitive dissonance as persons seek integrity but are engaged in actions that contradict their own belief systems (see Dobel 1999, pp. 27–29; Festinger 1957). The judicial inability to articulate a coherent theory of state action (that offers consistent criteria to determine when private parties collaborating with government in fact assume public legal responsibility) likely wears upon the professional images of public servants committed to standards of open and accountable governance. Similar frustration might be found among human service administrators who discover that the "guaranteed" techniques emerging from new public management advocacy simply do not pan out in assuring the quality of particularly sensitive services for the most vulnerable in society. Other individuals, at some level of consciousness, might perceive contextually ambiguous blind spots opportunistically as a "blank check," or some sort of "contextual bye," that arises since the well-understood standards of ethical conduct appear not to fit the situation. High-ranking political appointees—or "cowboys" in Peter deLeon's characterization—may well exploit the ambiguities of privatization as a "bye" in a self-serving manner to circumvent generally understood public standards of morality.

Bailey stressed the imperative to *recognize* the ambiguities of context, but perception is especially elusive in dilemmas that pit prevailing societal, cultural, and nationalistic norms against universal principles. As noted by Adams and Balfour, Weber correctly observed that the technical-rational motive in Western societies leads to a moral inversion that can tear at the human fabric in the name of progress and efficiency. Yet the ambiguity between sociopolitical norms and moral principle is fundamental to analytical treatment of transnational ethics. On one hand, it may indeed be the case that public managers can agree upon core sets of anticorruption policy goals and reform strategies (see Gilman and Lewis 1996). On the other, surgically precise definitions of "corruption," as Caiden suggests, are hard to come by. And it is not surprising that the "toughest sell" for transparency measures is among Western nations where business interests and influences are so intermeshed in public policy (Galtung 2001). The ambiguity of public ethics is particularly apparent when values and obligations lodged within national sovereignty collide with international conventions and when national purposes preempt humanitarian concern.

To restate, Bailey saw the person as morally ambiguous under the most clear-cut of circumstances, not to speak of the usually cloudy contexts of decision choices. The ambiguous natures of people and contexts in turn lead to an inherent paradox in policies and administrative strategies, and nowhere is that more apparent than in reform efforts designed to encourage ethics and curb corruption in government. The ethics-reform experience suggests that the grand, one-size-fits-all intervention may offer symbolic resonance yet impedes implementation. Despite the appeal of openness revered as fundamental to ethical governance in the United States, Transparency International (TI) has developed a deliberate strategy that avoids confrontational exposé in favor of more discreet, cooperative negotiation. Galtung comments on the TI approach as follows: "This policy is uniquely adapted to aspects of the corruption scene. It is not the tool itself, but its finely tuned adaptability to the given context that makes it so effective" (2001, p. 199). In a similar vein, Dwivedi and Mancuso explain Canadian success in maintaining ethical public service that more often relies upon low-profile, behind-the-scenes consultation than on a U.S.-styled, explicit legalism (2001). The inference here—one that reverberates within Anechiarico's discussion of facilitating ethics in the compromised New York City contracting environment and in Denhardt and Gilman's treatment of reasonability with respect to employee gift policies—is that ethics reformers need to factor context into their policy strategies.

Second, in regard to a more generalized context of public-sector decision making, it is instructive to draw upon Dwight Waldo's idea of *cooperative rationality*. In *The Study of Public Administration* (1955), Waldo coaxes insight out of some fundamental concepts—such as "administration," "public," "organization," and "management"—from the more encompassing phenomenon of *cooperative human action*. Cooperation is vital to bureaucratic administration, but it implies much more—that two or more persons *willingly* roll that stone in public service. Perhaps the ethical significance of the cooperative context is all too often lost. Game theorists deduce that an individualistic strategy ultimately fails and that the cooperative pursuit of conscience leads to a realistic (rather than a merely sentimental) goal attainment (for example, see Rapoport 1964, p. 287). Human cooperation therefore rises above conventionality as the foundation of norms and socialization processes. The implication of cooperative human action as the generalized context of public service appears twofold. First, research findings based upon aggregates of *individual* cognitive development scores might take on broader meaning in a cooperative context. Certainly, undue allegiance to hierarchical authority and conformance to group pressures detract from healthy ethical environments. Nonetheless, ethics need to focus on a vibrant, collective responsibility in the public service as the essential platform for individual moral conduct. Second, cooperative action enables a leadership dynamic that extends beyond bureaucratic authority to cultivate ethical climates that are decisive in aligning internal resources with external legitimacy in pursuit of effectiveness.

What then does emphasis on *context* contribute to comprehending the ethical nature of persons in public-management settings? First, it reminds us that people are prone to moral ambiguity in complex and turbulent situations, and that individuals vary regarding their abilities to recognize the ambiguous elements of circumstances and to act upon them. Ambiguity can in turn create "blind spots" that obscure one's view of morally responsible action. Third, there is cause to reassert that the cooperative nature of public administration in practice carries its own ethical significance. Such a high scale of interpersonal cooperation needs to be recognized as a significant moral asset in itself, although it is certainly true that group-conforming behaviors can sometimes contribute to ethical failures. And last, personal responsibility requires one to cultivate a mental attitude that recognizes one's potential for moral ambiguity.

Making Ethical Decisions: An Extended View

Stephen Bailey in his classic essay on public administration ethics identified three essential mental qualities needed to work through the contextual ambiguities and procedural paradoxes inherent within public life: optimism, courage, and fairness tempered with charity. Bailey clearly tapped into the significance that Paul Appleby had placed upon attitudinal virtues as vital to public service. Bailey by inference reasoned that those who enter public (governmental contract and nongovernmental organization) service as successful fast-starters in business without these mental qualities are often ill-equipped to navigate the complexities of public life. To what extent are these vintage ideas germane to empirically based ethics research in the twenty-first century? On the surface, it would appear that empiricists would find attitudinal constructs difficult to operationalize—a set of Likert-type survey questions measuring "courage" would prove interesting. Nonetheless, Appleby and Bailey believed that decision making in the public sphere *is different*, largely due to contextual ambiguity, and that moral accomplishment depends upon a range of factors that includes the attitudinal along with the cognitive.

In chapter 2, Donald Menzel raises the fundamental question of how broadly or narrowly "moral development" should be understood. As Menzel attests, much (although not all) of the empirical work on decision making has focused on the Kohlbergian model using the Defining Issues methodology developed by James Rest and others (for example, see Rest and Narváez, 1994). Certainly, this body of work provides a secure anchor for the cognitive discernment of moral issues amid the ambiguous contexts of government and other public operations and public policy. Yet it is no reflection upon this important research to suggest that the model of ethical decision making—at least one that strives to integrate the cognitive, the attitudinal, and other pertinent ethical attributes—remains substantially underidentified. In chapter 3, Dennis Wittmer integrates several streams of decision literature, some of which propose strategies that tap into the interaction between the person and situation. And Carole Jurkiewicz's research forges a pertinent link between cognitive development and the attitudinal toughness (that Bailey prescribed) in her correlations between Defining Issues scores and leadership effectiveness measures. Jurkiewicz includes the administrative power (Mach score) variable, thereby adding to the array of variables important in executive decision making.

Some recent literature on emotionality suggests that cognitive capability to assess the reality of context depends upon a person's emotional capacities. In *Emotional Intellgence*, Daniel Goleman argues that modern psychology concentrates on the cognitive dimension of the mind while leaving the emotional side unexplored. He reasons, "The cognitive scientists who [ignore emotion] have been seduced by the computer as the operative model of the mind, forgetting that, in reality, the brain's wetware is awash in a messy, pulsating puddle of neurochemicals, nothing like the sanitized, orderly silicon that has spawned the guiding metaphor for the mind" (1995, pp. 40–41). If optimism, as Goleman suggests, is the capacity to interpret frustration and failure as temporary and changeable, it follows that optimists are those who recognize and master their emotions and who can factor in the emotions of others in contexts of interpersonal relationships (1995, pp. 87–90).

Can emotional capacity be learned? Goleman answers in the affirmative, that "temperament can be tempered by experience" (1995, p. 89). Although the emotional intelligence literature is primarily focused on the development of school-age children, emotional (in)capacity should not be discounted in public decision making. In charting the careers of public administrators, Douglas Morgan and Henry Kass use focus-group research that reveals how experience shapes managerial style in functioning in adversarial contexts. Those in early career stages are inclined to depend upon "a prevailing management ideology of efficient control" while others in later stages are more apt to "involve the language of a public, communal interest" (1993, pp. 180, 184). It is obviously not possible to measure how much of this experiential growth is attributable to cognitive skill as distinct from emotional seasoning. However, it appears that both contribute to one's ability to accommodate the ambiguities of democratic governance.

These speculative comparisons of cognitive and emotional influences serve the larger claim here, a need to broaden the array of issues treated in research on ethical decision making. First, it is clear that the accumulated body of research pertaining to cognitive development contributes substantially to understanding individual decision-making behavior in public life. Nonetheless, a review of some large ideas in public administration theory points to overarching attitudinal qualities as requisites of moral competence. References to the writings of Appleby and Bailey characterize moral decision making as an undertaking of the "whole person" in cooperative relationships with other whole people. It can be said then that the impressive body of empirical work pertaining to cognitive development calls for much complementary effort devoted to identifying other key variables affecting ethical decision making. Presumably, emotional capacity can contribute to a broader perspective of how persons, individually and collectively, interact in decision-making settings.

Administrative Ethics in the Twenty-First Century

As discussed in the Introduction and chapter 1, there is reason to take collective stock of research in administrative ethics in terms of its topical coherences and scientific rigor. The critical question is whether a sufficient body of quality empirical work exists to support accumulating knowledge in core areas that identify a domain of administrative ethics. Terminology is problematic. In the graduate classroom setting, conversation directed toward professional ethics in public administration often gravitates toward issues of personal morality that, although germane, obscure the distinctive focus on professionalized public service. Regarding definitions, Dennis Thompson writes that "administrative ethics involve the application of moral principles to the conduct of officials in organizations." Administrative ethics is a species of political ethics "that applies to political life more generally" (1985, p. 555). Some theorists, such as Kathryn Denhardt, argue that such an organizational orientation renders a narrow, legalistic approach toward controlling illegal behavior (particularly that concerning fiscal misconduct) and related issues of corruption (Denhardt 1991, pp. 97–99).

Other definitive treatments of administrative ethics characterize this subfield as more open-ended—shaped over the decades by broader debates on such issues as administration versus politics, administrative discretion versus internal controls, "inner checks" versus external codes of ethics, and organization conduct versus administrative citizenship in the public arena. In addition, the subfield is comprised of numerous thematic foci—for example, in an introductory article to the *Handbook of Administrative Ethics*, Terry Cooper (2001) identifies seven themes: (1) citizenship and democratic theory, (2) virtue ethics, (3) founding thought and the constitutional tradition, (4) ethics education, (5) the organizational context, (6) philosophical theory and perspectives, and (7) cognitive moral development. Although these themes lend coherence and identity to administrative ethics somewhat parallel to Thompson's organizational definition, the open-ended nature of each of these seven categories—along with the prospect of additional concerns—leaves room for this subfield to accommodate emergent new public issues. It is instructive to probe some of the "pressure points" that challenge the identity of administrative ethics as a subfield.

First, the politics-administration dichotomy reemerges to challenge an organizationally grounded administrative ethics, this time reopening the question of the nature of accountability as it relates to context. Although legalistic conceptions support the widely held notion that public accountability amounts to a universal principle of answerability, "messy" situations—such as the "new normalcy" in the aftermath of the September 11 terrorist attacks—command a more nuanced view of accountability that calls for responsibility appropriate to context. The notion of universal principle compromising the public interest runs counter to conventional thinking about administrative ethics. Perhaps the ethical expectations of liberal democracy can be regarded as logical appendages of technical-rational administration, because both in effect narrow the range of stewardship and responsibility of the public. Yet in the context of a developing nation divided by adversarial cultural identities, the prospect of what Yoder and Cooper call "thin trust" (translatable as public accountability based upon internationally accepted ethical principles) appears workable in achieving a national identity that is founded on civic trust. As a contemporary manifestation of the traditional dichotomy, the textural nature of accountability—whether as "thick" within context or "thin" as universal answerability—blurs the boundary between administrative ethics and policy concerns. Given the momentous events so far in this new century, the case for stretching those boundaries appears compelling.

As applied in transnational settings, dilemmas that pit universal standards against contextual norms direct attention toward a second pressure point, relating to the relative weight of alternative normative foundations as authoritative on a global scale. Now candor requires serious reflection about what "universal" means in the lexicon of public ethics. Does that adjective simply imply that American-style ethical norms are extended on a global scale, or does it connote binding commitments to factual truths and protocols that emerge through international deliberation? Does global interdependence to some extent eclipse national sovereignty in a manner that erodes constitutionally based regime values? Administrative ethics will be ill-served by flippant reactions to these tough questions. Simply to discount the substance of these global issues as irrelevant to an administrative ethics viewed as process-oriented (to counteract corruption—assuming that it can be universally defined) is to retreat to the bankruptcy of neutrality. On the other hand, the identity of administrative ethics must rise above the ever-present normative appeals of international politics. A collective prudence is needed to guide a continuing conversation about how (to paraphrase Terry Cooper), American administrative ethics fit into a global context (Cooper, 2004).

A third pressure point relates to the problem Dennis Thompson describes as "the moral responsibility of many hands," in light of issues discussed in previous chapters and of contemporary public events generally. At the heart of the issue are the locus and scope of moral agency, which in the U.S. political culture typically focus on the person as an individual agent. After reviewing the "many hands" problem (that is, the conundrum of the individual in a collective setting), Thompson concludes that the pursuit of personal moral responsibility offers the strongest foundation for promoting ethics and accountability in government (1987, p. 65). Such a perspective is widely shared among scholars of administrative ethics (see, for example, Stewart 1990; Doig 1990).

Few would dispute the proposition that public employees at various levels of authority should be held personally responsible for their actions and for organizational outcomes. Yet is it the case that the practicality of tracking individual responsibility and actions in essence reduces administrative ethics merely to "thin" answerability within the organization and beyond it? Stated another way, it is unclear if the increasingly complex textures of public issues—such as the ideological preferences for private-sector involvement in government, the potentially destructive nature of the technical-rational imperative in administration, and the conflict between national sovereignty and global accountability—can be factored into individualistic assumptions of moral agency.

It is noteworthy that theorists in other arenas of ethical inquiry are beginning to question whether moral agency is inherently individualistic or may in particular circumstances be shared collectively within institutions. In the subfield of ethics and international affairs, for example, Toni Erskine presents a model of collective moral agency wherein (a) the collective is a conglomerate, (b) the collective must be able to deliberate and sustain a degree of decision making toward a common goal, and (c) it has an identity of continuity over time. Further, Erskine argues that collective moral agency does not negate individual responsibilities of members, but that "rather it arises because some duties cannot be distributed among individuals at all" (2001, p. 73). Do parallels arise in public-sector organization wherein duties, or blame, cannot be reasonably distributed among individuals? Such a question appeals for a reassessment of moral agency in administrative ethics, which extends consideration to textural issues.

Public-administrative ethics of the twenty-first century confront a number of substantive questions, aside from those related to the rigor of its empirical inquiry. First, there is reason to focus upon the nature of moral responsibility as it applies to what Dubnick and O'Kelly distinguish as a "thick accountability," within the context of particularly sensitive and complex situations. Second, there is need to assess whether American ethical norms appropriately fit public ethics on a global scale, or if there is reason to reconsider particular values and assumptions in administrative ethics within international perspectives. And third, it is worth considering whether administrative ethics should accommodate more nuanced perspectives regarding moral agency open to the possibility of collective responsibility.

Research Implications

The intent here is to comment upon how each of the three preceding discussions might affect the course of ethics research. In its emphasis on the contextual dimension of the person as moral actor, the first discussion advocates that ethics researchers devote more attention to contexts, in an effort to support generalizations about the moral significance of human responses in particularly ambiguous or complex settings. Although some may point to the folly of generalizing on the ambiguous, it may help to construct some typologies (however crude) that identify some familiar sources of moral confusion that public officials confront—for example, those attributable to unresolved policy and/or legal determinations, to cultural and ideological traditions, as well as to the hierarchical pressures of public authority. And certainly, issues of textural complexity have their counterpart in the more general literature of organization theory. In their classic essay on the causal texture of organization environments, Emery and Trist (1965) differentiate among four densities of complex settings as functions of the randomness or connectedness of goals and noxiants—or "goods and bads." The parallel challenge in government ethics research would involve developing some general models of ambiguity that could offer predictive insight on circumstances that lead the person as a moral actor into dissonant, defensive, or otherwise problematic behaviors.

Another way to pursue the ethical significance of the ambiguous setting is to explore norms and values adapted for the purpose of making sense of complexity. Emery and Trist point out that organizations impose rules and norms as clarifying strategies for coping within contextually dense fields (1965, p. 28). Similarly, institutional leaders inculcate values to be shared as a means of charting mission and direction in the face of environmental turbulence. Attention to the moral implications of the enactment of shared values and meanings, or how ambiguous situations are portrayed and understood, can amplify the relationship between the moral ambiguities of context and of persons.

Research into the context of ethics decision making confronts formidable methodological challenges. With regard to typological work, perhaps meta-analysis of existing research, especially ethics case studies, could provide means for sorting out the sources and determinants of complexity among public-sector settings. Nonetheless, the exploration of ambiguity and how it is perceived appears to be the work of the ethnographic researcher who conducts observer-participant inquiry in the midst of those studied. Among numerous skills needed is the ability to gain access through trust (see Laine 2000, pp. 36–66). Only then can fieldwork acquire the scripts and narratives needed to reveal how settings are interpreted and acted upon. Clearly, the scale of such efforts, if not prohibitive for many, extends considerably beyond that of questionnaire-based survey research.

Emphasizing the dimensions of context with regard to decision making, the second discussion above asserts that government ethics has primarily to do with cognitive moral development. This is understandable since the (neo-)

Kohlbergian approaches differentiate among hierarchical stages (and levels) of reasoning to resolve moral dilemmas. Yet an exclusive reliance on moral cognition understates the importance of mental attitudes (such as those Bailey discusses) in approaching the context of action. There is some evidence, for example, that positive affect relates to flexibility in framing situations. Affect theorist Alice Isen suggests that "before the problem is actually addressed, some command decisions or evaluations may be made regarding how important the task is, what the utility may be, or whether the person has any control over the eventual outcome, as well as what the hedonistic consequences may be, how disruptive of ongoing feelings it may be, and so on" (Isen 1993, p. 269). These comments appear especially pertinent to decisions within the context of thick accountability (as developed by Dubnick and O'Kelly), such as that which guided John Scarlett's actions in stretching factual claims to support his prime minister's position regarding Saddam Hussein. Conceivably, affect may be instrumental in working through context prior to cognitive judgment of moral obligation.

Collectively, researchers in administrative ethics may opt to remain focused on accessible instruments that tap the Kohlbergian levels of cognitive development or venture into muddier waters in pursuit of affect and emotion. The latter would lead ethics research to psychodynamics or, to paraphrase Michael Diamond, it would call for understanding context [in addition to bureaucracy] as an "externalized self-system as viewed from the psychological interior" (1984, pp. 195–214). The notion of context as self-system implies that it supports defensive behaviors, especially among those Diamond labels as "performers . . . who demonstrate an extraordinary ability to conceal and deceive contradictory thoughts and action" (1986, pp. 659–60). Both the constructs of self-systems and as-is-performers become intriguing if applied to the contextual dimension of ethical decision making—and more broadly to scientific imperatives for rational-technical thinking (Denhardt 1981, pp. 35–58). It would follow that the thickness of context offers particular opportunities for risk-aversive and security-oriented behavior to deflect moral responsibility onto others. Accordingly, thick accountability depends upon emotional capacity, distinguishable from cognitive levels, as a basis for moral attitudes of optimism that work through the contours of interrelationships. And to reiterate, researchers engaged in these issues will be better served by interactive strategies such as focus groups and observer-participant fieldwork than by questionnaire surveys.

Finally, after some thirty years of research, the subfield of administrative ethics in public service has now reached brawny adolescence, if not full maturity. At this point, it is fitting to evaluate this body of research, as Donald Menzel does in chapter 2, particularly in terms of its empirical contribution to theory building. This collection includes contributions that add to the accumulating base of knowledge in established research categories, but it also contains other works that challenge the boundaries and/or the underlying premises of administrative ethics, at least as interpreted by many scholars in the subfield. Although these issues have already been treated, some additional comments speak to the research implications of these challenges as raising some paradoxical and provocative questions.

First is an essential question of research priorities concerning the relative merits of shoring up the scientific rigor of the empirical base within well-established topical categories and of incorporating emerging issues—even though sound research methodologies have yet to surface.

A second question relates to the issue of model (under-)identification, particularly in regard to ethical decision making, and accompanying methodological problems. Is it, in the interests of theory building, more advantageous to encourage empirical contribution to an accumulating body of knowledge that supports an underidentified model, or to seek more complete models based upon less elegant research? And third, the distinction that Dubnick and O'Kelly raise between "thick" and "thin" accountability has the potential to reopen numerous questions of ethical obligation presumably resolved. Are, for example, public-service principles (or perhaps laws) thin in comparison to cultural traditions and societal ideologies—whether recognized as inherently good or potentially evil? Nowhere do Dubnick and O'Kelly's constructs have more resounding implications than in the projection of administrative ethics onto a transnational world. On one hand, ethical reformers prescribe thin anticorruption interventions even though corruption takes on varying shapes and forms within thick national context. On the other, administrative ethics maintains the thick normative contours of its American roots as the basis of its professional relevance. Whether—and under what circumstances (or calculations)—does thickness, within regime values of national sovereignty, extend credence to principles derived from international deliberations?

Some Conclusions

Concern for the ethics of government and public service remains strong among citizens and scholars in the twenty-first century. In concluding *Ethics and Public Administration*, George Frederickson contrasted recent ethics reform with the earlier good government agendas as the latter typically reduced political influence and explained administrative controls. Much of the current ethics movement, however, calls for the opposite—increasing political control of public bureaucracies. On a continuing trajectory, this trend becomes even more evident with the emergence of profound issues related to globalization and international terrorism wherein policy imperatives and government operations converge seamlessly in the public mind. The ethics movement in public management thrives as robust, maturing at an impressive rate. It nonetheless confronts a number of vexing but interesting challenges that will likely affect how public management is practiced, studied, and researched in future years. Both the Introduction and this Conclusion discuss these problems—some related to the quality of empirical research and others to substantive issues—in some depth. Listed below are some of these challenges summarized as constructive dilemmas that warrant reflection by practitioners and scholars as individuals and deliberation among communities of those with sustained interest in public-service ethics.

Definitions

Contributors to this volume use various terms such as "public-service ethics," "government ethics," "administrative ethics," and "political ethics." Although they are most likely intended as synonyms, some may be interpreted as connoting particular assumptions that would steer research in some directions but not others. In particular, the term "administrative ethics" appears most parallel with the classical politics-administration dichotomy—even though policy issues related to democratic theory and social equity are generally regarded as important themes within administrative ethics. Questions as to whether definitions matter (how?) and if terminological boundaries can remain porous (particularly between administration and policy) warrant more consideration.

Research Priorities

Issues regarding the quality of empirical research in public-service ethics are frequently raised in this volume. Clearly, the goal to establish a body of scholarship on a par with standards of social science research is a commanding priority. Does this goal exact costs regarding other research priorities such as constructing more robust explanatory models or applications to a widening array of governance contexts in a changing world?

National Perspective

The international scopes of globalization and even terrorism force reflection about how expansive public ethics ought to be, not merely in miles but in societal ideologies and national traditions. How essential are such norms as civic virtue, utilitarian rationality, and regime values as assumptive parameters of public-service ethics, particularly as issues of transnational morality gain salience? Ethics in public management currently confront the formidable challenge of reconciling perspectives within U.S. culture and national experience, on one hand, with external vantage points that assess ethical governance in broader contexts, on the other.

Principles and Contexts

This concluding chapter argues the case for more fastidious attention to context as an important element in ethics study and research. Nonetheless, concern for the ambiguities of circumstance could be construed as counteracting the educational purpose of conveying standards of public official behavior and conduct in a forthright manner. Consequently, public-service ethics needs to accommodate stronger concern for various contextual issues without sacrificing the clarity of its educational mission.

These enumerated points do not explicitly refer to agendas for future research (although chapter 16 does so with regard to global ethics). Within these challenges we express confidence, or at least hope, that researchers will be motivated to pursue topics treated in this volume—or to engage in work that addresses these challenges in a manner that adds coherence to public-service ethics.

References

Appleby, Paul H. 1945/1970. *Big Democracy.* New York: Russell and Russell.
Bailey, Stephen K. 1965. "Ethics in the Public Service." In *Public Administration and Democracy*, ed. Roscoe C. Martin, pp. 283–98. Syracuse, NY: Syracuse University Press.
Cooper, Terry L. 2001. *Handbook of Administrative Ethics.* New York: Marcel Dekker.
———. 2004. "Big Questions in Administrative Ethics: A Need for Focused, Collaborative Effort." *Public Administration Review* 64, no. 4: 394–407.
———. 1986. "Psychological Dimensions of Personal Responsibility for Public Management: An Object Relations Approach." *Journal of Management Studies* 22: 649–67.
Denhardt, Kathryn G. 1991. "Unearthing the Moral Foundations of Public Administration: Honor, Benevolence, and Justice." In *Ethical Frontiers on Public Management: Seeking New Strategies for Resolving Ethical Dilemmas*, ed. James S. Bowman, pp. 91–117. San Francisco: Jossey-Bass.
Denhardt, Robert B. 1981. *In the Shadow of Organization.* Lawrence: Regents Press of Kansas.
Diamond, Michael A. 1984. "Bureaucracy as Externalized Self-Systems: A View from the Psychological Interior." *Administration and Society* 16: 195–214.

Dobel, J. Patrick. 1999. *Public Integrity.* Baltimore: Johns Hopkins University Press.
Doig, Jamison W. 1990. "Placing the Burden Where It Belongs." In *Combating Corruption/Encouraging Ethics*, ed. William L. Richter, Frances Burke, and Jamison W. Doig, pp. 292–96. Washington, DC: American Society for Public Administration.
Dwivedi, O.P., and Mancuso, Maureen. 2001. "Governance and Corruption in Canada." In *Where Corruption Lives*, ed. Gerald E. Caiden, O.P. Dwivedi, and Joseph Jabbra, pp. 57–67. Bloomfield, CT: Kumarian Press.
Emery, Fred E., and Trist, Eric L. 1965. "The Causal Texture of Organizational Environments." *Human Relations* 18, no. 1: 21–32.
Erskine, Toni. 2001. "Assigning Responsibility to Institutional Moral Agents: The Case of States and Quasi-States." *Ethics and International Affairs* 15, no. 2: 67–86.
Festinger, Leon. 1957. *A Theory of Cognitive Dissonance.* Evanston, IL: Row, Peterson.
Galtung, Fredrik. 2001. "Transparency International's Network to Curb Global Corruption." In *Where Corruption Lives*, ed. Gerald E. Caiden, O.P. Dwivedi, and Joseph Jabbra, pp. 189–206. Bloomfield, CT: Kumarian Press.
Gilman, Stuart C., and Lewis, Carol W. 1996. "Public Service Ethics: A Global Dialogue." *Public Administration Review* 56: 517–24.
Goleman, Daniel. 1995. *Emotional Intelligence.* New York: Bantam Books.
Isen, Alice M. 1993. "Positive Affect and Decision Making." In *Handbook of Emotions*, ed. Michael Lewis and Jeannette M. Haviland, pp. 261–77. New York: Guildford Press.
Laine, Marlene de. 2000. *Fieldwork, Participation and Practice: Ethics and Dilemmas in Qualitative Research.* Thousand Oaks, CA: SAGE.
Morgan, Douglas F., and Kass, Henry D. 1993. "The American Odyssey of the Career Public Service." In *Ethics and Public Administration*, ed. H. George Frederickson, pp. 177–90. Armonk, NY: M.E. Sharpe.
Rapoport, Anatol. (1964). *Strategy and Conscience.* New York: Harper and Row.
Rest, James R., and Narváez, Darcia, eds. 1994. *Moral Development in the Professions: Psychology and Applied Ethics.* Hillsdale, NJ: Erlbaum.
Ruggiero, Vincent R. 2004. *Thinking Critically about Moral Issues*, 6th ed. Boston: McGraw-Hill.
Stewart, Debra. 1990. "The Moral Responsibility of Individuals in Public Sector Organizations." In *Combating Corruption/Encouraging Ethics*, ed. William L. Richter, Frances Burke, and Jamison W. Doig, pp. 297–300. Washington, DC: American Society for Public Administration.
Thompson, Dennis F. 1987. *Political Ethics and Public Office.* Cambridge, MA: Harvard University Press.
———. 1985. "The Possibility of Administrative Ethics." *Public Administration Review* 45: 555–61.
Waldo, Dwight. 1955. *The Study of Public Administration.* New York: Random House.

About the Editors and Contributors

Guy B. Adams is professor and associate director of the Harry S Truman School of Public Affairs at the University of Missouri-Columbia. Adams's research has focused on organizational symbolism and culture, and on public-service ethics, history and theory. His book, *Unmasking Administrative Evil* (SAGE, 1998; M.E. Sharpe, 2004), with Danny L. Balfour, won the 1998 Louis Brownlow Book Award, the National Academy of Public Administration's highest award for excellence in public administration scholarship, as well as the 1998 Best Book Award from the Public and Nonprofit Division and the 2002 Best Book Award from the Social Issues in Management Division, both of the Academy of Management. Adams also co-authored *The Tacit Organization* (JAI Press, 1992), and has over sixty scholarly publications, including books, book chapters, and articles in a variety of public-affairs journals. He currently serves as co-editor-in-chief of the *American Review of Public Administration.*

Frank Anechiarico is Maynard-Knox Professor of Government and Law at Hamilton College. He is author of numerous articles on corruption control and co-author with James B. Jacobs of *The Pursuit of Absolute Integrity: How Corruption Control Makes Government Ineffective* (University of Chicago Press, 1996).

Danny L. Balfour is professor and director of the School of Public and Nonprofit Administration at Grand Valley State University in Grand Rapids, Michigan. He is co-author of *Unmasking Administrative Evil* (SAGE, 1998; M.E. Sharpe, 2004) and winner of the 1998 Brownlow Book Award from the National Academy of Public Administration. He has published widely in the areas of organizational theory and behavior, social policy, administrative ethics, and the Holocaust.

Pitima Boonyarak is a doctoral candidate in the Department of Political Science at the University of Utah. Her dissertation is entitled "The Impact of National Culture on the Accountability Verification Processes: A Comparative Case Study of an International NGO in Thailand, India, and UK." Her primary research interests are in the areas of nongovernmental organizations, accountability in multicultural settings, and civil society and development in the Southeast Asia region. She teaches courses in administrative theory, comparative politics, public administration, Third World development, and politics and development of Southeast Asia.

Gerald E. Caiden has published over 30 books and manuscripts and over 260 journal articles, and has acted as editorial consultant to several leading journals in the field of public administration and as a reader for notable publishing houses. He has acted as consultant, researcher, and administrator of a wide variety of public organizations ranging from the World Bank and the United Nations Organization to local authorities and public utilities. He is known best for his research in administrative and public service reform, corruption and administrative ethics, and administrative culture and organizational diagnosis.

Terry L. Cooper is Maria B. Crutcher Professor in Citizenship and Democratic Values in the School of Policy, Planning, and Development at the University of Southern California. He is the author of two books, *The Responsible Administrator: An Approach to Ethics for the Administrative Role* (Jossey-Bass, 1998), and *An Ethic of Citizenship for Public Administration* (Prentice Hall, 1991); and the editor of two other volumes, *Handbook of Administrative Ethics* (Marcel Dekker, 2001), and *Exemplary Public Administrators: Character and Leadership in Government* (Jossey-Bass, 1992).

Peter deLeon is professor of public policy at the Graduate School of Public Affairs at the University of Colorado (Denver), and author of *Thinking about Political Corruption* (M.E. Sharpe, 1993). He is presently working on a book manuscript dealing with democratic issues in policy implementations as well as a series of articles on voluntary environmental programs.

Kathryn G. Denhardt coordinates the Organizational Leadership area of specialization for the Masters in Public Administration Program at the University of Delaware. Her teaching and research interests include administrative ethics, performance management, and human resource management. Through the Institute for Public Administration she works with practitioners in the public and nonprofit sectors, particularly in the areas of facilitating decision making involving multiple stakeholders.

Lisa A. Dicke is assistant professor in the Department of Public Administration at the University of North Texas. She was formerly an assistant professor and MPA director at Texas Tech University. Her primary research interests and publications are in the areas of government and nonprofit accountability in human services contracting, civil society and globalization, nonprofit development, and service learning. She teaches courses in nonprofit and government management, organization theory, human resources management, and public-private partnerships.

Melvin Dubnick has been writing on the subject of accountability and ethics for more than two decades. A former managing editor of *Public Administration Review* and co-editor of the *Policy Studies Journal*, he also published works on administrative reform, regulatory policy, federalism, civic education, and has co-authored textbooks on public administration, American government, and policy analysis. A professor of political science and public administration at Rutgers-Newark, he was a Fulbright fellow at Queen's University, Belfast, when this chapter was written.

H. George Frederickson is the Edwin O. Stene Distinguished Professor of Public Administration at the University of Kansas. In 2003–4 he served as the Winant Visiting Professor of American Government at the University of Oxford, and as a Fellow of Balliol College, Oxford. He is a co-author of both *The Public Administration Theory Primer* (Westview Press, 2003) and *The Adapted City: Institutional Dynamics and Structural Change* (M.E. Sharpe, 2003). He received the John Gaus Lecturer Award from the American Political Science Association in 1999.

Richard K. Ghere is associate professor of political science at the University of Dayton and is a core instructor in the Master of Public Administration Program there. He is an author of articles on public-sector ethics and private-public partnerships.

Stuart C. Gilman is an independent consultant. He is the former president of the Ethics Resource Center and special assistant to the director of the United States Office of Government Ethics and has had professorial appointments at the Federal Executive Institute as well as St. Louis University, the University of Richmond, and Eastern Kentucky University. He has co-authored several books and monographs and has published articles in a number of edited books and journals. He has worked as an ethics expert for the World Bank, the Organization for Economic Cooperation and Development, the Inter-American Development Bank, and the United Nations.

Laura S. Jensen is associate professor of political science and a faculty associate of the Center for Public Policy and Administration at the University of Massachusetts, Amherst. She is the author of *Patriots, Settlers, and the Origins of American Social Policy* (Cambridge University Press, 2003), and articles in the *Review of Politics, Public Administration Review, Polity,* and *Studies in American Political Development.*

Carole L. Jurkiewicz is the John W. Dupuy Endowed Professor and the Women's Hospital Distinguished Professor of Healthcare Management at Louisiana State University. Her research and teaching interests focus primarily upon leadership, ethics, and organizational performance, areas in which she is widely published and for which she serves as an organizational consultant.

Sheila Suess Kennedy is associate professor of law and public policy at Indiana University Purdue University at Indianapolis. Ms. Kennedy is the author of *What's a Nice Republican Girl Like Me Doing at the ACLU?* (Prometheus Books, 1997) and *Free Expression in America: A Documentary History* (Greenwood, 1999), and co-editor of *To Market, To Market: Reinventing Indianapolis* (University Press of America, 2001), an analysis of Indianapolis's privatization experience under former mayor Stephen Goldsmith.

Marsha A. Marley is associate director and instructor at the School of Social Work, University of South Florida. She was assistant professor at the University of Tennessee College of Social Work from 1994 to 1999. She has published in the areas of human services management, macro practice, and kinship care.

Donald C. Menzel is president-elect of the American Society for Public Administration and emeritus professor of public administration, Northern Illinois University. He served in the U.S. Air Force 1962–67, and currently resides in Tampa, Florida. He has published widely in the field of public administration with a particular interest in local government management and ethics and has lectured on these subjects in China, Thailand, France, Germany, Portugal, and Italy and presented numerous professional papers at conferences in the United States and abroad. He is currently writing a book on ethical governance, conducting research on public administration and governance in China, and coordinating public management training for Chinese government officials.

Ciarán O'Kelly is a research fellow at the Institute of Governance, Public Policy and Social Research in Queen's University, Belfast. A political theorist, his research focuses on ethics and responsibility in public administration. He also specializes on the ethics of migration, specifically on the relationships that states should forge with settled migrants. He has written on nationalism and identity politics, most recently in 'Being Irish,' for a series in *Government and Opposition.*

Ann-Marie Rizzo is professor and director of the Institute of Government at Tennessee State University. She has written research articles and reviews on public administrators' ethics, teaching public administration, gender issues in administration and management training in *Administration and Society, Policy Studies Review, Public Personnel Management, American Review of Public Administration,* and *Southern Review of Public Administration,* among others. She was formerly associate professor and director of the Institute of Government at Florida International University.

Laura Lee Swisher is assistant professor at the University of South Florida in the School of Physical Therapy. She is also a physical therapist and co-author of *Legal and Ethical Issues in Physical Therapy* (Butterworth-Heinemann, 1998).

Dennis P. Wittmer is currently associate professor, Management Department, Daniels College of Business, University of Denver. He received his Ph.D. in public administration from the Maxwell School of Citizenship and Public Affairs at Syracuse University in 1992. His research has included empirical and conceptual studies of managerial ethics, comparative studies of public and private organizations, project management effectiveness, reward preferences among employees, R&D science policy, economic development policy, and the design of effective teaching methods in business education.

Diane E. Yoder is a Ph.D. candidate and instructor at the University of Southern California School of Policy, Planning, and Development. She has authored several articles on environmental policy and administrative ethics, which have appeared in *Policy Studies Review* and the *Journal of Administrative Theory and Praxis,* and is working on a study of environmental justice in cities nationwide.

Index

Los Angeles Police Department, 4, 204
Lugar v. Edmondson Oil Co. (1982), 225–26,
   228, 240

Machiavellianism, 60, 99–100
Machiavellian Scale (Mach V), 101–6
Maine, 228, 230
Market competition
   contract services, 251–52, 254
   new public management (NPM), 172–73,
      177–82
   transnational ethics, 316, 317, 318–22
Maryland, 270–73
Massachusetts, 348, 349
McDonald's, 266–69
Mediated corruption, 261–64
Medicaid, 223–24, 226, 227
Medina v. O'Neill (1984), 227, 240
Merck Pharmaceuticals, 269
Merit system, 244, 246
Merit Systems Protection Board (MSPB)
   (New York), 246
Mexico, 279, 283, 303, 309
Microsoft, 177
Middle East
   Arab Administrative Development
      Organization, 312
   Arab Business Council, 312
   Arab Organization for Human Rights, 312
   League of Arab States, 312
   Organization of Petroleum Exporting
      Countries (OPEC), 312
   transnational ethics, 312–15
   See also specific country
Minimalist public ethics, 130–31, 134, 150
Moderate Rehabilitation Program (MRP),
   210
Moose, Charles, 270–73
Moral agency, 156–58, 365
Moral ambiguity, 357–59, 360–62, 365–66
Moral episode, 21–22
Moral Judgment Interview, 72, 77
Moral reasoning assessment
   cognitive moral development (CMD), 57,
      72, 77–78
   Defining Issues Test (DIT), 57, 72, 77–78
   ethical judgment, 72, 77
Moral reasoning research
   age differences, 79
   Defining Issues Test (DIT), 79–81, 84–90
   educational differences, 79, 81–84, 86–87
   gender differences, 78–79, 81–86

Moral reasoning research *(continued)*
   law-duty reasoning, 78
   maintaining norms reasoning, 78, 81–87
   postconventional reasoning, 78, 81–87
   principled reasoning, 78
   racial differences, 79
   research, 79–81, 84–92
   See also Empirical research assessment;
      Ethics research
Moral reasoning theory, 70–78
   See also Cognitive moral development
      (CMD); Defining Issues Test (DIT)
Moral world view, 70–71
Motivation
   official corruption, 281–84
   power, 100–101

National Academy of Public Administration,
   227–30
National Air Traffic Services (Great Britain),
   34
*National Collegiate Athletic Association v.
   Tarkanian* (1988), 223, 224, 240
National Council for Public-Private
   Partnerships, 33
National Partnership for Reinventing
   Government, 4, 177
National Performance Review (NPR), 167–68,
   177, 186, 210
Nazism, 114–15, 123
Netherlands, 255–56, 343
Neutrality ethic, 122–23
New Mexico, 224, 227
New public management (NPM)
   characteristics of, 165, 167–82
   contract management, 175–80
   contract services, 166–67, 170–76, 178–82
   defining assumptions, 166–72
   deregulation, 166–70, 178–82
   downsizing, 173–75, 178–82
   ethical consequences, 178–82
   legal accountability, 220–21, 235–39
   market competition, 172–73, 177–78,
      178–82
   principal-agent theory, 207–9, 211–14,
      235–39
   privatization
      corruption, 166–67, 170–73, 178–82
   research, 9, 14, 165–66
   See also Human services accountability
      measurement; Political corruption
New world order, 115, 125–28

Political corruption *(continued)*
  See also Corruption control (New York);
    Gift policy; Official corruption;
    Transnational ethics
Polk County v. Dodson (1982), 226, 240
Powell, Jonathan, 146, 155
Power
  corruption link, 95–96, 100, 109–10
  effective leadership correlation, 96–99,
    360, 361
  ethics correlation, 99–101
  Machiavellianism, 99–100
  operationalizing ethics, 101–3
  operationalizing power, 100–101
  organizational politicization, 97
  power motive, 100–101
  psychological theory, 100–101
  research, 103–10
Principal-agent theory, 207–9, 211–14,
    235–39
Privatization
  human services accountability
    measurement, 184–85, 186, 187–89,
    191
  legal accountability
    Indianapolis experiment, 231–37
    state action, 222–33
  new public management (NPM),
    170–75
  research assessment, 30, 33–34
  See also Contract services; Public-private
    partnerships
Procurement Policy Board (PPB) (New
    York), 248, 251–52, 255
Procurement system. *See* Contract services;
    Corruption control (New York)
Professionalism
  administrative evil, 120–21, 122–25
  American Progressive Movement, 243–46
  human services accountability
    measurement, 187–90, 193–96
  See also American Society for Public
    Administration (ASPA)
Program on International Policy Attitudes
    (PIPA), 341
Prosocial behavior, 57–58
Proxmire, William, 212–15
Psychological theory, 100–101
Public good, 342–46
Public Integrity Annual, 16–17, 38
Public Integrity (Dobel), 357
Public Management, 271

Public management ethics
  contextual dimension, 357–62, 365–70
  ethical decision-making, 360–62, 366–70
  research, 356, 363–65, 367–72
  theoretical perspective, 362–65, 367–70
  See also New public management (NPM)
Public opinion
  accountability, 140–41, 144–47, 155–56,
    157
  gift policy, 262–65
  global ecology, 338, 340–46
  official corruption, 293
Public-private partnerships
  human services accountability
    measurement, 184–87
  legal accountability, 221–22, 231–39
  research assessment, 33
  See also Contract services; Privatization
Public-private sector differences
  cognitive moral development (CMD), 57
  legal accountability, 223–24, 231–39
  political corruption, 208–11

Racial differences, 18–19, 79
Reagan, Ronald, 171–72, 176, 203–4, 209–10,
    212
Regan, Donald, 210
Regulatory agencies
  corruption control (New York), 248–57
  new public management (NPM)
    deregulation. 167–70, 178–80, 209–13
  research assessment, 18, 22–25, 30, 37
  See also Bureaucracy; Ethics law-
    regulatory agency research;
    Privatization
Reinventing government, 4, 177, 299
Reitman v. Mulkey (1967), 228, 240
Rendell-Baker v. Kohn (1982), 225, 228–29,
    240
Rest, James. *See* Defining Issues Test (DIT)
Rethinking Public Administration (Emery &
    Trist), 330–35
Richardson v. McKnight (1997), 225, 240
Ridge, Tom, 340
Rohr, J., 206
Russia, 19–20, 78–79, 85, 279, 283
Russian Academy of Public Service, 19–20

Sagebrush Revolution, 186
*San Francisco Arts & Athletics, Inc. v.
    United States Olympic Committee*
    (1987), 224, 227, 240